CHARLES
IVES
AND HIS
AMERICA

CHARLES IVES AND HIS AMERICA

Frank R. Rossiter

LIVERIGHT   NEW YORK

Library of Congress Cataloging in Publication Data

Rossiter, Frank R
  Charles Ives and his America.

  Bibliography: p.
  Includes index.
  1. Ives, Charles Edward, 1874–1954.   I. Title.
ML410.I94R68   780'.92'4 [B]   75–12663
ISBN 0–87140–610–1

PRINTED IN THE UNITED STATES OF AMERICA

1 2 3 4 5 6 7 8 9 0

To My Mother
and to the
Memory of My Father

CONTENTS

ILLUSTRATIONS

❦

PREFACE

THE FIRST TIME THAT Charles Ives became more than a name to me was during the summer of 1958, when I was serving as a midshipman in the Naval Reserve Officers Training Corps on board the U.S.S. *Bristol*. A fellow midshipman, an undergraduate at Columbia University, excitedly informed me one night when we were standing the midwatch that a certain American named Charles Ives had been the greatest composer since Johann Sebastian Bach! The incident has remained with me, for it is a striking instance of the recurring tendency for Ives's music to arouse unrestrained admiration in each new "younger generation."

Like many other Americans, I first actually heard Ives's compositions during the great upsurge of interest in his music in the 1960s. I soon discovered that apart from the intrinsic interest of his music, Ives himself was a fascinating figure in American cultural history.

Ives's life (1874–1954) presents a remarkable set of paradoxes. He was a businessman whose spare-time composing was done in nearly total obscurity during the early years of the twentieth century; yet after his death, he came to be widely recognized as America's greatest composer. His compositions were extremely advanced, anticipating many of the innovations of Stravinsky, Schoenberg, and other European modernists; yet his music quoted old-fashioned American tunes and looked back nostalgically to the simplicity of New England Yankee life in the nineteenth century. He was a wealthy insurance executive; yet he held radical political and social views, advocating the substitution of direct for representative government and a redistribution of wealth and income.

When I decided to undertake serious research on Ives and began to delve into his papers, I became more and more convinced that the Ives Legend which has grown up around him gives a very imperfect picture of the man. I think that the key to an understanding of his place in American culture lies in his extreme artistic isolation. The creative artist in America has a tradition of being isolated, of lacking an audience. But nearly all such artists have had at least a small circle of friends who sustained them artistically and intellectually. Ives had nothing of the kind during his creative years; he was about as close to complete isolation as it is possible for a creative artist to be.

Ives's isolation is generally attributed to the action upon him of powerful pressures and forces in the American culture. But did these forces act upon him from without or from within? According to the Ives Legend, they operated upon him almost entirely in an external way. In the late nineteenth and early twentieth centuries, it is said, Ives was confronted with an American musical profession that was unoriginal, conservative, and commercialized, a profession that had no use for his innovative music. Unwilling to compromise his principles, he had no alternative but to break with the profession and go his independent and lonely way. But his isolation from musicians and other artists might also be seen as an internal process. Ives was deeply affected by the widespread feeling in his culture that high art and the artists who made it were somehow unmanly, undemocratic, and un-American. His inner acceptance of this value judgment about art and artists made it difficult for him even to reach the point where he could accept himself as an artist—a problem that would hardly have existed for a European. In a very real sense his music is a record of his struggles with this problem and his attempts to work out a solution to it. Ives's artistic isolation, then, arose not only from his desire to write experimental music, but also from his desire to be a good American; this is perhaps the central paradox of his career as a composer.

Most of what has been written about Ives's career has consisted of surmises based upon his music and his published writings. The extant records of his life give a somewhat different picture. I have tried in this study to capture something of the texture of his actual life, apart from the rhetoric of his music and his prose.

Some may feel that I am hostile to Ives in my treatment of him. His extraordinary anticipation of later developments in twentieth-century music has led many present-day musicians and music enthusiasts to admire him extravagantly. There is naturally a tendency to assimilate him to the trends of the present and to see him as a modern artist. Aspects of his life which seem old-fashioned, or which are otherwise incompatible with the image of the modern artist, are too often overlooked or treated patronizingly as eccentric and amusing quirks. But many of those aspects were an integral part of his life. It is fairer to Ives, I think, to see him frankly in the context of his own era and to see him whole than to idealize or patronize him. His artistic misfortunes and contradictions were, after all, more of a reflection on American culture than on the man himself.

Ives often wrote out his letters, essays, memoranda, and diary entries in a fast and careless way, making a good deal of editing necessary if his prose is to be easily read. In quoting from these unpublished prose writings, I have exercised a free editorial hand (without specifically indicating that I have done so) in matters of spelling, punctuation, capitalization, grammar, interpretation of his handwriting, and choice from among two or more alternatives that he may have given for a passage; words that I have added are placed in square brackets. A similar procedure has been followed with the letters and diary entries of Harmony T. Ives, although these required less editing.

I wish to thank the following: the National Institute of Arts and Letters for permission to quote material from Charles Ives's letters, music manuscripts, and other personal papers, as well as for permission to quote passages from Ives's published *Memos,* edited by John Kirkpatrick (New York: W. W. Norton & Company, Inc., 1972); George G. Tyler for permission to quote from letters and other writings of Harmony T. Ives and George E. Ives; Lehman Engel for permission to quote from a letter written by him; Monique Schmitz Leduc for permission to quote from a letter written by her father, E. Robert Schmitz; Ruth E. Riegger for permission to quote from letters written by her father, Wallingford Riegger; Edith M. Sansom and the Henry H. Bellamann Foundation for permission to quote from letters written by Henry Bellamann; and Sparkle M. Furnas for permission to quote from letters written by her brother-in-law, Clifton Joseph Furness. Mrs. Furnas also kindly supplied me with copies of some Charles Ives letters that are in the Furnas Memorial Room at the State University of New York at Buffalo.

The Horace H. Rackham School of Graduate Studies at the University of Michigan has aided the research and writing of this book with a faculty research grant in 1971 and a faculty research fellowship and grant in 1972. The book was completed while I held a fellowship from the National Endowment for the Humanities in 1973–1974.

I should like to express my gratitude to several people who have helped me in the writing of this book.

My friend Michael G. Patty has greatly facilitated several research trips and given much encouragement in the writing. Koit Ojamaa kindly made the translation from the Russian article in chapter seven.

Three members of the faculty of the Department of History at Princeton University read the manuscript in its earlier dissertation form and made useful suggestions for its improvement: Martin Duberman (now of Herbert H. Lehman College of the City University of New York); James M. Banner, Jr.; and James M. McPherson.

Ruth L. Schaefer, Librarian of the Mutual Life Insurance Company of New York, made available to me the Ives material in the

Research Library of that company. Judith Schiff, Chief Research Archivist in the Manuscript and Archives Department of the Sterling Memorial Library, Yale University, helped me to locate pertinent material in the Yale University Archives.

At the John Herrick Jackson Music Library of Yale University, my protracted research in the Ives Collection was greatly facilitated by Harold E. Samuel, Librarian, and by Alfred B. Kuhn, Head Librarian, Cataloguing Section. At the Yale School of Music, Vivian Perlis, Director of the Oral History of American Music Project, shared much valuable information with me and gave me an opportunity to "talk out" a number of Ives problems.

My greatest debt is to John Kirkpatrick, Curator of the Ives Collection and Professor Emeritus of Music, Yale University. Not only has Professor Kirkpatrick made available to me the Ives materials that I have requested, but he has also generously shared with me the results of his own research on Ives over many years. I have benefited from his reading of my manuscript and from many conversations with him, both about Charles Ives (on whom he is the leading authority) and about the social aspect of American music in the twentieth century.

Part One

DEVELOPMENT
1874–1921

I

DANBURY

To a remarkable degree, Charles Ives's mind revolved throughout all his life in the orbit of his childhood. The music that he composed as an adult constantly reverted to the tunes and the experiences that would have been encountered by a boy growing up in a New England town in the nineteenth century. The boy was Charles Ives himself. The town was Danbury, Connecticut, where Ives was born on October 20, 1874. To understand the cultural source of Ives's art, his thought, and his mode of living, it is first necessary to know something about Danbury.

Danbury is an inland town; it lies in the extreme western part of Connecticut, near the New York border, a little more than twenty miles north of Long Island Sound. Settled by a few pioneer families who came north from Norwalk in 1684, Danbury grew slowly for the next 150 years.[1] Until just before the Civil War it was still a largely rural community, its people living an existence relatively undisturbed by the outside world; the town's population in 1840 was only

4,504, including the outlying rural areas of the township.[2] About the middle of the nineteenth century, however, a series of sudden economic and social changes began to disturb the tranquillity of the town, so that by the end of the century its entire character had been altered. These changes took two principal forms: first, the rapid physical and industrial expansion of the town into a city; second, the shift of the town's ethnic pattern through the arrival of new immigrants from Europe.

The making of hats had begun in Danbury in the late eighteenth century; and the town had long been the leading center of hat production in the United States when, about the middle of the nineteenth century, the introduction of machinery revolutionized the industry. At approximately the same time, in 1852, Danbury's first railroad gave the town a connection with the Sound and New York City. After the Civil War came the most rapid expansion of the hatting industry, the erection of large hatting mills, and the parallel growth of such allied trades as the manufacture of hat cases and hat trimmings. As Danbury became an industrial town, its population increased at a startling pace. In the 1870s, it grew from 8,753 to 11,666—an increase of one-third. And during the extraordinary decade of the 1880s, Danbury experienced a growth of population unprecedented in its history, from 11,666 to 19,473—an increase of two-thirds.[3] Along with industrial and population growth went the founding and building of many new civic institutions, such as churches, schools, and hospitals. Then, during the depression decade of the 1890s, the city's growth slowed down and its population remained stable.

Thus Ives's years in Danbury, from 1874 to 1893, were the very period when the town experienced its greatest growth. Ives lived in the heart of the city, and his family contained some of the business and professional men who were most energetic in helping the city expand and acquire the advantages of "civilization."

As Danbury grew and prospered, and as its general standard of living rose, it also became less socially cohesive and homogeneous. At the beginning of the nineteenth century, when the population of the town was between three and four thousand and the property gap between even the wealthiest men in the town and their fellow citizens was not great, the possession of a respected name and a reputation for integrity might enable a man to secure an honored position in town and church even if he was merely a farmer, a tavernkeeper, a blacksmith, or a tailor. As the town grew rapidly in population and industry in the latter half of the century, however, economic criteria became much more important as standards of admission into the elite. By the time of Ives's boyhood, success in a sizable business or specialization in one of the professions, particularly the law, had become the almost indispensable prerequisite to a place near the top of the social hierarchy; the town's elite was now made up of wealthy manufacturers, merchants, bankers, and builders, along with the lawyers and other skilled professionals who served them. At the same time, the gap between men of large property and those of average or below-average wealth had become greater and more socially unbridgeable.[4]

The evolution of the word *hatter* nicely illustrates this whole process. Early in the century a hatter was an entrepreneur who made hats by hand in his house or a small shop with the help of a few journeymen and apprentices, who could themselves hope to set up a small business in a few years. By the last quarter of the century, large mechanized factories having replaced small shops, the term *hat manufacturer* was applied to the capitalist who owned and ran a hat factory, the term *hatter* being then reserved for his wage laborers; the latter could hardly hope to raise enough capital to establish themselves as manufacturers and were, therefore, destined to remain wage workers.[5]

With a decrease of social cohesion came a breakdown of social deference in Danbury. Early attempts to organize labor in the hat factories led to a protracted series of disputes between employers and workers; in 1887 an annual report of the Connecticut Bureau of Labor Statistics summarized the situation by noting that "previous to 1885 there was almost continual war between the hat manufacturers and the hat makers and finishers of Danbury."[6] Further troubles following that date led to a nine-week lockout not long after the onset of the panic and depression of 1893. The most famous of Danbury's labor disputes was the Danbury Hatters' Case, of the early twentieth century, in which the courts imposed a heavy fine on union members for damages resulting from a boycott. Labor relations in Danbury, then, were far from tranquil.

Just as the hat workers of the city fell behind in the march of progress, so those people who remained in the outlying rural parts of Danbury town and its tributary area were regarded as backward and unprogressive by the hustling and improvement-minded members of the city's elite. Nor did the competition for elite status spare those who bore an ancient and honorable name but could not make the grade. In 1895 the treasurer of the Hat Makers' Society, the hatters' labor union, was Albert B. Hoyt, who had the family name of one of the "original eight" men who had settled Danbury in 1684.[7] Again, Charles Ives's boyhood hero John Starr, of the nearby rural community of Brookfield, bore one of the most esteemed names in Danbury, yet he was nothing but a country fiddler.

The second great social change that engulfed nineteenth-century Danbury was the coming of large numbers of non-British immigrants from Europe. From the time of Danbury's founding in 1684 until well into the nineteenth century, it was an ethnically homogeneous community made up almost entirely of Protestants of British origin. The first real portent of a challenge to the hegemony of these old Americans came with the arrival of the Irish, the first of whom, one Peter O'Brien, appeared in town about the 1820s.[8] The first Catholic priest began to hold services in Danbury in the 1830s, and the first "regular place of worship" for Catholics was set up in the 1850s.[9] By the time of Ives's boyhood, Danbury's Irish-Americans made up a considerable portion of the town's population. By that time, too, Germans had settled in Danbury in sizable numbers; and by the end of the century, there were groups of Italians and Hungarians and smaller numbers of other nationalities from southern and eastern Europe. Needless to say, the newcomers comprised the bulk of the city's lower economic class; many of them worked in the hat factories.

The immigrants and their children made up a steadily increasing proportion of the total population of Danbury, a proportion that had reached about one-half by the time that Ives left Danbury in 1893. In 1890, foreign-born whites and native-born whites with at least one foreign-born parent made up together 48.8 per cent of the white population of Danbury.[10]

Charles Ives must have been recalling the social gulf and the hostility between older and newer ethnic groups in Danbury when he wrote years later: "O Prejudice. . . . You enter into the little boy of a N[ew] E[ngland] town and make him stand and gape with the same horror at [the] man going into a Catholic church as the man going into a saloon." [11] Coming from a family of older English stock, Charles Ives and his brother seem to have played mainly with other children of similar background. Yet as he grew up in Danbury, Ives's experiences on school teams and in musical activities gave him some contact with the newer immigrant groups. Indeed, hostility among Danbury's ethnic groups was no greater than in other New England towns that had experienced a similar development; it was perhaps somewhat less than the average. Both the Germans and the Irish had been partially assimilated—through business and professional life and voluntary organizations like the fire companies—into the older community by the end of the century. But the prevailing climate of opinion toward the despised Italians was eloquently set forth in a news item—intended to be humorous—in the *Danbury News* of July 16, 1890: "Those who have noticed a peculiar flavor about the water this summer will be glad to learn that it is caused by the Italians who go in swimming in Padanaram reservoir on Sunday." [12]

In the twentieth century Danbury's elite of older American stock would have to meet the demands of the newer ethnic groups—particularly the numerically powerful Irish and Italians—for recognition at all levels of the city's political, social, and economic life. Charles Ives's brother, Moss, who remained in Danbury and became the city's most eminent lawyer and jurist between the two world wars, proved to be one of the most effective members of that elite in bridging the gap between older and newer Americans, largely because of his genuine tolerance and his deep admiration for the Roman Catholic religion.

As the leading men of Danbury in the 1890s looked back upon the changes that had transformed their town, they were of two minds about it. Their spokesman in this ambivalence was James Montgomery Bailey, the editor of the *Danbury Evening News* and probably Danbury's best-known citizen. Famous as the "Danbury News Man," Bailey had acquired a reputation far beyond Connecticut for his newspaperman's humor, which was similar to Mark Twain's. In his *History of Danbury,* published in 1896 not long after his death, Bailey took an obvious pride in what Danbury had become during his lifetime; he boasted of its industries, its buildings, its public improvements, and its charities. But his detailed treatment of the earlier and simpler Danbury was directed toward the nostalgia of Danbury's people; and his care in listing the names and residences of those who had lived in the town in preceding eras was intended to satisfy that desire for family roots which often comes over men in a time of rapid social change. The immigrants, the factories, and the rapid pace of modern life were not looked upon as an unmixed blessing, even by the most prosperous of Danbury's citizens. One's daily work was supposed to be aimed at progress and improvement; but in leisure-time activities—in music, for example—one might dwell nostalgically upon the past. It was this ambivalence toward "progress" that Charles Ives absorbed in Danbury and carried with him in later life.

Throughout the nineteenth century, Danbury was led by an elite, just as a similar elite led any other American town or small city of the time. The members of this elite, who were often related to one another by marriage, held the positions of power and prestige in the various areas of Danbury's life as a town and city; they were the employers of labor and controllers of wealth, the leaders of the professions, the holders of office in local and state government, the foremost laymen in the churches, the promoters of Danbury's public improvements, and the honored members of its charitable committees. A relatively small number of families—some long in power and some more newly arrived—made up this elite and regarded themselves as socially superior to their fellow citizens. Among these elite families in late-nineteenth-century Danbury was the Ives family—or, more exactly, that branch of the large Connecticut clan of Ives to which Charles Ives belonged. Although the Iveses established themselves in Danbury at a comparatively late date, they soon became,

8

through the enterprise of the first two generations, one of the few families "who *were* the town," [13] as one of their descendants put it.

The Iveses could trace their ancestry back to the earliest days of the Connecticut colony.[14] The first member of the family in America was William Ives, who came from England to Boston in 1635 and was later one of the original settlers of New Haven in 1638; from that time on, the Ives name has been a common one in numerous parts of Connecticut. William's sons helped to found Wallingford, Connecticut, and Ives descendants lived in the Wallingford-Meriden region throughout the eighteenth century. One of these descendants, Isaac Ives (1764–1845), was Charles Ives's great-grandfather. Having graduated from Yale and studied law, Isaac came to Danbury in the 1790s and took there as his second wife Sarah Amelia White, the daughter of Joseph Moss White, one of the town's most prominent citizens. (It was common, at that time and later in New England, for an ambitious young man who was just starting out in life to move from his native town to another—often a larger—one.) Isaac must have made a strong impression on his adopted town, for he had been there only a few years when he was selected to be one of Danbury's two representatives in the Connecticut House of Representatives for two successive sessions (October, 1795, and May, 1796).[15] His ambitions, however, could not be satisfied in Danbury, and he soon moved to New York City, where he was a successful entrepreneur for thirty years, chiefly in the hat and grocery businesses. Having made his fortune, Isaac Ives retired to Danbury in 1829, bought the house on Main Street which was to remain the family homestead for a century (and in which Charles Ives was born), and settled down to the life of a deacon of the Congregational church and one of the most eminent men in the town.

Isaac's son, George White Ives (1799–1862), who was Charles Ives's grandfather, was born in New York and went into business with his father. He retired to Danbury, where his family roots were strong, soon after his father did. Since he was still a young man and was comfortably fixed, George devoted the second half of his life to that combination of businesses of a public character and community endeavors which was regarded by Danburians as providing the proper activity for a man of means if he wished to attain public eminence. The spirit of improvement was abroad in the land during the several decades before the Civil War, and George W. Ives joined a small group of like-minded men—Frederick S. Wildman, Edgar S. Tweedy, Eli T. Hoyt—in a vigorous effort to improve Danbury. Thus, as early as 1835, he was one of the ten grantees of a charter for a railroad to be built from Danbury to Long Island Sound; and when the Danbury and Norwalk Railroad was finally built in the 1850s, he served as the first treasurer of the company. He was a director of the Danbury Bank; a director and one of the original incorporators, in 1857, of the Danbury Gas Light Company; and a founder and director of the Mechanics' Association, a library company. His two favorite projects were the Savings Bank of Danbury and the Danbury Cemetery Association. He was the principal organizer of the Savings Bank of Danbury and its first secretary and treasurer; the bank's business was first conducted in his home. He served as a director of the Danbury Cemetery Association, and he helped to lay out and superintend its Wooster Cemetery grounds during the first decade of its existence. When he died in 1862, a Danbury newspaper called George W. Ives "one of our most valued and respected citizens." [16] His widow, Sarah Hotchkiss Wilcox Ives (1808–1899), survived him by thirty-six years, devoting herself to such good works as saving the Danbury Home for Destitute and Homeless Children by a public appeal for contributions when it was burdened with debt, serving on the board of managers of this home, and raising money to restore the town's original burial ground on Wooster Street.

Of the four children of George W. and Sarah Ives who survived to maturity, the three eldest followed their father's pattern of economic success and membership in Danbury's elite. The oldest, Joseph M. Ives (1832–1908), was a hustling merchant whose J. M. Ives Company, a store that sold home furnishings and hardware, became one of Danbury's largest and most successful enterprises. He was also in the forefront of the promoters and improvers of Danbury, serving as a director of the Danbury Cemetery Association and as an officer and director of the Danbury Farmers' and Manufacturers' Company, which sponsored the annual Danbury Fair; and he had the distinction of knowing James Russell Lowell and Ralph Waldo Emerson.[17] His wife served on the board of managers of the Danbury Hospital. Joseph's younger brother Isaac W. Ives (1835–1910), whose tastes were more sporty than literary, pioneered in the manufacture of hat cases and was one of Danbury's most successful builders during the period of its rapid growth. In his early twenties, through his father, Isaac became associated in the project for gas lighting in the town, and he was one of the original incorporators of the Danbury Gas Light Company, of which he served as a director and the first clerk and treasurer; from that time on he was an inveterate promoter of railroads and other public-spirited enterprises that he thought would contribute to the progress of the town. Joseph and Isaac had a sister, Sarah Amelia (1837–1918), known to her nephew Charles as "Aunt Amelia," who married Lyman D. Brewster (1832–1904); her husband became the most eminent of Danbury's lawyers, a state representative and state senator, the first judge of the Court of Common Pleas of Fairfield County, a leader in the American Bar Association, and chairman of the committee that drew up Danbury's new city charter in 1888–1889. Amelia Brewster herself served with her mother on the board of managers of the Danbury children's home, of which her husband was the legal adviser. In the 1880s the Brewsters lived in the family homestead on Main Street, along which Joseph and Isaac also had their homes. The three houses were symbolic of the solidity and superiority that the family had achieved.

Among George W. Ives's children, the exception to the pattern of financial success and social respectability was the youngest child, George Edward Ives (1845–1894), who was Charles Ives's father. George E. Ives showed an early talent for music, although no such bent was to be found among any of the other members of his immediate family or among his direct forebears. By the time he had reached his middle teens, he was playing with the Danbury Brass Band and giving solo performances at Danbury musical "soirées" [18]—that is, he was following the same pattern of musical precocity that his son Charles was to pursue at an even earlier age a quarter of a century later in Danbury. Instead of attending Yale, as his grandfather and his older brother Joseph had, George was sent

11

to Morrisania, in Westchester County, New York, when he was only fifteen, to study with a German-American "professor" of music, Charles A. Foeppl. That such a serious study of music was permitted him by his father does not prove that the latter was capable of rising above the notion, then generally held by Americans, that music was no more than an amusement that could hardly be made a man's life's work. The father may have been merely indulging his son's whim to study music; the boy was so young that his music lessons scarcely amounted to a vocational commitment.

George Ives studied with Foeppl from 1860 to 1862. Meanwhile, the Civil War had broken out, and in 1862, although he was barely seventeen years old, he undertook to recruit and organize a volunteer band, drawing especially upon German-American musicians of his acquaintance. The youthful leader then led his band through the remainder of the war. It was attached to the First Connecticut Artillery, a regiment of which Nelson L. White, his father's first cousin, was lieutenant colonel; and it served as a siege artillery brigade band during the Union siege of Richmond. It was during this siege that General Grant is supposed to have remarked to President Lincoln that Ives's band was the best in the Union army.[19] The war must have been a hard, as well as a maturing, experience for the young man, for he later recorded in a notebook: "A space of Three years servitude as Leader . . . & one year sick, from Sept/62 to Sept/'66." [20]

In 1866–1868 George Ives continued his studies with Foeppl, this time in New York City. He then returned to Danbury and, after trying his hand at business, took up the life of a professional musician. His father had died during the war, and one can only speculate upon the degree of opposition that the rest of his family exerted against his career decision. In the eyes of Danbury, the professional nature of his new role was fundamentally different from the amateur nature of his youthful role as boy prodigy in the town or the "emergency" nature of his role as bandmaster during the war. His commitment, as an adult in Danbury, to music as his life's work was a breach of the traditions of his family and society—a violation of what they expected of an American, a man, and an Ives. In making this career decision in favor of music, George Ives showed an independence that his more talented son was not able to muster up when a similar choice fell to him some thirty years later, although the fact that the son was a composer and the father was not makes the two situations not strictly comparable.

As a professional musician, George Ives participated in many aspects of Danbury's musical life—sacred and secular, classical and popular—for the next twenty-five years. Danburians knew him in a variety of musical roles, not all of which were held at the same time: leader of the Danbury Band and other bands (the role in which he was probably best known to most of them); musical director at the Methodist church; leader or member of several small theater orchestras; teacher of music (which is the profession by which he was listed in the Danbury directory in the latter 1880s); soloist on the cornet and violin (his two principal instruments); and many other positions. A man who wished to make his living by music in a small city in nineteenth-century America had to be versatile and willing to take on a large variety of musical odd jobs. Yet Danbury's musical life was quite rich for a community of its size, and George Ives was only one among many makers of music there. It is certainly not true that the musical life of Danbury centered around him.[21] On the other hand, he was unquestionably the single most original figure among Danbury musicians.

There is no evidence that George E. Ives brought to music the uplifting attitude of such American musicians as Lowell Mason or Theodore Thomas—no evidence, that is, that he sought to use his position as a professional musician to train up the musical taste of his fellow citizens in Danbury. In his *personal* musical preferences, however, he differed from other professional musicians in and around the town in that he was not satisfied merely to play the accepted music, classical and popular, of his era. George Ives was, in fact, a restless musical experimenter who was interested in all kinds of sounds.[22] His interest was not that of a composer who employed these sounds in written music, or of a theorist who studied sound in a scholarly fashion, but simply that of an enthusiast who was fascinated by new and unusual aural experiences, both those produced by nature and those artificially created, both the accidental and the planned.

13

After his marriage in 1874 and the birth in 1874 and 1876 of his two children, George Ives drew his family into his musical experimentation; Charles Ives grew up in an atmosphere in which musical innovation, so rare in America or anywhere else at the time, was taken for granted. In an article published in 1925, the son described some of his early memories of his father's unconventional musical behavior:

> My father had a weakness for quarter-tones [roughly, the tones between adjacent keys on a piano, not reproducible on the piano]—in fact he didn't stop even with them. He rigged up a contrivance to stretch 24 or more violin strings and tuned them up to suit the dictates of his own curiosity. He would pick out quarter-tone tunes and try to get the family to sing them—but I remember he gave that up, except as a means of punishment—though we got to like some of the tunes which kept to the usual scale and had quarter-tone notes thrown in. But after working for some time he became sure that some quarter-tone chords must be learned before quarter-tone melodies would make much sense and become natural to the ear and so for the voice.
>
> He started to apply a system of bows to be released by weights, which would sustain the chords—but in this process he was suppressed by the family and a few of the neighbors. A little later on he did some experimenting with glasses and bells and got some sounds as beautiful sometimes as they were funny—a complex that only children are old enough to appreciate. . . .
>
> A friend who was a "thorough musician"—he had graduated from the New England Conservatory at Boston—asked him why with his sensitive ear he liked to sit down and beat out dissonances on the piano. "Well," he answered, "I may have absolute pitch, but, thank God, that piano hasn't." One afternoon in a pouring thunder storm we saw him standing without hat or coat in the back garden—the church bell next door was ringing. He would rush into the house to the piano and then back again. "I've heard a chord I've never heard before—it comes over and over but I can't seem to catch it." He stayed up most of the night trying to find it in the piano. It was soon after this that he started his quarter-tone machine.[23]

George Ives's experiments became, in fact, an important part of his son's musical education, over and above the training in the clas-

sical musical tradition and the great German composers of the eighteenth and nineteenth centuries that his father gave him from the
time he was five. Believing that most people were too beholden to
musical custom, George Ives encouraged independence of mind and
a greater use of native musical abilities in his family through such
ear-stretching exercises as having them sing *Old Folks at Home* in the
key of E♭ while being accompanied in the key of C; he was not, however, thinking in terms of polytonal composition.[24]

His experiments were also conducted outside his home. For example, he would play musical instruments over the pond at Danbury, captivated by the tone quality of the echo that returned to him
across the water [25]—an experience that his son attempted to recapture, years later, in his chamber-music piece *The Pond*. Sometimes he
even tried out his ideas on the townspeople of Danbury—probably
not to stretch *their* ears, but rather to satisfy his own musical interests
and his own sense of humor. His son recalled an example:

> The writer remembers hearing, when a boy, the music of a band
> in which the players were arranged in two or three groups around
> the town square. The main group in the bandstand at the center
> usually played the main themes, while the others, from the neigh-
> boring roofs and verandas, played the variations, refrains, etc. The
> piece remembered was a kind of paraphrase of "Jerusalem the
> Golden," a rather elaborate tone poem for those days. The band-
> master told of a man who, living near the variations, insisted that
> they were the real music and it was more beautiful to hear the
> hymn come sifting through them than the other way around. Oth-
> ers, walking around the square, were surprised at the different and
> interesting effects they got as they changed position. It was said also
> that many thought the music lost in effect when the piece was
> played by the band altogether, though, I think, the town vote was
> about even. The writer remembers, as a deep impression, the echo
> part from the roofs played by a chorus of violins and voices.[26]

The influence of this experiment by the father appears in his son's
later interest in the tonal effect of placing instruments offstage or at
varying distances from the auditor, as in his Fourth Symphony or
The Unanswered Question.

The best-known case of George Ives's trying out his musical innovations on the town occurred when two bands, his own and another one, marched past each other while each one played a different piece, so that the separate keys and rhythms were brought together in cacophonous conflict.[27] Charles Ives's memories of his boyhood musical experiences were often inaccurate; but in 1968 the Danbury architect Philip Sunderland, who had known both George E. and Charles Ives, recalled distinctly the clash of the two bands as they marched in opposite directions around the park.[28] Sunderland thought that George Ives had not planned the event deliberately; but whether he had or not, he found the effect fascinating, he communicated his sense of fascination to his son, and his son later captured the effect in one of his most famous works—*Putnam's Camp,* the second movement of his First Orchestral Set, *Three Places in New England.*

The reaction of people in Danbury to George Ives's aural experiments was probably more indulgent than hostile, but it was certainly not sympathetic. Sunderland recalled that they were not particularly interested in the effect produced by the two bands that played simultaneously, and he felt that they found Ives's experiments in general merely "discordant." [29] In 1891, after George Ives had given up the leadership of the Danbury Band, two bands passed each other accidentally in the street; the *Danbury Evening News,* reporting the event humorously, saw no inherent interest in the combination of sounds that resulted:

> The National band was giving a brief concert in Wooster House Square Saturday evening to advertise its dance at Cosmopolitan Park, when the Danbury band marched up the street on a similar mission for its entertainment in the City Hall. For a few moments there was a clash of brass instruments, and war seemed imminent, but good humor prevailed and each gave way to the other.[30]

Charles Ives gave evidence of an even more unsympathetic reaction among Danbury's citizens when he recalled that although his father had not inflicted his contrivances on the public very often, some had called him a crank when he had done so.[31]

George Ives's acoustical innovations did little to change an opinion which people in Danbury would have held even if he had been more musically conventional. They thought that he was not to be taken quite seriously simply *because* he was a professional musician. Socially, he was seen as somewhat *déclassé* in comparison with the rest of his family. It is true that a local newspaper, in an obituary for his brother Isaac in 1910, gave George equal rank with his two brothers and attributed his lack of eminence only to his relatively early death:

> The Ives family, through its representatives, Joseph M., merchant, George E., musician and Isaac W., philanthropist, for many years enjoyed in several villages on this side of the Connecticut line, not only popularity and confidence but enthusiastic support. George, by reason of death was not permitted to enjoy the benefit of his study and labor.[32]

This assessment may, however, be discounted as an attempt to pay tribute to the whole family upon the death of one of its most prominent members. A fairer view can be obtained from those who lived in Danbury when George Ives was active in music there. Philip Sunderland recalled that Danburians did not take George Ives "very seriously," a fact which Sunderland seemed to think arose naturally and understandably from the fact that he was the bandmaster; except for the latter role, George did not take an important part in the affairs of the town, according to Sunderland, although he was "without reproach." [33] All this was in strong contrast with George's brothers, Isaac and Joseph, and his brother-in-law Lyman Brewster, all of whom were among the most prominent and successful men in the town.

Again, Amelia Ives Van Wyck, George E. Ives's grandniece, who was ten years younger than Charles Ives and who spent her childhood and youth in Danbury, recalled in 1968 that in George's day Danburians thought it "foolishness" to make music one's life's work, since it was entertainment. Danbury did not have a high opinion of musicians; to be a musician or an artist was something a bit odd and not entirely respectable. Thus, Mrs. Van Wyck concluded, George failed to receive from his town the recognition that was his due; and she remembered that when he served as the last-minute replacement for the conductor of a visiting orchestra, he did better than the townspeople had anticipated—a remark that says as much about

Danbury's low expectations as it does about George Ives's high achievement.[34]

Contemporary printed sources give further evidence of Danbury's doubts about the serious value of music and musicians. Bailey's authoritative *History of Danbury* presents a picture of a society that thought it incumbent upon a man to go into business or to take up a useful profession such as law. Music was thought to be at best a leisure-time activity; and even in that category it was a merely pleasant and self-indulgent appendage to life, to be ranked far below charitable and community-improvement projects. Even though Danbury had an active musical life, and even though there was then considerably more direct, popular participation in music making than in the later age of the phonograph and the radio, nevertheless the serious-minded and work-oriented middle class of the town could not admit that music might be an individually or socially important matter. The professional musician, although he was invariably accorded the title of "professor," was too often reduced to a role in the town somewhat similar to that of the jester at a medieval court.

Thus the *History of Danbury* devoted considerable portions of its many pages to manufactures, railroads, banks, public improvements, the bar, medicine, religion, education, newspapers, charitable activities, and useful organizations of a public character; but to Danbury's musical history and contemporary musical life it gave scant attention—a bare listing of the names of five musical organizations in existence in 1895 and the statement that "Danbury has two colleges of music, both in a flourishing condition." [35] The last comment seems to say more about the business success of the colleges than about their cultural value.

After George Ives's death in 1894, Danbury was willing to accord him the honor that was his due by virtue of his background and character—provided that it was not required to recognize that he had been a professional musician. Both the *History of Danbury* and the *Danbury Evening News* chose to imply that he had been "in business" and that his musical experience had been that of an amateur. Thus they both turned his life upside down and avoided mentioning what had been most important about him, both in his own eyes and in those of the townspeople—that he had pursued the career of "town musician" for a quarter of a century. The *History of Danbury* gave him a separate write-up in its chapter on the Civil War, probably because he had died shortly before the book's publication; it spoke of his "thorough musical education" and his wartime activities, after which "Mr. Ives returned to Danbury, where he resided until his sudden death on November 5th, 1894. At that time he held the positions of Cashier and Director in the Danbury Savings Bank, of which his father was one of the founders." [36] There was not a word about his musical activities in Danbury. The obituary in the *Danbury Evening News* was only slightly less myopic; after a similar account of his early life, it continued:

> He was mustered out September 25, 1865, and returned to New York city. He then came to Danbury and embarked in the hardware business.
>
> He afterwards was bookkeeper for a number of local business houses, and in January accepted a position in that capacity in the Danbury Savings Bank. Ever since the close of the war he has demonstrated his love for music by being connected with many bands as leader.[37]

Thus did Danbury choose to pass lightly over a man's life's work because it could not regard that work as valid.

As for George Ives's activities in business, both Amelia Ives Van Wyck and Philip Sunderland believed that he had never been trained as an accountant.[38] He was forced, from time to time, to take various nonmusical jobs around the town because he could not make enough money from music to support his family. On one such occasion he was reduced to working as an assistant to his own nephew, Howard Merritt Ives, who was head bookkeeper in the office of the wealthy and prominent hat manufacturer Charles H. Merritt. Merritt, who was George Ives's second cousin, could not claim to occupy a higher social position in the town than the Iveses did; yet on at least one occasion, George Ives chose to play the role of Merritt's employee rather than his theoretical social equal. Philip Sunderland, who was also working in the office at the time, heard him address Merritt under his breath, so that the other employees, but not Merritt, could hear it, as "you damned old monopolist"—a remark that

Sunderland thought both irrelevant and, in its irrelevance, typical of George Ives.[39]

At the end of 1890, George Ives gave up his leadership of the Danbury Band, with which he had been so closely connected for a number of years; and at about the same time, he took a full-time position in the Savings Bank of Danbury in order to support his family more adequately. He became a teller and, in 1893, a director; but these positions were given him, as his grandniece later pointed out, because of the close connection which his father had had with the institution.[40] Philip Sunderland remembered him as a "clerk" in the bank until the end,[41] and this seems to have been the position that he in effect occupied when he died at the age of forty-nine in 1894.

If George Ives's chosen career made his social position in the town that of the *déclassé,* his position within the Ives family was equally anomalous. His marriage to Mary ("Mollie") Parmelee in 1874 was an alliance with a family a good distance below the Iveses in social standing. The Parmelees were a family not long removed from the farm, and the few extant letters written by Mary reveal, in their misspellings and lack of punctuation, a level of education considerably below that of her husband and his family. She is remembered as a simple person, her life entirely devoted to domestic concerns; beyond the narrow world of her household she had no interests, and she knew nothing of music. As is usual in such marriages, the life of George Ives, his wife, and his sons was dominated and monopolized by the more socially prominent family, the Iveses, and not by the Parmelees. All these circumstances must have made it difficult, at least at first, for Mary Ives to fit into her new round of life after her marriage, especially because the pace of that round of life was bound to be set by the imperious temper and exalted notions of George Ives's sister, Amelia Ives Brewster.

Charles Ives's Aunt Amelia had very definite ideas about the role that the Ives family should play in Danbury. She let it be known that Joseph H. Ives, a lowly florist in the town, was not related to *her* family, although he was in fact her second cousin.[42] If it can be surmised that she was not happy with her brother's marriage, it is even more likely that she was displeased with his musical activities—for example, when he led the Danbury Band in a parade for the butchers' barbecue, or when his Standard Orchestra was hired to play for the Ancient Order of Hibernians' St. Patrick's Day ball and at the opening of Sam Harris's new store.[43] Nor is it recorded that her genteel notions of religious worship allowed her to attend the outdoor camp meetings at which her brother led the farmers and their families as they let out their pent-up feelings by singing *In the Sweet By-and-by* and other gospel hymns.

George Ives was, nevertheless, much closer to his sister and her husband than he was to his two brothers, Joseph and Isaac. George and Mary Ives and their sons tended to do things with the Brewsters; and although the two families did not live together, much of the life of George's family centered around the "old house" on Main Street where Judge Brewster and his wife lived with George's and Amelia's aged, widowed, and venerated mother, Mrs. Sarah Hotchkiss Wilcox Ives. In their interaction with the Brewsters, George and his family inevitably took on the character of poor relations. The clearest example of this relationship occurred each summer when a group of interrelated and socially prominent Danbury families—Whites, Seeleys, Demings, Iveses, Brewsters—occupied their adjoining family houses, known collectively as "Cousins' Beach," at the seaside town of Westbrook, Connecticut. George Ives, of course, owned no such house, and his family stayed, therefore, with his sister and brother-in-law as guests in their place. It was a relationship of dependence which the closeness of the two households made it unnecessary to define, but which George Ives probably understood. Eventually, in 1888–1889, George's and Amelia's mother had the barn behind her home on Main Street converted into a house, Amelia supervising the work; George and his family then moved into the converted building, a move that brought them next door to the Brewsters.[44]

The well-off but childless Brewsters also lavished attention on George Ives's sons, in whose development they took a keen interest. In 1893, for example, Lyman Brewster was appointed by the governor of Connecticut to the state's new Commission for Promotion of Uniformity in Legislation in the United States, and in this capacity he attended a conference of such commissions from the several states that met at Milwaukee along with the convention of the American Bar Association. He took his nephew Charles along as his secretary, thus giving the latter his one and only look at the interior of the country as well as a trip to the Columbian Exposition at Chicago, where he heard the celebrated French organist Alexandre Guilmant. The scholarly Brewster also supervised his far-from-scholarly nephew's studies when Charles was preparing for Yale the next year. On the whole, however, Uncle Lyman took a greater interest in Charles's brother, Moss, grooming him for the bar and taking him into his law firm; ultimately, Moss Ives practically duplicated his uncle's career by becoming an eminent Danbury lawyer, a member of the state legislature, a local judge, and an amateur scholar. It was Charles Ives, however, who duplicated, in the next generation, Lyman Brewster's more-than-avuncular relationship to his nephews; wealthy but without male children, Charles took a paternal interest in his less successful brother's five sons, furnishing them a home, money, and guidance at crucial stages in their maturation.

Amelia Brewster, too, bore an important relationship to her nephew Charles. Especially after her brother's death, she took advantage of his wife's reticent nature in order to exert a commanding influence in the lives of her two nephews. It was generally understood in the family that it was futile to try to oppose her will. When Charles came home from college or visited Danbury after he had gone to work in New York, it was at Aunt Amelia's house, not at his mother's, that he stayed. When he became engaged, it was the impression that his fiancée would make on Aunt Amelia, not the one that she would make on his mother, that he worried about. The climax—and the collapse—of Aunt Amelia's efforts to dominate Charles's life came at the time of his marriage in 1908, when she made an abortive attempt to get him and his new wife to live with her in Danbury.[45] It was soon clear, however, that in Charles's wife, Harmony Twichell, Aunt Amelia had met her match.[46]

Although Charles Ives did not articulate his views about his father's anomalous social position as a professional musician, there is some indication that he was disturbed by it. His awareness of his father's social, professional, and economic difficulties undoubtedly accounted in part for Charles's going into business, not into music, as a vocation; in his father's career he had a vivid example of society's general attitude toward the professional musician.

The lavish praise and admiration that Charles, in his later life, heaped upon his father may also be partially explained by a feeling in the son that injustice had been done his father in Danbury. Of course, Charles *was* extraordinarily close to his father. His mother, whom he never mentioned in his later writings, was limited both in personality and in understanding; her grandniece recalled later that Mary Ives had had so little sense of the importance of music for her son that she had often taken him away from his practice to run errands for her.[47] As a result, George Ives loomed inordinately large in his son's early life. Almost all of Charles's formative musical experiences, as well as many important experiences of other kinds, were intertwined with his father's guidance, support, and encouragement; it is not surprising, then, that the son came to idolize his father, especially after the latter's untimely death, believing that whatever was of value in his own compositions was primarily the result of his father's influence.[48] Nor is it too much to say that "the germ of every new type of musical behavior that Charles Ives developed or organized can be found in the suggestions and experiments of his father." [49] But Charles Ives claimed even more than this for his father, attributing to him a musical depth that he probably did not have, apologizing for his having left behind so little of permanence, and exaggerating his influence upon the youth of Danbury.[50] He also made sure, when his own music began to be known and written about by musicians, that accounts of his musical development began with a generous tribute to his father's influence upon him—with the result that most people today who know something about Charles Ives's music are also acquainted with George Ives and his musical experiments.

George Ives lived an obscure life in Danbury, and its people treated him badly, both socially and musically. When his son acquired a reputation as a composer, he felt justified in using that reputation to secure for his father some small posthumous recognition.

If a clear reaction to the *social* implications of George Ives's position as a musician is not to be found among his son's writings, a reaction to the *sexual* implications of that position is one of the most articulate themes in Charles Ives's life and work. This theme—the connotation of effeminacy that art music had for Americans in the nineteenth century—is a crucially important means of approaching Charles Ives as a composer. To understand the subject, it is first necessary to consider the social development of music in nineteenth-century America, particularly the division between classical and popular music.

In America, "classical music" suggests a music that is artistic, edifying, and enduring, a somewhat exotic music that must be appreciated or "cultivated" with effort. "Popular music," on the other hand, is merely entertaining, utilitarian, and ephemeral, a more home-grown music that is entered into naturally and without effort. The music historian H. Wiley Hitchcock has used the terms "cultivated tradition" and "vernacular tradition" to refer more exactly to these two bodies of music in American history.[51] While a given piece of music is generally thought of as belonging either to one tradition or to the other, it is nevertheless possible for the selfsame composition to be classical on one occasion and popular on another, since the determining factors are the social situation in which it is played and the attitude of the performers and listeners toward it. Thus the bandmaster John Philip Sousa, comparing himself with the famous American symphony conductor Theodore Thomas, wrote that Thomas "gave Wagner, Liszt, and Tchaikowsky, in the belief that he was educating his public; I gave Wagner, Liszt, and Tchaikowsky with the hope that I was entertaining my public." [52]

The division of music into cultivated and vernacular traditions did not really assume its familiar form until the nineteenth century. In the eighteenth century, to be sure, a few urban sophisticates who were cognizant of European musical developments, such as Francis Hopkinson of Philadelphia, probably looked disdainfully upon the folkish compositions of self-taught New England composers like William Billings. But throughout the towns of rural New England, the roughhewn sacred compositions of Billings and other native-born singing-school teachers were acceptable to all levels of society. Harriet Beecher Stowe, although born as late as 1811, recalled with what vigor the "fuguing tunes" of Billings and the others had been sung during her childhood in her father's very proper Congregational church at Litchfield, Connecticut.[53]

Early in the nineteenth century, American musicians began to feel the impact of the European romantic sensibility, with its new emphasis on the sublime and the spiritually exalted in the arts. Influenced by the romantic ideal, advanced arbiters of musical taste in America adopted a higher and purer standard for acceptable music, turning particularly for models to the "scientifically correct" compositions of such German composers as Handel, Haydn, and Beethoven. The old fuguing tunes, with their crudities, were banished from proper New England churches, to be replaced by more correctly harmonized hymns. The appearance of a musical life that was distinctly in the cultivated tradition occurred first in the larger eastern cities, where it was encouraged by the immigration of many German musicians and patronized by a wealthy and growing upper middle class with pretensions to "culture." Yet smaller communities like Danbury, as they grew in wealth, population, and leisure, also felt the pull of the cultivated tradition.

Meanwhile, the less affluent classes in America clung to a more popular music, while the westward movement, which removed many Americans from contact with the cultivated-tradition music of the more civilized centers, constantly reinvigorated the vernacular tradition through fresh contact with folk and indigenous sources. People of cultivated taste might look askance at revival hymns, minstrel-show songs, band marches, and popular dances, but most Americans loved this music far more than art music.

The split between these two musical traditions had several unfortunate results. American composers of classical music were trained in Europe or by Europeans in America, and their compositions tended to sound Germanic, imitative, and somewhat academic. Lacking an American tradition of art music comparable to that of Germany or Italy, they felt cut off from the popular culture of their own country and often retreated (as did John Knowles Paine and Horatio Parker) within the walls of the university or conservatory. Nor were they likely to have their compositions played, for there were no aristocratic patrons with court orchestras, and the audiences at public concerts found European composers more exotically appealing—if not Mozart, Beethoven, and Wagner, then Spohr, Meyerbeer, and Raff. But concert-hall audiences with limited musical tastes also found such music rather "heavy" and shifted their attention from the composer to the more obvious and more spectacular virtuosity of the performer. Hence appeared the cult of the virtuoso, which European artists like the violinist Ole Bull and the singer Jenny Lind took advantage of in their highly successful tours of America before the Civil War.

To satisfy the demand of amateur performers for a music simpler than that played by the great virtuosos, but of equal cultivation, there arose what Hitchcock calls "genteel household music," of which two American examples would be Stephen Foster's song *Beautiful Dreamer* and Louis Moreau Gottschalk's *méditation religieuse* for piano, *The Last Hope*. Although professing noble artistic ideals, such household music was too often characterized by banal melodies, rippling arpeggios, and other tasteless decorations. Danbury's growth from town to city gave some of its citizens aspirations to "culture," aspirations which were fed by its proximity to Boston and New York; but it was still too small and too far from the big cities to participate in more than a diluted form of the cultivated tradition. Since Danbury rarely got to hear a genuine virtuoso, household music was also very largely the music of public concerts, which were usually given by the Danburians themselves. Thus Charles Ives grew up surrounded by such music; and he tended all his life to judge art music in general on the basis of the sentimental household music he had heard and played as a boy.

The separation between cultivated and vernacular traditions in nineteenth-century America was by no means absolute. Especially outside the great cities, in provincial communities like Danbury where public taste and musical resources were limited, a given musical program might contain elements of both the cultivated and the vernacular. What is significant for Charles Ives's development is that different sexual connotations became attached to each tradition.

Excluded from the more prestigious business and professional positions in nineteenth-century America, refined women of the "better classes" turned increasingly toward music to fill their leisure time, to satisfy their desire for "accomplishment," and sometimes also to make a living. But they were, of course, excluded from taking an active role in vernacular-tradition music because of its vulgar connotations. Instead, they threw themselves into cultivated-tradition music; and by the latter part of the century, they had come to dominate this aspect of the country's musical life. Women were, above all, the "appreciators" of good music, making up most of the concert and opera audiences and forming musical clubs throughout the country. By the early twentieth century, through their sustained interest, women exercised considerable power over the policies of the great American orchestras. It was ladies active in the New York Philharmonic who hounded Gustav Mahler out of the conductorship of that orchestra in 1911.[54] Women also made up the majority of music students in America, furnished many of the music teachers, and wrote much of what was written about classical music. They could sing in public, both as soloists and in groups; and they could play instrumental solos or accompaniments, especially on the piano or organ. The farther one got from the cities, moreover, the more sheer necessity allowed women to occupy other performing roles in classical music. "I do not think," wrote the American conductor Walter Damrosch, "there has ever been a country whose musical development has been fostered so almost exclusively by women as America."[55]

Women became dominant in cultivated-tradition music because the European system of selecting out and educating a body of males to carry on artistic traditions had never caught hold in America. And as women's dominance grew, American men retreated from classical music as a threat to their masculinity, regarding it as "essentially the province of females, foreigners, or effeminates."[56] A very large number of American men—including many whose social and educational backgrounds should, from a European point of view, have drawn them toward art music—took their musical values instead from the vernacular tradition, with its preference for utilitarian, uncouth music and its disdain for the cultivated.

The resultant situation became an American joke, as in the later comic strip of Jiggs and Maggie (called, significantly, "Bringing Up Father"): the wife did her duty to culture and the higher values by dragging her husband to a concert or to the opera; her husband

27

maintained his masculinity by protesting all the way and by falling asleep during the music. It was an old game with him: when he had been a boy, his mother had done *her* duty to culture by giving him piano lessons and forcing him to practice, while he had done *his* duty to his manhood by playing truant and protesting that only sissies played the piano.

In Danbury, in the 1880s and 1890s, women appear to have exercised a commanding role in music of the cultivated tradition, particularly two women: Miss Ella Hollister and Miss Isabelle Fayerweather. A relatively enlightened view among Danburians about the role of women in society, combined with a scarcity of the male (mainly German-American) musicians that would have been available in a large city, allowed a remarkable degree of freedom to these women in their attempts to fulfill the aspirations of Danbury toward musical culture. In March, 1888, for example, Miss Hollister actually conducted a group of amateurs in public in Haydn's Toy Symphony.[57] Miss Hollister and Miss Fayerweather were teachers of music; in the fall of 1887, along with the Norwalk organist Alexander Gibson, they opened the Danbury School of Music. They also served, at one time or another, as directors of music (sometimes called "choristers") in several of the churches of Danbury. The school of music, the Protestant churches, and the YMCA formed the axis around which cultivated-tradition musical life, both sacred and secular, revolved in Danbury, and it was in these institutions that the numerous genteel concerts, recitals, and "entertainments" were held.

As musical director at the Methodist church in the 1880s, as well as in many other tasks as a professional musician, George Ives naturally participated in the making of cultivated-tradition music in Danbury; when he did so, however, he was forced to enter the province of women, and his son Charles clearly saw that he was doing so. The performance of Haydn's Toy Symphony, for example, was part of a concert that Miss Hollister and Miss Fayerweather got up for the benefit of the YMCA; on the same program Miss Hollister also conducted the players, among whom was "Master Charlie Ives" on the drum and musical glasses, in F. X. Chwatal's *The Happy Sleighing Party*. The printed program for this concert appears in one of the musical scrapbooks that Charles Ives put together years later; at the bottom of the program is written, in his hand: "I remember Father did all the work, rehearsing, arranging, etc., for this, and showed Miss Hollister how to conduct—as this was a ladies' society concert!" [58] George Ives's name, of course, appeared nowhere on the program. What his son was complaining of—what he must have had to witness again and again in those years—was the spectacle of his father's being musically emasculated by the genteel women of Danbury.

Charles had his own emasculation to worry about as well. Although many of his early musical appearances in town were made under the sponsorship of his father, he was nevertheless compelled, as a performer and composer of cultivated-tradition music, to venture into a field dominated by women. For example, in 1887, when he was twelve, he appeared in a recital given by pupils of the Misses Hollister, Fayerweather, and Rice; Charles, who was a pupil of Miss Hollister's, gave a piano solo, a tarantella by Heller, on a program that also included Lange's *Chirping Crickets* and Behr's *Fire-balls* Mazurka.[59] In February, 1889, when he was fourteen, he became regular organist at the West Street Congregational Church, where Miss Hollister was in charge of the music. In October of the same year, on his fifteenth birthday, he became regular organist of the Second Baptist Church; the *Evening News* noted that he was "the youngest organist in the state." [60] He held this post at the Baptist church for three and a half years, until he went away to school; from May, 1890, the musical director under whom he served at the church was Mrs. Thomas Smyth, who played an active part in the cultivated musical life of Danbury and whom Ives's wife later described as a woman who put on airs.[61]

As a church organist, Charles played a great deal of music of the cultivated tradition (including some of his own) at the regular and special services. He also played numerous organ solos for concerts at the Baptist and other churches. Although men participated in these concerts, there was a noticeably feminine aura about them and about the reaction to them. A case in point is a concert, for the benefit of the New Church Fund, that was given at the Baptist church on June 11, 1890. A review of the concert, evidently written by a woman, appeared in the *Danbury Evening News* the next day; it is given here in full, exactly as it appeared, for it captures perfectly the character of the cultivated-tradition musical world in which Ives grew up:

LAST EVENING'S CONCERT.: THE GREATEST
ARTISTIC SUCCESS OF THE SEASON.

The weather last evening was anything but inspiring to an artist who is called upon to face an audience such as assembled in the Baptist church to listen to and mayhap criticize those who were to appear in the concert. But there was much to praise and little to criticize. There was a fair and intelligent and appreciative audience, every one of whom seemed to think that the programme was all too short.

The programme opened with the overture to "William Tell," by Rossini arranged by Dudley Buck. It was rendered on the organ by Master Ives with brilliancy and precision.

The duett, "Estudiantina," Lacombe, was sung by Mrs. Carrie Allen-Baker and Luther G. Allen in a perfection of voice, tone, and taste, the clear, bird-like notes and the full, deep chest tones harmonizing beautifully.

The organ solo, "Toccato," Bach, was finely executed by Master Ives.

"Welcome, Pretty Primrose." Pinsuti, as rendered by Master George Moore, the boy soprano, was a dream of delight, for his wonderful voice rung like a silver bell, and rippled along like the murmurings of a gently-flowing brooklet. In response to an encore, Master Moore gave the gem of the evening in "Angels Ever Bright and Fair," in so charming a manner that one could almost fancy he heard the flutter of white wings and heard the music of distant harps.

The next number was a solo by Miss Adelaide Haight. She has a deep, powerful and well managed voice, and her selection was greatly enjoyed.

The "Song to the Evening Star," from "Tannhauser" was given by Mr. Allen in a delightful and artistic manner; but even more enjoyable was "Come to Me My Love," which he sang charmingly in response to an encore.

The duett "Eben a Te," from Rossini's "Semiramide," as given by Mrs. Baker and Miss Haight, was most brilliantly rendered, and thoroughly appreciated, the memory of the bird-like trills and clear notes like the falling of crystal waters will be pleasant for many days.

"La Capricciosa" by T. Mattei, as sung by Master Moore, held the audience breathless with delight.

The organ solo, "Home, Sweet Home," arranged by Dudley Buck, was exceedingly well rendered by Master Ives.

The Sonata, in F minor, by Mendelsshon, was superb, as was also the march "Pontificale," in D major, by Lemmens.

Master Ives deserves and receives great praise for his patient perseverance in his study of the organ, and is to be congratulated on his marked ability as a master of the keys for one so young. We predict for him a brilliant future as an organist.

The concert was brilliant throughout—perhaps a song or two of quiet pathos would have given variety—and suited the tastes of those who now are old; but it was a success as it was, however. Prof. Gibson as accompanist deserves much credit, for without him the concert would not have been so great a success.[62]

Charles Ives may well have been thankful that he did not have to experience the even more explicit emasculation at the hands of women undergone by the boy soprano, Master Moore.

In the midst of such an atmosphere, Ives had to assert his masculinity and to try to grow up as a normal boy. It was a problem for him, because boys in Danbury, like boys all over America, were naturally going to consider him a sissy if he played "Mendelsshon" in public and got patted on the head for it by nice ladies. In his autobiographical *Memos,* written forty years later, Ives explained his ambivalent feelings toward music:

> As a boy [I was] partially ashamed of it—an entirely wrong attitude, but it was strong—most boys in American country towns, I think, felt the same. When other boys . . . were out driving grocery carts, or doing chores, or playing ball, I felt all wrong to stay in and play piano. And there may be something in it. Hasn't music always been too much an emasculated art? Mozart etc. helped.[63]

Charles Ives maintained his manhood by becoming a baseball player. His informal efforts in this direction were later institutionalized in the spring of 1889 when he joined a juvenile team called the Alerts. His activities that summer and the next were a strange combination of music and baseball. For example, he played center field for the Alerts on June 27, 1890, and then on the next afternoon gave his own organ recital at the Baptist church.[64] He also played football; and in the early 1890s, as a student first at the Danbury High School and then at the Danbury Academy, he outshone most of his fellow players at the two sports. In 1892 he was captain of a combined Danbury High School–Danbury Academy football team; in the team picture taken that year, he attempted to cover up his baby-faced appearance by scowling and looking tough.[65]

Ives continued to play football and baseball at the Hopkins Grammar School (in New Haven) and at Yale, and he participated in a baseball team made up of his business associates even after he went to work for a life insurance company in New York City. Undoubtedly he enjoyed these sporting activities; but he seemed to place an unnatural and strained emphasis, both for his own benefit and for that of other people, upon his role as a player and enthusiast. And there is good reason to believe that this emphasis was a counterweight to the connotations of emasculation and effeminacy which his activities in music of the cultivated tradition had in his own mind and which, he knew, they had for other people as well.

One of the many stories about Ives is that when, during his boyhood, someone who had heard that he was a musician would ask him what he played, the embarrassed Ives would reply, "Shortstop!" [66] But, as with many other aspects of his thought and feeling, Ives was not really articulate about this subject until middle age. Yet it is not a matter that begins to bother a male only after he has grown up; it arises rather from a boy's life among other boys. It seems justified, therefore, to extrapolate back from Ives's later writings to obtain an idea of his thoughts about masculinity and music when he was growing up. Certainly his mature life is full of embarrassed attempts to make excuses for his sensitivity as an artist by asserting his masculinity as a sportsman. During his last thirty years, in letters about music written to his musical friends, Ives turned with great frequency to metaphors drawn from baseball. In his seventies, for example, he wrote to E. Power Biggs that in playing his own

Variations on *America* on the organ as a boy, he had enjoyed playing the fast pedal part in the last variation almost as much as playing baseball.[67] He could not quite equate the two experiences, for the masculine role had to be kept dominant.

Baseball, football, and other sports, then, helped Ives to maintain his masculinity as a boy; but the danger, from the point of view of the future composer, was that Ives's boyhood musical experiences would sour him on music of the cultivated tradition and cause him to be perpetually embarrassed by his connection with it. His musical thinking might have taken a different turn if he could have had the opportunity to share "great music" with other men in a thoroughly masculine atmosphere, cut off from genteel women. His father provided a great deal of help in this direction, but Ives needed, even more, the companionship of peers—other boys or young men who were also searching for a way in which a male could love art music without losing his masculinity. The composer Roy Harris, growing up near Los Angeles a quarter of a century later, faced an even more difficult situation, for he received only disapproval from his father for his musical efforts. Harris, too, went out for school sports in order to stave off the hostility of his male peers toward his penchant for classical music; but he managed to preserve his respect for his own artistic sensitivity by finding musical companionship in other males of his own generation, with whom he had a separate existence apart from his day-to-day life:

Meanwhile, my two worlds of growing up continued. I became a solo clarinet player, and learned to dance well. With great pride I boasted that I was not at the top of my class in my studies.

But there was another hidden world which few knew about: the "Bachelor's Club." There were six of us, headed by a young Scotchman who was the best organist in town and a first-class certified public accountant. He liked the way I played the piano and the clarinet, and that I was not a sissy, that I went to dances with the girls. In this group I learned to play chess, and I learned about philosophy. Most important of all, I heard great virtuoso performances (on His Master's Voice records). On Sunday nights we would congregate to hear Caruso, Chaliapin, John McCormack,

Galli-Curci, Schumann-Heink, Kreisler, Ysaÿe, Paderewski, de Pachmann. We went to see and hear operas and symphonies on tour in Los Angeles.[68]

It was just this sort of companionship that Ives lacked in Danbury. He was born too early to find in the social fabric of the American town or small city the interstices for independent artistic development that Harris found only twenty-five years later in a similar environment. If Ives could have received the requisite support from other males of his peer group, he might have concluded that a separation could be made between the most serious European classical music and the genteel household music that he so despised, that only the latter was worthy of the aversion that American males felt for all music of the cultivated tradition, and that this foolish blanket aversion on the part of men was the real reason that all music of the cultivated tradition had come to be socially dominated by women. Lacking any peer-group support, however, Ives accepted the connotations of sociosexual effeminacy that American males attached to all cultivated-tradition music and thus allowed an emotional barrier to form between himself and such music. In doing so, he gave way to tremendous social pressures that weighed upon him and forced him to conform to the mores and attitudes of Danbury people, pressures which are evidenced more generally in his lifelong compulsion to idealize and identify himself with Danbury life in his music and his writings.

Ives's emotional rejection of all cultivated-tradition music was of immense importance, for it left him essentially truncated as an artist. Although he loved and played Bach, Beethoven, and Brahms all his life and drew upon the tradition that they represented for much that he put into his own music, he always protected his masculinity by avoiding a too close identification with that tradition. On the one hand, this attitude allowed him to make the radical experiments that were a decisive break with the eighteenth- and nineteenth-century European musical tradition; on the other hand, his attitude was an important reason for the tragic isolation of his active musical life. This emotional aversion to the effeminacy that he saw in cultivated-tradition music took shape in him while he was growing up in Danbury; it was refined while he was studying at Yale and after he went to work in New York City; but it was not articulated until his thirties and forties, when he first overcame his shyness on the subject and began to pour out onto paper the pent-up feelings of his earlier years. He gave perhaps the most reasoned statement of his position in the autobiographical *Memos* of his late fifties. Here he argued that all music—even that of Bach, Beethoven, and Brahms—had been too much bound by unthinking authority and tradition because of composers' dependence on the approval of the ladies and the lady-like music critics. "Music is a nice little art just born," he wrote, "and they ask 'Is it a boy or a girl?'—and one voice in the back row says 'It's going to be a boy—some time!' " [69]

A more strident, and potentially more violent, note of frustrated masculinity was sounded by Ives in the following passage from his *Essays before a Sonata* (issued privately in 1920), which must have embarrassed the more self-consciously cultivated among his readers. Ives is discussing concert artists and composers who attempt to impress their audiences:

> The pose of self-absorption, which some men, in the advertising business (and incidentally in the recital and composing business) put into their photographs or the portraits of themselves, while all dolled up in their purple-dressing-gowns, in their twofold wealth of golden hair, in their cissy-like postures over the piano keys—this pose of "manner" sometimes sounds out so loud that the more their music is played, the less it is heard. . . . The unescapable impression that one sometimes gets by a glance at these public-inflicted trade-marks, and without having heard or seen any of their music, is that the one great underlying desire of these appearing-artists, is to impress, perhaps startle and shock their audiences and at any cost. This may have some such effect upon some of the lady-part (male or female) of their listeners but possibly the members of the men-part, who as boys liked hockey better than birthday-parties, may feel like shocking a few of these picture-sitters with something stronger than their own forzandos.[70]

Ives could not leave the subject alone; again and again he returned to it in his letters, his formal writings, and his personal memoranda. He referred to the dean of Boston's music critics as "she, Philip Nathan Hale" and as an "old lady." [71] Indeed, "old ladies"

became his standard term of contempt for those musicians who submitted themselves to female domination by keeping music conven-
tionally genteel, while the most acid adjective that he could bestow
upon the music itself was "nice"—probably the standard term of
praise that the ladies of Danbury had once bestowed upon the music
that he had played for them. A sentimental passage incorporated
into Ives's Second String Quartet as a joke on "the ladies" was
marked by him "Andante emasculata." [72] Many more examples
could be given, but perhaps the one that shows him at his most inventive is the series of nicknames connoting effeminacy that Ives,
who loved puns, thought up for leading performers of the standard
repertoire of cultivated-tradition music. Josef Hofmann became
"Josy Hofmann," Toscanini became "Toss the ninny," Ossip Gabrilowitsch became "Osssssssipy Gabrilowitsch," and Rachmaninoff became "Rachnotmanenough." [73]

An important aspect of Ives's assertion of his masculinity against a
feminized musical culture was his strong liking for musical dissonance—that is, for what his generation regarded as cacophony.
Drawing upon both his admiration for his father's experiments in
sound (themselves an assertion of masculinity and independence)
and his dislike for the conventional genteel music of "the ladies,"
Ives erected in his mind a dichotomy between manly dissonant music
and effeminate "easy-on-the-ears" music. To write or perform or listen to a dissonant work became, for him, an act of courage and
manhood, while to be content with a "nice," soothing, conventional
work was to be a "cissy." John Kirkpatrick, the leading authority on
Ives, has even suggested that as Ives grew older, he felt an ever
greater need to express his rebellion through ever greater dissonance in his music; this need was so great that it later led him on several occasions to find in his early musical works, the manuscripts of
which were often in a sketchy and inexact state, a dissonance which
they had not contained when he had written them.[74] And this was
true even though some of the music he had written as a boy in Danbury had, in fact, contained startling dissonances. The point being
made here is crucial to an understanding of Ives as a musical pioneer. Instead of his having first rejected cultivated-tradition music
on aesthetic and moral grounds—lack of idealism and originality,

concern for pure "effect," lack of ear-challenging dissonance—and then having attached connotations of effeminacy to what he had already rejected, it appears that the actual process was just the reverse: he first rejected such music for its sociosexual implications of effeminacy, and only then did he develop an aesthetic and moral rationale for that rejection. Only in this way can the underlying paranoia about masculinity and femininity in his writings about music be adequately explained.

So far, Ives's musical experiences in Danbury have been examined in relation to music of the cultivated tradition. There was, however, another tradition of music in Danbury—the vernacular tradition—and with it Ives could wholly identify himself, because it did not have popular connotations of effeminacy. Vernacular-tradition music can best be approached in terms of the four principal institutions through which he encountered it: the town band, the theater orchestra, the barn dance, and the outdoor revival meeting.

Charles naturally regarded his father as an extraordinary bandmaster. His Civil War band had drawn the admiring comments of Lincoln and Grant because he had put something special into the playing of the usual band pieces.[75] He continued this craftsmanlike approach to band music after he returned to Danbury; it was as leader of the Danbury Band that George Ives was best known to his fellow Danburians during the 1880s, when Charles Ives was growing up and receiving his early musical impressions. The boy himself played the drum in his father's band, although not as a regular member of the group; and several of his own youthful pieces received some of their earliest performances by the band. George Ives himself composed very little for his group, although he did some arranging of other music for it. Among the band music that most impressed Charles Ives was that of the composer David W. Reeves, whose *Second Regiment Connecticut National Guard March* always retained for him its power to conjure up vivid memories of his father and his boyhood in Danbury.

The Danbury Band was squarely in the vernacular tradition of American music. One clear indication of its lack of pretensions to cultivation was its including at least five or six Irishmen—and in 1892, after George Ives had left its leadership, even an Italo-

American! (In fact, according to the rector of the town's Catholic church, the Danbury Band had evolved from what had once been that church's temperance society band.[76]) The band thus provided for George Ives and his son what other Danburians of their background and class often did not have—a bridge to the non-Anglo-Saxon part of the community. In a more general sense, however, the band was part of the mainstream of the American vernacular tradition because it played music which was not regarded as edifying and worthy of appreciation in itself. The music was merely a utilitarian accompaniment for festive or solemn public occasions, such as the Fourth of July parade or the procession to the cemetery on Decoration Day to lay flowers on the soldiers' graves; and often the band simply supplied a relaxing entertainment, in the form of a concert in the park, after a hard day's work. Perhaps it was more for his activities in *vernacular-tradition* music than for his position as professional musician per se that George Ives's musical career was soft-pedaled in his obituaries in the *Danbury Evening News* and the *History of Danbury,* which were here acting as exponents of genteel culture. If so, George Ives was damned for both sides of his musical life—psychically emasculated by the ladies in his making of cultivated-tradition music and socially declassed by the arbiters of "society" and culture for his making of vernacular-tradition music. Charles Ives, however, had a very different view. He came to feel that the ideals and uplift to which genteel music of the cultivated tradition aspired were generally quite superficial, but that real (although un-self-conscious) ideals and depth were to be found in music of the vernacular tradition, the music of that daily life of the people of Danbury in which he found a transcendental and mystical significance.

George Ives also played in several theater orchestras in the 1870s and 1880s, notably the Standard Orchestra, and he led some of them as well. The small theater orchestra of the American town of that time was an ill-defined institution, generally made up of whatever instruments happened to be available at the time. At Taylor's Opera House in Danbury, the theater orchestra of the moment would provide instrumental interludes or accompaniments for comedies and variety shows, which might then be followed by a dance for which the orchestra also supplied the music. At such an evening of vernacular theater and dance, presented by the German Dramatic Association at the opera house on January 16, 1888, the Standard Orchestra gave Charles Ives's *Holiday Quickstep* its first known performance.[77] The theater orchestra was also closely connected with two other forms of music in Danbury, that of the minstrel shows and that of the popular town dances, both of which made their impression on young Ives; and although ragtime, which arose partly out of a combination of these two forms, had not yet made its formal appearance as such by the time he left Danbury, he later came to enjoy it, play it, and incorporate it into his own compositions.

While the bands and theater orchestras were town institutions, the barn dances were held in the country and had a strong attraction for farm people. Barn dances were not mentioned in the Danbury newspapers, probably not so much because of the ungenteel character of the music played at them as because of the "class of people" who attended them from among the Anglo-Saxon community. Although he was an accomplished violinist, George Ives is not known to have sunk so low as to fiddle at country dances. Charles Ives's hero in this part of popular music, therefore, was the country fiddler John Starr, who came from the nearby rural community of Brookfield.[78] Shrinking from a description of Starr as a mere barn-dance fiddler, but unable to call him anything else but a musician, the *Danbury Evening News* in his obituary searched hard for euphemisms and came up with this description: "He was a well-known musician, being a skillful violinist, and was from his youth up identified with orchestral music at sociables and other entertainments in Danbury and neighboring towns." [79] For Charles Ives, however, John Starr's position as country fiddler was not one of ignominy, but one of pride, for the music that he played was more masculine and vital, and more meaningful to those who danced to it, than anything presented at the genteel "entertainments" of Miss Hollister and Miss Fayerweather.

The outdoor camp meetings were also held in the country, at nearby Redding, with George Ives leading the singing and his son sometimes accompanying on the melodeon (small reed organ). As reported by the *Danbury News,* these camp meetings were Methodist gatherings under fairly staid leadership. But Charles Ives chose to remember the more popular, rural, and vernacular aspects of them, particularly how deeply moved he had been by the fervor with which the farm families had sung the revival and gospel hymns. The stonemason John Bell might bellow off key and everyone have his own version of the words and tune, but their sincerity imparted to the music a substance that trained singers could not have given it. In their excitement the singers would sometimes raise the pitch of the notes, and George Ives "had a sliding cornet made so that he could rise with them and not keep them down." [80] "There was power and exaltation in these great conclaves of sound from humanity," Ives later recalled; it was "a man's experience of men!" [81]

What distinguished the vernacular tradition from the cultivated tradition in Danbury's musical life was not really the actual music played. The Danbury Band and Standard Orchestra undoubtedly played some of the same genteel pieces that were presented at Miss Hollister's pupils' recitals; and Lowell Mason's *Missionary Hymn,* a proper hymn of the cultivated tradition, became a staple of the revival meetings. The distinguishing factors between the two traditions were the attitudes that people brought to the music, the resultant manner in which the music was performed, and the atmosphere surrounding that performance. In the vernacular tradition Charles Ives found a music that had no popular connotations of effeminacy, a music by and for men. The bands and theater orchestras were made up solely of men; the country fiddlers had to be men; and in the congregational singing at camp meetings, the women's role was at best only equal to that of the men. Miss Hollister and Miss Fayerweather were excluded by the genteel associations of their sex from leading such uncultivated music; and thus George Ives could lead it without suffering emasculation in his son's eyes. No greater compliment could have been paid to George Ives, from his son's point of view, than that of one Manlove, a player on the Danbury baseball team, "who was our idol, partly because he caught fouls with his left hand, but [mainly] because he spoke to us instead of the Scully boys, who were carrying the bat, and said he had rather play a cornet like father than make a home run every inning." [82]

From this music of the vernacular tradition, Charles Ives later drew many elements—particularly quotations of tunes and programmatic "stories"—that he incorporated into his own works. In *Decora-*

tion Day, for example, Reeves's *Second Connecticut March* is quoted to
mark the martial return of the townspeople to Danbury after they
have decorated the soldiers' graves in the cemetery. Theater-orchestra music suggested the instrumentation of a number of Ives's
works, notably the Set for Theatre Orchestra. More substantially, the
spirit of theater-orchestra music was the inspiration for a number of
ragtime dances that Ives wrote for small theater orchestra early in
the century; one of these was incorporated into the second movement of his Third Violin Sonata, of which movement Lou Harrison
has written that "it contains much that later composers were to do in
theater music . . . and is itself an almost ideal overture to the
brightest of musicals. That is, it would be now." [83] Country fiddlers'
tunes and vagaries were drawn upon for the hilarious "Barn Dance"
section of *Washington's Birthday.* Finally, the mystical democratic experience of the outdoor revival meeting furnished both hymn-tune
quotations and programs for two major works: the Third Symphony
(*The Camp Meeting*) and the Fourth Violin Sonata (*Children's Day at
the Camp Meeting*). In drawing upon vernacular-tradition music in
these works of his mature years, Ives sought not only to glorify his
father, but also retrospectively to identify himself with the vital vernacular life of Danbury, a life from which he had felt himself partially removed as a boy because of his activities in music of the cultivated tradition.

Young Charles's sensitive ear also noted the occasions when
players and singers of popular music departed from harmonic and
rhythmic proprieties—when an amateur in the band played in the
wrong key and missed the beat, for example, or when some of the
players at a barn dance would play for a polka while the other
players were accompanying a waltz. He associated these "wrong
notes" with the masculine vitality of popular music, seeing them as
another affront to the genteel ladies. Along with his father's experiments, they were an important source of his emotional attachment to
dissonance, and they later became the basis for a number of his harmonic and rhythmic innovations.

It may be concluded from this analysis of Ives's youthful musical
experience in Danbury that by the time he left the town in 1893, at
the age of eighteen, there was already present in his mind, however

inarticulate, a vision of music as divided into two great opposing camps. On the one side lay music of the cultivated tradition—effeminate, aristocratic, pretentious, easy on the ears, commercial and lacking in ideals in spite of its pretensions, only rarely breaking its bondage to women. On the other side lay music of the vernacular tradition—masculine, democratic, down to earth, fervent, speaking to men of the substance of their daily lives.

Faced with this division, Ives gave his heart and his allegiance to the vernacular tradition. The vernacular commitment, however, posed an ugly dilemma, for when he came to compose, he had to write within the cultivated tradition. The Western tradition of "great music" was the one in which his father had raised him, and neither father nor son ever doubted that the son's music must be composed within the framework and assumptions of that tradition, which was the cultivated tradition in America. These assumptions—the assumptions of the nineteenth-century romantic movement in the arts—were that music, to have any real value, must aspire to be serious, enduring, moral, and idealistic, and that to achieve these aspirations it must remain separated from the hullabaloo of mundane existence. Those were the Ives family's assumptions about music, as they were the official assumptions of other genteel, middle-class families of the time, and Charles Ives never seriously questioned them; in fact, when he later began to write about music, he revealed that he held the assumptions of the cultivated tradition in a peculiarly pure form. What bothered him about the music of his boyhood was that the artistic ideals of romanticism, in which he deeply believed, seemed to him missing in the very cultivated-tradition music that pretended to embody them. On the other hand, he found that vernacular-tradition music, which made no claims to having such ideals, was thoroughly imbued with them.

Ives never faced the contradiction between his intellectual adherence to the formal ideals of the cultivated tradition and his emotional preference for the real substance of the vernacular tradition. He never saw the irony that the very absence of effeminate connotations in the vernacular tradition, an absence that made him strongly sympathetic to that body of music, was only possible, in the context of American society, because such music was not supposed to have any ideals and was not meant to be taken seriously. He *did* realize, however, at least intuitively, that people would not pay serious attention to music that was written within the vernacular tradition. If one was in earnest as a composer, one must write within the framework of the cultivated tradition.

Ives's solution to his dilemma made musical history. On the one hand, he wrote his compositions within the cultivated tradition, laid them before the public on the basis of the claims to recognition and approval made by that tradition, and adopted the vocabulary and many of the forms of that tradition. On the other hand, he drew into his music from the vernacular tradition, and from the more general vernacular American life of which it was a part, much of that tradition's character—musical quotations, rhythms, forms, amateur mistakes in performance—and also what he conceived to be its values—idealism, humor, religious feeling, democracy. To this mixture he added the elements of dissonance and musical experimentation, which were closely connected in his mind with the vitality of the vernacular tradition, and which in his music often reflect the difference between the formal written vernacular-tradition music and the real quality of an actual performance of it, mistakes and all. The remarkable result of this synthesis may be seen in Ives's Third Violin Sonata. Made up of the traditional three movements, it was first performed in Carnegie Chamber Music Hall and was later issued by an avant-garde music publishing firm; yet its themes are quotations of gospel hymn tunes (*Beulah Land, I Need Thee Every Hour*), and its first movement is in the standard form of a revival hymn: four verses, each followed by the same refrain. It is this extraordinary combination of elements from different musical traditions which has done much to earn for Ives his unique place in the history of American music.

If the conflict between Ives's intellectual acceptance of the cultivated tradition in music and his emotional need to adhere to the vernacular tradition accounts in large part for the nature and greatness of his compositions, it also helps to explain much about other elements in his life: his staying away from music as a profession; his philosophy of music and of art in general; his political thought; and, most tragically, his separation from other musicians and his composing in utter musical isolation for twenty years.

Yet Ives's emotional aversion to cultivated-tradition music was also something of a red herring. Economically successful males in America—and those who were headed for success—made fun of classical music as effeminate and pretentious, and Ives naturally accepted the judgment of these his peers. But beneath their jokes lay a deeper reason for their hostility, a reason which Ives never grasped: they regarded classical music as a commercial failure and professional musicians as outside the pale of respectable society.

Charles Ives's earliest musical compositions seem to have been inspired by the funerals of family pets.[84] One of these dirges, a *Slow March* in the form of a song for the Ives family's dog, was preserved and later published by Ives; it set a precedent for the quotation of well-known tunes, a characteristic of many later Ives works, by quoting the *Dead March* from Handel's *Saul* in the piano accompaniment.[85]

The title page of a *Schoolboy March* of September, 1886, was proudly labeled "OP. 1," [86] and over the next seven years the young composer produced a considerable body of music. In contrast to the works of his mature years, these early pieces were in many cases actually performed. The forms in which they were cast were a direct response to the roles that Ives and his father were playing in the vigorous musical life of Danbury; thus there were pieces for band and for theater orchestra, solos for piano and organ, and a large number of sacred choral compositions (for performance at local church services) and solo songs (for performance by Carrie Allen Baker and other local singers of note). The all-purpose *Holiday Quickstep* neatly bridged the gap between cultivated and vernacular traditions. It was played by George E. Ives's theater orchestra on January 16, 1888; by the young people's orchestra of the Methodist Sunday school on December 25, 1888; by the Danbury Band on October 11, 1889; and by the composer himself, as an organ postlude, at the Baptist church services on May 25 and June 15, 1890.[87]

These early works had something of the character of *Gebrauchs-*

musik, and many of them were written in accordance with the musical conventions of the time; nevertheless, Ives was already injecting into some of them that musical radicalism toward which his father's experiments were steering him. The result was not altogether to the liking of the local public. He later recalled playing the somewhat dissonant accompaniment to his song *At Parting* at a concert in the nearby town of Brewster, New York, in 1889. The text he had chosen ("The sweetest flow'r that blows . . .") undoubtedly prepared the audience for the usual conservatively harmonized, genteel song of the period; but Ives wrote next to certain notes on a later manuscript of the piece that "I played this way in Brewster Concert—and they thought I was aplaying wrong notz—so cut them out of copy." [88]

It is difficult to believe that the ingenuous-looking boy who stares out from a photograph taken of the Alerts in 1890 [89]—the boy whom Philip Sunderland remembered as "the most modest, retiring person imaginable" [90]—could have perpetrated the musical rebellion that is to be found in some of these early compositions. Beneath his self-effacing surface, however, Charles Ives was struggling both to maintain his masculinity in a female-dominated musical environment and to protect his creative independence in the face of popular disapproval of musical experimentation. His clever method of responding to both challenges at once is clearly apparent in the most renowned work of his Danbury period: Variations on *America*.

Ives wrote these organ variations on the national hymn "My country, 'tis of thee . . ." in 1891 or early 1892. He gave what was probably the first performance at a very proper concert of cultivated-tradition music in the Methodist church at Brewster, New York, on February 17, 1892.[91] The idea for the piece may have come from a work on the same theme, the German composer J. C. H. Rinck's Variations on *God Save the King,* which Ives had played as an organ prelude at the Baptist church on the preceding July 5.[92] In spite of some resemblances between the two works, however, Rinck's variations are relatively staid and proper, while Ives's are audacious and full of humor. The most famous sections are the two interludes, each of which is in two keys at once, which have prompted the judgment that the piece is "the earliest known work using polytonality." [93] About these interludes Ives later remembered that "Father would not let me play them in the Brewster concert, as they made the boys laugh out loud," [94] although there is other evidence that the interludes were actually added to the work several years later.[95] At any rate, there were plenty of other features in the music that were sure to startle an audience of 1892: some cross rhythms and unconventional harmonization (including sliding "barbershop" harmony from the vernacular tradition), a polonaise in a minor key, and—above all—the awkwardness and the breathless exuberance of youth.

In 1948, in a sketch for a letter that his wife wrote to the organist E. Power Biggs, Ives recalled his youthful performances of the Variations on *America:*

> It was so long ago when he [Mr. Ives] first played this, that recollections of his earlier performances are not fully remembered.
>
> Mr. Ives' father would occasionally play with him; but always insisted that the fourth variation should be omitted, because it was, in his father's opinion, a kind of Polonaise which had no place in our country and also was in a rather sad minor key. The Brass Band joined in and the loud pedal variations [Variation V] were considered more appropriate. Sometimes when "America" would appear to their ears, some of the listeners would join in, even if it occasionally made the boys go marching down the aisles. Usually, as he remembers, many of the boys had more fun watching the feet play the pedal variations than in listening to the music.[96]

While obviously not applicable to the performance of the work at the Methodist church in Brewster, this description sounds almost equally fantastic as an account of performances in Danbury; it is a good example of Ives's tendency to idealize in his recollections of his youth. What is important here, however, is not the inaccuracy of Ives's memory for facts, but rather the likelihood that the underlying anxiety implied in the words of the articulate old man in 1948 had been present in the mind of the inarticulate boy in 1892. The young composer feared that his deep interest in serious music might alienate him from the common people of Danbury and, in particular, from his male peers. His ingenious response to the threat was the Variations on *America,* in which he not only used musical unorthodoxy to assert his independence from the genteel musical life of the ladies of Danbury, but also, by the very act of doing so, asserted his oneness with the democratic and masculine vernacular life of the town. In his experimentation he was just "cutting up," just "being one of the boys." At the same time, he was being seriously patriotic. "The jumping up and down, hard and fast, from the Great to the Swell manuals and down again, is in a way a kind of take-off, in part, of the Bunker Hill fight," he later wrote of a passage in which off-accents are created by the combination of two different rhythms.[97] Thus did Ives wrap the cloak of patriotism around his musical radicalism! But his nostalgic nationalism was as much cultural as political; it was an unconscious harking back to a time before the appearance of cultivated and vernacular traditions—the time of the tune *America* itself—when Americans had been united musically as well as nationally.

In Ives's early Variations on *America,* then, there appeared in embryo several important characteristics that were to reappear again and again in his mature work. First, there was the apparently paradoxical joining of pioneering technical experimentation with nostalgia for the past, the latter expressed through a musical "program" and the quotation of an old tune. For Ives there was no paradox here, however, for he saw his "modern" techniques not as the expression of rarefied up-to-dateness, but rather as a form of rebellion against overrefined and fussy modernity and as an assertion of solidarity with a more down-to-earth and culturally more democratic past. Second, there was a combination of apparently uncombinable elements—the serious and the humorous, the cultivated and the vernacular—in the transcendental belief that all things were ultimately one. Third, there was the role of the composer as boy. He wanted to be taken seriously, but he was also so shy about his outrageous innovations that he wished always to be able to escape accountability for them by taking up the pose of irresponsible boy.

Unlike his brother, Moss, who accomplished the remarkable feat of earning a Bachelor of Laws degree from Yale after only one year of formal academic study beyond high school, Charles Ives was no more than a mediocre student of the standard school and college subjects of his day. If he hoped to fulfill his family's plans for him to go to Yale, he was going to need a good deal of specialized coaching. In the spring of 1893, therefore, he withdrew from the Danbury Academy, moved to New Haven, and entered the Hopkins Grammar School, an institution whose academic program had long been directed toward the specific goal of getting boys past the Yale entrance examinations.

The next year and a half was not a happy time in Ives's life. It is true that he shone as an athlete at Hopkins, especially as pitcher on the baseball team. But the threat of his impending examinations, along with the knowledge that at best he could only hope to squeak by, hung over his head constantly. In addition, he was dissatisfied with his job as organist of St. Thomas's Episcopal church in New Haven, a position he had taken to help his father pay his expenses. With his evangelical background, Ives found the Episcopal church music unfamiliar and difficult to get used to; [98] and the choir director under whom he served, Charles Bonney, was an Englishman and a martinet.[99] Finally, he was living away from home for the first time; and even though he was in his nineteenth year when he left Danbury, his parents expressed toward him the solicitude that is usual in such situations. They wanted to be sure that he was getting regular exercise (as opposed to participating in dangerous sports); [100] they sent him telegrams when he failed to write promptly or was slightly injured in a football game; [101] and they worried about his academic progress.

The nadir of this period came for Ives in the spring of 1894. He was not doing well academically at Hopkins, and he was about to give up his organist's job (and thus lose the use of the organ) without a prospect of getting another. Downhearted, he wrote to his father:

> I am bound that I will not let all of these things interfere with my musical studies, in the end, and if possible to take advantage of it, although it does make one feel blue, etc. . . . . I think if anything the work at St. Thomas had a tendency rather to deaden than to give ambition and I think that my aim ought to be now to improve in the things that I would not have time to with the church work, and also to see and look out for some place in N.Y. for next year.[102]

Although Charles was mainly concerned with his musical problems and wrote that "I don't see now why things at school hadn't ought to go all right," [103] his father saw matters in a different light. Unsympathetic to his son's need to excel at sports as an offset to his public identification with serious music, George Ives could not understand how the boy could spend his time pitching his baseball team to victory instead of concentrating on his studies. For once, the extraordinarily close relationship between father and son was strained, as Charles revealed in some of the letters he wrote to his father that spring:

> I have just received your letter. Why do you think that I don't understand your letters? Maybe I don't write as if I did, but I think I understand what you have advised and what I have got to do. You know after the first of May, which is nearly here, I can come up over Sunday. Of course, if your writing won't do until then, I could come up some afternoon, and you might come down. The best I can do now is to study and exercise, with the church work. . . . I don't see how things could go better now either at church or school.[104]

> Your last letter with envelopes and paper just rec'd. I can't think of anything in my last letter that wouldn't do for the family to hear. Don't they know I am taking singing lessons, and if they don't, don't you want to have them know? I don't remember writing anything about extra [academic] lessons in that letter, as I thought that you understood from what I have written before, that if I considered it necessary to have any tutors at all, it would be towards the end of the term, and I will look out and attend to that at the proper time. . . . I . . . exercise as you said every night and morning. I have succeeded in getting up about 6:30 every morning lately and get quite a little studying done then. I have been playing tennis for the last week or so, as I don't need to go to the field to practice with the nine, except the day before the game. And don't see why you insist on blaming everything on ball, or at least because I didn't write a good letter last Sunday. I usually study in evening until 9:30 or 10, and then go to bed. And this is the programme as far as I can state it for the day. Mr. Fox [rector of Hopkins] has not complained to me at all for a long while, and I am sure he thinks I am

doing all I can. I will try and write to Uncle Lyman soon about studies, but as much as I can say will be what we are studying, etc., and how I am getting along with them (that is, as to what my opinion is), but as to what Mr. Fox or the teachers think, of course I can't say.

Sunday after I had gotten lessons out of the way, I was working on a little song that I am trying to write for Garrison [a friend]. I worked later than I expected to, and then wrote that letter; I was rather tired and probably that was the reason it was so poor. I will try to have better ones in the future. . . . The last part of this letter is not written perhaps as well as I can, but hope otherwise it is satisfactory.[105]

In spite of these misunderstandings and anxieties, things turned out all right in the end. Ives secured, for the fall, a job as organist at Center Church on the Green, the oldest and probably the most prestigious church in New Haven—although at first he was taken on only as a substitute, and the church ultimately got their twenty-year-old organist for a mere fraction of what his more eminent predecessor had been paid.[106] At considerable expense to himself, George Ives hired tutors for his son that summer;[107] Uncle Lyman contributed his services by hearing his nephew's lessons;[108] and Charles himself dutifully (although obviously without enthusiasm) crammed at his English, Latin, Greek, and German. With these efforts he succeeded in passing his entrance examinations, although only with conditions which he was required to work off later.[109] (One of his tutors expressed the belief that his teachers at Yale would understand his merits better than those at Hopkins had.[110]) In September, 1894, then, the young man finally entered into the exciting and self-consciously superior existence of an undergraduate at Yale College.

A few weeks later, George E. Ives died very suddenly of a stroke. His son's sense of loss—made greater, perhaps, by a feeling of guilt for the recent roughness in his usually smooth relationship with his father—was so great that Charles Ives never fully recovered from it. "I went around looking and looking," he later wrote, "for some man to sort of help fill up that awful vacuum I was carrying around with me."[111] Again: "Father died just at the time I needed him most. It's been years since I've had an older man that I felt like going to when things seem to go wrong or a something comes up when it's hard to figure out which is the best or right thing to do." [112] For the rest of his life, Ives mourned and eulogized his father. His nephew noted that "Uncle Charlie" seemed always to be aware of the presence of his father, so much so that he sometimes presented the strange spectacle of almost physically talking to the dead man; [113] and his wife pointed out that "every now and then he'd exclaim, 'How I want to see Father again!' " [114]

The loss was musical as well as personal, of course. The story is told that shortly after it was composed, the *Holiday Quickstep* was performed by George Ives's band in a Decoration Day parade; but Charles, too embarrassed to play the drum in the performance, was found shyly throwing a ball at the barn door, apparently oblivious as the band passed by playing his piece.[115] The story may not be entirely true, but it captures the essence of the musical relationship between George and Charles Ives. Ives never ceased to be that shy boy composer; he never outgrew the youthful need for a paternal figure—a patron—who would not only encourage him in his experimental composing, but also, by taking responsibility for having his works performed, act as mediator between him and the public whom he feared to face alone.

George Ives filled this role perfectly. In his autobiographical *Memos*, Ives traced several of his innovative techniques back to "boy's fooling" [116] that he had done under his father's direction. For example, some of his dissonant chords (especially those used for their rhythmic, rather than their harmonic, effect) derived from his using the piano to practice the drum parts for his father's band and his discovery that certain dissonant chords—having "little to do with the harmony of the piece" but "used only as sound-combinations as such"—provided the best "takeoff" of the drums.[117] Again, his melodic lines with large skips in them between successive notes had their origins in his youthful practice of "playing the chromatic scale in different octaves, and seeing how fast you could do it." That is, his father had him play the chromatic scale on the piano so that there was an octave and a half tone, rather than just a half tone, between successive notes: "If you must play a chromatic scale, play it like a man." [118]

Ives later expressed very clearly his sense that his early works—some of them now accounted masterpieces—were the products of an exuberant boy prankster in need of firm but understanding parental guidance. His father insisted that he first know how to write music according to the accepted rules; but he also encouraged him to think independently, provided that he knew what he was doing. Thus Charles experimented in rhythmic syncopation and the construction of new chords; furthermore, "if you can play a tune in one key, why can't a feller, if he feels like [it], play one in two keys?" These experiments resulted in much more than mere exercises, especially in Ives's settings of some of the Psalms under his father's guidance.[119]

Perhaps the culmination of this collaboration between father and son was *Psalm 67,* a work not datable exactly, but very probably written during the year and a half before George Ives's death. Like Variations on *America, Psalm 67* makes use of polytonality, but uses it in a considerably more mature way. This a cappella work begins in two keys, the men's voices singing in G minor and the women's in C major: "I remember father saying that this (as a basic formation and among some other combinations we had worked out) had a dignity and a sense of finality."[120] A bitonal relationship between the two groups of voices is maintained throughout the piece, except for a short section in the middle. The result is a work of incredible sophistication for 1894—"a prophetic masterpiece," as John Kirkpatrick has called it.[121] "Father, I think, succeeded in getting a choir in Danbury to sing this without an organ—but, I remember, I had difficulty in the New Haven choirs. The two keys gave trouble. It seemed for some reason more difficult for the ladies to hold their key than the men."[122]

With his father's death, Charles Ives lost the support that had been so vital to his work. No one appeared to take his father's role in his musical development. Almost all his major compositions, with their extraordinary innovations, had to be written in a strange isolation. He continued, into manhood, to be the prankish boy, but now bereft of anyone who would encourage him, discipline him, and make him feel that what he was doing was serious. He continued, also, to be the shy boy, but now lacking anyone who would sponsor his works before the public when he lacked the personality to do it himself. It was not until he met Henry Cowell (a much younger man than himself) in 1927 that he found anyone who could even begin to provide the needed professional support, particularly in introducing his works to other musicians. By that time, however, having wandered in the musical wilderness for a third of a century, Charles Ives had ceased to compose.

2

YALE

❦

THERE IS SURPRISINGLY LITTLE evidence available about Ives's personal life during his four years at Yale. Undoubtedly he continued to write home, although perhaps less frequently, after his father's death; but hardly any of his letters were saved. Of his musical life at college, however, Ives left a good account in his *Memos,* from which it can be seen that his experience in music divided itself naturally into three parts: his theoretical study in the classroom, his organist's job at Center Church, and his extracurricular music making among his friends.

Ives's teacher of theory and composition at Yale was Horatio W. Parker, who came to New Haven to assume his new post as Battell Professor of the Theory of Music and (in effect) head of the Department of Music at the same time that Ives entered the freshman class. Parker was only eleven years older than Ives, but he had already composed his masterpiece, the oratorio *Hora Novissima,* and had acquired a considerable reputation as a composer of church music.

The Department of Music was only four years old, and music still held only a tenuous place as a formal and respectable discipline at Yale; but Parker had exceptional energy and will, and he immediately set about revising the curriculum and bringing the study of music into conformity with his own exacting standards. He succeeded so well that he dominated Yale's musical life for the next twenty-five years, until he worked himself to death in 1919. Although highly regarded in his own time as a composer, Parker is now chiefly remembered as a teacher of younger composers in Yale's Department (later School) of Music, of which he was appointed dean in 1904.

Ives later recalled that he had studied under Parker all four years,[1] which was not formally true, since the regular academic program at Yale College did not permit electives during the first two years of study. Ives may have sat in on some of Parker's courses earlier; but it was not until his junior year that he was able to elect courses in counterpoint and in instrumentation for four hours a week throughout the year, while during his senior year he took Parker's classes in strict composition and in instrumentation (again) for four hours a week.[2] At the very beginning of his freshman year, however, Ives showed Parker some of his compositions.[3]

Parker had received a rigorous musical education under Josef Rheinberger in Munich, and he had come out a perfectionist in his ideas. It was said that he could "detect consecutive fifths [forbidden according to nineteenth-century notions of harmony] 'around two corners.' "[4] Neither by temperament nor by training was he prepared for Ives's experimental works when he saw them. Parker felt that there was "no excuse" for an unresolved dissonance in the song *At Parting;* and when he was confronted with "a couple of fugues with the theme in four different keys," he "took it as a joke (he was seldom mean)." Ives soon learned that Parker would simply ignore anything that departed so radically from the rules: "He would just look at a measure or so, and hand it back with a smile, or joke about 'hogging all the keys at one meal' and then talk about something else." In fact, "Parker, at the beginning of Freshman year, asked me not to bring any more things like these into the classroom." As a result, "I didn't bother him but occasionally after the first few months," and "I kept pretty steadily to the regular classroom work, occasionally trying things on the side"—that is, outside Parker's purview.[5]

Ives was a well-behaved student, but he privately balked at some of the exercises that Parker required of him. On the sketch of an "Organ Fugue for Prof. H. W. Parker," he wrote: "a stupid fugue and a stupid subject." [6] He had studied harmony and counterpoint with his father for many years, and now he had to do it over again with Parker, even using the same textbook—although John Kirkpatrick has remarked that "the surviving counterpoint exercises show clearly that those for Parker maintain a more exigent level than those for his father." [7] "I think," reflected Ives, "I got a little fed up on too much counterpoint and classroom exercises," for he came to feel that counterpoint was "a kind of exercise on paper, instead of on the mountains." Remembering George E. Ives's receptivity to experimentation, the young man inevitably compared Parker with his dead father: "I felt more and more what a remarkable background and start Father had given me in music. Parker was a composer and widely known, and Father was not a composer and little known—but from every other standpoint I should say that Father was by far the greater man." [8]

Ives composed parts of his First Symphony as a senior project in connection with his course work for Parker. The symphony was, to use John Kirkpatrick's expression, "well behaved," and it was obviously influenced by the great nineteenth-century European symphonists; but in its original form it was too much for Parker. Although the symphony was supposedly in D minor, "the first subject went through six or eight different keys, so Parker made me write another first movement." Feeling that the substitute movement was inferior, Ives asked to be allowed to use the original one; Parker "smiled and let me do it, saying 'But you must promise to end in D minor.'" Parker was also disturbed by the slow movement, for instead of beginning on F, as it was supposed to, it began on G♭; also, "near the end, 'the boys got going.'" So once again, Parker convinced Ives to substitute for this slow movement "a nice formal one—but the first is better!" In its final state, not only is the symphony formally correct and harmonically relatively conservative, but it is remarkable among Ives's larger compositions for the absence of quotations from well-known tunes. When, in later years, he remembered this early symphony, Ives grew bitter against Parker, feeling that he had been pressured into turning out an imitative work in order to be sure of getting his degree.[9]

As for the rejected slow movement, its quotation of standard hymns had undoubtedly displeased Parker, who held that "the hymn tune is the lowest form of musical life." [10] Ives had originally written the movement as part of a revival service and played it on the organ at Center Church.[11] Parker, however, felt that it lacked the dignity to be part of a proper symphony; and Ives was not immune to the effects of Parker's criticisms, for after he left Yale, this movement (which ultimately became part of the Second Symphony) was revised "à la Brahms, at Parker's suggestion." [12] Still later, Ives rued these changes and noted on the earlier manuscript that "when scored later, it was made better and spoiled (by advice HWP). . . . P said—a movement in Key of F should start in Key of F. So change and weaken it!!!!!!!!!!" [13]

Parker could be far from benign with his students. He was well known for his biting sarcasm. Although he mellowed somewhat in his later years at Yale, he was very rigid in his viewpoints and manner when Ives knew him. John Tasker Howard, the historian of American music, gave an unpleasant picture of Parker's method of running his classes:

> His brusque manner frightened the timid, and he despised those who were afraid of him. In this he was something of the bully; he would often wilfully confuse his pupils in class, and then scoff at their confusion. But for those who stood on their two feet and talked back to him he had the profoundest admiration.[14]

Ives, on the other hand, was always subject to fits of shyness, particularly in formal situations. He is unlikely to have "talked back" to Parker, and one can only speculate on the awkward scenes to which he may have been subjected in the classes of his imperious and sharp-tongued teacher.

On the whole, however, Parker appears to have ignored Ives as a composer, regarding him as an amusing and inconsequential aberra-

tion. The Battell Professor of the Theory of Music had more important matters upon which to expend his extraordinary energies. He
was building up the New Haven Symphony Orchestra, of which he
was conductor, from practically nothing. (He even gave a private
reading of Ives's Postlude in F with his orchestra, according to Ives's
note on the manuscript, but was apparently not interested in playing
it at a regular concert.[15]) Parker's attentions were also absorbed by
his full-time professional students of music at Yale; and in Yale
College itself, from among Ives's fellow undergraduates in the regular academic program, Parker was bringing to light a young man
who had *real* talent as a composer: David Stanley Smith, of the Class
of 1900. Smith, who was a friend of Ives's, took more advanced
music courses than Ives did and got higher grades in them. While
Ives averaged a low B in his music courses, never got an A, and
received no honors at all at graduation, Smith graduated with
honors in music as well as in his general studies.[16] Smith went on to
become Parker's protégé and his successor as dean of the School of
Music. He composed diligently for many years; but even in his own
time his music was considered "academic," and he is now almost entirely forgotten.

While he was at Yale, Ives did have one triumph over Parker,
which he carefully recorded. One afternoon during Ives's senior
year, George Chadwick, one of the most eminent composers in
America and a former teacher of Parker's, stopped into a music class
after he had had lunch at Heublein's Café. Smelling heavily of beer,
he seated himself behind Ives and observed the class. At that period
Ives had a habit of setting his art songs to texts that had been used
by great European composers, and Parker was engaged in comment-
ing to the class upon two such Ives songs, *Ich grolle nicht* (set to a text
used by Schumann) and *Feldeinsamkeit* (set to a text used by Brahms).
Parker was saying that the middle section of *Feldeinsamkeit* had "too
many keys"—here Chadwick "grinned at it and HWP"—and that it
was not so close to Brahms's song as *Ich grolle nicht* was to Schumann's. At this point Chadwick spoke up and contradicted Parker,
maintaining that "the Summer Fields [*Feldeinsamkeit*] was the best."
He said (as Ives quoted him): "The melodic line has natural continu-

ity—it flows—and stops . . . , as only good songs do." He also pointed out that Ives's song was attempting to express something very different from Brahms's—something more difficult too, "for active tranquillity of outdoor beauty of nature is harder to express than just quietude. In its way, almost as good as Br[ahms]." Chadwick also "winked at HWP and said, 'That's as good a song as you could write.' " When Ives got back to his room after class, he took down the whole story "carefully on the margin" of his manuscripts of the songs, "as at that time . . . Chadwick was the celebrated man of American music." [17] Charles Ives had gained a small victory over Horatio W. Parker.

Thirty-five years later, Ives was generous in his opinion of Parker, noting that he had "great respect and admiration for Parker and most of his music," which was "seldom trivial"; Ives found in his choral works a "dignity and depth" that was often lacking in other sacred and choral music composed in the same era. "Parker had ideals that carried him higher than the popular"; nevertheless, "he was governed too much by the German rule, and in some ways was somewhat hard-boiled." [18] This estimate was kinder than that of John Tasker Howard, for whom Parker "was often trivial." [19]

But it was not so much Parker the individual as Parker the symbol that had an important influence upon Ives at Yale. First of all, Parker symbolized European training. In those days it was considered necessary for an American composer to study in Germany if he wished to be a finished musician. Parker completed the process, begun by Ives's father,[20] of turning Ives against this tradition of European study; after his encounter with Parker, he was unlikely to want to go to Europe and deal at first hand with those who made the rules. At the same time, this conviction conveniently allowed him to be more American, since European musicians and European ways were considered somewhat *outré* by most Americans. Here is an example of that curious process by which Ives's vaunted independence of musical convention actually tended to ally him with the unmusical mass of his fellow countrymen; behind his musical individualism there often lay social conformity.

In a broader sense, Parker symbolized for Ives the plight of the professional musician (particularly of the academic variety) in America—the man who was considered too refined by the masses and not refined enough by the arbiters of social standards. Confronted by a people that had no use for his high artistic purposes, Parker retreated into the university and the Episcopal church and lost contact with much that was vital in American life. Even his friends admitted that he struck people as "cold and aloof." [21] David Stanley Smith praised his music for its "clarity and reserved elegance and formalism" and for "a Northern grayness of tone, . . . a kind of modernized Puritanism." [22] Parker's dignity and overrefinement were also a reaction to his fear that because he was a musician, he might be taken for a Bohemian. Howard caught this point exactly when he described him as "quite the man of the world. Fastidious, immaculate, he commanded a social standing often denied musicians of his time." [23] His English was spoken with impeccable enunciation; as his daughter noted, he was "always thought to be an Englishman by strangers." [24] For fear that it would contaminate him (for he was not, after all, a town bandmaster), he kept his distance from Yale's vernacular music—that is, from the only music that meant anything to all but a handful of the students. His attempts to understand the music of the people were pitiable in comparison with Ives's:

> There are humbler levels of popular taste which are surely significant in measuring our progress. . . . The recently acquired Ethiopian characteristics in our folk music may have their uses, but as yet their benefits are hidden from me. It is indeed stirring to hear a great mass of people, including a seven-foot policeman, singing "Brighten the Corner" at Billy Sunday's. The policeman's eyes and attitude show sincerity and devotion beyond any chance of doubt. He is moved by his vocal efforts and enjoys his emotion and his singing. So do I, but I wish the music were such as I could swallow without gagging.[25]

Thus Parker went his way, writing his cantatas and oratorios and operas, accepting from wealthy women a prize for his music and a building for his school—and having little contact with the pulse of everyday life in his country. If Charles Ives ever seriously considered becoming a professional musician while he was at Yale, he certainly did not find a model for his aspirations in Horatio Parker.

The second part of Ives's musical experiences in New Haven revolved about Center Church, where he was organist during his en-
tire undergraduate career. His superior there was the choirmaster,
Dr. John C. Griggs, who came to the church at the same time that
Ives did. Griggs was nine years older than Ives and had recently returned from study in Germany, where he had taken his Ph.D. in
music at the University of Leipzig. His dissertation, *Studien über die
Musik in Amerika,* does not, on its surface, give the impression that
Griggs would have been sympathetic with Ives's musical ideas.
"American music," he felt, "cannot, for the present, have any distinctive national character." Instead of American composers' trying to be
distinctively *American,* they should draw from the best in the different European traditions. He naturally approved of their studying
in Germany.[26] Griggs also placed an emphasis on liturgy that was
somewhat out of place in a Congregational institution like Center
Church.[27]

In spite of these appearances, however, Griggs proved to be surprisingly receptive to Ives's music. His choir sang Ives's choral compositions, he himself sang some of Ives's solo songs in Center
Church and elsewhere, and Ives was free to play his own organ
works at the regular services. "After Father's death, Dr. Griggs . . .
was the only musician friend of mine that showed any interest, toler-
ation, or tried to understand the way I felt . . . about some things
in music." It is doubtful that Griggs understood very well what Ives
was trying to do or was able to give him specific advice about his
compositions. It was rather his "open-mindedness" for which Ives
praised him. "He didn't like all the things I wrote by any means, but
he was always willing to listen and discuss anything seriously." [28]

Griggs was also a religious man whose faith went beyond the
bounds of denominationalism, and there was in his thought a strain
of idealism and transcendentalism similar to the one that was developing in his younger colleague; [29] years later, when he was in his fifties, he went to China as a teacher-missionary. These similarities between the two men help to account for the growing affection that
Ives felt for Griggs, an affection that he expressed openly in a sketch
for a letter to Griggs many years later. Ives recalled that after his father had died, "I went around looking and looking for some man to

sort of help fill up that awful vacuum I was carrying around with me." He had even had "a kind of idea that Parker might—but he didn't. I think he made it worse—his mind and his heart were never around together." It had been Griggs who had come closest to meeting Ives's need: "You have put into the lives of others greater things than you know—and without trying to. . . . You didn't try to superimpose any law on me, teach me, or admonish me, or say very much—but there you were." [30]

Since he was allowed relative freedom at Center Church, Ives continued his experiments in art music there rather than in Parker's classroom. During his many years as a church organist, he often got bored with the conventional harmonic progressions of most church music; and at Center Church he would on occasion fill out the interludes between verses of a standard hymn with dissonant chords, played very softly in the upper registers.[31] This practice was certainly disconcerting to some of the congregation, but Ives had learned to be self-asserting and aggressive in certain musical situations even while he was still shy or merely easygoing in ordinary social intercourse.

On a more serious plane, Ives wrote his First String Quartet (1896) while he was at Center Church. He played it in part on the organ there (sometimes with strings) on several occasions, one of which was a "mild" revival service.[32] (It must have been mild indeed to be held at such a staid and respectable church!) This quartet was the first of Ives's extant works in the larger musical forms. Although its overall structure was not that of a standard string quartet, the first movement was a fugue and each of the other three movements followed a classical form. But Ives called the work *A Revival* and gave to its four movements the titles Chorale, Prelude, Collection, and Postlude; [33] and into the traditional forms he injected hymn tunes—*Coronation* ("All hail the power of Jesus' name! . . ."), *Webb* ("Stand up!—stand up for Jesus! . . ."), *Nettleton,* Lowell Mason's *Missionary Hymn,* and *Beulah Land*—the last of these a rousing gospel hymn that was not likely to have been heard before in Center Church.[34] This pattern of using vernacular tunes as themes to be developed within classical forms was again followed by Ives, a few years later, in his Second Symphony.

The First String Quartet contained rhythmically and harmonically daring passages—some of them quite subtle, others merely awkward and immature; but on the whole, it was a fairly conservative work, and it had about it the unmistakable note of middle-class America in the 1890s. Ives had not yet made a decisive break with the genteel tradition in music. A new departure was apparent in the Prelude and Postlude for a Thanksgiving Service, played at Center Church in November, 1897.[35] In his *Memos,* Ives placed these two organ pieces among "the first serious pieces quite away from the German rule book"; and he was particularly proud of them, calling them together "the first piece that seems to me to be much or any good now." Here again he quoted hymn tunes; but he was trying to express his admiration for the Puritans, whose "inward beauty" was covered by "a rather harsh exterior," and the only way to do it was to use harsh dissonance. Thus the Postlude began "with a C minor chord with a D minor chord over it, together, and later major and minor chords together, a tone apart." He was trying "to represent the sternness and strength and austerity of the Puritan character, and it seemed to me that any of the major, minor, or diminished chords used alone gave too much a feeling of bodily ease, which the Puritan did not give in to." [36] Typically, Ives defended his harmonic, rhythmic, and contrapuntal experiments not as artistic ends in themselves, but as necessary means for representing the extramusical ideals and values whose expression was the true purpose of the music.

Ives also contrasted the reactions of his two mentors to these organ compositions. "Parker made some fairly funny cracks" about them; but Griggs felt they "had something of the Puritan character, a stern but outdoors strength, and something of the pioneering feeling." When Griggs told Parker that he admired the pieces for this reason, "Parker just smiled and took him over to Heublein's for [a beer]." [37]

During his years at Yale and for several years thereafter, Ives wrote a good deal of music whose matrix was the religious atmosphere in which he worked. He continued his experimental practices in his settings of the Psalms. By the spring of his senior year, he had started a cantata, *The Celestial Country.*[38] And before he left New

Haven that summer, he had begun the first of three *Harvest Home* Chorales; these pieces for chorus, brass instruments, and organ were a veritable revolution in music, embodying nineteenth-century remembrances of Puritanism in extraordinary dissonances and rhythmic complexities.[39] The chief significance of Ives's career at Center Church lay in the fact that it was not in the academic classroom, but in the institutions of American evangelical Protestantism, that he continued to find an outlet for his creative expression in art music.

Of the third phase of Ives's musical life at college—his music making with his friends as part of the social life of Yale and New Haven—it should first be pointed out that it was almost entirely within the vernacular tradition. It is true that his somewhat "arty" folk song *A Scotch Lullaby,* to a poem in dialect by his classmate Charles Edmund Merrill, Jr., was published in the *Yale Courant,* an undergraduate literary magazine, in December, 1896; [40] but its effect was perhaps canceled out when the two of them collaborated on *A Song of Mory's,* published in the same journal the following February.[41] With a few such negligible exceptions, the works that Ives composed with and for his college friends were vernacular-tradition music; and this was so almost by definition, for these young men were not interested in music for its aesthetic or idealistic values. The compositions that they demanded and that Ives produced— humorous pieces (*The Circus Band*), sentimental love ballads (*For You and Me!*), and college songs (*Battell Chimes*)—had, above all, a utilitarian purpose: the strengthening of the bonds of collegiate fellowship.[42] The origin of *Tarrant Moss,* Ives's setting of a poem by Kipling, lay (at least in part) in the same social purpose, although it is regarded today as one of his finest art songs. The Kipling Club (for men "who thirst for Kipling or tippling") was a social organization made up of some of the most influential leaders in Ives's class.[43] In a poll of the class in its senior year, moreover, Kipling came in fourth in the vote for "favorite poet"; and in the poll for "favorite prose writer," he was barely squeezed out of fourth place by Professor Ladd, author of the unreadable textbook used in the psychology course that was required of all juniors.[44] It was surely no coincidence, then, that Ives set three poems of Kipling to music around 1898.

During his junior year Ives was kept particularly busy writing music for the shows put on by Delta Kappa Epsilon, his junior fraternity. The music for these humorous performances was of an ephemeral nature, and little of it has survived.[45] During his senior year Ives's song *The Bells of Yale* (also called *Battell Chimes* and *Chapel Chimes*), a setting of verse by his friend Huntington Mason, of the Class of 1899, was sung regularly at the programs given by the Glee Club.[46] Since the club spent the Christmas vacation making a concert tour of the country that took it as far west as Colorado Springs, it has been remarked that *The Bells of Yale* must have been heard more widely than any other work by Ives down to the 1930s.[47] In addition to the two songs published in the *Courant,* three works by Ives were commercially published as sheet music in 1896: a McKinley campaign song, the "barbershop" song for male voices *For You and Me!,* and a March *Intercollegiate* for band.[48] In 1903 *The Bells of Yale* was published by the director of the Glee Club in a book of *Yale Melodies.*[49] These were the last works of Ives's to be published (aside from his private printings) until 1929.

Much of the vernacular music that Ives wrote at Yale was conventional, some of it of the "potboiler" variety. But he succeeded in bringing his taste for experimentalism into some of his utilitarian music making. At Poli's, New Haven's vaudeville house, the piano player was George Felsburg, who "could read a newspaper and play the piano better than some pianists could play the piano without any newspaper at all. . . . I used to go down there and 'spell him' a little if he wanted to go out for five minutes and get a glass of beer, or a dozen glasses." Here Ives played and became imbued with the rhythm of ragtime music, which was then beginning to sweep the country. He traced back to his association with Felsburg and Poli's the ragtime dances that he wrote early in the new century—"germ" pieces of crucial importance in his development, for their rhythmic and harmonic textures were used in several of his most original larger works.[50] Ives's song from his Yale period *In the Alley,* although not ragtime, was also redolent of the atmosphere of Poli's. In the version that he later published, the subtitle is "After a session at Poli's. Not sung by Caruso, Jenny Lind, John McCormack, Harry Lauder, George Chappell or the Village Nightingale"; and in one measure the music occupies the pianist's left hand alone, with a note ("Attention! Geo. Felsburg!") that the right hand is to be used to turn the newspaper. Ives published it (in 1922) "for association's sake" and "to help clear up a long disputed point, namely:–which is worse? the music or the words?" [51]

At the Hyperion, a somewhat more legitimate theater, "Professor" Frank Fichtl and his theater orchestra played some of Ives's experimental pieces. Ives remembered "some short overtures and marches, some brass band pieces, and short orchestra pieces." Some of these works were "composed" extemporaneously by running two or three well-known tunes against one another, resulting in "two or three different kinds of time and key and off-tunes." The pianist (who might be Ives himself) would keep "a kind of shuffle-dance-march (last century rag)" going while he gave "the cue for the impromptu counterpoint parts" to the other instruments, "the violin, cornet, and clarinet taking turns in playing sometimes old songs, sometimes the popular tunes of the day, as *After the Ball,* football songs, *Ta-ra-ra-boom-de-ay.*" [52]

At the amateur fraternity shows given by Delta Kappa Epsilon, some outrageous departures from "regular music" were also performed—"but not very successfully"; more successful were milder "marches with college tunes in the trio against the original themes," along the lines of his march *A Son of a Gambolier.* At the Hyperion Theater, however, the more radical experiments sometimes caught on, and then "Prof. Fichtl, in the theater orchestra, would get students in the audience whistling and beating time . . . to the off-key and off-time tunes." Such moments of democratic rapport with his peers meant a great deal to Ives. A few of his fellow students and fraternity brothers actually liked these "stunts" and requested that they be repeated; Sid Kennedy, president of the Banjo Club, thought that "it made the music stronger and better, after he had got used to it." These instances showed Ives "what the ears can handle, when they have to" and convinced him that the layman could appreciate his music. At Yale, as at Danbury, he found that his friends would accept his experiments if they were presented as fooling.[53]

It would seem, then, that at Yale Ives was remarkably successful both in bridging the gap between cultivated and vernacular musical traditions and in preserving his integrity as an experimenter. It was a considerable feat not only to introduce harmonic and rhythmic innovations into the music of college social life, but also to bring dissonance *and* vernacular vitality into the staid precincts of Center Church—and to get away with it all! His Second Symphony, mostly completed during the first few years after his graduation, seemed to proclaim the unity of his musical experience at college: the first and third movements were drawn from organ pieces originally played at Center Church, while the first, second, fourth, and fifth movements derived from overtures played by Fichtl's orchestra and by a New Haven brass band.[54]

Henry Seidel Canby, who graduated from Yale's Sheffield Scientific School in 1899, later looked back on his college years and concluded that college faculties in America at the turn of the century "had one of the great opportunities of educational history, and muffed it. . . . The future political, social, commercial, and industrial leadership of the United States was in college." But the professors believed "that their sacred knowledge was a temple set apart from everyday life," and they had no "understanding that this science, this scholarship, was deeply relative to everyone's future." The result was "the country-wide failure to teach Americans the control of their own culture." [55]

Canby's criticism was as applicable to Horatio Parker and his classical music as to any other part of Yale at the time; and Ives, realizing the problem in its musical aspect, offered a solution. In *A Yale-Princeton Football Game,* for example, he presented a musical picture of an event that was vitally relevant to his peers: the bassoons gave a takeoff of the "fat guards pushing and grunting," the trumpet was a "running half back," a wedge of notes on paper depicted a wedge formation on the field—and the crowd was brought into the music by using the songs and cheers of the two colleges. Naturally, the work was extremely dissonant, for "in picturing the excitement, sounds and songs across the field and grandstand, you could not do it with a nice fugue in C." [56]

Ives wrote this work at Yale and played it over on the piano for his friend Hunt Mason and others at the Spot (the meeting place of the sophomore society Hé Boulé). As Ives quoted him, Mason's reaction was sympathetic: "That may not be good music, but those sounds make sense to me. Why shouldn't a Symphony (?) give out in new sounds our experiences today, common or supreme, . . . and not always those of Ariel or a Classic . . . ?" [57] Mason "quite agreed with me that music could 'proclaim' any part of the human experience." [58] These were the same things that Canby was to realize about the arts and sciences in general after he graduated and began to teach; he little thought that one of his own Yale contemporaries had come up with a viable means for uniting the academic and the popular in music.

But before any conclusions can be drawn about Ives's success in handling his musical experiences at college, it is first necessary to examine the context of Yale's social life in the 1890s.

In the 1890s Yale College was a conservative institution.[59] The president and most of the members of the corporation were clergymen, and they held to the older ideal of a Christian institution whose purpose was to bring together a small body of men in isolation from the outside world, mold their characters by a common and all-embracing discipline, and send them out for altruistic service in a Christian commonwealth. Thus undergraduates at Yale College were still required to attend chapel daily, and their first two years were still spent entirely in a common body of disciplinary subjects centered in the classics.[60] Electives for juniors and seniors had been admitted into the curriculum in the 1870s and 1880s, but only over the objections of the old guard.

Such an educational system was ludicrously out of date by the 1890s. Entering classes had grown to three hundred or more in number. Many young men in each class came from wealthy families and intended to go not into the older professions, for which Yale had traditionally prepared, but into business—often into their fathers' businesses. A growing, modern, industrial America lay just outside the Yale campus, demanding recognition from an institution that claimed to train men for service in the everyday world.

Instead of a clash between the old guard of administrators and the new generation of students, however, a tacit compromise was reached. As Henry Seidel Canby (who lived through it all as student and teacher) later pointed out, there were really two colleges and two systems of education that existed side by side in the 1890s. One was the official Yale of the catalogue and the classroom. The other was the unofficial Yale of "college life"—a system of athletics, extracurricular activities, and styles of living that had become highly elaborated and was the real educative force in the life of the great majority of students.[61] "College life for us was at least 90% of our felt experience, and therefore 90% of the college as we knew it." [62]

The existence of these two Yales meant "a dual education in which college life and the college curriculum pretended each to be unaware of the other's existence, except when they met head on in a collision over the marking system." On one side, "the undergraduates in the education they preferred had worked out a compromise with formal study very much like the tacit agreement to go to church without being religious which their elders had made with the church." [63] The senior class always voted in favor of requiring daily attendance at chapel, even while they read newspapers during the morning services. Year after year, with scarcely a protest, the undergraduates memorized or bluffed their way, with a minimum of effort, through required courses in Greek and Latin that bore absolutely no relation to their own lives; it was the sacrifice one had to make to become a Yale man. They even clothed their intense extracurricular competitions for personal prestige in phrases like "loyalty to college" and "doing something for Yale," which sounded like the official purposes of idealism and service for which the college stood.

On the other side, the administrators were not displeased with the compromise. They had always believed in the moral training of character rather than in mere academic learning—look what was happening to Harvard!—and they noted with pleasure that student disorders decreased as college life became more organized and Yale men learned to discipline themselves in their feverish pursuit of activities. A little later, President Hadley remarked that "if the chairman of the *Yale News* Board is a man of the right type,—and he almost always is,—he is the most efficient disciplinary officer of the university." [64] As for the faculty, they regarded the undergraduate body as a pack of barbarians and devoted themselves to their research and to the few students who would become scholars.

If "college life" was the real educative force at Yale, what was the nature of this life? Here again, Canby pointed out a curious ambivalence.[65] The students thought of themselves as irresponsibles and hedonists, drinking away their nights at Mory's and enjoying themselves for a brief time until they had to enter the world of work. They created a mood of romance and nostalgia and sang of "bright college years." This mood, however, was largely an illusion, for they were actually caught up in an intensive round of activities. "Some voice seemed always to be saying, 'Work, for the night is coming.' " [66] These activities were not undertaken for the pleasure they gave in themselves, but in order to secure the tangible honors that the system offered. Freshmen and sophomores wore themselves out gathering items for the *Yale Daily News,* or turned out regular quantities of original material for one of the literary magazines, in hopes of securing a place on the editorial boards of these publications. Others devoted every afternoon for three years to practice on a scrub team, with the object of making the varsity in their senior year. The verb *to heel* acquired a double meaning. To heel a person was a cowardly act unworthy of a gentleman; but to heel the *Lit.,* the football team, the Glee Club, or the YMCA was an admirable effort expected of a Yale man. Competition was the lifeblood of Yale; and as with the football team, so with all other activities, the purpose of competition was to win.[67]

Almost as impressive as the energies which these activities harnessed was their extraordinary degree of organization. The students' athletic teams—even the Freshman Baseball Nine [68]—were organized like their fathers' business corporations, with an elected president (acting as manager), vice president, and secretary, in addition to the captain and the members of the team. When Canby arrived at Yale, he had pointed out to him "the Big Men, the [varsity] managers, the powers behind college life, more important, because brainier, than the athletes. These were the real masters of this new state." [69] The Yale Glee Club, too, was a big business, its manager having the responsibility of arranging for the club, among other concerts, an elaborate tour by chartered Pullman car of numerous cities during Christmas vacation. And at the apex of the whole college organization lay the senior secret societies, the ultimate symbols of achievement.

There were three senior societies—Skull and Bones, Scroll and Key, and Wolf's Head—and each of them took in only fifteen members out of a senior class of about three hundred. Membership in them was rarely a reward for scholarship. In fact, one student of the subject, who divided all graduates of Yale College between 1882 and 1905 into members of senior societies and nonmembers of senior societies, found that the first group contained a much smaller percentage of academically high-ranking students than did the second group. [70] The senior societies existed, rather, to reward success in athletic, musical, managerial, journalistic, and religious activities. Few dared to ignore the tremendous power that they wielded. Toward the end of each school year, in an impressive public ceremony known as Tap Day, forty-five juniors (soon to be seniors) were selected by the outgoing members of the three societies and admitted into the sacred precincts of their tomblike halls. For three years the hopes of the whole class, and particularly of its more ambitious members, had been centered on this awarding of what everyone acknowledged to be "the highest social honor of Yale College"; yet 85 per cent of them were destined to leave the ceremony disappointed. Even friends of the Yale system conceded the harshness of the judgment rendered on Tap Day:

> That afternoon has left in the hearts of a score and more of men as sharp and painful and deep wounds as perhaps they will ever suffer in all the battles of life. They have lost, generally for reasons which they cannot tell, that which they most desired of all the honors their fellows could give them. Their friends, and the college at large, have seen them conspicuously fail. The decision is irrevocable. A peculiar mystery is closed to them, a peculiar experience denied them, and a certain choice and helpful association prohibit-

ed. There is no undoing it all. The word has been given, and judgment has been passed.[71]

Yale in the 1890s, then, was a sort of adaptation of the British public school to the competitive American industrial world.[72] All in all, the college was proud of itself and its system and could point to the conspicuous successes achieved by its graduates, even by those who did not come from wealthy families, in the larger world. Yale men saw themselves as democratic. Did not students come to Yale from all over the country? Were there not undergraduates who worked their way through? Did not every man have an equal chance to win the rewards offered by college life? The Yale man also felt himself to be religious (in a practical, active way), idealistic, college- and public-spirited, manly, optimistic, and loyal to his fellows. Underneath these proud self-evaluations was the fear that the opposite qualities lay hidden in himself and in his times; and these fearful qualities were projected upon Harvard. There President Eliot had made a decisive break with tradition by introducing the elective system and setting up a modern university with specialized and professional training. The results could be plainly seen: Harvard men had become irreligious, self-centered, individualistic, decadent, cynical, overintellectualized—and snobbish and undemocratic to boot! The Yale man knew he was different. And at least one visitor from Harvard agreed. George Santayana wrote in 1892:

> Nothing could be more American . . . than Yale College. . . .
> Here is sound, healthy principle, but no overscrupulousness, love
> of life, trust in success, a ready jocoseness, a democratic amiability,
> and a radiant conviction that there is nothing better than one's self.
> It is a boyish type of character, earnest and quick in things prac-
> tical, hasty and frivolous in things intellectual. But the boyish ideal
> is a healthy one, and in a young man, as in a young nation, it is per-
> fection to have only the faults of youth. There is sometimes a beau-
> tiful simplicity and completeness in the type which this ideal pro-
> duces.[73]

There was, however, a darker side to this Yale system. It was absolute and all-pervasive in the lives of the undergraduates; it demanded exclusive loyalty and had no place for the outsider. "College ideals are for the time being his only ideals, college successes the only successes," wrote Santayana of the Yale undergraduate. "Everything is arranged to produce a certain type of man." [74] The university's official historian who wrote of this period was less kind:

> Yale conformed. . . . Individualism was not encouraged. Campus sentiment was against it, and traditions stood in the way. A man's classmates valued his cooperation far more than his criticism. Originality of ideas was suspect and, outside of a tolerated range, eccentricity of dress or conduct was frowned on. To succeed at Yale one must avoid queerness, make friends, do something.[75]

The student body contained considerable talent; but the young man who wished to indulge himself freely in creative expression, or to engage in original scholarship, or just to let his mind wander in new paths, had no place in the scheme of things. The all-powerful senior societies did not reward such activities.[76] Even in the 1890s a few courageous cries were heard, usually from the *Yale Literary Magazine,* against the conversion of all worthwhile endeavor into counters in the game of success. One sensitive undergraduate, daring to take the unpopular pessimistic view, spoke out in bitterness against Yale's materialism: "Under the outward appearances, below all the so-called joys of these few years lurks a poisonous undercurrent, that spreads itself into all the roots and fibres of our college life." Feeling that every undergraduate was affected by this undercurrent, he spoke of the "simple scholar" whose "life at Yale has been embittered, his struggles for victory over himself and his work . . . left without a recognition." He spoke also of the student whose only purpose was "to broaden himself into a Man"; "but if he lacks the ambition to attain position by questionable means, if he has not in him the worshipful spirit of reverence to a would-be Hero, his life here is dwarfed, narrowed, browbeaten into a sullen silence, and he leaves at the end with tears in his eyes, perhaps, for the tender associations of the few friends as noble and as independent as himself, and with inward cries of rage at the system of things that has brought it thus." [77]

Again, Yale prided itself on its democracy; but quite aside from the question of whether a system that ended in such stratification could really be democratic, some were suggesting that there was not even "a free field and no favor" for all students at the beginning of the process. Owen Johnson, of the Class of 1900, watched the way things worked from his chairmanship of the *Lit.*, and in 1911 he published *Stover at Yale* in the muckraking *McClure's Magazine*. *Stover* could be read as a Frank Merriwell romance, but it was actually an attack on some aspects of Yale's system of secret societies through the story of a boy who goes to Yale with the certainty of becoming a "big man," but decides that he must oppose the Establishment.[78] The book was specifically directed against the sophomore societies, of which there were three,[79] taking in seventeen men from a class in the spring of its freshman year. Like the senior societies, they were cloaked in secrecy.

There were two undemocratic effects of the sophomore societies.[80] First, each class at Yale was tightly organized within itself, and there was relatively little connection among the classes; on the other hand, it was the class ahead that determined the social status of the class below. A man who had connections in the classes ahead of him had an inestimable advantage in the competition for college honors. The sophomore societies provided such connections; they were a means by which the big men in the upper classes, but in particular in the sophomore class, could select the coming big men from the freshmen and pave their way for eventual election to a senior society. The members of sophomore societies tended to win out in college competitions and ultimately to become members of senior societies. Nor did the process begin only in freshman year, for there were secret societies in the large preparatory schools that supplied many of the college's entering students, and membership in them was an advantage in the competition for the sophomore societies at Yale. The result of the whole system was cliquishness, an aristocratic attitude, and a distinct lack of democracy. On the day that Dink Stover comes to Yale, a sophomore friend takes him aside and explains to him how things are run:

> You'll hear a good deal of talk inside the college, and out of it, too, about the system. It has its faults. But it's the best system there is, and it makes Yale what it is today. It makes fellows get out and work; it gives them ambitions, stops loafing and going to seed, and keeps a pretty good, clean, temperate atmosphere about the place.

As a potential big man, Stover's friend has a "frankly aristocratic" way of looking at things:

> This college is made up of all sorts of elements. . . . And it is not easy to run it. Now, in every class there are just a small number of fellows who are able to do it and who will do it. They form the real crowd. All the rest don't count. . . . You're going to be judged by your friends, and it is just as easy to know the right crowd as the wrong.

The right crowd, the sophomore goes on to say, is "about the crowd you'll want to know all through life." There are practical considerations of the future, too. "You may think the world begins outside of college. It doesn't; it begins right here. You want to make the friends that will help you along, here and outside." Dink Stover's dream of democracy is shattered.[81]

Johnson pointed out the second evil connected with the sophomore societies when he identified the two types of men who were taken into the society system at Yale: "big men" and "lame ducks." [82] The big men were the achievers; the lame ducks were the friends of the big men, the latter pulling the former along on their coattails, first into a sophomore and then into a senior society. Naturally, there was a great deal of toadying by those who desired election. The prestigious managerships and assistant managerships of the varsity teams were contested only by candidates from the three sophomore societies, and it was not unknown for a society to put up a lame duck for such a position just to increase his prestige and boost him into a senior society. Again, Dink Stover's friend Dopey McNab spends his years at Yale doing nothing but drinking and cutting up, but on Tap Day he is promptly tapped for "Locks and Keys" (Scroll and Key). He is a good fellow, and he has kept the big men among his Andover classmates constantly amused for three years. In spite of protests to the contrary, money and social position in the outside world (as well as a tradition in one's family of belonging to a certain society) also exercised an influence upon society elections. In Yale's vaunted democracy there were many flaws.

In analyzing Charles Ives's place in the context of Yale's social life, the first thing to look at is the undergraduate activities in which he participated. He was in the Freshman Glee Club [83]—and that was all, through the end of his junior year.[84] Yet on Tap Day in 1897, James Lineaweaver marched solemnly into the crowd of juniors gathered by the Yale Fence, slapped Ives on the back, cried "Go to your room!" and pursued him to 76 South Middle—and Ives found himself a member of Wolf's Head.[85] True, it was the least prestigious of the three senior societies; but it is remarkable that after having "done" so little for three years, Ives was numbered among the elect forty-five.[86]

Of course, quite apart from the question of his abilities, Ives had been busy holding down a job and writing a great deal of music during those years; in addition, there was no place for the composer of music as such within the system of college competitions. It would be good to believe that Ives's election was a recognition of important musical contributions that he had made to Yale outside of the established system; but the evidence suggests that his music played little part in his election. He certainly was not chosen for the *art* music that he wrote, for he did not generally share such music with his undergraduate friends, tending to keep it in a separate compartment of his life. But neither was his utilitarian music a sufficient reason for his receiving the highest honor that Yale could bestow. In the musical write-up in his senior classbook, only passing reference was made to him, as the composer of *Chapel Chimes;* furthermore, he was only one of several composers mentioned, and none of the others made a senior society.[87] It was not unusual for an undergraduate to write utilitarian poetry or music whose purpose was to increase good-fellowship; but such an activity was a peripheral matter, not the sort of thing that was recognized by election to a senior society.

It must be concluded that Ives was more a lame duck than a big man, that his election was a recognition not of his achievement, but of his personal popularity and his closeness to the big men. This conclusion is strengthened by an examination of Ives's social progress from 1893 to 1897. At Hopkins Grammar School there was only one secret society that had any prestige or staying power over the long run: Pi Sigma Tau.[88] Its members often retained their connection with the society even after they had left the school. Ives was

a member, and so was a boy named Elisha Ely Garrison; [89] and the
two became close friends. Garrison entered Yale a year ahead of
Ives, quickly became a big man, and was eventually elected president
of the Yale University Football Association (that is, manager of the
varsity team).[90] Meanwhile, Ives had remained friendly with Garrison and had given him some elementary lessons in music.[91] Garrison
was a member of Hé Boulé, the most important of the sophomore societies, and he was undoubtedly influential in securing Ives's
election to Hé Boulé toward the end of Ives's freshman year.[92] Another big man whom Ives got to know was his future brother-in-law
David Twichell, who had entered Yale with the Class of 1897 but
had later switched to '98 (Ives's class) and had thus acquired crucial
friends in the class ahead; he, too, was in Hé Boulé and became
president of the University Football Association.[93] Garrison went
into Skull and Bones and Twichell into Scroll and Key; [94] but in
Wolf's Head itself Ives had two important contacts in the class
ahead: Ebenezer Hill, Jr., his former teammate at the Danbury
Academy, and James Lineaweaver, who had been in Pi Sigma Tau at
Hopkins and who actually tapped him on Tap Day.[95]

To say that Ives was a lame duck is not to denigrate his personal
qualities. He undoubtedly had what was then called "character."
Whether or not he was clubbable in his personal tastes, it is obvious
that he was the sort of person who, if he is set down in a strange environment, is almost immediately accepted into its most prestigious
and exclusive groups. His class as a whole liked him, too, for when
he was put up at a class election, along with seven other seniors, for
the Ivy Committee (a purely ceremonial position), he received the
highest number of votes.[96] It is difficult to give a simple explanation
of why he was so popular, for he had a complex personality with several sides to it. Although he had apparently "opened up" somewhat
since his Danbury days, he was still basically shy and was to remain
so for the rest of his life; yet that shyness, combined as it was with
humor, was a winning trait. Not being a self-centered person, he was
also capable of a large amount of team spirit, and he no doubt
increased his popularity by showing much enthusiasm for sporting
events at Yale.

Perhaps the most admirable of Ives's qualities were his kindness and transparent genuineness, carried sometimes to the point of real innocence. Thirty years later, his Italo-American secretary was insultingly called "Mussolini" by an office supervisor; Ives not only severely reprimanded the supervisor, but also talked to the girl about the pride she should take in her Italian ancestry.[97] This sensitivity to the feelings of others probably characterized Ives even in his Yale years. It is hard to believe that he did not remain aloof from the cruelties and conspiracies of the Yale society system.

His independence seems, in fact, to have proved attractive to those who decided his social fate at Yale. The *Horoscope,* a publication that predicted with a high degree of accuracy the elections to senior societies from his class, actually placed Ives's name on the list of likely candidates for Skull and Bones (the most prestigious of the senior societies), although it admitted that he "is not a sure man." Noting that "he has much to recommend him," the anonymous astrologer wrote that Ives "has never been at all changed by his Sophomore [society] success, has put himself through college very creditably by acting as organist at Center church, and always acts with a becoming independence"; nevertheless, "he is not a big man in any way and the chances are a trifle against him." [98]

But Ives's independence could obviously not be carried too far. He seems to have made it acceptable by combining it with qualities of humor and innocence, thus suggesting that he was not to be taken altogether seriously. There was a bit of Dopey McNab in Charles Ives. Dr. Edwards Park, of the Class of 1900, who roomed with Ives in New York after they had both left Yale, remembered him as an original and even eccentric young man who entertained his more sober and practical roommates: "I had not the slightest intimation that Charley was a musical genius . . . I regarded him as a most delightful man and companion, completely unpredictable . . . one never knew what to expect next." [99] In all probability his friends had much the same impression of him while he was at Yale.

If, as seems to have been the case, Ives's social success at Yale was based not upon what he *did,* but upon what he *was,* then he was under peculiarly great pressure to conform to prevailing standards and to avoid "queering" himself by any behavior that was too outlandish or independent. The later Ives of argumentative opinion on every political and social question was not the Ives of Yale days. It was not until twenty years later that he burst forth in a diatribe against Yale that was worthy of the rebel Brockhurst, Dink Stover's friend:

> I remember . . . that before I went to college, I was interested. I found a pleasure . . . in browsing in my father's library that I never found in college. My mind seemed to stop at my first fresh-man recitation as soon as I felt smothered by the compulsory con-stant proximity of 300 classmate minds. Compulsory ideas of tu-tors, compulsory traditions of professors, compulsory courses, compulsory freedom of thought, compulsory chapel—I learned not a thing that I ought. Whatever thoughts I had came out of some others' mouths, or didn't come out at all. I learned not to have a "shy foot" in batting (at the plate) and that the Freshmen could always rush the Sophomores at "Thermopylae"—valuable, but all four years in complete dulness of mind. But after receiving the sheepskin (the most appropriate thing I had received for a long time), I felt free to think again, and I'm gradually getting straight-ened out.[100]

Ives probably felt some of these things during his undergraduate days, but to have uttered them then would have been heresy—and Ives was not a heretic.

If Ives did not wish to queer himself with his friends, it was in-cumbent upon him not to reveal to them the depth of his love for art music, for the boys of Yale were almost as fearful of effeminacy in classical music as the boys of Danbury had been. In 1895 the *Yale Daily News* assured its readers that "more or less knowledge of art is expected in college men." It was admitted that until recently "a criti-cism was frequently heard to the effect that the Yale graduate had little taste for higher culture, as shown in literature, music and the other fine arts." But "the great body comprising the University is beginning to appreciate that every man has something refined in his nature from which Yale can produce power. Let the students re-member that real culture is not inconsistent with democracy or any-thing for which this institution stands." But the paper also revealed the masculine fears that made these bland assurances necessary: "Yale stands for everything that is practical, for everything that has a distinctive American flavor, and we should deeply regret if the student here should lose any vigor of manliness for the sake of developing his appreciation of the fine arts. This, we regret to say, has elsewhere been the case [i.e., at Harvard], and as history is apt to repeat itself we should be on our guard." [101] In this complex of authoritative student attitudes can be seen the matrix of that musical " 'arrested development' among nice Yale graduates" and of those "soft-headed ears running the opera and symphony societies in this country" against which Ives was to rail years later.[102]

The fine arts in general might be cultivated as socially useful graces; but since music posed a greater threat to "manliness" than did the other arts, the Yale man (and particularly the type of man in the senior societies) preferred to deal with it only in its vernacular form. Ives was under pressure from his "crowd" to accept their opinion that music was essentially an amusing entertainment. An undergraduate might be self-consciously "artistic" in a poem or story written for the *Lit.,* but the socially powerful Yale Glee Club of the 1890s (unlike present-day college glee clubs) did not sing cultivated-tradition music. When Ives's friend Sid Kennedy, who was president of the Yale Banjo Club and was regarded as the "class musician," reviewed the Class of 1898's musical activities for the senior classbook, he confined himself to a humorous account of vernacular music. His review contained the only reference made to Ives in any of the classbook write-ups of the different undergraduate activities; buried in the list of the humorous, sentimental, and college pieces written and composed by members of the class was the note that "Charlie Ives composed 'Chapel Chimes,' which has been sweetly sung under several aliases." Emphasizing the good-fellowship of the glee and banjo clubs, Kennedy concluded on a surprisingly unmusical note: "The impression which the Ninety-eight clubs have made is very gratifying. The reason for this is as follows. The men most prominent in the social life of the club[s] . . . have always in my opinion stood for everything that a typical Yale man should be, and I think that they have given to all before whom they have sung and played a true idea of what they are." [103]

But music at Yale was not just fun—it was organized fun. Canby pointed out that although competition at Yale was a preparation for competition in the business world and successes at Yale often meant successes in that larger world, nevertheless the thing that was most desired in business competition was not regarded as a legitimate goal at Yale. "Of all the talents useful for success in the college community the gift of money-making was least esteemed." [104] As a result, those who sought the prizes of college life converted the accomplishments of that life in athletics, literature, religion, and music into symbols and substitutes for money. In the literary competitions a semblance of creativity was required, but in music it was only performance—a good voice or the ability to play the banjo—that counted. The energy that men like Kennedy threw into their musical activities should be seen as a temporary striving after musical counters, which could be turned in, after graduation, for more tangible rewards. Music would then be dropped for more important things; and a Yale man was considered odd indeed if he continued his interest in music by making it his career. In 1950 Kennedy wrote to Ives that while he certainly could claim no critical taste in music, his presidency of the Banjo Club had been a fine preparation for his life in business; and he went on to give examples of other presidents of the Yale Banjo Club who had made good in business.[105]

At Danbury Ives had learned that the man who was enthusiastic about classical music endangered his reputation for masculinity and that the middle-class man who became a professional musician became also a *déclassé*. At Yale he was confirmed in these opinions. Faced with the whole complex of musical attitudes held by his college crowd, he suppressed in their presence the expression of his interest in the serious side of music and emphasized, instead, its merely humorous or sentimental aspects—not because he *chose* to, but because he *had* to. It was the only basis on which his musical interests would be accepted by his friends. The Glee Club was glad to sing *The Bells of Yale,* but would it accept a more serious work? The answer appears on the manuscript of *The All-enduring,* a semireligious piece written about 1896: "For Yale glee club and orchestra. . . . But they wouldn't sing it. T. G. S. N.G."—that is, Thomas G. Shepard, the director of the Glee Club, said it was "no good." [106] (Dr. Griggs, however, sang it at Center Church.[107]) Even Hunt Mason, who earned Ives's gratitude for his support of his friend's experimentation in college, had a curiously ambiguous attitude toward Ives's compositions: "I had Hunt Mason's encouragement, even enthusiasm, when all the shysters had gone down—and the sun was beginning to show over East Rock. At least we amused ourselves. Hunt would declaim in blank verse." [108] The context of college life was the governing factor in Mason's reaction to Ives's music. It would seem that Mason appreciated *A Yale-Princeton Football Game* and other experimental pieces more as college stunts, or sources of fellowship, than as serious pieces of music. Since Ives was obviously appealing to prevailing collegiate attitudes when he wrote these works, it cannot be said that Mason was entirely wrong.

Ives's habitual shyness and embarrassment about expressing his true feelings are important reasons why he did not reveal his inmost musical aspirations even to his close friends. Besides, who among them would have understood him? The average Yale undergraduate—not to speak of the average Wolf's Head member—was abysmally uninformed about serious music. In *Stover at Yale,* the rebel Brockhurst hurls a challenge at the musical ignorance of his classmates: "I won't ask you the tendencies and theories of the modern schools—you won't know that such a thing as a theory in music exists. You know the opera of *Carmen*—good old Toreadore song. . . . You have a hazy knowledge of Wagner, and you know that Chopin wrote a funeral march. That is your foothold in music; there you balance, surrounded by howling waters of ignorance." [109] Brockhurst's criticism seems a fair estimate of the state of musical knowledge at Yale in Ives's day.

There were, of course, a few undergraduates of Ives's acquaintance who were devoted to classical music: Bass Brigham, who played the violin in Parker's orchestra; Max Smith, who became a music critic; David Stanley Smith, who became Parker's successor. They were not, however, senior society men or men of Ives's crowd. And he knew very well that they had little taste for experimentation—as they all proved some years later, when he showed them his music and they cut him to the quick with their derogatory comments about it.

Ives, then, stuck to his own crowd, both at Yale and after graduation. For ten years after he left New Haven, he lived in a cooperative bachelors' apartment in New York City with a group of Yale men, many of them senior society members from various classes. Ives was composing all the time that he lived in Poverty Flat, and the names of his fellow tenants appear in joking notes on his manuscripts. For example: "Keyes says these notes are O.K. He is the best critic—for he doesn't know one note from another." [110] Again: "Bill Maloney [is] mad at this. . . . [He] says [it] just hammers—[and he] can't sleep." [111] For their part, his friends probably regarded Ives's music as a humorous and harmless pastime. As they got married and took on greater responsibilities, they gave up their youthful amusements; and perhaps they thought that Ives would give up his music for the same reason. Marriage was the time when the Yale man put away childish things like music and followed his wife into the ranks of the patrons of the New York Philharmonic.

At Yale, then, Ives lived to a large extent in musical isolation. Much worse, because less inevitable, was the false picture of himself that he gave to his friends. The price of social success was the dividing of his experience into two separate lives. On the outside was Charlie Ives—a well-liked and amiable companion, not an intense and serious person. On the inside was the developing artist and idealist, who felt more deeply about music than about anything else—and who had no one to whom he could communicate his feelings.

The process by which Ives's life was being severed into two parts was accelerated when, upon graduation, he went into business rather than into music. In his *Memos* he gave several reasons for doing so. Typically, he placed first in his list the shame he had felt in his boyhood at being associated with such a feminized thing as music. He drew no conclusion from this consideration, assuming that it was self-evident: no real man would allow himself to be publicly identified with a vocation regarded as effeminate. His second reason was the obvious one that he could not have supported a family without prostituting his art in the commercial market; since "writing sellable music" had a bad effect on his experimental work (although it had not seemed to bother him at Yale, when he had been able to do it without appearing to be a professional musician!), he had decided to "keep his music-interest stronger, cleaner, bigger, and freer" by staying away from music as a vocation. A subsidiary reason had been his desire to enlarge his "sensibilities" through the contact with "people of all conditions" that was possible in business, but not in music.[112] Enough has been said about Ives's experiences at Yale to make it clear that he had several other reasons for avoiding music as a vocation; nevertheless, since his vocational choice is one of the least understood parts of his life, three further points should be made about it.

First, it is doubtful that there was a conscious decision at all. The very fact that Ives and his parents planned from the first that he should go to Yale, a liberal arts college and a widely recognized means of entrance into the business and professional world, rather than to a conservatory of music, is good evidence that he never intended to make music more than an avocation. There were three paths open to Ives in the professional musical world: that of the small-town musician (like his father), that of the academic and church musician (like Parker), or that of the Bohemian. Ives was unfitted by temperament, background, and training for the second and third of these possibilities; and none of them offered any inducement to depart from the tested path of success that led from Yale into the business or accepted professional world. Ives later became very defensive about having gone into business;[113] and if he then remembered that he had seriously considered taking up music instead,[114] that remembrance may be discounted as an attempt to soften the criticism of those who could not understand "why and how a man who apparently likes music so much goes into business." [115] It is worth noting that Horatio Parker believed the primary purpose of college music courses to be the training of composers— that is, professional composers; [116] perhaps Parker failed to take Ives seriously as a composer partly because he realized that Ives was not going to make music his life's work.

Second, it seems unjustified to say, as some have implied,[117] that Ives made a conscious sacrifice when he went into business instead of music. It was by no means a clear-cut case of his defending his artistic integrity against the commercial "lily pads"; there were positions in the music profession that would not have required him to compose for money, positions that would have given him more time for his private experimentation than the business world ever did. The real choice lay between barely eking out a living at music or taking his chances on the business world, with all the advantages that his Yale associations would give him in business. Ives chose the second alternative and became a wealthy man. It would be perverse to call his action a sacrifice. Nor was a career in business uncongenial, as a musical career would have been, to the friendships and style of life that he had acquired at Yale. The real sacrifice was made by David Stanley Smith, who could have gone into business, but came under Parker's influence at college and decided to devote his professional life to music.[118] Ives, on the other hand, avoided appearing before his Yale friends as a "professional musician," with all the connotations of loss of social status, eccentricity, and even Bohemianism that were bound up in that concept.

The corollary, however, was that his friends were allowed to think that he did not wish to be taken seriously as a composer. Ives's vocational choice is today seen as a sacrifice on his part because it is now known what was going to happen to him. He was, in a sense, walking into a trap laid for him by his society and culture. Few musical positions could have demanded of this musical genius the degrading and irrelevant tasks that the insurance business imposed upon him. And the business world cut him off from what he might have found in the professional world of music: persons of artistic sensitivity (not necessarily professional musicians themselves) who would have encouraged his ideas and his musical experimentation.

Third, it is a crucial fact in this whole argument that Ives did not return to Danbury. His brother, Moss, did, and he became an eminent lawyer and judge there, but he never had quite enough to support his six children as he would have liked to, and he was glad to accept his brother's financial help.[119] Charles, however, like his great-grandfather Isaac Ives, had ambitions that were too big for Danbury and could only be satisfied in the metropolis. The towns and small cities of New England could no longer hold their Lyman Brewsters, their young men of talent. Industrialization had created a truly national business system, centered in a few great cities. Between 1890 and 1900, while the total population of the city of Danbury remained almost exactly stable at about 16,500, the number of native whites both of whose parents had been native-born decreased from 8,358 to 7,223.[120] Young people from older families were leaving Danbury to find greater opportunity elsewhere. Yale, which had once supplied clergymen to the towns of Connecticut, was now supplying businessmen and lawyers to New York City. According to Yale's historian, in the last years of the century Yale "undergraduates knew that, provided they first learned the rules of the game, they were destined for great prizes, sure to make fortunes, and bound for the managing posts in society." [121] And Canby remarked on the opportunity that social success at college offered to the young man "from a commonplace family in a commonplace town" to make his way "into the brave, translunary world of great cities and the gilded corridors of their privileged sets. . . . If there was a good job in a brokerage firm he would get it, because of his connections." [122] In heading for New York, Ives indicated that he understood all these things and that he found the prospect of success not at all distasteful.

Ives left Yale as a Yale man should, striving for success. Like the friends in his crowd, he had what Santayana called "this buoyant faith in one's divine mission to be rich and happy." [123] He was, however, unprepared to face the contradictions in his life, to accept the fact that a part of himself was already alienated from the life of his fellows. Thus his quest for achievement in the business world was destined to have damaging effects upon the integrity of his experience. The man who believed that "the fabric of existence weaves itself whole" and that "you can not set an art off in the corner and hope for it to have vitality, reality and substance" [124] was to exist in such utter musical isolation that even those in close contact with him would not realize that he was a serious composer.

3

THE COMPOSER

❦

When Charles Ives came to New York City in 1898, he went to work for the Mutual Life Insurance Company of New York. For eight years he was an "organization man"; but in 1906 he and a fellow employee, Julian S. Myrick, decided to strike out on their own in the selling of life insurance. After one false start in association with another company, they were set up by Mutual in 1909 as joint managers of an agency in New York City; and throughout the next decade, the Ives & Myrick Agency was extraordinarily successful in increasing its sales of life insurance from year to year.

From 1898 to 1908, Ives shared a bachelors' apartment in Manhattan with some other Yale men and their friends. New tenants arrived and old ones left over the course of the decade, while Poverty Flat itself changed its location twice. One of Ives's fellow inmates was his classmate and friend David Twichell, and somewhere between 1905 and 1907 Ives became seriously interested in Twichell's sister Harmony. Her father, the Reverend Joseph Hopkins Twichell, was one of Hartford's leading citizens and a close friend of Mark Twain, having served as the model for "Harris" in Mark Twain's book *A Tramp Abroad*. In the fall of 1907, Ives and Miss Twichell confessed their love to each other and became engaged; and her father married them in Hartford in June, 1908. After their honeymoon the young couple moved into an apartment in Manhattan.

In 1912 the Iveses bought a piece of land in the countryside at West Redding, Connecticut, not far from Danbury. They had a house and barn built; and for the rest of his life Ives and his wife lived at West Redding (from which he commuted into New York) from April or May to October or November of each year, staying in Manhattan during the winter months. Naturally, they became deeply attached to their country life in Connecticut. While Ives was still well, it allowed him to fulfill his desire for agricultural and rural pursuits.

Charles and Harmony Ives had no children of their own. In 1915 they allowed the cottage on their West Redding estate to be used by the Fresh Air Fund, which took poor children from the city and placed them in the country for part of the summer. One of the families that lived in the cottage that summer, the Osbornes, left their infant daughter in Mrs. Ives's care when they returned to the city. The Iveses became increasingly attached to Edith and in 1916 legally adopted the little girl as their own. Ives was, above all, a family man, and the circle of his familial happiness was now complete. It was perhaps unfortunate that he adopted no male children, but he lavished a great deal of attention on his brother's five sons.

A constant underlying factor that inevitably affected Ives's life during the 1910s was the extraordinary growth in his personal wealth. Even more remarkable, however, was his refusal to take up the "Yale man's burden"—the round of civic and social responsibilities that most of his Yale friends, particularly those who had been successful in business, assumed as a natural concomitant of their wealth and social position. Ives and his wife had little interest in becoming patrons of the opera, leaders in public affairs, prominent sponsors of charitable activities, or participants in high society and club life. They stayed at home and did a good deal of reading, particularly of eighteenth- and nineteenth-century English "classics."

Ives even shunned social contacts in the business world, leaving them to his partner. As a result, he became isolated from his Yale classmates and friends.

Ives devoted his spare time—evenings, weekends, and vacations—to intensive musical composition. Working in total isolation and continuing to experiment in many directions, he produced, during the years when he was most active in business, those works which are now regarded as the masterpieces of American music of the early twentieth century. When he finished a work, he put it away. Even without much of a social life, Ives's devotion of long hours to composition in addition to his regular business activities put a strain on his health.

In a very private way, Ives also became concerned about political and social questions during the 1910s. He increasingly identified himself with Woodrow Wilson and with Wilsonian idealism between 1914 and 1917. When the United States went to war with Germany, his emotions became entirely involved and he threw himself into the Liberty Loan drives and other war work. About a month before the armistice, in the midst of this work, he suffered a severe heart attack that proved to be the great physical turning point of his life. Within three years he had practically given up composing music and had moved into semiretirement in his business.

In 1921, at the age of forty-seven, Ives's active life was effectively at an end. Although he was to live for another third of a century, he would produce little more of significance in the fields in which he was interested. His social isolation was in marked contrast with the popularity of the gay young blade from Yale that he had been twenty years before. The new era of the 1920s was uncongenial to his temperament; but he was a very wealthy man, and in his wife and daughter he found great personal happiness and fulfillment. Almost all his music had been written; yet his musical reputation was at its nadir. Charles Ives the composer was unknown.

The music that Charles Ives composed between 1898 and 1921 is especially remarkable when it is compared with the compositions that other Americans were writing during the same period, for Ives was the only one who did not work in the shadow of Europe. On the one hand, he turned to American subject matter, American experiences, and American tunes as the basis for his compositions. On the other hand, he broke decisively with the nineteenth-century European procedures in harmony, melody, and rhythm that were accepted almost without question by other American composers. The connection between his Americanism and his experimentalism is the key to Ives's musical development.

"Our day of dependence, our long apprenticeship to the learning of other lands, draws to a close," Emerson had announced in his "American Scholar" address of 1837. "We have listened too long to the courtly muses of Europe," he had declared, and had urged Americans to develop a native literature: "We will walk on our own feet; we will work with our own hands; we will speak our own minds." [1] But music was the last of the major arts in America to break away from European dominance and find an indigenous mode of expression. Down through World War I, American composers, like Horatio Parker and Edward MacDowell, were trained in Germany and wrote a Germanic music, although French influences began to be felt around the turn of the century. The result was generally a weak imitation of the original article.

Germany and Austria gloried in that which America lacked: a traditional musical culture, built up over centuries out of national folk sources and culminating in an art music the love for which was widespread among the population. Although Italy and France nourished their own national traditions, German musical practices became dominant in Western culture during the nineteenth century. In England, where national musical traditions were quiescent, this German dominance was particularly noticeable; but it was even more pronounced in the United States. As a predominantly middle-class country that was weak in folk sources and lacking in discriminating aristocratic patronage, America had to import its higher "culture" from Europe; this culture, however, never seemed to take hold among the mass of Americans, whose attentions were absorbed in making money. The lack of a traditional musical culture exposed the United States to the worst results of the split between cultivated and vernacular. While most Americans stuck to popular music, art music became a plaything of the rich. The situation had been bad enough in Danbury, but Ives was even more appalled in New York by institutions like the New York Philharmonic and the Metropolitan Opera, whose wealthy patrons adulated the great "personalities" among imported virtuosos as a means of advertising their own social superiority. Ives felt that this situation emasculated the art of music by commercializing it and cutting it off from a vital relationship to the general American culture. As for American composers, no matter how well they hewed to the European line, they were scarcely taken seriously by American performing organizations and their audiences.

Aaron Copland has written that "the entire history of modern music . . . may be said to be a history of the gradual pull-away from the Germanic musical tradition of the past century." Although the ideals and the forms of expression of this modern movement ultimately became international in nature, the movement had its beginning with certain nationalist composers who turned to the folk music of their own countries as the means of breaking away from the Germanic tradition. But many of these nationalists, such as Grieg in Norway, were unsuccessful in their attempts to become independent of the German ways that they had been taught. "The way out was found by those few composers who, taking their native songs as the basis for their work, were able to construct a music on formal and emotional lines independent of the German tradition." [2] The first of these was the Russian Moussorgsky; another of great importance was the Hungarian Béla Bartók, who abstracted from Hungarian folk music such elements as its peculiar scales and incorporated them into his own work.

"Natural objects and phenomena are the original symbols or types which express our thoughts and feelings," Thoreau had written, "and yet American scholars, having little or no root in the soil, commonly strive with all their might to confine themselves to the imported symbols alone." Ives was fond of this passage, for he too knew "American scholars" who despised "all the true growth and experience, the living speech" as "Americanisms." Rejecting such a conventional approach, Thoreau had called upon Americans to coin words out of their intimate experience of their own environment.[3]

But where was a native source of *musical* expression to be found in the United States? The Czech composer Antonin Dvořák, who taught in America in the 1890s, suggested to American composers that they make use of Negro tunes, as he himself had done in his *New World* Symphony. A few composers took his advice. Henry Gilbert, for instance, used Negro music, and Arthur Farwell turned to American Indian material; Farwell even set up the nonprofit Wa-Wan Press in 1901 for the purpose of issuing this music and other unpublishable American compositions.[4] But such folk music came from "folk" who were essentially alien to the composers themselves, and the melodies that were quoted were too often placed in a European texture that was inappropriate to their nature. According to Copland, folk music "can be successfully handled only by a composer who is able to identify himself with, and reëxpress in his own terms, the underlying emotional connotation of the material."[5]

Working independently of these local colorists, Ives turned to the vernacular-tradition music of his own people, the New England Yankees. He was no narrow patriot or local colorist in his music; but he believed that if a composer attempted to reflect in his art the spirit of the universal people as expressed in music, it was natural that he should turn first to the music that he knew most intimately.[6] For Ives, Thoreau's advice meant that an American popular tune was a worthy symbol of an American's experience and might be quoted meaningfully in a symphony, much as one would use an Americanism meaningfully in a sentence. "I embrace the common, I explore and sit at the feet of the familiar, the low," Emerson had said.[7] The American music that interested Ives was European in cultural origin, but what caught his ear was the spirit in which it was sung or played locally and the subtle departures from the formal written music that occurred in actual vernacular performance—departures that were not so much "mistakes" as they were the result of fervor and the accidental concurrence of events. Exploiting the musical possibilities of such quirks in performance, Ives developed many of his technical innovations.

Another source of those innovations was Ives's attempt to reflect his natural surroundings in his music. Pointing forward to John Cage, he also looked back to Thoreau: "I wish to hear the silence of the night, for the silence is something positive and to be heard. . . .

A fertile and eloquent silence. . . . Silence alone is worthy to be heard. . . . The silence rings; it is musical and thrills me." [8] Ives has been called both a realist and an impressionist in music, the distinction between the two being not so great in an art form that does not usually represent objects and events. In *The Housatonic at Stockbridge*, for example, he used orchestral polytonality and polyrhythms to portray a human event (the singing from a church across the river) as experienced through a haze of natural events and objects: the leaves, "the mist" which has "not entirely left the river bed, . . . the colors, the running water, the banks and elm trees." [9] Drawing on his favorite philosophy, Ives could even think of fainter musical notes that departed from the usual rules of harmony as transcendental overtones of natural events and objects.

Ives's experimentation was undoubtedly in part a way of venting his anger at the conservative musical establishment; but it also arose naturally and logically from his pursuit of American sources. This connection between Americanism and experimentalism set Ives apart from the principal line of American musical development in the quarter-century after 1920. The younger composers of the 1920s were experimental enough, but the source of their innovations was Europe, not America; and when American composers turned back to their own land for inspiration in the 1930s, their music also became more conservative and less experimental.

Without knowledge of what was being done in Europe—and often in anticipation of the Europeans—Ives worked out in an unsystematic way most of the new resources that are used in modern music: polytonality, atonality, dodecaphony (the twelve-tone system), polyrhythms, the spatially divided orchestra, unusual combinations of instruments in chamber music—even an element of the aleatory (chance). These were the departures from musical tradition that were to prove so disturbing to the conservative musicians to whom he first showed his compositions. Not only his technical devices, but also the way he put them together to make a piece of music, were extraordinarily innovative. Impressionism, expressionism, primitivism—all these styles can be found in Ives's work, developed independently of the Europeans with whose names they are associated. In both their construction and their total effect, Ives's more complex works have been compared by Lou Harrison with Joyce's *Finnegans Wake;* there are such similarities as quotation, punning, stream-of-consciousness association, mixed perspectives, objectivity of treatment, and many-layered meaning.[10]

Ives had a remarkable mind that could find sufficient order in what was for most people violent disorder. His music had a visual analogue in the bulletin board that he kept in later years on the door of his music room at West Redding, an extraordinary hodgepodge of pictures and printed matter concerning personal, family, musical, college, business, and historical subjects. His music is inclusive enough to extend even to the banal, as when it drifts into a passage of grandiose Lisztian romanticism.

It is startling, then, when one looks behind this daring music to examine the man who composed it, to find that Ives's mind was very old-fashioned. It was not simply a case of his searching for traditional roots for his new departures; Ives was actually oblivious to the leading artistic and intellectual movements of his time. It is in this respect that he came nearest to being a "primitive." In relation to the nineteenth century, he was no primitive, but a fairly well educated man. But he was isolated from the art and thought of the first two decades of the twentieth century, even though his compositions are now seen as an important product of that era. He was utterly on his own, and the naiveté resulting from such a situation certainly appears in his work. Ives stands in starkest contrast with Arnold Schoenberg, also born in 1874, whose innovations (although begun a bit later than Ives's) were conceived and propagated in highly intellectual terms and became central to the development of twentieth-century music. Unlike Ives, Schoenberg was closely involved with the innovations in thought and in the other arts in Europe during these two decades.

It is difficult to find a figure analogous to Ives in the other arts in America. He has been compared to Melville, Whitman, and Frank Lloyd Wright, among others, but none of these figures had his extraordinary combination of naiveté, experimentation, and (above all) utter isolation from the currents around him. One is tempted to compare him to such an American inventive genius as Eli Whitney or Edison, in contrast to the European theoretical scientist like Faraday or Lord Kelvin. But perhaps it is most useful to compare Ives with two American political and social thinkers of the period before the Civil War, two men whom Ives greatly admired: Henry David Thoreau and William Lloyd Garrison.

The necessities of organized society weighed heavily upon revolutionary thinkers of nineteenth-century Europe, such as Karl Marx. Desirous of overthrowing the existing organized system, they opposed to it their own organized system, backed by an intellectual theory that took account of all elements in existing society. For the Americans Garrison and Thoreau, however, organized society could be easily dismissed. Anarchically, they counseled the individual to follow his own conscience without worrying about the chaotic consequences for law, government, force, and social order. Similarly, for Schoenberg the European musical tradition was overwhelming and all-pervasive; to overthrow its harmonic system meant to deal with it intellectually, in its own terms, and ultimately to produce an opposed system—the twelve-tone system. It may be argued how thorough Ives's musical education at Danbury and Yale was; but clearly the very provincialism of American culture, his father's experimentalism, his own early experiments, and his need to preserve his masculinity all combined to allow him to treat the European musical tradition with a certain insouciance. He was under no obligation to deal with it intellectually and systematically. He felt free to take from it what he wanted, work the rest of his art out on his own, and not worry about the consequences. The attenuated cultural air of America gave a very special freedom to a few Americans, then, but it also made their thought and art somewhat irrelevant to the mainstream of European development, and they were regarded as eccentric by their own countrymen. Yet Garrison and Thoreau were ultimately discovered by Tolstoy and Gandhi, somewhat as Ives was later taken up as a "find" by the younger European modernists of the 1960s.

The old-fashioned philosophical and emotional impetus that lay behind Ives's advanced compositions is not so apparent in the music itself as it is in the music's literary concomitants—the song texts that he wrote and, most important, the programmatic explanations of his instrumental works. From a purely musical point of view, these nonmusical elements can be discounted. When a musician assesses the value of a piece of music, he is not concerned with the composer's choice of literary subject matter or his point of view toward that subject matter, but only with the expressiveness of the music itself. To the historian assessing Ives's role in cultural history, however, these extramusical elements must be considered—especially because Ives's own view of the matter, a very unusual one, was that the music itself (as sounds) had value only in terms of the mental or spiritual idea out of which it grew.[11]

Not all of Charles Ives's music is about Danbury; *Central Park in the Dark,* for example, reflects his life in the city. But most of his major compositions had their inspiration in either the music or the life of his boyhood town. Yet there is a curious discrepancy between what is known historically about Danbury between 1874 and 1893 and what Ives said about it in this music. The music is not concerned with the life of a rapidly growing small city, with its business and professional men, mill workers, immigrants, manufacturing, and railroads. Instead, it presents elements that were already outmoded or fast disappearing when Ives was growing up: farmers, camp meetings, barn dances. It was not so much his own boyhood that Ives was telling about, but rather that of his father before the Civil War, when Danbury had still been rural, Emerson had lectured at the lyceum, farmers had come to town meetings to speak their minds, and men had been sturdy and independent. Yet the boy Charles Ives was the center of the music. He was putting himself in his father's place, transferring his own boyhood experiences back into the social context of pre–Civil War Danbury, and thus recapturing in music a life that he had never actually lived.

In his Second Symphony, for example, Ives quoted a large number of tunes that were associated with Connecticut rural life and with his father's musical life in Danbury; among them were *The Red, White, and Blue* ("O Columbia! the gem of the ocean . . ."), *Bringing In the Sheaves,* and *Turkey in the Straw,* along with Ives's own takeoffs on barn-dance fiddling and Stephen Foster songs. There were also takeoffs on nineteenth-century European classics. This symphony, finished about 1902, was the first large-scale instrumental work that

Ives composed after leaving Yale, although much of the material in it was drawn from church, theater-orchestra, and band music written in college; part of it even dated back to 1889, when it had been played by George Ives's band and orchestra.[12] In this relatively conservative work, Ives showed that he had not yet found a musical style of his own. His model was the nineteenth-century European symphony, but the vernacular tunes did not exactly fit into the grandiose form and texture. Ives was a young man with a Yale degree, social success, and everything to look forward to in the business world; he was never to live in Danbury again. Like many another man who has left his home town to seek his fortune, he looked back nostalgically, perhaps even feeling a twinge of guilt over having abandoned his ancestral home for the temptations of the great city.

The Third Symphony, mostly finished in 1904, was titled *The Camp Meeting*, its three movements being *Old Folks Gatherin, Children's Day,* and *Communion*. Here Ives quoted only camp-meeting hymn tunes, such as *Erie* ("What a friend we have in Jesus . . ."), *Woodworth* ("Just as I am, without one plea . . ."), and *Cleansing Fountain* ("There is a fountain filled with blood . . ."). The work is scored for chamber orchestra, and the quoted hymns are set in a naive and intimate context that is highly appropriate to them; much of the work has the purgative and ultimately optimistic quality of a revival service. By giving up the European symphony as a model, Ives achieved a style that was both more indigenous and more personal than that of his first two symphonies.

The Third Symphony was drawn from organ pieces that Ives composed while he was an organist at Central Presbyterian Church in New York from 1900 to 1902. His four violin sonatas also arose from this church work, although parts of them were not written until much later. All four of them, like the symphony, harked back to the outdoor camp meetings near Danbury at which Ives had assisted his father with the music. The Fourth Violin Sonata (*Children's Day at the Camp Meeting*) was described by Ives in a way that suggests how hard he was trying to recapture the immediacy of his boyhood experiences. The first movement, in which a fugue by George E. Ives and a hymn tune are woven together, recalls an occasion when the boys marched around singing a hymn (*The Old, Old Story*) between services. Young Charles was meanwhile engaged in a "post-lude organ practice" on the melodeon; and the march and the practice "got to going together, even joining in each other's sounds." The boys "started this tune on 'ME' so the boy organist's father made him play 'SOH' hard even if sometimes it had to be in a key that the postlude was not in just then." Finally, "the organ would be uncovering 'covered 5ths,' breaking 'good resolutions' faster and faster, and the boys' march reaching almost a 'Main Street Quick-step.' " [13]

The second movement of this same sonata is based on the children's hymn *Jesus Loves Me*. The hymn is, to use Lou Harrison's phrase, "recomposed"—that is, the melody is taken apart and its possibilities explored by the violin—until, at the end, the straight hymn tune is stated. The piano accompaniment, on the other hand, has little to do with the harmony of the original hymn, but is an attempt "to reflect the out-door sounds of nature on those Summer days." Ives noted that at these camp meetings the evangelical shouting of some of the grown-up men would get the children stirred up, and "at times these 'confurorants' would give the boys a chance to run out and throw stones down on the rocks in the brook!" Thus the contrasting middle section of the movement is atonal and is to be played "Allegro conslugarocko!" [14] But the boys (and Ives) having been given the opportunity to prove their manhood and independence, the music returns to the quiet *Jesus Loves Me*. [15]

Ives later came to believe that the Third Symphony and most of the movements of the violin sonatas were too restricted and conservative. In writing these hymn-tune compositions, he had known that "if played at all, they would probably be played in church"; and he had not felt that he could inflict his dissonances on a congregation that was not free to get up and leave. It was not, then, until he turned to "secular" music, "whose subject matter has to do with the activities of general life around one," that his work was able to be "freer and more experimental in technical ways." [16] He would become tired of the idioms in which he had been working, finding that they no longer allowed him to express himself, and so he would invent new ones. For fifteen years after he left his organist's post in 1902, he produced a series of shorter experimental works for chamber groups—for example, the ragtime dances (c. 1902), the

Country Band March (c. 1903), the Overture and March *1776* (1903–1904), *In the Cage* (1906), *The Unanswered Question* (c. 1906), *Central Park in the Dark* (1906), *In Re Con Moto Et Al* (1913)—many of whose innovations were then incorporated into his larger "secular" works. Of the latter, one of the most important is the First Piano Sonata (1902–1909), which included some of the ragtime dances as its second and fourth movements.

What Ives had in mind in the First Piano Sonata can be seen in the description that he wrote on a manuscript page of the first movement:

> What is it all about?—Dan S. asks. Mostly about the outdoor life in Conn. villages in [the] eighties and nineties—impressions, remembrances, and reflections of country farmers in [the] Conn. farmland.
>
> . . . Fred's Daddy got so excited that he shouted when Fred hit a home run and the school won the baseball game. But Aunt Sarah was always humming *Where Is My Wandering Boy,* after Fred and John left for a job in Bridgeport. There was usually a sadness—but not at the Barn Dances, with [their] jigs, foot jumping, and reels, mostly on winter nights.
>
> In the summer times, the hymns were sung outdoors. Folks sang (as *Ole Black Joe*)—and the Bethel Band (quickstep street marches)—and the people like[d to say] things as they wanted to say, and to do things as they wanted to, in their own way—and many old times . . . there were feelings, and of spiritual fervency! [17]

John Kirkpatrick has recalled that Ives gave him a different description as "one possible aspect of the scenario: the family together in the first and last movements, the boy away sowing his oats in the ragtimes, and the parental anxiety in the middle movement." [18]

The sonata is certainly a romantic work and one into which Ives threw himself very freely. It is obviously about the secular life of Danbury, and most of it would not be appropriate for church services; but it cannot be far from religion, for the tunes quoted in the sonata are hymn tunes. His artistic viewpoint is reminiscent of Mark Twain's remark that " 'Tom Sawyer' is simply a hymn, put into prose form to give it a worldly air." [19] In fact, Ives made no real distinction, in his music or his philosophy, between the sacred and the secular. The fervor of a barn dance and the fervor of a camp meeting were for him merely different forms of the outpouring of man's inner spirit—different reflections of the human soul and of the Oversoul. The most heterogeneous elements of life were ultimately bound together in an invisible, transcendental order. The lowest and most insignificant event had its divine meaning.

This philosophy was similar to that set forth by another Yale man, Thornton Wilder, in his experimental play *Our Town* (first performed in 1938). Ives's music and Wilder's play offer many points of comparison. Both deal with a New England town before it has become engulfed by modernity. Both avoid the unpleasant or more "realistic" features of the town. Both the play and the music are perhaps more notable for their "manner" than for their "substance" (to use two Ivesian terms). Transcendentalism is an important element in *Our Town,* particularly in the graveyard scene, where the dead "get weaned away from earth" and wait "for the eternal part in them to come out clear." Wilder sketches the invisible hierarchy that links the human with the divine by means of the address on a letter received by a girl from her minister: "Jane Crofut; The Crofut Farm; Grover's Corners; Sutton County; New Hampshire; . . . the United States of America; Continent of North America; Western Hemisphere; the Earth; the Solar System; the Universe; the Mind of God." Wilder has written that his play "is an attempt to find a value above all price for the smallest events in our daily life. I have made the claim as preposterous as possible, for I have set the village against the largest dimensions of time and place." [20] Ives was making a similar point in the ragtime movements of his First Piano Sonata, for the tunes that he "ragged" into the most exuberant and secular rhythms were gospel hymns: *Happy Day, Bringing in the Sheaves,* and *I Hear Thy Welcome Voice.*[21]

Ives tried to express not only the transcendental unity that bound all things together at a given moment, but also the link among past, present, and future. In *Putnam's Camp* (1912), the second movement of his First Orchestral Set (*Three Places in New England*), he presented an event of the American Revolution that still had great significance for him and other Danburians. During the winter of 1778–1779,

Gen. Israel Putnam and his Continental soldiers had camped at Redding (near Danbury). "Long rows of stone camp fire-places still remain to stir a child's imagination," wrote Ives. "The hardships which the soldiers endured and the agitation of a few hot-heads to break camp and march to the Hartford Assembly for relief, is a part of Redding history." The camp was subsequently made into a memorial park, of which Ives's uncle Lyman Brewster served as a commissioner. Ives composed *Putnam's Camp* at a time when he was having a house built a few miles from the park. He based the work on two earlier experimental compositions, the *Country Band March* and the *Overture and March 1776*, the latter of which had been an overture for an opera that he had intended to write on his Uncle Lyman's blank-verse play, *Major John André*. But the real origin of all this music was that moment in his boyhood when he heard two bands pass each other playing different marches. In *Putnam's Camp* he represented the opposition between Putnam and the mutineers by setting against each other not only different march tunes in clashing dissonance, but also different rhythms; at a certain point, two march meters are going simultaneously, the one at a rate one and a third times as fast as the rate of the other. Even more remarkable, both the clashing bands and the story of Putnam and his men are focused upon through the eyes of the boy Charles Ives. Ives's program note tells of a child who wanders away from a Fourth of July picnic at the campground into the woods, where he falls asleep (the falling asleep being represented literally as the music grows slower and softer). Then he sees the Goddess of Liberty, sorrowfully "pleading with the soldiers not to forget their 'cause' and the great sacrifices they have made for it." But the mutineers "march out of camp with fife and drum to a popular tune of the day. Suddenly a new national note is heard. Putnam is coming over the hills from the center,—the soldiers turn back and cheer." The boy wakes up and rejoins the festivities.[22]

Among Ives's most nostalgic works is his *New England Holidays*. Three of the pieces that make up this orchestral "set"—*Washington's Birthday, Decoration Day,* and *The Fourth of July*—were written between 1909 and 1913; Ives called them "pictures of a boy's holidays in a country town" and wrote that they were "but attempts to make pic-

tures in music of common events in the lives of common people
. . . , mostly of the rural communities." [23] In these compositions, as
in *Putnam's Camp*, Ives showed that he had come a long way from the
clear quotation of popular tunes that he had used in the Second
Symphony. He seemed to feel that it was not sufficient to view his
childhood through the sentimental haze of a comfortable middle
age; what he wanted to grasp was the immediacy of the boy's experience as it was being lived. He expressed this desire in prose in a
memo that he wrote to himself in 1914. When he was commuting
daily from Redding to New York that year, he occasionally jotted
down memos, which John Kirkpatrick has called a "commuter's
diary." This was a time when Ives was enjoying enormous success in
business, writing his best music, and beginning to take a strong interest in current events; but as he heard the familiar station names
called out on June 5, 1914, his mind reverted to the make-believe
railroad that he and his brother had once built in their backyard.
"The only hard part of commuting now," he wrote, "is that each
time I fear I may get further and further away from my boytime
dreams." After dwelling lovingly on each detail of the railroad, including his father's important role in the game, he concluded:

> How thankful we feel now that father dreamed with us; how cir-
> cumspect our lives would be now if he hadn't. I have an idea that
> we felt then subconsciously [that] the fun was when the sunrise
> would start to throw its color and hope into our attic bedroom. We
> would lie awhile and live ahead the day to come. It was our enthusi-
> asm and plans [that] seemed most inspiring, and throughout the
> day an . . . underlying stimulant was the hope of "grasping a real
> throttle." . . . It is always the "minute after life" that everyone
> lives. Immortality is but a hope, a complementary substance we
> have *now* that must be full of hope. Riding up and down from
> Redding as I do now might stifle it if we hadn't had our RR under
> the clothesline.[24]

It was the effect of living this "minute after life" that Ives was
searching for in many of the works of his middle and later periods.
Since his greatest sensitivity as a boy had been aural sensitivity, it was
through representing in an artistic form the *aural* experiences of his
childhood that he sought to recapture the excitement and hope of

the boy's *total* experience. The simultaneity of different musical events had impressed him deeply in Danbury; his use of this simultaneity as a device in his art can perhaps be seen best in *The Fourth of July*. The effect that he sought here was, as he said of another work, "not something that happens, but the way something happens." [25] "I remember distinctly, when I was scoring this, that there was a feeling of freedom as a boy has, on the Fourth of July, who wants to do anything he wants to do, and that's his one day to do it." [26] Out of an impressionistic background arise many quotations from patriotic and popular tunes, the whole being woven together into an incredible complex of simultaneous melodies, harmonies, and rhythms; the cacophony reaches its climax with the explosion and skyrocket at the end. Ives paid particular attention to incorporating into the piece the mistakes in key and rhythm that were made by players in country bands. His program notes are almost as good as the music itself:

> It's a boy's "4th"—no historical orations—no patriotic grandiloquences by "grown-ups"—no program in his yard! But he knows what he's celebrating—better than some of the county politicians. And he goes at it in his own way, with a patriotism nearer kin to nature than jingoism. His festivities start in the quiet of the midnight before and grow raucous with the sun. Everybody knows what it's like,—if everybody doesn't,——Cannon on the Green, Village Band on Main St., fire crackers, shanks mixed on cornets, strings around big toes, torpedoes, Church-bells, lost finger, fifes, clam-chowder, a prize-fight, drum-corps, burnt shins, parades (in and out of step), saloons all closed (more drunks than usual), baseball game (Danbury All-Stars vs. Beaver Brook Boys), pistols, mobbed umpire, Red, White and Blue, runaway horse,——and the day ends with the sky-rocket over the Church-steeple, just after the annual explosion sets the Town-Hall on fire.[27]

Works like *The Fourth of July* raise the question of whether Ives's aural sensitivity as a boy had not erected a barrier between him and the people of Danbury—not an insuperable barrier, to be sure, for his father had overcome a similar problem, but still a real barrier. During his youth, Ives perhaps did not realize the philosophical significance to be found in the simultaneous experience of apparently incongruous things; but he certainly felt the *aural* appeal of such an experience, as his early experiments showed. The citizens of Danbury, on the other hand, were not attracted by music in two keys or by mistakes in pitch and rhythm; and they thought that church music and dance music ought to be kept in separate compartments of life. Mark Twain, in a version of *Pudd'nhead Wilson,* expressed the reaction of the average American to "Ivesian" effects through a widow who complains about the noise made by her two foreign boarders the night before. While one brother has sweetly sung Lowell Mason's *Missionary Hymn,* the other has simultaneously sung *Old Bob Ridley,* a "common rackety slam-bang secular song, one of the rippingest and rantingest and noisiest there is." The widow admits that she is "no judge of music." But she hopes "they will both sing the same tune at the same time, for in my opinion a duet that is made up of two different tunes is a mistake; especially when the tunes ain't any kin to one another, that way." Her daughter only overcomes the widow's opposition by advancing the unanswerable argument that "it must be a foreign custom" and "the best way," because "it don't stand to reason that with their education they would do anything but what the highest musical authorities have sanctioned." [28] Her argument offers one important reason why European experimentalism (such as Stravinsky's) came to be accepted in America by some of those who rejected Ives's works.

In Danbury, as later in his adult life, Charles Ives's ears were on wrong.[29] And perhaps only the insider who has become partially an outsider can appreciate the deeper significance in vernacular life. As a creative artist, then, Ives occupied an ambiguous position. He was not a folk artist, even in relation to a bourgeois "folk," for he did not create music that ordinary people among his contemporaries could enjoy. On the other hand, he was not an alienated artist, for he refused to admit his separation from the people among whom he had been raised. Instead, he tried to occupy a tenuous position between the two alternatives. Even as a boy, he sensed his alienation; and he resisted it by taking an ever more vigorous part in the vernacular life of Danbury. Still sensing that alienation as an adult, he continued to resist it by asserting in his music that in Danbury he had been an insider full of un-self-conscious expectation—that he had been part of the common life all along.

Several of Ives's later instrumental works, although they drew upon his musical background in Danbury, were not attempts to re-create in music his boyhood experience, but rather statements of his mature philosophy. That philosophy was New England transcendentalism. He approached it first from a literary point of view in his Second Piano Sonata, *Concord, Mass., 1840–60,* composed mainly in 1911 and 1912; it was his "impression of the spirit of transcendentalism that is associated in the minds of many with Concord, Mass., of over a half century ago." [30] The first movement, the deepest of the four, he called *Emerson;* in it he gave a general impressionistic portrayal of his hero Ralph Waldo Emerson, whom he regarded as America's greatest philosopher. The second movement, *Hawthorne,* was rather surprisingly a lighter scherzo. Ives knew that Hawthorne's "basic theme" had been "the influence of sin upon the conscience"; but that theme was completely alien to Ives's own optimistic temperament. Therefore, "this fundamental part of Hawthorne is not attempted in our music," which was "but an 'extended fragment' trying to suggest some of his wilder, fantastical adventures into the half-childlike, half-fairylike phantasmal realms." [31] In the third movement, *The Alcotts,* Ives gave a brief and relatively simple sketch of the family life in Bronson Alcott's home. Finally, in the fourth movement, *Thoreau,* a general picture was again presented, the music being more intimate and less grand than that in *Emerson.* Ives admired no one so much as Emerson; but sometimes he seemed to love Thoreau more [32]—the Thoreau of *Walden,* of course, rather than the Thoreau of "Civil Disobedience," for Ives was a majoritarian. In the life of the philosopher of Walden, Ives seems to have sensed an analogy to his own musical isolation and his own tendency to reclusion.

The trouble with the literary approach to transcendentalism, from Ives's point of view, was that the Concord philosophers had stayed aloof from traditional Christianity.[33] Ives was far from being an orthodox Christian. But he had seen the inner spirit of men find its fullest expression in the old camp meetings; religion, in the most general sense, had to be a part of his philosophy. Furthermore, he denied "that religious services have a tendency . . . to make a man conservative—that they restrict . . . freedom of thought and action." He felt that the "pioneers in most of the great activities" had been "essentially religious-minded men." Thus in the Fourth Symphony (1909–1916), the most vastly conceived and transcendental of his finished compositions, Ives turned to a frankly religious subject and found that he could compose without the sense of restriction that had marred some of his earlier religious works.[34]

Something of the philosophical maturation that lay behind the Fourth Symphony can be seen in a passage from Ives's *Essays before a Sonata* in which he describes how "a boy" wakes up one Memorial Day morning to the sounds of the band playing Reeves's glorious march. As the music draws near, "he seems of a sudden translated— a moment of vivid power comes, a consciousness of material nobility, an exultant something gleaming with the possibilities of this life, an assurance that nothing is impossible, and that the whole world lies at his feet." His vision passes as the music fades away. But "later in life, the same boy hears the Sabbath morning bell ringing out from the white steeple at the 'Center,' and as it draws him to it, through the autumn fields of sumach and asters, a Gospel hymn of simple devotion comes out to him—'There's a wideness in God's mercy.' " The Memorial Day vision returns to him, "but the moment is of deeper import":

> There is no personal exultation—no intimate world vision—no magnified personal hope—and in their place a profound sense of a spiritual truth,—a sin within reach of forgiveness—and as the hymn voices die away, there lies at his feet—not the world, but the figure of the Saviour—he sees an unfathomable courage, an immortality for the lowest, the vastness in humility, the kindness of the human heart, man's noblest strength, and he knows that God is nothing— nothing but love! [35]

The first of these experiences was what lay behind *Decoration Day* or *The Fourth of July;* the second of them, which seems to have been an adult experience, was what lay behind the Fourth Symphony. His pictures of a boy's holidays had "no message for the cosmic world," [36] but the symphony had an explicitly philosophical program.

Ives found meaning and beauty through nostalgia. He cherished those moments—whether they were "flashes of transcendent beauty" of "universal import," or merely "some common sensation"—that brought an "intimate personal experience" of "indescribable effect." [37] It was when he heard gospel music and other hymns that Ives experienced such moments most vividly; thus he drew heavily upon this religious music of the people when he wrote the Fourth Symphony. With its many simultaneous quotations, the work is (in places) more complex than anything else that Ives wrote. Technically, he experimented (in all movements but the third) with a divided orchestra whose sections would pursue independent rhythms, thus sometimes requiring more than one conductor. He also wanted to try the aural effect of placing the separate orchestral sections at different distances from the audience. This idea of a divided orchestra dated back to his earlier experimental pieces *The Unanswered Question* and *Central Park in the Dark*.

"The aesthetic program of the work is that of the searching questions of What? and Why? which the spirit of man asks of life. This is particularly the sense of the prelude. The three succeeding movements are the diverse answers in which existence replies." [38] In the short Prelude (first movement), the questions (which may have been related in Ives's mind to the unsatisfied questioning of the trumpet in *The Unanswered Question*) are represented by a chorus of voices that sings Lowell Mason's hymn *Watchman* ("Watchman, tell us of the night . . .").

The second movement, drawn partly from the *Hawthorne* movement of the *Concord* Sonata, takes its program largely from Hawthorne's story "The Celestial Railroad." In Hawthorne's satire, modern men improve on John Bunyan's *Pilgrim's Progress* by building a railroad from the City of Destruction to the Celestial City. Ives's movement is a "comedy," "in which an exciting, easy and worldly progress through life is contrasted with the trials of the Pilgrims in their journey through the swamps and rough country. The occasional slow episodes—Pilgrims' hymns—are constantly crowded out and overwhelmed by the former." This "dream, or fantasy, ends with an interruption of reality—the Fourth of July in Concord—brass bands, drum corps, etc." [39] Surprisingly, Ives used dissonance to represent the villains and relatively simple music to portray the heroes. And whether or not the composer realized it, Hawthorne's story makes fun of the very passion for public improvements and the very philosophy of optimism that had characterized Ives's grandparents. (It even mocks transcendentalism!)

For his third movement, Ives rewrote and orchestrated the fugue from his First String Quartet, originally composed in college. The movement is based on hymn tunes, but is nonexperimental—and rightly so, for this third movement "is an expression of the reaction of life into formalism and ritualism." [40] In this description Ives indicated his dissatisfaction with the answers that the traditional Protestant churches gave to man's questions about life.

"The last movement is an apotheosis of the preceding content in terms that have something to do with the reality of existence and its religious experience." [41] In this transcendental vision, Ives reached his greatest heights, both technically (a separate percussion group maintains an independent rhythm throughout) and philosophically. He called it "the best, compared with the other movements, or for that matter with any other thing that I've done." Yet it was based on hymn tunes and was connected in his mind "with a Communion Service, especially the memory of one, years ago, in the old Redding Camp Meetings." Toward the middle, "there is something suggesting a slow, out-of-doors march, which has for its theme, in part, the remembrance of the way the hymn, *Nearer My God To Thee,* sounded" at the old services.[42] As in the whole symphony, this peculiar combination of vernacular religion and transcendental philosophy was again Ives's way of looking back at the pre–Civil War era in New England, the era in which his grandparents had been active and in which his father had grown up.

In the early 1910s, Ives began an even more transcendental work, a *Universe* Symphony. Its three sections were to represent the "formation of the waters and mountains"; the "earth, evolution in nature and humanity"; and "heaven, the rise of all to the spiritual." Technically, Ives intended the music to parallel the visual effect of seeing the earth and the heavens from different perspectives. The vastness of his conception appears in his envisioning, for only *one part* of his playing forces, "from 5 to 14 groups of instruments or separate orchestras, each to know its own part before coming together in conclave." [43] Apparently Ives imagined that the work would be performed by a number of choruses and orchestras distributed around mountains and valleys.[44]

But the *Universe* Symphony was unfinished when America entered World War I in 1917 and Ives set aside his compositions. After his heart attack in 1918, he found that he lacked both the strength and the inspiration to continue composing. In 1920 and 1921 he wrote a number of songs, but scarcely anything was finished after 1921. In the 1920s a Third Orchestral Set was worked on but not completed; a Third Piano Sonata, written during the same period, was destroyed. Around the end of 1926, as his wife recalled, "he came downstairs one day with tears in his eyes, and said he couldn't seem to compose any more—nothing went well, nothing sounded right." [45] His creative period was over.

4

THE BUSINESSMAN

❧

THERE WAS GOOD REASON for Charles Ives to go with the Mutual Life Insurance Company of New York in 1898. His father's second cousin Dr. Granville White, who was highly placed in the medical department of the company and later became second vice president, was instrumental in getting him this position; and Robert A. Granniss, vice president of Mutual, was also a relative of his, on his grandmother Ives's side of the family.[1] That Ives started out as a mere clerk in the actuarial department is not very significant; his "proper" ethnic and social background, his Yale diploma, and his social contacts from college all made him an excellent prospect for an executive position.

Proving unsuited to actuarial work, Ives was transferred in 1899 to the Charles H. Raymond Agency, which handled most of Mutual's business in New York City. He did not do well as applications clerk there, but he was soon given more congenial work that provided him an opportunity to prove himself. At the Raymond Agency he met and became fast friends with another clerk, Julian S. Myrick. Although Myrick was not a college graduate, he came from a well-to-do family, and he had a smoothness in dealing with people that Ives lacked. Little is known of the work that Myrick and Ives carried on in the Raymond Agency between 1899 and 1906. Neither of them sold insurance directly. Ives worked with the agents who went out into the field, while Myrick seems to have supervised clerical work. By the end of the period, both were undoubtedly what would now be called junior executives.[2]

Meanwhile, in 1905, an outcry of the progressive movement against the malpractices of life insurance companies had led the New York state legislature to appoint a committee of investigation, headed by Sen. William W. Armstrong. The committee's chief counsel, Charles Evans Hughes, mercilessly subjected the officials of Mutual and the other large firms to questioning which revealed that they had been guilty of nepotism, reckless investments of insurance funds, arrangements for giving lucrative commissions to favored agencies, political influence, and many other underhanded practices. In the aftermath of the inquiry, New York adopted the Armstrong laws (1906) to regulate insurance business in the state.[3] But the directors of Mutual, frightened by the public's loss of confidence, effected their own reorganization and got rid of some of their more corrupt executives in 1906. Since Colonel Raymond had been a party to particularly shady dealings with these executives, his agency was abolished. In spite of these reforms from within, however, new business for the company fell off, there was a general demoralization, and good insurance men left Mutual in droves.[4] The disorientation of Mutual, and of life insurance companies in general, in the four or five years after 1905 was probably the key factor that enabled Ives and Myrick to come to the fore in the business during this period.

In the midst of Mutual's reorganization, Ives suffered a slight heart attack. In order for him to have a rest, Myrick accompanied him to Old Point Comfort, Virginia, at Christmas, 1906.[5] There they decided to get out of Mutual and open their own agency. Their friend John Tatlock, who had formerly been with Mutual, was now president of the Washington Life Insurance Company, a smaller firm; he offered Ives a general agency with his company covering New York City and Connecticut. The agency of Ives & Company, with Ives as manager and Myrick as his assistant, was set up in January, 1907. The two men worked hard recruiting agents and building up their territory, and they did well. They emphasized the low basic rates that resulted from Washington Life's being a nonparticipating (non-dividend-sharing) company. But a financial recession set in that fall; they were dependent upon their own financing; and in Washington Life they had little to offer against the larger insurance companies except the assurance that they were obeying the new Armstrong laws. In 1908, Washington Life was bought up by Pittsburgh Life and Trust, which did not carry on business in New York; and before the year was over, Ives and Myrick found themselves without a job.[6]

Turning back to Mutual, they discovered a friend in George T. Dexter, who headed the agency department; he was impressed with their assiduous work for Washington Life and offered them an agency in New York with Mutual. The firm of Ives & Myrick, with the two men as joint managers, was established on January 1, 1909. The Raymond Agency had been under Mutual's old general-agency system, in which the general agent was largely independent of the parent company and worked for large commissions. Under the new branch-office or agency-manager system (which included Ives & Myrick), the agency managers were salaried and received much smaller commissions; furthermore, their activities and those of their agents came under strict control from the home office.[7]

It was a good time to be setting up a life insurance agency. Public confidence was beginning to return to the large firms, which were now under stricter state control. The years during which Ives was associated with Mutual as an agency manager (1909–1929) were years of general prosperity in the United States, and the growth of life insurance was very rapid during the period.[8] Ives & Myrick was fully prepared to get a large portion of the new business. In 1909, as one of eight Mutual agencies in New York, it sold $1,600,000 worth of paid-for insurance.[9] Quickly pulling ahead of these other Mutual agencies in the city, the firm became, by the end of its first decade, the leading life insurance agency of all those in New York City.[10] By

1929, when it sold $49,000,000 worth of paid-for insurance, it was the largest life insurance agency in the entire country.[11]

Such phenomenal success, particularly in the early years, was due in large part to the great energy and enthusiasm which the two men put into building up their business. But the device in which they pioneered, and which was the key factor in their success, was the recruitment of a large number of general insurance brokers, who were scattered throughout the city and its environs, to sell Mutual policies. Far more numerous than Ives & Myrick's own full-time agents, these brokers dealt in types of insurance other than life, and they handled the policies of different companies. Thus they had valuable contacts with people who might buy life insurance. Ives & Myrick induced them to open life insurance departments by offering them, without any diminution of their commissions, the services of its staff of trained supervisors and clerical personnel, along with selling information and training in "scientific" sales techniques. In addition, Ives & Myrick was always located either in the same building as the Mutual home office or very nearby in the financial district of Manhattan; and the agency was thus in a position to expedite the company's acceptance of an application secured by a broker. It was through these independent brokers, then, that the agency did much of its business.[12]

In addition to their salaries and commissions as managers, Ives and Myrick also received a sizable income from the purchase of renewal commissions. The agent who sold a policy received from Mutual, besides a large portion of the first year's premium as a commission, smaller renewal commissions for several subsequent years (provided the policy remained in force). Since agents (especially brokers) wished to realize these renewal commissions at once when they sold the policy, Ives and Myrick would pay them (as a lump sum) a percentage of what they would have received if they had waited; in return, the two managers received the right to collect the renewal commissions themselves as they became due in subsequent years. The purchase of these renewal commissions proved to be very profitable to the two partners.

Referring to their division of work, Myrick later recalled that "Ives looked after the production, taking care of the agents' side of the business, and my activities were with the clerical, home office and outside contacts." [13] It could just as well have been said that Myrick dealt directly with people while Ives stayed at one remove from them. Ives was the "idea man"; but although he handled the firm's public relations and supervised its agents, he did so almost entirely in writing. In the mass of advertising copy, letters to agents, and training material for salesmen that Ives wrote in the 1910s and 1920s lies important evidence of his personal relationship to the insurance business.

According to his wife, Ives did not become a professional musician partly because of his shyness at appearing before an audience.[14] Probably a more fundamental reason was his inability to depart deliberately from the successful Yale man's standard route to the top and his preference for working with people among whom he was comfortable. What is ironic is that by following the Yale crowd and avoiding music, Ives found himself in a line of business far more unsuited to his temperament than music would have been. Charles Ives was basically a gentle, innocent, shy, aloof man who loved to compose music; nothing could have been more alien to his personality than the flamboyant, enthusiastic, foot-in-the-door salesmanship—not to speak of the selfish commercialism and pursuit of the almighty dollar—that was expected of the insurance agent in 1910. The surviving insurance men who worked most closely with Ives are agreed that he was utterly incapable of selling anyone an insurance policy.[15] He did not have to, of course, but he had to supervise others in doing it. Ives could only throw himself into an enterprise if he could depersonalize it—remove from it any selfishness or self-projection—and erect it into a noble general cause. As he had depersonalized athletics at school and was to depersonalize politics later, so at Ives & Myrick he depersonalized insurance selling. The contributions that he thus made to the insurance business were not any more a reflection of the needs of the business itself than they were a reflection of his own personal needs. The two aspects of life insurance that he chose to emphasize, in order to remove from it the element of selfish commercialism, were altruism and science.

Altruism was nothing new in the insurance business, but Ives raised it to a truly transcendental level in the literature that he wrote. He was no hypocrite; notions of the "service" that life insurance companies were performing for mankind—notions that became clichés in the mouth of the ordinary Babbitt—were among Ives's most sincerely held beliefs. He naively wrote (in a *private* essay) that Ives & Myrick had prospered because it had operated on the assumption "that *most* men were honest and most men were intelligent." [16] Specifically, life insurance was "doing its part in the progress of the greater life values" because it was the fulfillment of an altruistic aspiration that man had long ago felt but had lacked the means to act upon. Once it had been developed as an institution, life insurance served as a challenge to a man to do his duty to his family and fellow man, and at the same time it offered him a practical means of meeting that obligation; this was the period when the life insurance gospel was being spread by "an emotional appeal to the moral and altruistic side of human nature." By the 1910s, however, American men were well enough informed about life insurance that they admitted their duty to carry it. Ives believed that selling was now moving into a new scientific phase. The old guesswork and emotion were being replaced by a formula so simple and convincing that, given a man's financial and family situation, it was possible to determine exactly how much insurance he should carry.[17]

Ives suggested that the agent open his scientific presentation with an approach such as this one: "I want to talk life insurance to you for four minutes. I will tell you something no agent has ever told you. I can answer scientifically the one essential question. Do you know what that is?" Once the prospect could be induced to take pad and pencil and apply to his own financial figures the formula that the agent gave him, he would sell himself the necessary amount of insurance. There were actually three formulas, ranging from the minimum, which would guarantee a man's family the necessities of life if he should die, to the maximum, which would keep them in comfort. An example using the maximum formula will illustrate the procedure. The prospect was asked to write down his present income, say $5,000 a year. Since studies had shown that an average of 36 per cent of this income made up his personal living expenses (including insurance premiums), it was incumbent upon him to guarantee 64 per cent ($3,200) to his wife and children if he should die the next day. From this $3,200 he was to subtract the part of his present yearly income (from securities, real estate, business holdings, etc.) that would continue after his death, say $1,125. The remaining $2,075 a year was the part that had to come from life insurance; and it should be continued for his wife's present life expectancy—32.5 years, if she was then 34. The sum of money that would have to be invested to return $2,075 a year for 32 years was $39,160—and that was exactly how much insurance the prospect should carry. If he wondered how he could meet the premiums, Ives & Myrick also issued a chart showing how a family at a given income level could budget its domestic expenses in order to be able to afford the needed insurance.[18]

This scientific approach to a prospect's insurance needs and his capacity to pay for them was Charles Ives's major contribution to the life insurance business; it is now called "programming" or "estate planning." The idea was not original with him, but he was the first to apply it on a large scale in practical agency work. Clearly he was thinking of the agent who, like himself, lacked self-confidence and needed a structured sales presentation to fall back on. To the man who was temperamentally unsuited to the "psychological" sales approach, Ives offered the advice that "there seems to be, too often, a proneness to put more stress on the 'psychology of a sale' than on the 'science' of it." [19] As he elaborated his idea in the material that he wrote for agents in the 1910s and 1920s, it came to include such variations as provision for inheritance taxes and income for children only until they reached the self-supporting age; in the 1920s Ives & Myrick produced what they called an "Estate and Insurance Program," into which the pertinent figures could be readily fed to obtain the amount of insurance that was needed.[20] The best-known form which Ives's scientific approach took was *The Amount to Carry— Measuring the Prospect,* which he first published as an article in the *Eastern Underwriter* for September 17, 1920, and which Ives & Myrick subsequently issued as a pamphlet that received wide distribution in the insurance business. The many letters requesting this pamphlet (or other material by Ives) that the agency received from all over the country are strong evidence of how new and attractive his ideas were among insurance men.[21]

Ives did not ordinarily deal directly with his brokers and agents, but employed for that purpose a small corps of skilled supervisors, to whom he fed his training material and from whom he gained his knowledge of conditions in the field. These supervisors also conducted the training classes for agents, especially new agents, in which the fundamentals of life insurance and the techniques of salesmanship were taught; Ives seems to have preferred to meet with the trainees individually.[22] Again, the idea of such classes was not new with Ives, but he was the first to develop it within one of Mutual's agencies.[23] By the 1920s, several terms of classes were being conducted each year by the agency. Above all, Ives stressed the *service* that Ives & Myrick could offer to its agents in the field.

When the Armstrong investigation had been held in 1905, there had still been much "peddling" of life insurance in America, involving rebates, irregular agents, high-pressure salesmanship, and inside connections. By the time that Ives retired in 1930, life insurance agents had moved a long way toward becoming a group with professional standards.[24] Ives's innovations in the training of agents must be acknowledged as a key factor in this process of professionalization.

It was unusual for one of Mutual's agencies to have two managers, but Ives and Myrick were vitally necessary to each other. The agency could probably not have been nearly so prosperous without Ives's ideas; but it could hardly have continued on at any level of success without Myrick's ability to handle people. Ives was skillful in writing copy, for he knew how to arouse "human interest" through the discussion of matters such as personal finances and ordinary problems of living. He understood the life insurance business in the large and in detail, and he was resourceful in constantly coming up with new ways to recruit agents and identify prospects. Ives also took a strong personal interest in his subordinates and thought nothing of lending them money; but he lacked all capacity to regulate and discipline them, leaving that job to Myrick. As a result, the employees regarded Ives as something of a saint and were often hostile to Myrick.[25] Ives was extraordinarily aloof for a businessman; and as Ives & Myrick expanded, this aloofness increased. His office, where he stayed most of the time, was removed from the center of activity in the firm, while Myrick was in constant contact with both employees and outsiders. Ives could not bring himself to appear before large groups. He contributed a number of articles to trade journals; but if there was a speech to be made on an insurance subject, he would write it and Myrick would deliver it.[26] Nor did Ives take any real interest in the professional insurance groups to which Myrick devoted much of his time.[27] Ives had many good ideas for the modernization of Mutual's organization and services, ideas which had little chance of being adopted voluntarily by the conservative Charles A. Peabody, president of the company. But when, around 1920, Myrick (the "political" member of the partnership) joined with other managers in an unsuccessful effort to force new policies and personnel upon Peabody, Ives took little part in this organized effort;[28] instead, he satisfied himself with an ineffectual personal memorandum to the other managers and the higher-ups in the company, criticizing Peabody's policies.[29]

It was Myrick, not Ives, who took up the suburban, civic, sporting, and club life of the successful businessman. As a man of finesse and polish whose personality inspired confidence, he made his way up through the presidencies of the city, state, and national associations of life underwriters. This career in business organizations was paralleled, in his "leisure time," by his intense interest in the development of lawn tennis in America. He served as president of the United States Lawn Tennis Association and was chairman of the Davis Cup Committee for seven years. These activities brought prestige not so much to the partnership as to Myrick himself. Charles Ives was nearly unknown in the business when he retired, but Myrick went on to devote seventy years to life insurance, to become known as Mr. Life Insurance, and to be beloved by all—at least, by all those who were equal or superior to him.[30]

After his retirement, Ives presented a glowing picture of his business experience: "It is not . . . uncommon in business intercourse to sense a reflection of a philosophy—a depth of something fine—akin to a strong beauty in art. To assume that business is a material process, and only that, is to undervalue the average mind and heart. . . . I have experienced a great fullness of life in business."[31] He was also able to interject references to literary figures, transcendentalism, and his other interests into the copy that he wrote. But there is ample evidence that he experienced much that was distasteful to a man of his sensitivity. *The Amount to Carry,* for example, contained not only a scientific formula, but also a selling presentation, in which Ives was compelled to resort to commercialism, "psychology," and high-pressure salesmanship. "Generally speaking," he advised the agent in one place, "the more he debates this point, the more hold you have on him." Again: "Go to it hard now, with all the persuasive power you have—(in some cases it is well to use, at this point, the usual moral and emotional appeals)." "Then 'go to the mat' again, and go hard, saying perhaps something like the following—but whatever you do say—say *hard*." "Start to fill out the application, or just hand the prospect a pen and point to the dotted line." [32] In other aspects of his handling of agents, Ives also became involved in moral dilemmas. He abhorred contests for composers, regarding them as rank commercialism; but he thought nothing of instituting contests for insurance agents.[33] He believed that "a teacher of the humblest country school has a greater trust . . . than can ever rest on the world's greatest railroad pres[ident]"; [34] but he could casually consider weaning teachers away from their jobs to become insurance agents.[35] He considered it practically treason for a rich man to use legal means during World War I to escape paying inheritance taxes; [36] but he himself later set up a tax shelter for his renewal commissions in the form of a trust for his wife, and when the government tried to tax him anyway, he fought the case through the tax courts for years.

The people with whom Ives dealt in his business were undoubtedly more personally congenial to him than musicians would have been. But in some of his private memos he expressed his feeling that businessmen were often too insensitive, conservative, and hypocritical. Maddened by certain dicta handed down by Mutual's home office, he burst out against "these stupid, reactionary ideas." [37] When his partner was elected president of the Life Underwriters' Association of the City of New York, he noted that Myrick was "a different kind than most of them. He says what he means—at least. Most associations of businessmen have the same fault as the underwriters—they don't practice what they preach." [38] And when a businessman whom he knew strained his patience, he condemned him not simply as an individual, but as a type of the "American Business Man":

> He doesn't know much,
> But—*he thinks he knows a lot.*
> *Oh,* doesn't *he think he knows an awful lot!*
> *But—what he knows everybody knows,*
> *And what he doesn't know everybody knows too.*
> *And when it comes to talkin',*
> *He's there with both his jaws.*
> *An' the sounds you hear are the sounds you hear*
> *When the crows get going their "caws."*
> *Yes—he's a busy, buzzin' business man,*
> *Talkin' glib and continual.*[39]

The first ten years of the Ives & Myrick Agency must have been hectic ones for Ives. But after his heart attack in 1918, he was out of business for a year. After returning in September, 1919, he eased up in his work; and as his health gradually declined during the 1920s, he withdrew increasingly from active involvement in his agency. Finally, on January 1, 1930, he retired on disability at the age of fifty-five, Myrick continuing on as agency manager. Ives was certainly a wealthy man; but even in his most successful years, during the latter 1920s, his income apparently never reached $100,000 a year. Within a few years after his retirement, his income (from his pension and personal investments) had been reduced to a mere fraction of what it had been before. After his retirement, Ives gradually lost contact with life insurance. During the remaining twenty-four years of his life, he turned his attention instead to problems arising from his growing recognition as a composer.

It is often forgotten that during Ives's active years, his family and friends thought of him primarily as a businessman, not a composer; he probably took much the same view of himself. Ives belonged to a generation of business and professional men who appeared in urban America in the 1890s, often from small-town backgrounds, and who exercised increasing power in American life during the first three decades of the twentieth century. Two distinguished American historians have offered very different models to describe these men. For Robert Wiebe, the man of the "new middle class" was one who gave up the values of the older small-town communities and their social systems based on personal and informal interaction among homogeneous people; instead, frankly accepting the city as a place of many heterogeneous groups in continuous flux, he developed a bureaucratic approach to social order that used "rules with impersonal sanctions" and "a variety of flexible administrative devices" to bring about "continuity and predictability in a world of endless change." [40] For Richard Hofstadter, on the other hand, the values of much the same group of men were very different. Hofstadter's "Progressive" was a man who brought his small-town values with him to the city, who tried "to realize familiar and traditional ideals under novel circumstances." He "had been brought up to think of the well-being of society not merely in structural terms—not as something resting upon the sum of its technique and efficiency—but in moral terms, as a reward for the sum total of individual qualities and personal merits." [41] Appalled by the threat to individual moral responsibility that was posed by the great impersonal organizations of the city— business corporations, labor unions, political machines—he held up against that threat the ideal of the good average citizen who was altruistic and disinterested.

Probably many of Ives's contemporaries and associates can best be described as lying somewhere between these two models. On the one hand, they were skillful at developing bureaucratic and technological solutions to the problems posed by the rootlessness of the city. Ives himself, for example, developed formulas for a scientific and impersonal approach to life insurance. He helped to work out a system of family financial security upon which men could depend in an impersonal and urbanized era. Relying on the law of averages, he worked out intricate procedures for making constant and systematic contact with agents, prospects, and those who already held policies with Mutual. He also understood the importance of the immigrant groups in New York City as prospective policyholders, and he wisely sought to hire agents who were members of these ethnic groups.

On the other hand, many of those who were most successful in the highly organized urban world still held to values that reflected an older small-town or rural America. For some, particularly certain of the reformers during the period, this combination of the old and the new was not unfruitful. But for others it created painful and obvious conflicts—Henry Ford is often cited as an example. It was big business more than anything else that brought about the distinctive culture of modern urban America, based as it is on mass production and mass consumption. As businessmen and their professional allies worked out the finances, the technology, the organization, and the advertising of the new industrial order, they were actually creating a monster that was destroying the simpler America that most of them loved. The three Republican presidents of the 1920s—Harding, Coolidge, and Hoover—have been cited as men who urged on the development of business and industry even as they paid nostalgic homage to the older religion, morality, social beliefs, and tastes that were being undermined by industrial expansion.[42]

Similarly, for all his understanding of the life insurance business, Ives was not reconciled to the new urban America that he was helping to bring into being. When he returned from a day spent as an insurance executive in New York's financial district, he used his music to retreat back into small-town life in Danbury, where his heart lay. It was the simple, homogeneous Danbury of his father's youth, in which men had not been separated into occupational or ethnic strata, but had been united by common Protestant worship, common entertainments, and common closeness to nature. Ives's retreat from the city—"the Hell Hole," as he called it [43]—became physical when he and his wife built their house at rural West Redding in 1912–1913. The Iveses often spent more than six months of each year in Redding, which they far preferred to New York; only its extreme physical isolation and the problems of water supply forced them back to the metropolis in the fall. Many of Ives's ideas about society grew out of his small-town or rural set of values, which were moral, not structural or bureaucratic. The farmer, he felt, was the ideal man and citizen, who could be depended upon to think seriously about political questions. The city man was more likely to talk before he thought.

Apparently, then, Ives had much in common with other business and professional people (including reformers) of his time who could understand and handle the processes and institutions of the city, but whose emotional allegiances lay elsewhere. Yet in one crucial respect Ives differed from these others: he refused to assume the role of leadership that was expected of him. No matter how scientific and bureaucratized modern social organization may be, it is still dependent upon personal leadership. Its very flexibility demands constant interaction among the leaders of its segments, each leader representing the interests and concerns of his own segment; and the individual who can exercise personal leadership within an impersonal organization becomes the new society's indispensable man. He "makes things work" and "gets the job done." But Ives avoided personal, face-to-face contact wherever he could, whether in the exercise of authority over subordinates, in negotiation with his equals, or in dealing with his superiors. There was a large part of leadership that could not be sublimated into altruism or science, and such leadership was unacceptable to Ives.

In his business, Ives was able to be so successful while avoiding personal leadership because of the dynamic qualities of Julian Myrick, a born leader of men. In many ways it was the political conservative Julian Myrick, rather than the political liberal Charles Ives, who was the man of the "new middle class." In his continual re-examination of applications for policies that had been turned down by Mutual and in his constant interaction with his employees, with the home office, and with other leading life insurance men, Myrick was a practical exemplar of Wiebe's "techniques of constant watchfulness and mechanisms of continuous management" [44]—far more than was Ives, who stayed isolated in his office and handed down his insurance writings as from a scholar's study. Ives later wrote to a friend: "I think I was born without a 'committee' or 'associative' sense—not exactly an 'a-social' but an 'a-association' one. But I suppose to get some things done in certain stages, this 'groupilia' is necessary; but organically and constitutionally I'm 'agin it' and I feel the way you do—a 'lone wolf' is more natural." [45] Thus Ives avoided involvement in the organizations of life underwriters, although such trade organizations were key factors in the professionalization of the new middle class.[46] Ives even made fun of the concept of "efficiency" in business.[47] It is interesting that Julian Myrick was one of the most ardent admirers of Herbert Hoover, a man who exemplified the joining of new bureaucratic and technological abilities with older values; but Ives disliked Hoover, apparently regarding him as a humorless and cold-blooded model of modern efficiency.

With regard to his society's larger social and political problems, Ives eschewed a leadership role even more obviously than he did in business. He lived in New York City for more than fifty years without ever really becoming engaged in its problems or taking part in the interaction among its many heterogeneous groups. "Perhaps city life itself is an unessential," he wrote. "Perhaps it is caused nowadays more by curiosity than necessity—the restless, nervous curiosity of men that Thoreau may have had in mind when he said that rubbing elbows together does not necessarily bring minds closer together." [48] Ives's behavior toward the city can be profitably compared with that of his wife. During her twenties, Harmony Twichell had experienced a strange restlessness which had not allowed her to stay around her father's house and wait for the right man, as girls of her class were supposed to do. After taking training and qualifying as a registered nurse, she worked in the Visiting Nurse Association of Chicago, visiting houses in the slums, and at the Henry Street Settlement in New York.[49] It is true that in the midst of her service at the Henry Street Settlement, she wrote poetry about the way in which the beauties of the countryside sustained her "thro' all the city's noise and heat." [50] But at least she experienced some personal involvement with lower-class and immigrant groups. Not surprisingly, her attitude toward the poor was condescending and paternalistic, and her view of social work was moral and altruistic rather than scientific and bureaucratic.[51] It was undoubtedly her influence that drew her husband into personal acts of charity; how personal they could be can be seen in Ives's entry in his diary for New Year's Day, 1918, during the fuelless days occasioned by the war: "Piantidosi family from Bleecker St. Spent night. Three little children slept with Harmony. Very cold—no coal anywhere." [52]

Ives was very generous in his private contributions to charity. Yet neither the conservative's desire for social order nor the reformer's concern for the welfare of the unfortunate could impel him into a direct involvement with practical social problems through leadership in church and charitable work or in political and social movements. He believed that his business experience gave him contact with all types and conditions of men. But his isolation from field work and the recurrence of the word "salaries" rather than "wages" in his insurance literature suggest that he had little contact with persons outside his own class. (Mutual did not write group or industrial insurance, although Ives wanted the company to offer small policies to laborers.[53])

Characteristically, Ives stayed aloof from the progressive movement for most of its course; he failed to take an interest in Theodore Roosevelt's Bull Moose movement of 1912, in which many men of his background played a role. Then, during the middle and latter 1910s, he became intensely concerned about political and social questions, although in a purely private way. Not only were his extreme views anathema to his conservative business associates, however, but they were also closer to the western and rural branch of the progressive movement than to its eastern and urban branch. Ives's views seemed to strike directly at the very concept of leadership, for he proposed converting the whole structure of American government into a gigantic town meeting. Leadership in government was a positive evil; the important thing was to keep referring questions back to the whole people, for they would make good laws—it was their moral duty.[54]

It can be argued, of course, that Ives's abhorrence of leadership and personal involvement in social organization was a result of his shyness. It seems strange, however, that the young man who at Yale had made his way so successfully into Hé Boulé, Delta Kappa Epsilon, and Wolf's Head should have found himself temperamentally incapable of following the path taken by his Yale friends in business and civic life. The question cannot be resolved until his political views and his artistic isolation have been examined. But it is worth noting here that Ives was isolated not only from artists and intellectuals; during his active years, he also became isolated from the business and professional men who were his natural associates.

5

THE POLITICAL AND
SOCIAL THINKER

☙

CHARLES IVES'S POLITICAL and social views revealed the influence of his paternal grandparents, George White Ives and his wife Sarah Hotchkiss Wilcox. In addition to their activities on behalf of public improvements and charities, George and Sarah Ives had drawn far enough away from a background dominated by religion to take a small part in the "flowering" of speculative thought and social reform that occurred in New England for thirty years or so before the Civil War. George was sympathetic to abolitionism and (according to his grandson) "took an active part against the anti-abolitionists" in Danbury.[1] Sarah was an admirer of Emerson;[2] and when her son George (Charles Ives's father) brought a freed Negro boy home with him from the Civil War, she raised him and later helped to send him to Hampton Institute.[3] Charles Ives never knew his grandfather, but his grandmother did not die until he was in his twenties. From her and from his own father, Ives absorbed a transcendentalism and a kind of individualism that were more characteristic of the pre–Civil

War era than of the Gilded Age; he and his brother also absorbed a liberal tolerance for many diverse groups in society that went beyond the attitude shown by most New England Yankees.

But Ives was raised in the Gilded Age, and his immediate political inheritance, personified by his uncle Lyman Brewster, was that unquestioning adherence to the Republican party that characterized many Anglo-Saxon New Englanders of the business and professional classes in the late nineteenth century. It was as a child of this environment that Ives wrote the music for *William Will*, a campaign song for William McKinley, when he was in college (1896):

> *What we want is Honest Money,*
> *Good as gold, and pure as honey;*
> *Ev'ry dollar sound and true. . . .*[4]

Ives seems to have shown no further interest in politics until 1908, when he apparently wrote to his fiancée of his inability to bring himself to take part in public affairs in New York, for she replied: "No[body] is public-spirited in N.Y., it seems to me. When you get to living up in Connecticut, you'll feel like going in to all sorts of things, I'm sure."[5] From about that time, his interest in political and social questions began to grow steadily. There is no obvious reason why Ives should have suddenly taken an interest in such questions at the age of about thirty-three. But the form which that interest took—a passionate identification of himself with the masses—strongly suggests that he felt alienated from his own upper middle class. He began to adopt in politics a point of view that he had long taken in music: he looked over the heads of his "own kind" to "the people" as the arbiters of virtue and value.

Ives never did take a direct part in political or social movements. Down to about 1914, current events and party battles do not seem to have concerned him even in a private way. He was obviously a progressive; yet he ignored the progressive movement during its heyday. One reason was that he was interested in progressive reforms—the initiative, the referendum, and "direct democracy"—which were less popular in the northeastern part of the country, where a more elitist and paternalistic approach to reform prevailed. He was also repelled by the aggressive personality and rhetoric of Theodore

Roosevelt,[6] who personified national progressivism for most Americans down to 1912. The presidential election of 1912, sometimes described as the high-water mark of progressivism, held no interest for Ives. He sketched a wildly dissonant song for it, which he headed: "Vote for Names! Names! Names! Teddy, Woodrow, and Bill. All nice men!!" Part of the accompaniment he described as the "same chord hit hard over and over. Hot Air Election Slogan." [7] And on election day he made a memo to himself in which he indicated that the differences among Roosevelt, Wilson, and Taft were about as great as the differences among three chords that were exactly the same: "a sad chord—a hopeless chord—a chord of futility." [8]

Until 1914, then, Ives approached political and social questions in an abstract or historical way, and he approached them only in his music. His first inspiration came from an idealistic view of the slavery question as it had existed before and during the Civil War. In the piano piece *The Anti-abolitionist Riots* (c. 1908), he recalled his grandfather's role in the slavery controversy. About 1911 he composed *The "St. Gaudens" in Boston Common* (the first movement of his First Orchestral Set, *Three Places in New England*), in which he was inspired by Augustus Saint-Gaudens's bronze relief of Col. Robert Gould Shaw and his Negro regiment that had fought in the Civil War; Ives even wrote a free-verse poem to accompany the work:

> *Moving,—Marching—Faces of Souls!*
> *Marked with generations of pain,*
> *Part-freers of a Destiny,*
> *Slowly, restlessly—swaying us on with you*
> *Towards other Freedom! . . .*[9]

Ives found a theme even closer to his heart when he celebrated the common man in three works for chorus and orchestra written between 1912 and 1914: *Lincoln, the Great Commoner* (from Edwin Markham's poem); *Walt Whitman* (based on lines from Whitman); and *Majority*. The words for the last of these three pieces were by Ives himself and indicate the direction his thought had taken by 1914:

> *The Masses! The Masses!*
> *The Masses have toiled,*
> *Behold the works of the World!*

The Masses are thinking,
Whence comes the thought of the World!

The Masses are singing, are singing, singing,
Whence comes the Art of the World!

The Masses are yearning, are yearning, are yearning.
Whence comes the hope of the World.

The Masses are as legion;
As the rain drops falling together make the Rivers and for a space become as one,
So men seeking common life together for a season become as one,
Whence come the nations of the World.

As the tribes of the ages wandered and followed the stars,
Whence come the many dwelling places of the World!

The Masses are dreaming, dreaming,
The Masses are dreaming,
Whence comes the visions of God!

God's in His Heaven,
All will be well with the World! [10]

By the time he wrote *Majority*, Ives was starting to think seriously about current events. In foreign affairs, which came to the fore in America during 1914, he found a political subject that he considered truly worthy of idealistic thought and endeavor, for it dealt with the masses in *all* nations. And in Woodrow Wilson he began to discover a political leader capable of expressing that idealism. It was President Wilson's actions in bringing about the overthrow of the dictatorial Huerta regime in Mexico—his policy of teaching good government to the Mexicans—that first earned Ives's approval.[11] But it was the president's handling of the European war between 1914 and 1917 that made of Ives a real Wilsonian.

Ives was of two minds about the First World War in Europe. On the one hand, Germany's "rape" of Belgium in August, 1914, shocked him deeply. On Columbus Day of that year, he sketched a dissonant work for chorus and orchestra called *Sneak Thief*, directed against the kaiser. Some of his marginal notes were highly exaggerated, such as his equation of the kaiser's moral cowardice with the "aural cowardice" of German musicians who stuck to easy music. But the words of the song (which quoted several American patriotic tunes) were very prescient:

People of the World, rise and get the Sneak-thieving Kaiser and all those
  helpless mollycoddle negative medieval minds who became his slaves,
Because they are afraid to get up and act like real men.
So after this cursed war is o'er (all made by the Kaiser and his slaves)—
[Chorus:] Let all the people build a People's World's Union in a
  Free World for real men to live in! [12]

Again, Ives was deeply shocked by the German torpedoing of the
Lusitania in May, 1915, but this time he reacted more with sorrow
than with anger. On the day of the sinking, he had a democratic experience that deeply affected him. Having left work, he was waiting
for the elevated train at Hanover Square in the financial district,
where there was a large crowd on the platform. Everyone was appalled by the awful disaster, and there was fear that America would
now be drawn into the war. An organ grinder on the street was playing a tune, and one by one the people waiting—first a workman,
then a banker—began to sing or whistle or hum the chorus. The
singing swelled to great proportions, as a release for what everyone
was feeling. Even after the train had come and gone, "almost no-
body talked—the people acted as though they might be coming out
of a church service. In going uptown, occasionally little groups
would start singing or humming the tune." Ives was impressed that
the tune "wasn't a Broadway hit, it wasn't a musical comedy air, it
wasn't a waltz tune or a dance tune or an opera tune or a classical
tune, or a tune that all of them probably knew. It was . . . the
refrain of an old Gospel Hymn that had stirred many people of past
generations"—*In the Sweet By-and-by.* Out of this experience came the
third movement of Ives's Second Orchestral Set, *From Hanover
Square North, at the End of a Tragic Day, the Voice of the People Again
Arose;* he considered the movement "one of the best that I've done."
It reflected "the sense of many people living, working, and occasionally going through the same deep experience, together. It
would give the ever changing multitudinous feeling of life that one
senses in the city." [13] In this incident, what made the city comprehensible for Ives was his belief that its many different groups could
all respond to a Protestant gospel hymn that he remembered from
rural camp meetings. It is also significant that in this account, as in
his descriptions of the camp meetings, Ives mentioned no women in
the crowd; democracy for him was very much a masculine thing.

As the war in Europe continued on, Ives's desire to see Germany punished for its actions was counterbalanced by another set of ideas that he had been mulling over during the Mexican crisis, even before the war had started. He had begun to feel that "patriotism is in a sense a magnified form of personal vanity," that physical bravery could actually be a type of cowardice, and that "the stupidity of the politicians of [the] human race is the only cause of war." [14] His questioning of the ultimate allegiance due the sovereign state was given a further impetus as he observed the turmoil in Europe and concluded that "this war [was] started by rich . . . degenerates, fought for rich degenerates, but fought by the people against the people"; here he was criticizing all the European governments for their cowardly suspicion of one another.[15] On the very eve of America's entry into the war, he was writing a memo to himself attacking "gov[ernment] by property" and asserting that "compulsory service means fighting for the rich." [16] By this time his thinking had moved beyond mere political democracy to social democracy, and he had formulated the idea of society's imposing a limitation on the amount of property that its members could hold. This plan, to which he devoted much thought over a number of years, was suggested in his letter published in the New York *Evening Post* in December, 1916:

> The tragic results of traditional political expediency which the world is witnessing to-day—that kind of expediency which is reflected throughout the history of academic economics—suggest the following questions:
>
> Has there been a war, during, say, the last two or three hundred years, where the primal cause has not been the desire of a small number of men of large property to conserve or increase their property, and where most of the fighting has not been done by a large number of men of little or no property?
>
> Would a limited property right be a natural or unnatural, efficient or inefficient, means of increasing the unit of energy and the resulting economic goods, and the power of man to utilize and enjoy them in such a way that, as his material benefits increase, his mental, moral, and spiritual life can develop proportionately?
>
> Further, can a man of average social consciousness feel that he has a moral right to all the property he can acquire legally and honestly?
>
> Fundamental [17]

The two contradictory aspects of Ives's thinking about the war—his moral idealism that condemned Germany for its depredations and his moral idealism that condemned all the warring countries for their violations of social justice—were paralleled in the president's actual policy toward the war, for Wilson steered a course between the extreme noninterventionism of Robert La Follette and the extreme belligerence of Theodore Roosevelt. Thus Ives (unlike his brother) fully supported Wilson and the Democrats in the presidential election of 1916—not only because Wilson had "kept us out of war," but also because he proposed to use America's neutrality altruistically to bring about a just settlement of the war. In contrast to the election of 1912, Ives write on one of his music manuscripts: "Nov. 8, 1916—W. W. elected!" [18] Charles Ives had come a long way from the college boy who had written the music for *William Will.*

A few months later Wilson led the country into war, and Ives enthusiastically followed. As the political scientist Robert E. Osgood has pointed out, liberal reformers like Ives could not sanction a war fought for selfish ends like national security or national honor; only utopian goals of social justice and peace for the whole world could earn their support for a military venture. The president's rhetoric emphasized these altruistic purposes and thus drew such liberals into the crusade, although in the aftermath of the war Wilson would find it impossible to fulfill his noble promises.[19] The three war songs that Ives wrote in 1917 fairly seethed with Wilsonian idealism; one of them (the march *He Is There!*) was based upon American patriotic tunes and spoke of the "Yankee boy" who went abroad to fight so "that we may live / In a world where all may have a 'say.' " [20]

Ives was also quick to notice the activities of a small group of wealthy men—especially advocates of national military power (of the stripe of Henry Cabot Lodge) in the United States Senate—who were trying to embarrass the president and "get control of the war machinery" in order to solidify their "control of this country." In a document of August, 1917, called "Stand by the President and the People," Ives declared that "President Wilson has done more than any other President to voice the sentiments of the people rather than of politicians" and that "he has been quick to sense the great change that is going on throughout the world, the resentment and the growing social consciousness among the proletariat the world over against the medieval idea of government by property." Calling for direct rather than representative government and a limit on personal property, Ives went on to give the names and property values of some of the rich "reactionaries" who had "a great deal too much to say regarding the people's government." They included Elihu Root, Sen. Boies Penrose, Sen. Albert Fall (whom Ives singled out as a suspicious character long before Teapot Dome), Theodore Roosevelt—and Jim Wadsworth, Ives's old friend and classmate at Yale, who was now a United States senator from New York.[21] It is not clear what use, if any, Ives made of this document; perhaps he simply wanted to get certain things "off his chest" by writing them down.

The next year he produced a statement containing a number of alternative goals for the war and the peace that was to follow. Essentially inspired by Wilson's Fourteen Points, these "progressive" proposals arose from Ives's conversations with "about 100 men in all walks of life." Here he suggested "punishment" of "the criminals now in control of the Central Powers." But he also proposed: establishing a league of nations whose decisions would be enforced by an "international police"; subjecting the peace terms to ratification by a majority vote of the people of the Allied nations; submitting the question of a country's membership in the league to a vote of the people of that country, regardless of their government's attitude; and allowing an appeal from the league's decision to a majority vote of the people in all member states. He was even thinking of giving the league power to impose taxes and redistribute wealth. Ives sent part of this statement of war goals to the New York newspapers in 1918, and he was so caught up in his cause that he even brought himself to read it before a meeting of Mutual's agency managers.[22] Most of his subsequent political thought can be found in embryo in these two documents of 1917 and 1918.

Ives threw himself into the Red Cross and Liberty Loan drives carried on by his firm, wearing himself out even more than usual.[23] He drew up and distributed circulars urging people to limit themselves to a strict diet in order to conserve food; his nephew Richard has recalled that Ives imposed this diet on himself also.[24] He had already had a mild heart attack in 1906; and when, in the summer of

1918, he signed up to serve for six months in France with the YMCA, the doctor who examined him would not give him a clean bill of health.[25] On October 1, he suffered a severe heart attack. Ives was never in really good health again.

In the remarkable three years that followed this attack, Ives experienced a last great spurt of creativity, both in music and in politics, before sinking back into retirement and relative inactivity. During these three years he did his principal writing on both aesthetics and politics, and he made his principal efforts to get his music and his political ideas before the public. Yet he was already sinking back into that curious aloofness which removed him from the reality of day-to-day events. On February 18, 1919, while he was convalescing from his heart attack at Asheville, North Carolina, and busily writing his *Essays before a Sonata* and getting his *Concord* Sonata into shape, he recorded in his diary: "Read newspaper for first time since Oct[ober]. Things have gone on just about as one would imagine they would. Hence uselessness of reading newspapers but once every four months." [26] Yet these were the very months of the armistice and the beginning of the peace conference! It is no wonder that when Ives set about writing "The Majority" (his longest political essay) in 1919, he allowed his idealism to carry him away into impracticality and irrelevance.

Ives, of course, was totally in favor of American membership in the League of Nations, which was the principal political issue before the nation in 1919 and 1920. Unlike many of those who had followed Wilson, he experienced no disillusionment with the president's idealism after the war. But he did not realize that as a practical matter, the League could only be an association of governments, not of peoples. For him, the question of international association was vitally bound up with the questions of majority rule and direct government. Forgetting about the immediate issue of the League as it had been constituted at Paris, he devoted most of his political thinking and writing in 1919 and 1920 to speculations about direct government. In the vague belief that America's example in adopting direct, majoritarian government would influence other nations to do the same, thus bringing about a league of nations that would express the will of peoples and not of governments,[27] he limited most of his essay "The Majority" to an argument for the conversion of the American system of government from a representative to a direct democracy.

His plan was simplicity itself. Men were innately good; furthermore, "it must be assumed, in the final analysis and consideration of all social phenomena, that the Majority, right or wrong, are always right." Hence American democracy should be converted into one gigantic initiative and referendum. The people would vote directly on national laws, without regard to state lines. Political parties would be done away with, and all government officials would become "but an efficient clerical organization which shall carry out in detail the basic plans that the Majority propose." "Congress would become but a body of technical experts or specialists," preferably to be chosen through civil service examinations rather than by election; the president would be "executive head clerk." Elections would consist of two national ballots, separated by several months. On the first one, an initiative, the people would submit their suggestions for new laws. The "clerical machine" (Congress) would then select the most popular of these suggestions for inclusion on the second ballot and would make available to the people the "fundamental argument for and against each issue," avoiding unnecessary detail. The second vote would be a simple referendum on these issues. In discussing possible laws that the majority might approve under his scheme, Ives wrote favorably and in some detail of worker participation in the management of businesses, the nationalization of larger industries, and the imposition of limits on individual income and property.[28] But his detailed plans show that he was principally interested in taking corrupting wealth away from the rich rather than in applying the surplus to the needs of the poor; [29] and he tended to view all citizens, rich and poor alike, as good middle-class people like himself.

Like many progressives, Ives believed in an undifferentiated "majority" of sober and impartial citizens that lay above and beyond the clamoring few who made up each of the minority groups (capitalists, labor leaders, conservatives, etc.). "The whole country," he wrote, "is one great middle; the so-called upper and lower classes are as transitory and elusive as the proverbial flea." But although he was a city man, he obviously viewed the Yankee farmer in his town meeting—

the man who would devote himself to serious study of public questions—as the typical member of the majority.[30] Ives's optimism about the common man arose from his business life. He believed that his experience in insurance had "brought him in close relation with thousands of men of all kinds and conditions"; and "this association . . . gave him a high respect for, a deep interest and confidence in the average man's mind and character." [31] But his wife, who had participated in the social welfare side of progressivism (an aspect of it which held little theoretical interest for Ives), had a different view of the common man and did not agree with her husband's majoritarian views.[32] And his cousin Amelia Ives Van Wyck, who had some experience in social work in New York, argued against his scheme for direct government by flatly telling him that the people who came into his office to take out insurance represented only the more intelligent stratum of society.[33]

Ives's limited view of the common man led him to postulate an essential homogeneity of interests among all men. He gave this program for his Second String Quartet:

> S[tring] Q[uartet] for four men—who converse, discuss, argue (in re "politick"), fight, shake hands, shut up—then walk up the mountainside to view the firmament! [34]

Any difference of opinion which could be forgotten about so easily must not have been very great to begin with; perhaps it was significant that Ives marked the dispute in the quartet partly by using tunes suggestive of the Civil War. He was fond of pointing out that men were coming to agree on the fundamentals—if only the details that divided them could be eliminated.[35] But he failed to see that the details were often the important thing and that his bare fundamentals were sometimes so abstract as to be meaningless words.

The homogeneity of interests that Ives assumed among all men was only a part of his broader belief in a transcendental oneness that united all things. He felt that he could afford to espouse radicalism—even apparent incoherence—in both music and politics, for he was optimistically sure that there was a natural and divine order to things that was the more real for being unseen; radical schemes approved by the majority were merely a working out of this order.

There was no need for man to construct an *artificial* order—social or musical—and impose it on heterogeneity from outside in order to avoid chaos. A similar faith had sustained the philosophers and reformers of the pre–Civil War era whom Ives admired; and in America there had been a good deal of justification for this faith. Gilbert Highet has suggested that the few musicians who saw (and rejected) Ives's music early in the century may actually have been looking forward; their European training had brought them into contact with the "disruptive spiritual forces" that would soon engulf Europe in chaos and physical destruction. But "Ives, like Whitman, could hear only the remote echoes of the American Civil War, from which he extracted a complicated music in which dissonance did not mean enmity, nor conflict destruction." [36]

Whether or not this is an apt comparison of Ives with European-trained *conservative* musicians, it certainly suggests important differences between him and certain European *modernists*. Much of twentieth-century music has been a search for a principle of order that might be imposed upon the chaos of the revolutionary musical materials being developed. The best known of such efforts is the twelve-tone system of Arnold Schoenberg.[37] As John Kirkpatrick has pointed out, the sixth verse of Ives's choral work *Majority* (*The Masses*) was written "in a style pointing forward to" Schoenberg's row of twelve tones.[38] (This is the verse that begins: "As the tribes of the ages wandered and followed the stars . . .") But Ives's motives for using the technique in this composition were exactly opposite to those of Schoenberg and his followers:

> The plan of this in [the] orches[tral] parts is to have each in [a] different rhythm group complete the twelve notes (each on a different system) and end and hold [the] last (of twelve)—as finding its star. Occasionally something made in this calculated, diagram, design way may have a place in music, if it is primarily to carry out an idea, or a part of a program subject-matter, as in the above; but generally, or too much, or alone as such, it is a weak substitute for inspiration or music. It's too easy; any high-school student (unmusical) with a pad, pencil, compass, and log[ari]th[m] table, and a mild knowledge of sounds and instruments (blown or hit) could do it. It's an artificial process without strength, though it may sound

busy and noisy. This wallpaper-design music is not as big as a natural mushy ballad.[39]

Ives's "twelve-tone row" was not an attempt to impose order upon dissonance; it was simply the one means from his eclectic range of musical resources that he felt was best suited to express the extramusical "idea" at that particular point in the composition. Neither in music nor in politics was Ives engaging in that "search for order" which Robert Wiebe has found to be characteristic of urban business and professional men in the early years of the century.

In opposing the politicians, capitalists, and other leaders who (he felt) were frustrating the will of the people, Ives was placing himself in an old American tradition, the tradition of opposition to European autocracy and tyranny. Against the tyrant-politicians he set both individualism and democracy. But unlike Thoreau, he did not deal with the problem of the conscientious individual who found himself opposed to the democratic will of the majority. Assuming the transcendental oneness of things, Ives was sure that if the individual with a superior idea would only set it forth, the majority would eventually adopt it.

In 1920 Ives drew up his scheme for direct government in America, as outlined in his private essay "The Majority," in the form of a Twentieth Amendment to the Constitution. He sent this proposed amendment, along with an explanation of it, to eight New York newspapers, but none of them chose to print it. He also sent it to a number of leading politicians, such as President Wilson and Gov. Calvin Coolidge, and unsuccessfully submitted it for publication to the *Atlantic Monthly* and the *Outlook.* He had the amendment printed up as a circular and made an abortive attempt to have it distributed among the delegates at the Republican National Convention, but the circulars did not get to Chicago in time. All except one of the replies from the politicians to whom Ives wrote were polite but noncommittal. The exception was William Howard Taft, who bluntly told Ives of his strong opposition to the amendment; but Ives was so happy to have elicited a real reaction to his proposal that he wrote Taft a long letter in rebuttal.[40]

Meanwhile, American membership in the League of Nations had been twice rejected by the United States Senate, and President Wilson had declared that the presidential election of 1920 was to be a "referendum" on the League question. Returning partially to the question at hand, Ives submitted a letter to the New York newspapers shortly before the election—part of it was printed in the *Globe* [41]—suggesting that the election of the Republican Harding would not mean that the majority of Americans had thought seriously about the League and rejected it; what was needed was a method more accurate than political parties for informing the people about issues and recording their will.[42] But on November 2, when Harding was overwhelmingly elected, Ives knew that the League was dead for the time being. He expressed his bitterness in one of his most experimental and magnificently conceived songs, *Nov. 2, 1920,* in which he used dissonance to proclaim not only his masculinity, but also his unpopular and radical political and social views. His text tells of how "all the old women, male and female, had their day" when the American people took "the easy way" (these words being accompanied by a trite cadence), said "To Hell with ideals!" and voted for Harding and against the League. It concludes: "Oh Captain, my Captain! a heritage we've thrown away; / But we'll find it again, my Captain." [43] At the end of the song, music is quoted from Ives's earlier work *Lincoln, the Great Commoner.* Whitman's portrayal of Lincoln in his poem *O Captain! My Captain!* served as the basis for Ives's portrayal of Woodrow Wilson as the captain of the ship of state who lay stricken upon the deck while his vessel sailed safely into port after a stormy voyage.

But Charles Ives could not be a pessimist. When he included *Nov. 2, 1920* in the book of *114 Songs* which he put together in 1922, he placed a note at the bottom of the song: "The assumption, in the text, that the result of our national election in 1920, was a definite indication, that the country, (at least, the majority-mind) turned its back on a high purpose is not conclusive." The opinions of the people on great issues, he went on to explain, were being "somewhat emasculated" by the existing party system; but a more accurate method for recording those opinions might be found. "A suggestion to this end . . . in the form of a constitutional amendment" would "be gladly sent, by the writer, to any one who is interested enough to write for it." [44]

Throughout the 1920s and 1930s, although his interest in public affairs greatly declined, Ives refused to be disillusioned about Wilsonian idealism, and he continued to rank Wilson with Lincoln among the few statesmen who had risen above mere politics.[45] He frequently berated the Republican party for its expediency, and he found President Hoover (whom Julian Myrick idolized) particularly objectionable.[46] The rejection of both his music and his political schemes by the Anglo-Saxon Protestants of his own class caused him to look with greater interest toward other groups. He supported Al Smith for the presidency in 1928 not only because Smith was a liberal, but also because he thought it was time to have a Catholic president.[47] (He did not carry his pro-Catholicism so far as his brother did, however; Moss Ives, although a deacon in the Congregational church, wrote a book attempting to prove that the origins of religious liberty in America should be traced not to Roger Williams in Rhode Island, but to the Catholics who had settled Maryland.[48]) Ives had long admired Jews for their business abilities; and in the 1920s, he found that among the few musicians who took an interest in his music were several Jews—Jerome Goldstein, Anton Rovinsky, Nicolas Slonimsky.[49] In a memo written in the 1920s or 1930s, Ives noted that the people who had called his political ideas impractical had been mainly "those like Yale and Harvard graduates," but that "a good many and quite a number of Jews" had agreed with him that reforms of this sort ought to be instituted.[50] Ives was even a member of the Jewish Theological Seminary of America in 1925–1926.[51]

In the 1920s and 1930s Ives found a great deal of fault with his fellow Yale men, from whom he was now largely cut off. In 1922 the *New York Times* published a long letter from him, ostensibly expressing serious doubts about varsity athletics and the college spirit that was aroused to support them; in the letter's frequent digressions, however, he revealed his reservations about the very nature of exclusive places like Yale.[52] He was appalled by the increasing indulgence in materialism and hedonism that he observed in college graduates, particularly Yale graduates, with their snobbish club life and their appearance in the society columns. "Step on the gas, Lily Boy," he wrote in a private memo; "suck around the Rich—and get in

'Bones.' " [53] Colleges, he felt, had become standardized places that undermined the individualism of their students; somewhat surprisingly, in view of his own academic record, he accused them of neglecting Latin and Greek as they indulged in vast building programs.[54]

Unfortunately for Ives, his alienation from Yale men was only part of his more general alienation from the commercialism of the new American popular culture; in the course of the 1920s he became separated from the vernacular life of his fellow Americans. Movies, the radio, tabloid newspapers, popular music, best sellers, and the automobile were all the objects of his diatribes,[55] particularly in the 1930s, but he saved his special wrath for the airplane; [56] when a plane would fly over his house in West Redding in the 1930s, he would shake his cane at it menacingly and denounce it as an invasion of his privacy.[57] Ives believed that a man's life ought to be dedicated to production (including the arts, of course). He also assumed, with Whitman, that the masses would be a group of individualists. Thus the new culture, with its appeal to mass consumer taste, dismayed him; he called it a process of "emasculating America," and it is conceivable that his alienation from it was one reason why he stopped composing. Vernacular culture, from which he had long drawn much of his musical inspiration, became a thing to which he could no longer relate himself. It apparently never occurred to him that the movies, the tabloids, and the radio programs with their crooners were merely the modern urban counterparts (with a similar sort of appeal to ordinary people) of the old barn dances, camp meetings, and parades. Dissatisfaction with the way people were living, in combination with his physical disabilities, made Ives more and more of a recluse from the 1920s on.

Ives had the good fortune to retire from business a few weeks after the stock market crash of 1929. He rarely mentioned the Depression in his writings and correspondence. He was living in Europe during the period when Franklin D. Roosevelt was elected to the presidency and assumed office; but when he returned in July, 1933, he was not impressed by the New Deal. He thought Roosevelt a "nice fellow, kinda hysterical, messed up—ladybird, chatterbox"; Ives had never been much interested in programs of social welfare, and he found the president's strong leadership the very antithesis of his own ideas about direct democracy.[58] On the other hand, the new issues of foreign policy that arose in the 1930s reawakened Ives's interest in politics. Initially he was isolated from knowledge of these events, for he was surprised when Nicolas Slonimsky told him about Hitler's coming to power and the early atrocities of the Third Reich; [59] soon, however, he found in the actions of the European dictators a new outlet for his idealistic indignation.[60]

It was not so easy, however, simply to resurrect Wilsonian idealism in the 1930s. In the thinking of some political theorists, and later of some hardheaded politicians, internationalism was assuming a new and "realistic" form. This realism assumed that the sovereign state was the basic unit in international affairs; that the primary goal of such a state's foreign policy was necessarily its own national security; and that only national power, including the possible use of force, could guarantee national security. International cooperation had to be based upon these realistic premises, and international idealism had to be compatible with them.[61] This line of thought, which dominated American foreign policy from 1940 on, sounded very different from Wilson's appeals of the 1910s, and it obviously had little attraction for Ives. On the other hand, the isolationists were using majoritarian rhetoric, particularly in the proposed Ludlow Amendment to the Constitution, which would have required a national referendum before America could declare war (except in case of invasion). In the middle 1930s, as Congress was considering the Ludlow Amendment, Ives put some of his old political ideas into a new form; omitting his plan for international organization, which was not a popular idea in America at the time, he concentrated on the notion that if the people in all countries, rather than the politicians, were to be consulted on the question of war or peace, there would be no more war. In early 1938, at the time of the crucial vote in Congress on the Ludlow Amendment, Ives, apparently ignorant that he was playing into the hands of the isolationists, sent off his document to the president and other government officials, along with a direct appeal for passage of Ludlow's plan.[62] But the amendment was defeated in the House of Representatives.

In the end, Ives, as both an Easterner and a Wilsonian, took his stand with the internationalists. In 1940 he contributed to a fund being raised by one of his classmates to send ambulances to France and England.[63] On the front of an isolationist leaflet demanding a referendum on war and asserting that most Americans were opposed to entering the European war, he wrote in 1941: "An insult! No—if it's a move to defend and free the world from criminal sneak-thieving bosses and their slaves. Not [an] old-time War, but a fight against slavery." [64] After America's entry into the conflict, he reworked his earlier material into a new proposal for a "People's World Nation." [65] He also converted his march song from World War I (*He Is There!*) into a war song march for World War II (*They Are There!*); it was supposed to be played during the 1943–1944 season by the New York Philharmonic, but the performance never took place.[66] In its quotation of the rousing old patriotic tunes and in his own text for it, this work for chorus and orchestra represented Ives's last effort to recall Wilsonian idealism in the grim era of the war for survival:

> *Then let all the people rise, and stand together in brave, kind humanity.*
>
> *For it's rally 'round the Flag of the people's new free world,*
> *Shouting the battle cry of Freedom.*[67]

Even in relation to the first two decades of the century, Ives's political and social thought was rather naive for a man of his discernment. The naiveté undoubtedly reflected his isolation from the political thought and the other intellectual currents of his time. In spite of his disillusionment with the major parties, for example, he paid little attention to the socialist movement, which shared many of his goals; he innocently supposed that it was not necessary to have organized movements in order to accomplish social purposes. Even more significant, he seemed unaware in 1919 and 1920 that many liberals were critical of President Wilson for having made an unjust peace and then having embodied it in the League of Nations.

Ives was certainly sincere in his idealistic liberalism. What makes it difficult to take his views entirely seriously today is the obvious gap between his professed altruism and the actual system of capitalism and national power to which he gave practical support by his life as a middle-class businessman. An appreciation of this sort of tragic gap lay at the root of that new realism in foreign policy which Ives could not understand. Lacking a sense of human sin, a sense of the tragic in life, Ives faced the future optimistically, sure that freedom and progress would ultimately triumph. But he was actually looking back to an older America which had had the good fortune not to be faced with moral dilemmas and hard choices—an America where one had been able to be both idealistic and comfortable.

6

THE SELF-CONSCIOUS
ARTIST IN ISOLATION

❦

DURING IVES'S EARLY YEARS in New York, he continued his part-time
work in church music. From 1898 to 1900, he was choir director and
organist at the First Presbyterian Church in Bloomfield, New Jersey;
and from 1900 to 1902, he held the same positions in Central Presbyterian Church, a large and wealthy congregation on West Fifty-
seventh Street in Manhattan. These posts—particularly the one at
Central Presbyterian Church, which entailed his giving organ recitals
as well—presented Ives an opportunity to perform his own compositions. Congregations and audiences actually heard his choral works,
as well as his pieces for organ (sometimes with voice or another instrument); some of these organ compositions became the bases for
several of his larger works.

Ives later concluded that in the compositions written in connection
with his church work, he had been too conservative, because he had
worked with the constant knowledge of a captive audience; he had
not felt justified in imposing his experiments on a body of worship-

ers.[1] Certainly he encountered official resistance to his musical radicalism in these churches. On a manuscript of his organ prelude on *Adeste Fideles,* he wrote, with reference to his playing the work at a Christmas service at Bloomfield in 1898: "Rev. J. B. Lee, others, and Mrs. Uhler said it was awful." [2] Later, at an evening service at Central Presbyterian Church, he performed his Hymn-Anthem, for chorus, organ, and piano (the prototype for *In the Night,* the third section of the Set for Theatre Orchestra); it was "not successful," and the pastor, Dr. Wilton Merle Smith, "turned around and glowered at the choir." [3] This resistance, however, was only a part—indeed, an essential part—of the more important fact that during his years as a church organist, Ives had an *audience* for his works.

The culmination of Ives's career as a composer-performer came on April 18, 1902, when his cantata, *The Celestial Country*—"for solo, quartet, octet, chorus, organ and string orchestra"—was given its first performance at Central Presbyterian Church as part of an evening concert, Ives directing the work from the organ.[4] It was not performed again for seventy years. Obviously influenced by Horatio Parker's oratorio *Hora Novissima,* the cantata was fairly conservative—so much so that in his *Memos,* Ives was apologetic about its lack of experimentalism, although he insisted that he had departed from the copied score to "throw in" some dissonances in the actual performance.[5]

The cantata was favorably reviewed. The critic of the *New York Times,* noting the absence of a full chorus for the performance, wrote that "the composition seems worthy of a more complete hearing. It has the elementary merit of being scholarly and well made. But it is also spirited and melodious, and, with a full chorus, should be as effective in the whole as it was on this occasion in some of the details." He must have made Ives particularly angry by referring to the "pretty intermezzo for strings." [6] In a more extensive review in the *Musical Courier,* the critic wrote that "the work shows undoubted earnestness in study and talent for composition." He found the bass solo "lyric and full of grace" and the Intermezzo for strings "songlike" and "full of unusual harmonies and pleasing throughout," while the Finale "shows some original ideas, many complex rhythms and effective part writing." [7] Such conventional praise from established sources must have been an unpleasant reminder to Ives of how conventional the work itself was, for he wrote across his clipping of the *Musical Courier* review: "Damn rot and worse." [8]

Three weeks later, the Kaltenborn String Quartet, which had assisted in the performance of *The Celestial Country*, repeated the Intermezzo from the cantata at a concert in New Haven.[9] A few weeks more and Ives, apparently finding that his church work took too much time from his business and his composing, resigned his position at Central Presbyterian Church.[10] By doing so, he cut off his only outlet to the professional world of music and to the musical public. His long musical isolation had begun. In the file of programs and reviews in the Ives Collection at Yale University, there are no programs or reviews of any Ives work between the May, 1902, concert in New Haven and a concert of August, 1921. In the intervening two decades—the very years when Ives was writing his best and most innovative music—he lacked contacts with professional musicians, he was not himself a professional musician, and his music was therefore not performed. In Aaron Copland's opinion, Ives's greatest lack as a composer was the lack of an audience, "an audience which *demands* and *rejects* music—which acts as a stimulus and a brake"; his "weaknesses . . . arise from a lack of that kind of self-criticism which only actual performance and public reaction can bring." [11] Ives was even without anyone who could understand his compositions or show an intelligent appreciation of them.

When he finished a work, he would put it away and move on to another one. Understandably, Ives became confirmed in an unfortunate habit that was to prove disastrous to his musical recognition years later. Instead of putting each work into a single, final, finished form, he left his manuscripts disordered, inaccurate, illegible, and often incomplete; he even marked up the scores done for him by professional copyists. The strain of his isolation affected not only his music, but also his personality. On his artistic side, he became too insistently independent and rebellious, very lonely, and somewhat musically misanthropic. But there is a strong suggestion that his rebelliousness and his solitude were not simply necessary responses to his being cut off from meaningful dialogue with other musicians. His attitudes seem also to have reflected the needs of his own personality and of his system of cultural values. His isolation was, to a certain extent, self-imposed. But under the circumstances, it is amazing that he continued to compose and to turn out such a large number of compositions.

During his twenty years of isolation, Ives did make a few attempts to interest professional musicians and other musically knowledgeable people in his compositions; he even tried to secure performances of his works. These tentative efforts were almost uniformly unsuccessful. That Ives was unable to shrug them off afterward is obvious from the painstaking care with which he recorded them in his *Memos*. His account of these incidents makes clear the nature of Ives's musical aloneness in the 1900s and 1910s.

While Ives was living at Poverty Flat, from 1898 to 1908, he had a captive audience in his fellow inmates. Their friendly but untutored reactions to the works he was writing in the apartment—they called his composing "resident disturbances" [12]—must soon have proved unsatisfying to him; understandably, he wanted the opinions of people who knew something about music. Since he lacked wide contacts among professional musicians, it was natural that he should turn to his personal friends who were involved in music. Among them were three friends from Yale—David Stanley Smith, Bass Brigham, and Max Smith. Ives had come to know them through his activities in art music at college, but none of them had been part of his crowd of insiders at Yale; perhaps their obvious devotion to classical music had "queered" them.

Even before Ives gave up his church work, David Stanley Smith stopped in at Poverty Flat one day in 1900 or 1901 to visit a friend. Ives was then composing the Hymn-Anthem, which was to be performed at Central Presbyterian Church. The work was startlingly modern in its technical scheme, but it was based on the old hymn tune *Eventide* ("Abide with me . . ."). Ives, whose intentions in the piece were entirely serious, was temporarily disconcerted when Smith asked, "Why do you take a good tune like that and spoil it with a lot of burlesque?" About ten years later Harcourt ("Bass") Brigham, of the Class of 1897, stopped to see Ives and his wife and reacted unfavorably when Ives played his orchestral score *The Housatonic at Stockbridge* on the piano: "Well, that's a funny-sounding collection of sounds—your tonality and your chord relations are more wobbly than César Franck's, which are bad enough." Ives apparently lost contact with both Brigham and David Stanley Smith, but he long remained on terms of personal friendship with Thomas Max Smith, of his own class at Yale. Smith, who was music critic for newspapers in New York, listened to Ives play his compositions several times over the years. But even the mild Third Symphony was too much for him; and when Ives moved on to some of his more experimental things, the horrified Smith went "out on the stoop." Yet Ives was so anxious to communicate his musical feelings to someone else that he played all of his new *Concord* Sonata for Max Smith in 1912, trying to make him understand; he was, of course, disappointed at Smith's hostile reactions, which he carefully recorded on paper the next year along with his own counterjustifications of himself and the sonata.[13]

Mrs. Elizabeth Sprague Coolidge, a musically knowledgeable woman of great wealth, was close to Mrs. Ives because their fathers had been classmates at Yale. Stopping at West Redding with her parents in 1913 or 1914, Mrs. Coolidge asked Ives if he had continued with his music and insisted that he play her some of it; but the dissonance drove her, too, out of the room. She wanted to know how he could compose such awful things when he had studied with Parker. A few years earlier, Mrs. Coolidge had introduced Ives to Edgar Stowell, a violinist and a teacher at the Music School Settlement on Third Street. On social visits Stowell listened to Ives's works and tried over some of the violin music; but he complained that the style was not felicitous and facile for the violin, though admitting that one of the violin sonatas was full of ideas. A more challenging work like *Hawthorne* simply exasperated him: "Now what chord is that?—What key does that chord belong [to] there?—a C♯ and then D♭ [in the] next chord!" (Ives came to personify this sort of attitude in the character "Rollo," the name of a boy in a nineteenth-century series of children's books who asked many unimaginative and literal-minded questions.) The early and mild Introduction to the Second Symphony, however, suited Stowell better, and he conducted it with a string orchestra at the Music School Settlement—one of the few Ives performances during this period.[14]

Another professional musician of Ives's acquaintance was the violinist Franz Kaltenborn, whose string quartet participated in the performance of *The Celestial Country*. Detecting a certain sympathy for his music in the violist of the Kaltenborn Quartet, Ives dedicated to him "a little practice piece called *Holding your own*," which the quartet played at Poverty Flat in 1903. "One man plays the chromatic scale and another a diatonic [scale] in different time etc.—we played it over and had a laugh." The piece was a not atypical Ivesian experiment in sheer cacophony, but it was also an example of his frequent reversions to the role of musical bad boy.[15] Kaltenborn must have thought it sheer lunacy, inconceivable as the work of a serious composer. Kaltenborn also led an orchestra that gave summer concerts of "popular classics" in New York, and Ives hoped that some of his pieces would be included on the programs; but Kaltenborn refused, claiming that the pieces were too difficult and that he would lose his audience. He obviously had little interest in Ives's compositions.[16]

What is pathetic in all these incidents is the contrast between the earnestness with which Ives, shy and embarrassed but desperately needing approval, showed these works to his friends and the cool offhandedness with which they dismissed the music as worthless. Ives's personal writings leave no doubt about the great seriousness with which he approached his own music. But in presenting it to his friends, he may again have felt compelled, by temperament and by ideology, to play the role of musical prankster. His friends would hardly have been so cruel if they had suspected that music was anything more than a game for Ives. Yet they *were* his friends, so that it was not until he consulted a professional musician who was a stranger that he encountered the extremes of cruelty. In 1914, feeling that "it would be a good plan to get one of the supposedly great players" to try over his music, the Iveses invited to West Redding one Franz Milcke, whom Mrs. Ives had known in Hartford. This "typical hard-boiled, narrow-minded, conceited, prima donna solo violinist with a reputation gained because he came to this country from Germany with Anton Seidl as his concertmaster" dismissed Ives's compositions summarily. "He came out of the little back music room with his hands over his ears," complaining that "when you get awfully indigestible food in your stomach that distresses you, you can get rid of it," but that he could not "get those horrible sounds out of my ears." [17]

In addition to these "consultations" with other musicians, Ives also attempted, in the period from 1902 to 1921, to obtain performances of some of his instrumental works—mainly so that he himself could hear what they sounded like. Frank Fichtl and his Hyperion Theater orchestra played some of the theater orchestra pieces (chiefly the ragtime dances) in New Haven on several occasions; but mainly Ives was forced to turn to theater orchestra players in New York, whom he sometimes hired for the purpose and gathered together in the back of the Tams Copying Bureau. He might even conduct the players himself or lead them from the piano. These "first performances" (some of them even "first public performances") were Ives's only means for hearing such crucial works in his development as *In the Cage, In the Night,* the Second String Quartet, and even part of the *Universe* Symphony.[18]

One of his happiest experiences was with *Hallowe'en,* an experimental little work for string quartet and piano of which Ives was particularly proud from a technical standpoint. When he played it "with a little orchestra from a theatre just off the Bowery," this take-off of a group of small boys playing around a bonfire sounded just as he had intended, the players understanding and cooperating. But these performances were usually grossly inadequate because of the lack of talent and interest in the performers and the absence of some of the instruments. For example, his revolutionary *Central Park in the Dark,* with its two orchestral groups going their separate ways, "was cut down some in instrumentation for a theater orchestra . . . and . . . played between the acts in a downtown theater" about 1906 or 1907. Ives recalled vividly that "the players had a hard time with it—the piano player got mad, stopped in the middle and kicked the bass drum." On another occasion, a friend got the orchestra in a vaudeville house to perform some of Ives's ragtime dances, but "at the second afternoon performance, the manager of the theater came out and stopped them, saying it made too much of a disturbance." [19]

Washington's Birthday, for chamber orchestra, was played both at Tams's and in a theater, but Ives evidently wanted to hear it done by more expert players. His friend Reber Johnson, a violinist who was assistant concertmaster of the New York Symphony, brought some members of that orchestra to the Iveses' house on East Twenty-second Street about 1918 or 1919. They found *Washington's Birthday* so difficult, however, that the score had to be "practically emasculated" before they could play it, and Ives thought that the theater orchestra men had done at least as well. Still, Ives invited friends and relatives to his home around this time to hear portions of his compositions performed by Johnson and his men, and *Washington's Birthday* was probably among the works played. Johnson would not play Ives in public and he thought that modernism spelled the end of great music, but he and Ives remained on friendly terms. They had even played together for the troops at Camp Upton during World War I.[20]

None of Ives's compositions received a public performance by a symphony orchestra during the 1900s and 1910s, but he had a few brushes with large orchestras. In March, 1910, probably at the instigation of a friend, the last three movements of the First Symphony (composed at Yale) were conducted by Walter Damrosch at a Saturday morning rehearsal of his New York Symphony. Damrosch's every attitude and action that day came to epitomize for Ives the smoothness and the limitations of the celebrated orchestra conductor. He praised these harmless movements for their "workmanship" (which Ives interpreted to mean "groove made technique"), but he found them too complex to be played in public because of the rehearsal time required. Clearly Damrosch was not interested in this music and was not going to play it at a regular concert; nevertheless, Ives, seeming to court punishment, sent Damrosch the professionally copied score of his Second Symphony—and never got it back.[21]

The conductor of the other great orchestra of the city, Gustav Mahler of the New York Philharmonic, also had a brief encounter with Ives's music at about the same time. As Ives recalled, Mahler (himself an eminent composer) accidentally noticed the Third Symphony: "When this was being copied in, I think, Tam's office, Gustav Mahler saw it and asked to have a copy—he was quite interested in it." [22] A story has arisen that Ives lost his one good copy of the symphony because Mahler took it with him to Europe in 1911, but died there before he could perform it.[23] Yet twenty-five years later, Ives recalled that the score of the Third Symphony had also been sent to Walter Damrosch and therefore lost.[24]

During the 1919–1920 season, a newly organized New York group called the New Symphony Orchestra ran an offer in the newspaper to play over American orchestral works in manuscript. Ives saw the offer in the paper; and instead of submitting one of his earlier and more ingratiating works, he sent in *Decoration Day,* which was accepted. Paul Eisler, the assistant conductor who was to lead the work, later tried to back out of giving the reading; but through a sort of naive sarcasm, Ives apparently shamed him into doing it, and the Iveses were present when the work was played at "an invitation rehearsal-concert" in Carnegie Hall in the spring of 1920. The reading was a travesty. The players would start together at the beginning of each lettered section of the score, but by the end of the section most of them had dropped out. The piece was not really played; and Eisler, angry at Ives, returned the score with the remark, "There is a limit to musicianship." Painful occasions like this one made it distasteful for Ives to attend public performances of his works in later years.[25]

These pitiful occasions apparently marked the limits to which Ives would go in promoting his own music. He had only a tenuous connection with musicians in New York City, and his high sense of artistic integrity would not allow him to "push" his own works as one might push an insurance policy. His attitude stood in stark contrast with Stravinsky's self-promotion during the 1910s and after.

Ives's solo instrumental works were just as neglected as his chamber music and orchestral scores between 1902 and 1921; there were a few performances by Ives or a friend in semipublic or church concerts.[26] As for his songs, he must have shown them to professional singers, for he referred in the *Memos* to their objections to the difficulties of the songs; in the end, he was evidently left to sing these masterpieces to himself in private.[27] There is definite information about only one song performance, and it is interesting because of its subordination of musical considerations to those of the insurance business. In 1917 Julian Myrick, noting that Dr. John McCrae of the Canadian army, author of the popular war poem *In Flanders*

Fields, had been a medical referee in Montreal for Mutual, suggested that Ives set the poem to music. Giving vent to his strong feelings about the war that America was just then entering, Ives produced a challenging and dissonant song, complete with snatches of the tunes of *America, The Red, White, and Blue* (with one phrase put into a dolorous minor key), and *La Marseillaise* running into *The Battle Cry of Freedom.* Myrick got his friend McCall Lanham (an insurance man) to sing it at a Mutual managers' luncheon at the Waldorf only days after the American declaration of war. Neither singer nor accompanist was capable of meeting the demands of the music, and Ives was so disappointed by the performance that he thought he could have done better himself.[28]

Ives even had trouble with his copyists, especially with one named Price, who worked for him—and plagued him—for years. The composer's admonition to his copyist on the manuscript of *The Fourth of July* is justly famous: "Mr. Price: Please don't try to make things nice! All the wrong notes are *right*. Just copy as I have—I want it that way." [29]

Somewhere around the middle of this twenty-year period, Ives's isolation was further compounded when he largely gave up going to concerts in New York, limiting himself to an occasional program by one of the large symphony orchestras. Business was taking up much of his time, and he wished to devote what little leisure he had to composition. He also found that listening to others' music, particularly unfamiliar music, interfered with his own compositions that he was planning and carrying around in his head. A veritable musical revolution was occurring in Europe in the 1910s; and during that decade New York began to hear the music of Europeans who were working independently along some of the same lines that Ives was pursuing. But Ives heard nothing by Stravinsky until 1919 or 1920 and apparently never heard anything by Schoenberg.[30] His writings between 1919 and 1922 suggest that he was only vaguely aware of the modern movement in music and that he had difficulty relating himself to that movement; they reveal the embarrassment and hesitancy of a man who has found that he has wandered far from the beaten paths of music and who is not at all sure that others are going to come that way.

Ives's music was not totally without approval from others. Interest was expressed by the farmer Francis Ryder, Ives's neighbor at West Redding, who had no knowledge of music but liked to hear Ives play his compositions on the piano; by Dr. Griggs, whom Ives saw from time to time during these years; and by David Talmadge, a violinist whom Ives hired to teach the violin to his mentally ill nephew, Moss White Ives. Talmadge played several of the violin sonatas informally with Ives, and in 1917 he and the pianist Stuart Ross gave the Third Violin Sonata at a private concert in Carnegie Chamber Music Hall. In setting up this concert, Ives probably had no alternative but to invite either personal friends who were not musicians or musical friends who disapproved of his compositions; but it must have been a boost to his self-confidence to hear one of his works played by someone who really thought it worth playing.[31]

These few supporters were far from being vigorous Ives enthusiasts, however, and the friendly comments of such relatively lightweight musical figures can hardly have given Ives much consolation when compared with the consistent disapproval he received from more eminent musicians. This disapprobation occasionally caused Ives to doubt his own musical judgment and to fall back temporarily into a more conservative style; the traumatic session with Milcke, in particular, had this effect (he felt) on the Third Violin Sonata. Thus Ives came to feel that "if I wanted to write music that, to me, seemed worth while, I must keep away from musicians." [32]

Most members of his family were unsympathetic to what he was trying to do; his brother, Moss, joked about his music and asked him why he didn't write something "pretty." But Ives attributed his ability to keep going along his own way, in the face of criticism, principally to the confidence that his wife had in him. No matter what others said, she wanted him to be himself, and she never suggested that he change his musical ways. Mrs. Ives knew almost nothing about music, however, and Ives seems to have shared his music with her very little when he was composing it.[33]

Ives's musical isolation raises several questions about the man and his work. First, what was the effect of his isolation upon his music? Undoubtedly isolation was largely responsible for the communicative weaknesses of his compositions, as Copland has suggested. But the other side of the coin is probably more significant: isolation en- couraged innovation. As Henry and Sidney Cowell have pointed out, it "increased his concentration upon the music of the Ideal, of the Transcendental, music that was to be uninhibited by the limitations of people and instruments, satisfying to the composer even if un- heard." [34]

What, then, was the effect of isolation upon the man himself? For those who admire Ives, it is tempting to believe that he had so much integrity and independence that he went his own way relatively un- troubled by neglect or adverse criticism. Even Arnold Schoenberg seems to have subscribed to this view.[35] But Ives left considerable evi- dence that he was deeply troubled by his situation. Desiring to get things off his chest but lacking anyone to talk to, he addressed him- self in shrill tones. Before he burst into print around 1920, his music manuscripts were his principal outlet; he filled their margins with political opinions, judgments of other composers, justifications of his own music, records of criticism leveled at his work, humor, outrage, and nostalgia. Later he burdened the autobiographical *Memos* with elaborate self-justifications and long diatribes against men and insti- tutions. The former insider at Yale had finally learned what it was like to be a poet or scholar or rebel, what it meant to suffer neglect and contempt at the hands of the big men in control of the system. Later, in the 1930s, younger composers who admired Ives even claimed that lack of recognition had brought his composing to an early end; Mrs. Ives, however, disagreed, laying the blame on the breakdown in his health and the exhaustion of his creative vein.[36]

If isolation had such a devastating personal effect on Ives, then a third set of questions arises. Given that he wanted to compose such advanced music, was there no alternative to this terrible isolation that he suffered? Did that isolation grow inevitably out of the exist- ing musical situation in the United States? Or did it rather arise from nonmusical elements in Ives himself and in his relation to the total American society and culture? Ives gave his own answers to these questions in his *Essays before a Sonata* (c. 1919) and in the "Post- face" to his *114 Songs* (c. 1922), his principal writings on aesthetics and on the role of the artist in society.

Drawn from his broader transcendentalism, Ives's aesthetic philosophy was grounded in a basic dualism, which he found in all art, between "substance" and "manner"; this distinction was not unlike the more familiar dualism between content and form.[37] He believed that the basic purpose of art was that of "paralleling or approving . . . the highest attributes, moral and spiritual, one sees in life." The beginning of the art process lay in the artist's consciousness of spiritual and moral truths; the artist then summoned up an artistic intuition that reflected and approved these moral and spiritual truths. All this was the part of the art process that Ives called "substance." The other part of the art process ("manner") was the expression of this artistic intuition through a particular medium—for example, the translation of the artistic intuition into musical sounds. Ives valued substance much more highly than manner and thought it much more important in art. Personifying each element of his dualism in a famous author, he saw Emerson as nearly all substance and Poe as nearly all manner. Naturally, he valued Emerson more highly than Poe, just as "we prefer Whittier to Baudelaire—a poet to a genius, or a healthy to a rotten apple." [38]

Ives's theory gave him a philosophical justification for preferring the hymns sung in camp meetings to the same hymns sung in proper churches: "In two separate pieces of music in which the notes are almost identical, one can be of 'substance' with little 'manner,' and the other can be of 'manner' with little 'substance.' " Thus Ives sought the idea or ideal—particularly the moral point of view—behind any work of art. He had no objection to program music, for a scene in nature might have deep religious connotations for an artist. But he objected to "the extreme materializing of music"; he especially criticized tone painters like Richard Strauss, who allowed "the shining hardness of externals" and "the lure of the media" to betray them into writing music of trivial content and purely "sensuous" or "physical-emotional" appeal.[39]

From his platform of aesthetic idealism, Ives launched an attack against those artists who had little or no substance to express and who took refuge instead in "over-enthusiasm for local color—over-interest in the multiplicity of techniques, in the idiomatic." Not only was manner artificial and insincere, but it was also reactionary and too easy: "Beauty in music is too often confused with something that lets the ears lie back in an easy chair. Many sounds that we are used to, do not bother us, and for that reason, we are inclined to call them beautiful. . . . And unity is too generally conceived of or too easily accepted as analogous to form, and form (as analogous) to custom, and custom to habit." Perhaps Emerson's substance was the greater just because of its muddiness of expression: "Vagueness is, at times, an indication of nearness to a perfect truth." [40] But the aspect of manner that Ives detested most was the artist's concentration on the effect he would have upon an audience. Over the years he delivered protracted tirades against the pianist Josef Hofmann, the conductor Arturo Toscanini, and other artists who were the matinee idols of American concert life during the first third of the century. In his opinion, such men "hypnotized" the "nice ladies" by playing them "easy" music in order to "get the money." [41]

When Ives moved from his basic aesthetic philosophy to a consideration of the role of art and the artist in society, he found himself following two contradictory lines of thought. On the one hand, he idealized art, placing it on a pedestal above all mundane matters. Condemning composers who accepted the patronage of the rich or entered competitions for prizes, he dismissed as rank commercialism the most necessary of practical considerations for the artist. His extreme idealism led him to raise music above even physical limitations to the realm of pure idea: "My God! what has sound got to do with music! . . . Why can't music go out in the same way it comes in to a man, without having to crawl over a fence of sounds, thoraxes, catguts, wire, wood, and brass? . . . That music must be heard, is not essential—what it *sounds* like may not be what it *is*." [42] In the opinion of the composer Elliott Carter, Ives's idealization of music was part of "the 19th-century American dream of art and high culture" and was the great tragedy of his musical life. Seeing the artist "as a prophet living in the pure, transcendent world of the spirit, above the mundane matters of money, practicality, and artistic experience," Ives "cut himself off from music's reality. Too many of his scores, consequently, were never brought to the precision of presentation and scoring necessary to be completely communicative to the listener." [43]

The other, and opposite, line of Ives's thought about the social role of the artist led him to the conclusion that the artist and his art must be close to the people. From transcendentalism he had learned to have faith in the innate goodness—the divinity—within every man. The composer, then, should seek inspiration in the hopes and ideals of the common man. Ives also believed that the creative artist should live among the people. He feared the elitism that resulted when artists congregated together as a separate group, monopolizing art and placing themselves above the masses; such artists, he felt, would tend to become too wrapped up in their own personalities, and their art would degenerate into mere manner. He compared the hoax of discovering "the one great American poet" (and thus separating him out from the people) to the hoax of "discovering" leaders that was perpetrated upon the people in politics.[44] Naturally, he was hostile to the idea that American composers should form a separate profession, governed by standards peculiar to itself and accorded a special place and prestige within the society.

Ives's solution to the problem of artistic separatism was, of course, that the artist should not make a living from his art, but should work among the people: "We might offer the suggestion that Debussy's content would have been worthier his manner, if he had hoed corn or sold newspapers for a living, for in this way he might have gained a deeper vitality and truer theme to sing at night and of a Sunday." A man's art should be neither a separate activity nor his sole activity. It should be made part of a larger round of life and work among his fellow men; it would then have broader and more vital sources of inspiration, and it might "have a chance to be more natural, more comprehensive, perhaps, freer and so more tolerant." [45] "The fabric of existence weaves itself whole," he wrote of his own life in business. "You can not set an art off in the corner and hope for it to have vitality, reality and substance. There can be nothing 'exclusive' about a substantial art. It comes directly out of the heart of experience of life and thinking about life and living life. My work in music helped my business and my work in business helped my music." [46]

Ives had no fear that the people could not appreciate the best in music. What was the need for a system of patronage, special institutions for musical training, or a separate musical profession? He preferred to trust the intuitive judgment of the people: "For the amount of a month's wages, a grocery-clerk can receive 'personal instruction' from Beethoven, and other *living* 'conservatories.' "[47] Even modern music might be better appreciated by the common man than by the usual lazy-eared concertgoer, for the "unmusical" common man had not gotten used to the traditional musical procedures.[48]

But it was not enough for the average man to be merely an appreciator; he must become himself a creative artist, for in every soul there was an element of creative genius and a desire to bring it to expression. Musicians per se could well be eliminated, just as leaders could be eliminated in politics. The "one true art" could only come from "the direct expression of the mind and soul of the majority." Down with the Artists and up with the people as artists! Looking forward with his usual optimism to a time "when the school children will whistle popular tunes in quarter-tones," Ives concluded this line of thought with a grand utopian vision of "the day . . . when every man while digging his potatoes will breathe his own Epics, his own Symphonies (operas if he likes it)." Resting at the end of the day and "watching his brave children in *their* fun of building *their* themes, for *their* sonatas of *their* life," this common man would "look up over the mountains and . . . hear the transcendental strains of the day's symphony, resounding in their many choirs, and in all their perfection, through the west wind and the tree tops!"[49]

Ives pursued these two contradictory patterns of thought—the tendency to idealize art until it was removed from most people's idea of practical reality and the tendency to democratize it until it became integral to every man's experience—side by side in his writings. Philosophically, the contradiction could be traced to New England transcendentalism, which tended both to spiritualize all things and at the same time to find value in the most ordinary things. From another point of view, Ives shared his contradiction with other composers who had felt the powerful nineteenth-century combination of romanticism and nationalism. While opposed to nationalism in politics, Ives espoused it in music; he hoped for American musical independence from German influences, and he sought a fundamentally American expression in music that went beyond the mere use of local color. But composers like Ives and Moussorgsky, who came from non-Germanic, musically underdeveloped nations, were torn between the desire to express their unity with the vernacular culture of their own peoples and the allegiance to high-minded German artistic ideals that they had imbibed from the romantic movement.

The contradiction in Ives's thinking about art and society also had a peculiarly American aspect. In the 1910s the critic Van Wyck Brooks pointed out the division in American culture between "highbrow" and "lowbrow"—between a high art and culture that were far removed from ordinary life and an ordinary life that had little use for high art and culture.[50] This sort of gap was peculiarly great in America because Americans lacked that long historical development as an organic people that might have bound them together culturally. Brooks felt that Walt Whitman had begun the needed breakthrough to a new American literature that would disregard the distinction between highbrow and lowbrow. Brooks did not know it, but Ives was beginning a similar breakthrough in music; in fact, one reason for the prolonged resistance to his music was the general assumption that there had to be a division between highbrow and lowbrow, an assumption that was contradicted by his rarefied and experimental art music that quoted vernacular tunes. Ives never achieved a comparable breakthrough in his thought or his personal life, but in his own way he understood the problem posed by Brooks and wrestled strenuously with it. In his preference for the ethereal Emerson over the earthy Whitman, however, he tended to widen rather than narrow the gap between highbrow and lowbrow.

But Ives's contradictory desires both to idealize and to democratize art had their most significant source in his own emotional needs. They were two different ways of attacking the leading practitioners of classical music in America, whom he had long disliked and who had now rejected his music. These apparently contradictory tendencies were held together by their common masculinity; each was the assertion of a masculine principle against an opposing feminine one, as his frank use of sexual imagery showed. On the one hand, the art that he idealized was a high, manly art of content and substance; against it he set a lower, feminine art of mere form, effect, and manner—the kind of art practiced by sissified male performers and composers who sold themselves as exotic personalities to the concert audience. On the other hand, a democratic art which was part of people's daily life was also vital and masculine, while an aristocratic art that remained aloof from the masses was effete and effeminate. In Ives's view, the effete artist who turned commercialist was selling himself to an equally effete aristocracy, not to the manly people. (Ives's "people" were generally males.) And behind his diatribes against prominent artists lay an oblique attack against their patrons—Ives's own class of wealthy businessmen—who had also rejected or ignored his music; they too had lost their manhood, both by separating themselves from the people and by acquiescing as their wives degraded high art into a mere interest in artistic personalities. From 1910 on, Ives sprinkled his occasional essays and memos, his correspondence, and his public writings with the outcries of wounded manhood against an effeminate musical culture in which he feared he had become entangled. He thought nothing of referring to Chopin's music as "pretty soft, but you don't mind it in him so much, because one just naturally thinks of him with a skirt on, but one which he made himself." [51]

By attacking composers and other professional musicians from two sides at once, Ives was indirectly justifying his own nonprofessional solution to the problem of the artist, while at the same time obscuring the contradictions and unconscious ironies within that solution. As he presented it, his choice as a creative artist seemed admirable. Finding the field of professional musical composition too tainted by commercialism, he had become a businessman so that he would be free to be a purer and truer composer. Instead of wrestling with the question of how professional composers were to be able to make a precarious living in the capitalist society that he supported, Ives simply suggested that they follow his path and take up work among the people.

But this plausible solution contained two great flaws, by his own standards. First, his business and his musical lives were utterly sepa-

rate from each other. Far from the fabric of his existence weaving itself whole, it was in fact rent in two; and his art was indeed set off in
the corner, carefully insulated from his business life. Second, he did
not really escape commercialism, for in spite of his high-sounding
rhetoric about it, his business life inevitably became a not altogether
noble means of supporting his art on its pure and lofty plain. Elliott
Carter has even suggested that Ives's idealization of art was "an
American business man's view of the artistic profession, one that was
especially characteristic of that time of wealthy art-collectors." [52] Art
does indeed seem to have been for Ives an outlet for reaction against
the demands of his business life. Returning home to work on the
Thoreau section of his *Concord* Sonata after a day of pushing life insurance by clever sales techniques, he had every reason to exalt his
artistry high above the commercial world with its compromises and
its pettiness.

If Ives became confused when he attempted to explain how creative artists could be nonprofessionals, he was utterly at a loss to
explain how they were to find an audience among "the people."
Sometimes he seemed to say that such an audience was undesirable.
But it is inconceivable that Ives should not have wished the people,
with whom he was so emotionally and philosophically identified and
whose common life provided the inspiration for so much of his
work, to *hear* his music. The whole record of his reaction to the
public reception of his compositions is evidence that he desired to
make musical contact with the masses. But by thinking only in vague
and transcendental terms about the encouragement that the artist
needed from others, he neglected the vital institutions which were
the only practical means by which an artist might gain the attention
of the people. Obviously, however, his "people" were not the superficially sophisticated concert audiences, but rather the mass of men
living unpretentious lives throughout the length and breadth of
America and the world. Unfortunately, the only audience that it was
practicable for Ives and other serious composers to reach was the
concert audience. Ives was actually one of the last men in a tradition
of nineteenth-century American creative artists (such as Melville)
who looked beyond the *public,* which rejected them, to an amor-
phous *people,* with whom they ideologically identified themselves but

with whom they had no actual contact as artists.[53] Impotent (and temperamentally unsuited) to break through to the people, Ives could only dwell in isolation, shunning and shunned by the public, trusting optimistically that the natural (and divine) course of events would someday secure for the composer an audience in his beloved majority.

Whether or not anyone else thought so, Ives knew that his own music was music of excellence. But this assurance did not entirely satisfy him, and the *Essays before a Sonata* can even be read as a long justification by Ives of himself. His elaborate defense of Emerson's vagueness in content and style may have been an indirect defense of the supposed incoherence in his own music. When he bristled at criticism of Thoreau's isolation, he may have had his own in mind, as when he said of Thoreau that "living for society may not always be best accomplished by living *with* society." Mark Van Doren had charged that Thoreau had been so wrapped up in his own personality that he had failed to measure himself against other men. But Ives felt that Thoreau "cared too much for the masses—too much to let his personality be 'massed'; too much to be unable to realize the futility of wearing his heart on his sleeve but not of wearing his path to the shore of 'Walden' for future masses to walk over and perchance find the way to themselves." [54]

Ives's tremendous solitude as a musical modern and his tortured attempts to make an integral whole out of his music, life, and thought constitute one of the great personal dramas of American cultural history. This drama, Elliott Carter has written, "makes of Ives an artist really characteristic of America, not unlike Melville. Without the dimensions of this struggle and the quality it gave his scores, his *Emersons* and *Hallowe'ens* would be of superficial and transitory interest." [55]

When, about 1920, Ives set this conflict down in writing, he gave an unequivocal answer to the question of why he was musically isolated. He put the blame not on himself and not on American society and culture in general, but squarely on the American musical fraternity: "It is my impression that there is more open-mindedness and willingness to examine carefully the premises underlying a new or unfamiliar thing, before condemning it, in the world of business than in the world of music." [56] Given his own artistic convictions and the prevailing state of American music as a profession, Ives clearly thought that his isolation was inevitable. And in his defense of himself Ives used, consciously or unconsciously, rhetoric that portrayed him as he wished to be remembered. The reader of his writings invariably receives the impression of a cantankerous Yankee—radical, strong-minded, masculine, down to earth, cussing and mocking at refinement—who was condemned as disreputable by proper society.

There was, however, a very different side to Ives's personality that had something to do with his isolation. It can be approached best by asking whether the musicians who rejected his music down to 1921 were representative of all, or only a part, of the musical world at the time. Clearly, most of those who saw his compositions were second-rate musicians; and all of them (with the exception of Gustav Mahler) were thoroughly conventional in their musical tastes. These were the very "old ladies" that he was to denounce for forty years. Why, then, did he persist in showing them his music? Were there no other musicians, with different tastes, who would have been more likely to be sympathetic with what he was doing?

The answer lies in his remark that "Dave and Max Smith were old friends of mine, and real friends at that, whom I respected and liked and got along with, except when it came to music." [57] What is extraordinary about the people to whom Ives showed his music is the extent to which they were personal and family friends of his. Men like Max Smith, Edgar Stowell, and Dr. Griggs had styles of life similar to Ives's, and they and their families were welcome in the Ives home on a social basis. Ives's musical isolation arose not only from his being a nonprofessional, but also from his inability to have a comfortable musical relationship with anyone who was not personally and socially acceptable to him. The musicians to whom he showed his music were drawn mainly from "his kind" of people.

There were in New York City in the decade of the 1910s—the very years when Ives was at the height of his creative powers—a number of musicians who appreciated the significance of the new

European modernism represented by Schoenberg, Stravinsky, and Scriabin. They included the critics Carl Van Vechten, Paul Rosenfeld, and Hiram K. Moderwell; the musical amateurs Claire Raphael and Waldo Frank; and the composers Leo Ornstein and Charles T. Griffes. The European modernist composers Edgard Varèse and Ernest Bloch arrived in the city in the course of the decade. One can only conjecture whether or not any of these people would have given Ives encouragement had they seen his music; but it seems likely that two—Rosenfeld and Moderwell—would have been more than interested in it. In their articles in the *New Republic* and the *Seven Arts*, these two men revealed not only their enthusiasm for the latest European musical developments,[58] but also their desire for an American classical music based on vernacular sources; Moderwell's hope for such a music based on ragtime sounded very much like a call for Ives's First Piano Sonata.[59] Ives's music might even have been received more favorably in the 1910s than it was to be received in either of the following two decades, for the avant-garde of the 1910s combined the enthusiasm for experiment characteristic of the 1920s with the enthusiasm for vernacular sources characteristic of the 1930s.

Most of the figures in this incipient New York musical avant-garde were associated with a broader movement of the 1910s, a veritable "rebellion" in literature and art against the "genteel tradition" of nineteenth-century American romanticism.[60] The center of the rebellion was Greenwich Village, literally around the corner from Ives, for the Iveses lived on West Eleventh Street in 1908–1911 and 1914–1915 and on Waverly Place in 1911–1912. Even the reformer Amos Pinchot, Ives's old friend from Yale, contributed money and articles to the *Masses*, an organ of the rebellion.[61]

But in the 1910s Ives did not meet any of these proponents of modern music and probably did not know who they were. His separation from them was in part a result of his not being a professional musician, but it had far deeper causes. Had he known of them, he would have been doubtful about meeting them. Had he met them, he would not have been able to stand them, and they would have had difficulty in dealing with him. For they were Bohemians, and Ives was a man of gentility and conventionality. As any reader of

Essays before a Sonata can plainly see, he belonged to the very "genteel tradition" against which they were revolting.

Ives's conventionality—his commitment, in all matters except music and politics, to what was socially acceptable—is an aspect of his life that has been almost entirely neglected by those who have written about him, for it does not fit into the generally accepted picture of him as a rebel, nor is it congenial to the thinking of many of his admirers. Yet it was a crucial part of the man. Because he allowed himself to be drawn into a conventional pattern of life, he had no outlet for those parts of himself that were unconventional—his music and his politics. He seems to have felt compelled to hide away from public view these departures from the norm. Social convention made demands on him from one side that were stronger than the demands made by masculinity from the other, although Ives chose to speak much about masculinity and hardly at all about convention (apart from musical convention). Bohemianism and effeminacy were his Scylla and Charybdis, and his tortured self-justifications were actually attempts to negotiate the narrow passage between them. Those who move beyond his music to look at the man himself are mistaken when they say that his place in American cultural history is similar to that of Whitman or Frank Lloyd Wright. Whitman and Wright were Bohemians, "free souls"; Ives was a genteel businessman.

Ives revealed his allegiance to the genteel tradition very clearly in a private memo that he wrote in June, 1914. On the train down from Redding, he talked with Dan Beard, an older man of his acquaintance who had done the illustrations for Mark Twain's *Connecticut Yankee in King Arthur's Court*. Beard, who was a leading figure in the Boy Scouts of America, was far from a Bohemian, but he was still "more depressing than disappointing" to Ives. "His idea of manliness is *not* very wholesome. He cultivates the 'rough and ready man style,' but he is an artist (damn him—he can't get away from that)." Beard told Ives that in a class of his male students painting from naked female models, there had been one picture with "a strong sensual turn to it." Searching for the culprit, Beard had picked out a boy who "made a certain grimace" similar to the sensuality in the painting. But Beard's admirable concern for the proprieties did not satisfy Ives: "Seeing a trace of sensuality or any other weak trait immediately is not a form of innocence." And the incident stimulated Ives to pour out onto paper his feelings about art:

> Neither Dan, the boy, or anybody else need be painting from that kind of models. A bedbug or a monkey's ear ought to be a nobler stimulant for a true painter. God never intended his handiwork to be aped by a crowd of body-flatterers, sincere or insincere. The human anatomy can never be and has never been the inspiration for a great work of art. It's a medium to be used in God's service and not stared at by God's servants. I have felt that if a great painter could catch the radiance we see in some faces, be it homely or beautiful—that expression of a lifetime of faith, hope, and charity—the light we see in the faces of those in love—if a great painter could catch that and then gradually make invisible the things we have to look at—the eyes, the nose, the mouth, the cheeks—leaving in the picture the influence and benediction of the tender, strong, and beautiful soul—the bridge between heaven and earth would be only around the corner and almost in sight—the metamorphosis between earth and heaven would be now nearly understood. It never will be by painting the human body.[62]

This memo strongly suggests that Ives's aesthetic sensibility was severely limited by his fear of Bohemianism in art and that a certain narrow-mindedness and prudery lay beneath his transcendentalism.

Ives's attitudes were pervaded by an old-fashioned sentimentality which was lavished particularly upon the institution of the family. While he had an intellectual appreciation of women's demands for the vote and other reforms of their social position in the 1910s, he was emotionally drawn to a strongly traditional view of women's moral role in society. His sentimentality about family life also trapped him into judging composers on the basis of their devotion to their families. His admiration for Franck and his dislike for Wagner rested largely on these grounds. He felt that an artist who abandoned his family to follow his art would reveal his unwholesomeness in his work: "Look into this man's music, or any similar character's art—live with it long enough—and you will gradually feel the decadent part of the man's soul—making a strenuous, perhaps beautiful, sound—but you can't live with it long, any more than he could live with his family." [63]

Conventionality also affected Ives's practice of religion. He was wont to criticize the large and respectable churches; his personal preference ran to transcendentalism on the one hand and camp meetings on the other. Yet for many years he was to be found on Sunday mornings at the services of the proper and conventional denominations, particularly in the great churches of New York City. In his middle years, attendance at these churches was probably a duty that he felt he owed his wife. Ives's practice of going to church was entirely sincere; but it is doubtful that these particular services gave him much inspiration, either as boy or man.

Ives felt threatened whenever the subject of sex was broached; he rationalized his attitude, however, by choosing to believe that any appearance of sex in art, literature, or public discussion was a form of commercial exploitation. Sensuality was his bête noire. His fear of physicality and the bodily senses gave rise to his admiration of the ascetic Puritans and their " 'no-compromise' with mellow colors and bodily ease," his insistence on the "vileness" as well as the "sublimity" of Rousseau's *Confessions,* and his incapability of responding to the earthy poetry of Whitman.[64] His music is often exalted, but never sensuous. And although he wrote a great deal of program music, the theme of romantic love is notably absent in his mature works.

Ives believed that in music, there was no virtue in merely following custom and authority; but it would never have occurred to him to apply the same philosophy to moral questions. The point is not that he was more genteel than most successful businessmen of the time, for that is debatable, but rather that the combination of his advanced musical views and his conventionality in other matters gave rise to a tremendous incongruousness within the man.

Charles Ives had not always been so proper. During the ten years that he lived with his bachelor friends in Poverty Flat, his life was touched by a mild and innocent Bohemianism. There were evenings with his friends in saloons and beer gardens and walks through Central Park late at night (the inspiration for the piece *Central Park in the Dark*).[65] When Ives was about to leave for New Haven to attend the triennial reunion of his class, Edwards Park asked him what his address there would be, and Ives answered that he would be staying out the whole night and would be sleeping beneath a tree during the day.[66]

But life at Poverty Flat had to come to an end. Ives's friends were also marrying and settling down, and his own choice of Harmony Twichell as his wife was very much within the accepted pattern of life for the successful Yale man. Her father, a member of the Yale Corporation, stood in the great Yale tradition of Congregational clerical leadership in Connecticut. Although the old religious dogmas were being sloughed off in the Twichell family,[67] Harmony clung tightly to Victorian morality. When she traveled in Europe in 1905, her judgments of the art she saw were based largely upon her moral convictions. In Antwerp she found some paintings by Memling "charming—they have some of Fra Angelico's sweetness and purity of expression"; but Rubens's *The Assumption of the Virgin* was "not pleasing—the figures so sensuous and robust that they do not suggest spirituality." On the same trip she read Meredith's *Ordeal of Richard Feverel*, which she thought a "very strong portrayal of the loathsomeness of lust and the sweetness of purity." [68] Thus her marriage to Charles Ives assured that the rest of his life would be lived within the confines of gentility and respectability.

Ives's radical music, radical political views, and radical rhetoric can be seen as ceremonial gestures of rebellion carried on within a conventional pattern of life. They were "safe" forms of rebelliousness in that they posed no real threat to that larger pattern of life; in this respect they had their counterparts in Theodore Roosevelt's "strenuous life" or the singing of vernacular music by Yale undergraduates. Ives thought that Thoreau had gone too far: "Thoreau almost seems at times as though he liked to offend propriety—which is not a very commendable thing, for it is very easy to do." [69] But Ives also thought that music, being a more subjective art than literature, allowed the artist to express himself more "extravagantly" while still remaining within the bounds of propriety.[70] When his rebelliousness took a verbal or written form, he was careful to keep it very private or to tone it down for a limited circulation. He always tried to balance his loyalty to gentility against his assertion of his masculinity.

And above all, he avoided any public identification of himself as an artist.

Ives's musical isolation has generally been attributed to the advanced nature of his compositions; it is said that there was no one else in America at the time who could understand them. But this explanation cannot account for his more general isolation during the first two decades of the century. He was intensely concerned with questions of art and society and with a number of the social and political problems raised by the progressive movement. Yet he had no personal connection with his contemporaries in artistic, literary, intellectual, and reform movements; indeed, he was unaware of most of these movements and aware of the others only in the most marginal way.

In a sense, despite the differences, the only creative artists with whom it is logical to compare Ives are the other leading innovators in America in the 1910s: Frank Lloyd Wright in architecture; John Marin in painting; Alfred Stieglitz in photography; Isadora Duncan in the dance; Theodore Dreiser and Sherwood Anderson in fiction; Carl Sandburg, Vachel Lindsay, and Ezra Pound in poetry. Except for Pound, these figures were all of Ives's generation, several of them older than he; but he certainly had no contact with them, nor was he aware of their work (though his song *General William Booth Enters into Heaven* was a setting of part of Lindsay's poem that he discovered in the highly respectable *Independent*). It is very unlikely that he attended the famous Armory Show of 1913, which brought modern European painting to America. Ives might have found something in common with Frank Lloyd Wright; but Ives's counterparts in all the arts in the 1910s (including Wright) were clearly Bohemians, and what cut him off from them and their work was the conventionality of his life as an American businessman. (Ives's thought about art and life had much in common with that of the painter Robert Henri, another New Yorker; but here again, the two men moved in different worlds.)

Again, Ives's writings indicate that he had little knowledge of the major intellectual currents in America in these years. Figures like William James, Holmes, Dewey, Veblen, and Beard do not seem to have affected his thinking; indeed, the pragmatism and relativism of their work would have been anathema to him. Certain lesser figures in literature and reform thought would have been more congenial to him—the social worker Jane Addams, for example, or the realist novelist Brand Whitlock—for they stood somewhere between the old and the new, retaining a good deal of allegiance to the genteel past. But in this area, too, Ives's interest and knowledge were minimal. Although he proposed sweeping political and social changes in "The Majority" and other writings, his view of social reform was severely circumscribed by the experience and interests of a businessman.

Ives did greatly admire two nineteenth-century realists, Mark Twain and William Dean Howells; in Mark Twain, in particular, he must have found paralleled his own conflict between the cultivated and the vernacular. Ives and his wife read a good deal of nineteenth-century literature, especially fiction by English authors.[71] But his knowledge of the currents of his own time was picked up in a very haphazard manner. In the "Postface" to his *114 Songs,* for example, his quoting Henry Dwight Sedgwick reflected the fact that the Iveses rented Sedgwick's house in New York from 1917 to 1926. Ives might quote from an author for his own purposes, but he seemed to be less interested in entering into the author's point of view or trying to grasp his thesis. Like many another businessman, he relied for too many of his ideas on the daily newspapers (which also furnished several of the poems that he set to music).

If Ives was often naive in his thinking, it was because he had to work out everything—not just his music—on his own. Surrounded by mediocrities during these years of his greatest creativity, he lacked any close male friend with whom he could frankly and intelligently discuss his deepest concerns about art and society. The traditional isolation of creative artists in America has often been commented upon, but it would be difficult to find another great artist whose isolation was so extreme as Ives's. The nonmusical aspect of his isolation, however, resulted from his own choice, from his desire to remain a conventional businessman and not to submit his ideas to the dialogue or give-and-take that might have refined them.

Ives's rebelliousness, then, was kept within the confines of the genteel tradition. It was, nevertheless, a genuine rebellion which had immense importance for his life and work. At some point in the first decade of the century, Ives plainly began to be dissatisfied with the ways of his fellow Yale men and his business associates—not just with their attitude toward music, but with their whole approach to the conduct of life. Around the time of his marriage in 1908, he underwent two remarkable changes that indicate the importance of this dissatisfaction. First, by immersing himself in his family life and his music, he cut himself off from his friends. His marriage to Harmony Twichell was outwardly a proclamation of his allegiance to the Yale system; but more covertly, it was a conscious choosing of the means of rebelling against that system, for she had already made it clear to him how she hoped they would live:

> I've been thinking of ways and *longing* to make and keep my heart and life what our love would have it. For one thing, we must plan to have times for leisure of thought and we must try and read a lot, the best books—we can live with the noblest people that have lived that way—and we will have your music. But we must *do* these things, not only plan to. I have a horror of fitting into things in N.Y. . . . and of having no quiet hours and solitude—I think I *never shall,* for I hate it and I know so few people, but I so often see *unwilling victims.* With you as an *added disinclination,* tho, I'm pretty safe—and then, dearest, we must grow in our perception of the spiritual and unseen things thro our religion—and we can only do that by exercise in religion—by observance—I feel very deeply about that—I wonder if you do—we will talk about it. I think we have to hold *consciously* on to all good, or it slips away from us, or a thousand more immediate but less important interests blur it—the great question is, how to keep all these things fresh and real in a busy everyday life. We must find the way—we *have found* the way, and we must stay in it and know it better every day.[72]

These plans were largely carried out in the Iveses' married life. They went out little and shunned participation in the social and civic life which was so important to other couples of their background and class who lived in New York. Nor was Ives interested in the male club and sporting life that his business associates favored. Within a few years he had stopped seeing most of his Yale friends, as a few letters from them years later make clear. (He continued, however, to see many relatives.) The Iveses' home telephone number was always unlisted.[73] It is sometimes claimed that Ives's withdrawal from the world occurred after his heart attack of 1918 and his supposed "disillusionment" with World War I; but in a very real sense it had occurred ten years earlier, with his marriage.

If one may judge by the literary and philosophical themes that began to appear in his instrumental works around 1906 or 1907, Ives was starting to read and think more seriously in these years; his marriage certainly increased these tendencies. A related development was the second great change that came over him at about this time, a change in personality: he began to have strong views about all sorts of issues and to want to express them. Before, with his Yale friends, he had been merely humorous and unpredictable; now he became cantankerous and explosive. These new traits were, of course, one reason why the Iveses lived a curtailed social life.[74] By January, 1912, Mrs. Ives was writing him while on a visit to Hartford: "Fred Van Beuren [a Yale classmate and member of Wolf's Head] didn't sound very fruitful—aren't you bad to go on a Wagner tirade. I am afraid he will think your wild nature untamed. You probably laid it on thick for his benefit. I can hear you discussing literature, art, and music—poor old insurance coming out weak in the end." [75] Any issue that he felt strongly about could set him off; yet these explosions alternated with extreme shyness. For long periods of time, his wife was probably his only audience. Here, then, was the origin of that intense nervous excitability which was to be so debilitating to Ives during the last thirty years of his life.

As Ives thought more and more about politics in the 1910s, he revealed what it was about Yale men and businessmen that disturbed him. Of the whole range of questions raised by the progressive movement, Ives was little interested in efforts to alleviate poverty or improve the condition of the working class (although he was generous in his private contributions to charity). What monopolized his attention was direct democracy; the initiative and referendum were what "The Majority" and his proposed amendment to the Constitution were all about. He took up these reforms, moreover, in 1917–1920, at a time when public interest in them had been waning for several years and when the progressive movement itself was in sharp decline. Others thought of the initiative as a petition, gotten up privately by groups of citizens and presented to the government. But for Ives, this approach involved too much direction and leadership; he insisted that the initiative take the form of suggestions by all citizens on their regular ballots. Most of those who favored the initiative and referendum proposed to start with them at the state or local level. Ives, who showed little concern for state and local jurisdictions, was only interested in direct democracy at the national level. Many other progressives saw the initiative and referendum as a supplement to representative government, as one among many progressive measures, with direct government as perhaps a final and distant goal. Ives saw the immediate substitution of direct for representative government as the first step in reform. Some others thought direct democracy would work best in conjunction with a strong executive. Ives wanted no real executive at all.

Why did Ives become so intensely concerned with direct government? The only logical answer is that he wanted to destroy leadership in society and the power that goes with leadership. The hatred of leadership and elitism is the central theme in his political writings; leaders must be pulled down and denied their power, the money that enabled them to lead must be severely restricted, and all power must be returned to the people as a whole. But here he was rebelling against the very essence of the Yale system, whose whole tradition centered around training for leadership: leadership by the big men within Yale and leadership by all Yale men in the outside world after graduation. Ives was also rebelling very specifically against those Yale men (including his own relatives) who had assumed leadership positions in government and business; Sen. James W. Wadsworth, Jr., of New York, his old friend and classmate, was perhaps the best example of them. Sometime during his Poverty Flat years or early in his marriage, Ives had come to see the Yale life and its aftermath as no longer innocent, but as stained with evil. He had come to feel that leadership—the practice of taking responsibility for others and making decisions for them and exercising authority over them—was corrupting to both leaders and led.

During the 1910s Ives channeled his explosive cantankerousness into his hatred for leadership, finally coming up with his plan for abolishing it. He apparently believed that his own individuality (including his artistic independence) had been stifled by the Yale system of leadership, but that he had saved himself before it was too late. It was almost as if Ives had made a bargain with himself. After all the commitments he had made up to this point in his life, he could not bring himself to break away from the conventional pattern and become some sort of Bohemian; so he would work hard and make a success of his business. But he would retreat *within* the conventional system; he would confine himself to office and home and would refuse all the trappings and leadership positions of the system; he would not take any responsibility for the system. His solution seems a very limited response to the challenges of the progressive era. But it must be remembered that Ives did not have contact with gentle reformers. His friends from the Wolf's Head Society and the people to whom he was close in Poverty Flat appear to have been a very limited group, intellectually and in other ways; his and his wife's relatives were not notable for their liberalism in social matters; and at work he was surrounded by hardheaded businessmen with a philosophy of strong leadership and power. This was his world, and it must have seemed all-pervasive to him. Thus he carried on a long and lonely rebellion from within the conservative leadership system, much as he rebelled for years against the conservative economics that he had been taught at Yale in the nineties. But he could not make contact with the people and ideas that might have given his rebelliousness a more fruitful application. Both World War I and (especially) its aftermath became for Ives a sort of crusade against leadership at home; and when he extended his ideas abroad he also extended his attack on leadership, for his denial of national sovereignty was a denial that certain nations should take the leadership in world organization (although President Wilson had a very different viewpoint).

While Ives used democratic majoritarianism to attack leadership, there was another American tradition—a tradition of opposition to "legitimate" leadership in church, state, and society—with which he felt a good deal of sympathy. This was the New England come-outer tradition, the tradition of removing oneself from an institution which violates one's conscience. The Reverend Ebenezer White, Ives's great-great-great-grandfather and minister of the established

Congregational church in Danbury, had been such a come-outer. Becoming involved in a doctrinal dispute, White and his congregation had denied the authority over their church of higher ecclesiastical councils in Fairfield County; he and most of the members of the congregation had then come out of the established Congregational system in 1764 and founded an independent religious society.[76] The extension of this New England come-outer tradition to the secular realm had later culminated in the great abolitionist come-outers of the pre–Civil War period—Thoreau, William Lloyd Garrison, and Wendell Phillips—for all of whom Ives felt great admiration. Intellectually, Ives's education and experience did not allow him to face or come to grips with the civil disobedience of Thoreau and the nonresistance of Garrison. But emotionally, the come-outer tradition was part of Ives's family heritage; and he seemed to connect his paternal grandparents with it. It was this come-outer spirit that he was referring to when he lamented the decline in his contemporaries of the old New England independent tradition of standing up in town meeting or church and speaking out one's mind and conscience, without respect for the consequences.[77]

Not surprisingly, then, Ives's thought was not imbued with that desire for community which motivated many progressives. The insurance business had shown him that the law of averages could be used to spread a risk over larger and larger numbers of people; his intense concern with maximum and minimum property rights seems to have arisen from a desire to extend the same principle to economic relations in general. But the sweeping mechanical changes that he proposed in economic life, government, and administration became ends in themselves; he did not advocate them as the means of fulfilling a larger vision—of bringing about a more organic society, a Kingdom of God on earth. For an intense individualist like Ives, community (like tonality) would have to take care of itself. If he differed from many progressives in this regard, however, he differed even more from his brother, who devoted his scholarly energies in the 1930s to extolling the Roman Catholic contribution to America's early history. Moss Ives never lost his faith in the Republican party, of which he was a leader in Danbury; but he stood in that tradition of New England leadership, going back to John Winthrop, which held that the wise leader could best promote the good order of his community by encouraging as many of its members as possible to find an integral place within it. In the years between the two world wars, Moss Ives plainly saw that Danbury's Catholics (particularly those who were enjoying some economic success) must be integrated into their community to insure its coherence; and in doing perhaps more than any other member of the old Danbury families to give Catholics that sense of belonging, he earned their gratitude and respect. In the course of his work, he had occasion to denounce Roger Williams (perhaps the original New England come-outer) as both a religious bigot and a disturber of social peace.[78] But neither the desire for social order nor the goal of brotherly love could awaken a comparable sense of community in his brother, Charles.

In the years just following his marriage, Ives's personality developed in such a way that he played two rebellious roles (sometimes at the same time). The two roles corresponded closely to the two sides of his contradictory thought about art and society. One role, which he had long been accustomed to, was that of the prankish, outlandish boy; but now his wife encouraged this role by herself playing the proper woman shocked by his shenanigans and yet indulging him because he was a mere boy. "I am *very glad* you are really going to put a check on your profanity," she wrote to him in 1914 while she was away visiting. "I don't mind an occasional appropriate expression—but frequent consecutive cursing such as you've indulged in lately is what I don't like to hear. . . . You do get so mad, don't you." [79]

The other role, which was new to him, was that of the transcendental and crotchety old man on his mountaintop, a Bronson Alcott philosophizing while his wife took care of the practical details of life. Both Ives's wife and his partner seem to have taken a protective attitude toward him that confirmed him in this role of visionary; [80] and other business associates, who may not have known about his music, also regarded him as a saintly, aloof scholar. His Twentieth Amendment was probably not taken very seriously for this reason; and in a way, he may even have felt safe in distributing it because he knew it would not be taken seriously by those who were acquainted with him. It might be said that Ives passed from boy to old man within the space of a very few years. He was still a boy at heart when he left Poverty Flat in 1908; but he later wrote that he had become "middle-aged . . . long before the Hohenzollern hog-marched into Belgium"—that is, long before 1914, when he was thirty-nine! [81] Ives's swift passage from boyhood to old age allowed him to escape just what he wanted to escape: adult manhood, the time of responsibility and leadership and the guilt of authority. Both the boy and the old man were innocent; they were not responsible for the system of things. After his heart attack in 1918, his wife's role as trained nurse, her greater mobility, and her better health made her increasingly the dominant and responsible member of the household.

Ives began about 1908 to turn back to the larger musical forms, especially in works for large orchestra. And playing his two roles of rebellion, he produced in the years down to 1916 the compositions that are regarded as his masterpieces. They dealt predominantly with the innocence of boyhood experience (*Decoration Day, The Fourth of July, Putnam's Camp*) and with transcendental exaltation (the *Concord* Sonata, the Fourth Symphony). Both in his choice of a wife and in his use of his increasing wealth, Ives sought to protect his peculiar solution to the problems he faced as an artist and a man. But the terrible strain that arose from the contradictions and convolutions of his extraordinary situation took its toll, especially after the breakdown of his health in 1918. His creativity was brought to an early end. After 1921 he tended to repeat himself in his social and political thinking. Perhaps one reason that he stopped composing in the twenties was that he noticed a parallel tendency in his music. Long before 1921, certainly, he had developed that special temperament—a combination of the boy (shy, then explosive) and the old man (shy, then explosive)—which was so impressive to those who met him in later years. It was a pattern of defenses that he had developed to ward off those forces that threatened to challenge him with the contradictions in his own life. But in endlessly repeating this pattern of defenses during the years after 1921, he tended to stifle his own sensitivity and to become a caricature of himself.

The beginning of the end of Ives's isolation—and the most important event in the history of his public recognition—came in

1919–1920 with his decision to try to find an audience by having some of his compositions printed up and distributed free of charge.

After his heart attack in October, 1918, Ives decided to get the *Concord* Sonata into shape for private printing and distribution. Perhaps he realized that he would compose little more. He may even have suspected that, like his father, he would be dead before the age of fifty and that his music, existing only in manuscript form, would die with him. In any case, he was not averse to public recognition, although he would very much have preferred that others come to him for his music. But no one approached him; and given his temperament and his principles, he probably considered this method of private distribution the best way by which to go about finding a public for his work. During his recuperation, part of which he spent at Asheville, North Carolina, he made a good copy of the sonata and wrote the essays to accompany it, drawing his material partly from earlier papers.[82] In 1920 and 1921, the *Essays before a Sonata* and the *Concord* Sonata were mailed out. The former (a separate book) was printed up for him by the Knickerbocker Press and the latter by the music publishing company of G. Schirmer, which was careful not to allow its name to appear anywhere on the outlandish work. Twenty-five years later, Ives was to have the exquisite pleasure of watching the Schirmer firm beg to be allowed to publish some of his scores.[83]

Meanwhile, he had conceived a further project of a book of songs; *114 Songs,* containing almost all of his more important works in this form, was printed up in 1922—also by G. Schirmer, which was glad to take his money but must by this time have thought that Ives was an impossible crank. The volume was sent out in 1922 and 1923. "It is now generally agreed," Howard Boatwright has written, that this "song collection is the richest one of its kind by an American composer." [84] The critic Paul Rosenfeld called it "a book that must rank with *the* American books." [85] The pieces included in the book and their arrangement were a remarkable example of Ives's conviction that all things, no matter how heterogeneous they might seem, were ultimately part of a transcendental oneness. College songs, religious songs, war songs, street songs, art songs, sentimental songs, early songs, late songs; songs about music itself, about religion, about politics (including the election song *Nov. 2, 1920,* together with a printed offer to send Ives's proposed Twentieth Amendment to the Constitution to anyone who would write for it)—all were included and jumbled together without apparent order. Here was Ives's America assembled between covers. He had originally intended to begin the book with *Evening,* a delicate art song the text of which was from Milton's *Paradise Lost;* but he changed his mind and replaced it in that position with *Majority (The Masses),* an extremely advanced work full of tone clusters (chords made up of many adjacent white or black keys on the piano, played with the forearm or elbow). What prompted the change was criticism of similar tone clusters in the *Concord* Sonata, criticism which "made me feel just mean enough to want to give all the 'old girls' another ride—and then, after they saw the first page of *The Masses* as No. 1 in the book, it would keep them from turning any more pages and finding something 'just too awful for words, Lily!' " [86]

In order to send out these three books, Ives had to overcome his scruples about publicizing his own music. Thus he rationalized that *114 Songs* had been gotten up principally "in order to have a few clear copies that could be sent to friends who, from time to time, have been interested enough to ask for copies of some of the songs." [87] On discovering that the cost of printing a large edition would not be much higher, he had decided to send it out also to musicians—but mainly to get their "impressions, criticisms, or reactions"; in a letter that he prepared to be mailed out ahead of the song book, he laid great stress on its noncommercial character and on the fact that recipients were under no obligation to sing the songs.[88]

Perhaps even more terrible for this shy man was the necessity of standing musically naked before the public, with no mediator to protect him, after so many years of isolation. He attempted to cover his shyness by many humorous and self-deprecating remarks. The dedication of *Essays before a Sonata* is a good example: "These prefatory essays were written by the composer for those who can't stand his music—and the music for those who can't stand his essays; to those who can't stand either, the whole is respectfully dedicated." He also identified eight of the more sentimental songs in *114 Songs* as having "little or no musical value—(a statement which does not mean to imply that the others have any too much of it)." [89]

Ives's embarrassment was particularly obvious in the "Postface" to *114 Songs,* especially because he tried to mask it with a flood of words and poor jokes. Here his conflicting compulsions, his temperamental alternation between explosiveness and shyness, caused him both to expose himself and to hide himself, to write with both exuberance and self-distrust. On one level, the "Postface" was Ives's justification for his not being a professional composer; on another, it expressed his uneasiness about being a composer at all, for fear that by being one he was cutting himself off from the common life. "Some of the songs in this book, particularly among the later ones, cannot be sung," he warned. And he felt compelled to give forced and pathetic reasons for even putting the volume together and sending it out. For example, he wrote that the book "stands now, if it stands for anything, as a kind of 'buffer state,'—an opportunity for evading a question, somewhat embarrassing to answer,—'Why do you write so much ———, which no one ever sees?' There are several good reasons, none of which are worth recording." Again, he explained that he had not really written a song book: "I have merely cleaned house. All that is left is out on the clothes line,—but it's good for a man's vanity to have the neighbors see him—on the clothes line." Finally, the book was being "thrown, so to speak, at the music fraternity, who for this reason will feel free to dodge it on its way— perhaps to the waste basket." [90]

When the composer Aaron Copland and the critic Paul Rosenfeld encountered *114 Songs* a decade after it had appeared, they were struck by the loneliness and pathos that were revealed in the volume. Rosenfeld wrote of the "Postface" that "the tone bears witness to life driven back upon itself. It is half-apologetic, half-defiant, and altogether self-conscious, like that of a man who has found no support and anticipates an unsympathetic reception, and feels continually forced to explain and to justify an occupation which under normal conditions requires no explanation or justification." Copland felt that "Ives had every reason to be timid and to rationalize in a world which had no need for him as an artist." Impressed by the significance of the lack of any order or selectivity in the putting together of *114 Songs*, Copland thought it "self evident . . . that this publication was not designed to give the musical public a clear conception of Ives' gifts as composer." It seemed to Copland that "Ives . . . not only had no public in mind when printing this book, but he hardly had even the 'few friends' of whom he speaks in mind. The truth is he had only *himself* in mind. For after gathering together the fruits of thirty years' work (which, in effect, literally was a kind of 'house-cleaning') Ives found himself alone with his songs." [91]

Having spent several thousand dollars on putting out these three books, Ives had to decide whom to send them to. He had at least 750 copies of the *Concord* Sonata, and at least 1,500 of *114 Songs,* printed. Probably most, but not all, of these copies were sent out.[92] A certain number went to personal friends of Ives's or to professional musicians of his acquaintance; some of the people in both these categories he had not seen for years. The largest part of the books, however, went to musicians who were strangers to him. One of Ives's memos indicates that he intended to secure from the conservative *Musical Courier* a list of names and addresses of people to whom to send the *Concord* Sonata.[93] Whether or not he carried out this plan, he later relied heavily on *Who's Who in America* as a source of names of musicians (mainly singers) to whom to send *114 Songs,* although he supplemented it with other sources.[94] Those who received the books included composers, performers, teachers, and critics in Europe and America, as well as music schools and conservatories, music publishing houses, and musical journals. As both his sources for these names and the letters of acknowledgment that he received make perfectly clear, Ives—who had no contact with the musical public, much less the people—was compelled by his isolation to send his music to the selfsame conservative academics, composers, and performers whom he had damned for years and would continue to damn for the rest of his life. At the beginning of the 1920s, he neither knew nor knew of the growing avant-garde in American music; that a few Americans interested in experimental music were recipients of his works was largely an accident.[95]

Most of the extant letters from those who received his books were polite expressions of gratitude that showed little or no acquaintance with the actual music; some expressed or implied surprise at receiving such expensive books from a man of whom the recipient had never heard. Only a few contained serious criticism of the music; and of these, only two were from men whose names were at all well known in the musical world—the renowned teacher of theory and composition Percy Goetschius and the composer Charles Wakefield Cadman. Goetschius admitted that he thought the sonata overthrew the traditional procedures based on the natural laws of tone, which for him defined the only true music. But he tried to be positive; and on the whole he was encouraging, assuring Ives that he thought him entirely sincere and that he was much interested in his experimentation. There was, however, no further contact between Ives and Goetschius. Cadman, on the other hand, was frankly hostile to the sonata; it impressed him as ugly and confused, and he thought that it was not really music at all. Perhaps feeling that he ought to have something good to say to a man who had made him a gift of his music, Cadman commended Ives for all the time and effort he had spent on the elaborate notation of the score.[96]

Men like Goetschius and Cadman meant well; but they were committed, for professional and academic reasons, to the musical tradition of the nineteenth century. Their hostile and automatic reaction against music which broke with that tradition was largely a means of strengthening and preserving their own status in music and in the larger society. Even Wallingford Riegger, who became a modernist, recalled that he had had reactions of a similar kind during his student days in Berlin: "I blushingly admit to having upheld at that time [about 1910] good old academic tradition, so much so that at the first Berlin performance of Scriabin's *Poème de l'Extase* I hissed in exactly the same manner as did the Philadelphia boxholders twenty years later when Stokowski gave my own *Study in Sonority*." [97]

The letters of acknowledgment from Ives's personal friends cannot have given him much comfort either. Tom McLane, his old classmate from the Wolf's Head Society, was evidently very much surprised to receive a book of essays from Charlie Ives; it was just not the sort of thing one expected from the Wolf's Head crowd. He kidded Ives about his sudden burst of erudition, admitting that he did not think he would be able to follow the essays.[98] Perhaps the unkindest of these letters from personal friends came from Mrs. Elizabeth Sprague Coolidge, who had now assumed her role as the principal patroness of music in the United States. Her friend Mrs. Ives had sent Mrs. Coolidge the *Concord* Sonata, asking for her comments. Finding nothing in it that was comprehensible or appealing, Mrs. Coolidge had sent the music on to a composer friend (probably Henry Eichheim) who had a strong interest in the modern idiom. She could only reply that she did not wish to repeat the composer's evaluation of the sonata and of Ives's talent, for fear of hurting Mrs. Ives. Ives wrote out (but did not send) an answer to Mrs. Coolidge's letter that revealed how much it had hurt him. Insisting that her composer friend "can't hurt my feelings—I've been called all the names in the criminal code," he took the defensive position that the sonata was "but an experiment" and that he had been "surprised to find so many men were interested in a thing so repellent in form." [99] This incident is a concrete illustration of how Ives's music was drawn into the genteel world of people like Mrs. Coolidge not because he needed patronage, as was the case with many composers, but because his conventional way of life limited him to that world.

Ives's music and writings also received a few notices in the press. His old teacher Prof. William Lyon Phelps reviewed *Essays before a Sonata* in an article in the *Yale Alumni Weekly* devoted mainly to books by Yale men brought out in 1920 (including Sinclair Lewis's *Main Street*). But this short review was hardly more than an act of personal friendship. Phelps called the work "a brilliant and provocative book, full of challenging ideas, and marked by chronic cerebration," and he noted that Ives's father-in-law had been a member of the Yale Corporation, but he failed to say what the volume was about.[100] The New York *Sun*, which received a copy of *114 Songs* because it had granted permission to use certain newspaper poems as song texts in the book, took notice of it in a short article entitled "Here's a Chance to Get a Nice Song Book Free"; relying on a note at the back of the volume, the *Sun* informed its readers that Ives would send them a copy of *114 Songs* if they would just write for it, although the article did not say what kind of music it contained.[101] This publicity made Ives very angry, for he received "hundreds" of requests for the book. He felt, nevertheless, morally obligated to fulfill his promise to send a complimentary copy to anyone who requested one; but while he patronizingly noted in these requests "a sincere interest in the poets" whom the *Sun*'s article had mentioned as the authors of his texts, "particularly Wordsworth, Whittier and Shelley," he did not seem to realize that those who sent the letters were probably as close to "the people" as he was ever going to get.[102] In late 1922, then, he had 500 copies of *50 Songs,* selected from *114 Songs,* printed up; and these books were sent out to those who had responded to the article in the *Sun,* as well as to others.[103] The reactions of many of the recipients when they opened their "nice song book" can only be imagined.

Perhaps the most widely circulated reviews of Ives's works appeared in the form of humorous editorials in the *Musical Courier,* a conservative journal of the music "trade" to which Ives had sent copies. An editorial of 1921 called "Concord Unconquered" made fun of the *Concord* Sonata and its accompanying essays. Joking about Ives's avoidance of bar lines and time signatures, the writer suggested that "perhaps Charles aspires to become the Mark Twain of music"; and he even boasted that he had neither read the essays nor been able to play the music.[104] In spite of this unsympathetic reception, the *Musical Courier* received a copy of *114 Songs* the next year, and it was also treated as a joke. This time the editorial began: "Who is Ives? We have not the least idea"; and Ives was dubbed "the American Satie, joker par excellence." No attention was paid to the songs themselves: "As for the music, it was evidently not sent us for review, and to review it would be an impertinence, as much of an impertinence as to criticize a letter written by one man to another man neither of which is us." The writer did, however, quote several of Ives's footnotes and comments—not only his embarrassed and self-deprecating stabs at humor, but also (out of context) his serious remarks—in an attempt to ridicule him. The editorial concluded: "Perhaps old fashioned 'practical' methods are best after all." [105] *Musical America,* a journal similar to the *Musical Courier,* also printed a short humorous review of the sonata.[106]

It must have been a severe trial for Ives to see his music, which was such a personal testament, held up to public ridicule in this way.

After years of isolation, he had finally made what was for him a supreme effort to find a sympathetic audience; but instead of un-covering such an audience, his books of music were met by indiffer-ence and insult. These reactions may well have been more crushing for him than the preceding period of utter neglect.[107] After the last spurt of songs that he wrote in 1921 for *114 Songs,* he practically stopped composing. Throughout the 1920s he was joked about among musicians (many of whom did not know anything about his work) as the crazy composer of crazy music. For example, in the *Hawthorne* movement of the *Concord* Sonata he had indicated in a footnote that certain tone clusters should be played with "a strip of board" long enough to depress the requisite number of piano keys; [108] for this suggestion he became known as the man who ad-vocated "playing the piano with a stick." [109]

Hostile to the idea of self-promotion, Ives insisted on letting his music speak for itself; but his extraordinary combination of experi-mentation and naiveté allowed musicians to conclude that he had never been trained to compose "proper" music and that his modern-ism was therefore unacceptable. Ives's not being a professional musi-cian undoubtedly made it much easier to disregard him as a serious composer; among the avant-garde his nonprofessional status may well have been the clinching argument against him. When, in the 1920s, Henry Cowell heard about Ives from other modernists, such as Carl Ruggles and Charles Seeger, Ives was described to him as a crank, a musical wild man, and a charlatan.[110] The two large and solid books of music that Ives had put out were found by some teachers and pianists who received them to be very handy for raising the level of a piano bench; [111] the "obvious and vulgar jokes" which arose from this use of the music were the occasion for Henry Cow-ell's first hearing of Ives.[112]

It would seem, then, that Ives's decision to scatter his music broad-cast only served to bring home to him the depths of his own isola-tion. But the books were sent out in such quantities that they were more than likely to find their way, sooner or later, to someone who would be enthusiastic about them and who would also have contacts in the musical world. Even before *114 Songs* went out, the *Concord*

Sonata had fallen into the hands of Henry Bellamann and Clifton Joseph Furness, the two men who, although they were utterly unknown to Ives, were to be the first public proponents of his compositions. The long, slow process of Ives's recognition was about to begin.

Part Two

RECOGNITION
1921–1974

7

OPENINGS TO THE
AVANT-GARDE

1921–1932

❦

As CHARLES IVES GRADUALLY retired from business during the 1920s, he found that his health, although declining, permitted him to take some interest in the world of music and to continue the search for an audience for his own compositions. Surveying the musical scene, he found that the 1920s were an auspicious time for the reception of unorthodox music in America. Aaron Copland has observed that "contemporary music as an organized movement in the U.S.A. was born at the end of the First World War." [1]

In Europe, during the 1910s, a remarkable break with the musical past had been carried out by a number of younger composers—notably Stravinsky, Schoenberg, and Bartók. These practitioners of a "New Music" took a giant step beyond Richard Strauss and Debussy, who had previously been considered "modern." They had such a decisive effect on the development of Western music—and particularly on the composers who came just after them—that their startling technical innovations of polytonality, atonality, and complex rhythms have ever since been regarded by the layman as the marks of "modern music."

In America (where, of course, Charles Ives had already independently hit upon these technical innovations) the champions of the new European music during the 1910s were a very small and unorganized group largely confined to New York City. But in the next decade these champions—composers, performers, wealthy patrons, and audience—increased in number, came together, and achieved that degree of organization necessary to secure for "contemporary music" a place in American cultural life.

A crucial element in the formation of this American musical avant-garde was the organization of composers' groups. The International Composers' Guild (1921) and the League of Composers (1923) were formed for the purpose of bringing the new music to America. Even certain conductors of established orchestras, particularly Leopold Stokowski of the Philadelphia Orchestra and Serge Koussevitzky of the Boston Symphony Orchestra, were in contact with the avant-garde and had the courage to place the work of modernists before their startled subscribers. But most important of all was the appearance in the 1920s of the first truly original crop of native American composers.

These young composers apparently found an identity not so much in a sense of their own special "Americanness" as in a feeling that they were rejecting the previous tendencies in American classical music and breaking new paths. A number of them, such as Aaron Copland and Virgil Thomson, studied composition in the 1920s with Nadia Boulanger in France, and they absorbed there an enthusiasm for the new European approaches to music. Thus their work hurled a challenge at the conservative and generally Germanic tendencies of previous American composition. And their more Bohemian approach to the role of the American composer and musician[2] formed a contrast to the gentility of Horatio Parker, Walter Damrosch, and the other men who had dominated American music down to 1920; Aaron Copland, for example, did not teach at one of the respectable academic institutions in the 1920s, but instead depended for his income on a fellowship from the newly established Guggenheim Foundation and on lectures that he gave at the politically radical New

School for Social Research.[3] Yet the search for an *American* identity was not really lacking in these young men. According to Copland, he and the others wanted to write "music with a largeness of utterance wholly representative of the country that Whitman had envisaged." [4] Like George Gershwin, Copland incorporated into his compositions elements of jazz and American popular dance music.

Here, then, was a growing avant-garde that might well have been receptive to Charles Ives's work. If Ives had been capable of making a realistic survey of the American musical audience in the early 1920s, he would have understood that the great majority of Americans had no meaningful contact with, or interest in, classical music. Furthermore, the minority of Americans (the "musical public") which *did* patronize serious music—ranging from those who were interested only in the personalities of the performing artists to those who were actually familiar with Bach, Beethoven, and Brahms—was almost uniformly hostile or indifferent to modern music. It was the overwhelmingly conservative taste of this musical public that circumscribed the activities of America's musical institutions, such as symphony orchestras, opera companies, conservatories, and music publishing houses. On a different plane from the vast majority of this musical public, however, was a comparatively tiny avant-garde, led by a few composers and professional musicians and supported by a small number of interested amateurs. It was to this musical avant-garde, knowledgeable about contemporary compositions and anxious to encourage them, that composers like Ives had to look if they wanted an audience.[5]

Yet Ives was reluctant to approach this avant-garde. His hesitation arose partly from his shyness, from his merely amateur status as a musician, and from his belief that composers should not promote their own music. But he drew back mainly because of his commitment to certain values that would not allow him to make a realistic analysis of the American musical audience or to accept the cultural changes that were occurring in America.

On the one hand, Ives's belief in democratic majoritarianism rendered him hostile to the notion that an organized avant-garde would be the means of bringing pioneering music into the cultural mainstream. Ives was always opposed to organization of any kind; and the concept of a self-consciously separate avant-garde, alienated from the taste of the mass of Americans, would have seemed undemocratic and snobbish to him. Ives *did* reject the large concertgoing public, dominated as it was by "old ladies of both sexes"; but he rejected it not in the name of an avant-garde, but in the name of the masses, who would be open-minded enough to give experimental music a fair hearing if only they could gain access to it.

On the other hand, the growing avant-garde threatened Ives's gentility in the 1920s even more than it threatened his majoritarianism. Much of his dissatisfaction with American life in that decade arose from his feeling that the new mass culture was throwing off the genteel restraints of the past. Even his alienation from his Yale friends reflected not only his political and social radicalism, but also his belief that these men too had cast off traditional moral restraints and thrown in their lot with the hedonism and materialism of the age. Although Ives denounced the institutions of the new popular culture (tabloids, movies, and the radio) for their effeminacy and commercialized standardization,[6] he must also have been disturbed by their emphasis on sex and what he regarded as immorality.[7] As early as the writing of *Essays before a Sonata,* in condemning the proposition that "ragtime is the true American music," he revealed his foreboding about the new culture of the city that was to flower in the 1920s. Combining his gentility with his tendency to place art on a pedestal, high above the mundane and trivial, Ives greeted this extraordinarily rich decade in American culture with a rhetorical question: "Is it better to sing inadequately of the 'leaf on Walden floating,' and die 'dead but not dishonored,' or to sing adequately of the 'cherry on the cocktail,' and live forever?"[8]

It was inevitable that the new avant-garde in American music, as in all the arts, should be influenced by the mass-consumption culture of the 1920s, with its jazziness and its freedom from older proprieties. Advanced thinkers and artists condemned the domination of America by big business and the almighty dollar, but they could not help being influenced by the cultural products of that domination. In terms of Ives's categories of thought, the 1920s were the first time when Bohemianism posed a greater threat than effeminacy to American music and other arts, the era when a new generation of creative artists openly thumbed their noses at the genteel tradition in American society and culture. Perhaps Ives vaguely foresaw the growth of such an avant-garde when, in his *Essays before a Sonata,* he deprecated "these wrong choices, these under-values with their prizes, Bohemias and heroes." [9] It is not surprising, then, that he paid little attention to the progress of experimental music in America during the 1920s.

Because of his basic commitments and values, the very notions of an organization of avant-garde composers or of a concert of classical music given in a Greenwich Village theater were foreign to Ives. When he thought of the institutional channels for cultivated-tradition music, his mind ran naturally to the New York Philharmonic and to Carnegie Hall, in spite of (or perhaps *because of*) the delight that he took in railing against them. Thus he had no connection with the two important groups of avant-garde composers that were formed in the early 1920s, the International Composers' Guild and the League of Composers, even though the Guild offered to consider giving performances of any works by unknown composers that were brought to it. [10]

It was especially unfortunate that throughout the 1920s Ives's music remained hidden from the generation of young American composers who appeared on the musical scene in that decade. The principal figure among these new men, Aaron Copland, has described how they were searching for "a usable past" among the composers of the preceding generation, "a music that would speak of universal things in a vernacular of American speech rhythms." But they found nothing of this kind and concluded that "we were on our own": "Through a curious quirk of musical history the man who was writing such a music—a music that came close to approximating our needs—was entirely unknown to us." [11]

Ives's reaction to the new musical tendencies of the twenties was a continuation of his previous attitudes. He did not like the current system that existed to promulgate fine-art music in America, for he rightly felt that it made of music an innocuous plaything of the rich and fashionable. But his cultural commitments prevented him from tracing this problem back to the general defects in American society and American values, defects which were the root cause of the anomalous position of the arts in the United States. He would not, therefore, join the avant-garde rebellion against the existing system of disseminating music. Instead, he did what he had done before: he retreated from the existing system back into his own private musical world, where he could keep his anachronistic values pure.

Ives was not willing to become an active member of a composers' organization in which he would have been one among a number of equals. Such an organization would have required him to respond to others' interest in his compositions with a reciprocal interest in many different styles of music and (by natural extension) in many different personal approaches to the role of the artist in society. He was not prepared to expose his own values and style of life to such a threatening atmosphere. Of course he desired recognition. But he demanded not only that his music be accepted on *its* own terms, but that the man and composer Charles Ives be accepted on *his* own terms. Those who were interested would have to come to him and meet him on his own ground (which usually meant literally his own home or office), where he could be in complete control of the situation.

Since he distrusted the avant-garde as an organization, Ives could only make contact with it through certain of its individual members. These people would have to mediate between Ives and the organization. While shielding Ives from direct contact with avant-garde groups, they would pass along his compositions to these groups for performance, meanwhile assuring him that it was not improper for him to make use of such means. In judging both the individual and the group, however, Ives was incapable of limiting himself to objective and professional musical criteria. These mediators would first have to be *personally* acceptable to him—they would have to meet his standards of gentility and masculinity—or they would never be able to form a musical relationship with him.

It was through just such a process of individual contacts with members of the avant-garde that Ives achieved his musical recognition. He met the first of his musical champions, Henry Bellamann and Clifton Furness, through his distribution by mail of the *Concord Sonata* and *114 Songs* in the early 1920s. These two men actually had little immediate effect upon Ives's reputation, but they are important because they reveal the qualities that a person had to have in order to become Charles Ives's musical friend.

When Henry Bellamann received his copy of the *Concord* Sonata in 1921, he was serving as dean of the College of Fine Arts at Chicora College for Women in Columbia, South Carolina. Although languishing in this cultural desert, Bellamann was actually a highly sophisticated and learned man with a broad knowledge of the arts, particularly the contemporary arts. Best known as an exponent of modern piano music, he was also a poet; and he had connections with both the American artistic avant-garde and the respectable academic world.

Although he had never before heard of Ives, Bellamann was immediately impressed by the *Concord* Sonata. "An extraordinary work," he wrote to Ives. "One feels very happy to know that a creation of such calibre on an American subject may be done in America." [12] Ives, of course, was deeply gratified by Bellamann's interest; and he approved Bellamann's proposal to include the sonata in his coming series of lecture-recitals. Ives revealed his eagerness to have the work performed when he told Bellamann to "feel free to make any changes or revisions which meet your best judgment." Admitting that the first two movements "will arouse little enthusiasm with most audiences," he suggested that only selected parts of them be presented; "but it is not so difficult to make the 'Alcott' and 'Thoreau' acceptable to the average audience." It is clear that Ives was so happy to have found his first musical champion that he could for once be realistic and bend his high artistic standards a bit. He even offered to pay to have the lecture-recital given in New York City. [13]

Bellamann planned to give his lecture-recital in several southern cities, and at least two of these lectures came off. The sonata was first presented in Columbia, South Carolina, toward the end of 1921; then the large Atlanta Music Club heard it on January 4, 1922. Only portions of the sonata were given at these lecture-recitals; and the performances were not by Bellamann himself, but by Lenore Purcell, his assistant. Ironically, then, it was audiences made up of "the ladies" who first heard the *Concord* Sonata. [14]

Bellamann also wrote a lengthy critical review of the sonata, which appeared in the *Double Dealer,* an important avant-garde magazine of the arts published in New Orleans. Discussing the work in a frank manner, he was on the whole favorable to it. He had an almost uncanny feeling for the "substance" that Ives was trying to express in the music. Of the *Emerson* movement, for example, he wrote that its beauty "is a beauty of high and remote things. It is austere. It is informed with the stark and ascetic beauty of lonely and alien reaches of human imagination." [15] Bellamann was also in complete agreement with Ives about "American" music. Both rejected the local-color approach to national music, by which idiomatic elements (such as Negro or Indian harmonies, melodies, or rhythms) were introduced into a musical texture that was culturally alien to them. Both felt that a national music must arise *totally*—in spirit and ideals, not just in superficial characteristics—from "some mode of thought or manner of living essentially and exclusively American"; it would then be not only national, but also universal, in significance—as all music must be. Bellamann implied that the *Concord* Sonata was such music.[16] He concluded of the sonata that "one arises from a reading of it with much, much more of satisfaction than dissatisfaction. Its loftiness of purpose is evident; its moments of achievement elevating and greatly beautiful." [17] It is ironic that Ives read this review—practically the first sympathetic and understanding criticism from a musically knowledgeable person that he had received for more than twenty years—at a time when he had just finished his last spurt of creative activity (the songs composed in 1921). He was to compose very little thereafter.

These activities of 1921 and 1922 were Bellamann's principal efforts on behalf of Ives's music. He continued to write and talk about Ives, but it appears that what he did in the early twenties did not enlarge Ives's musical reputation or influence others to take up the cause.[18] Of greater significance was a personal friendship that developed between Bellamann and Ives.

During the 1920s Bellamann and his wife were welcome visitors at the Iveses' home in West Redding. Ives sent Bellamann's poems to Professor Phelps of Yale; [19] and he attempted to interest an old Yale friend who was an executive at Harper & Brothers in publishing them.[20] Mrs. Bellamann mastered and sang some of Ives's songs; [21] Ives, in turn, contributed several hundred dollars to a charity which she recommended to him.[22] After Bellamann moved to New York City in 1924, the two families had more opportunities to see each other. And when the Iveses were in Europe for more than a year in 1932 and 1933, they allowed the impoverished Bellamanns to live in their New York house.[23]

One thing that Ives undoubtedly found attractive in the Bellamanns was their devotion to each other. Their marriage seems to have been, like the Iveses' own, a combination of old-fashioned romance and mutual improvement—with an added element of practical collaboration.[24] Ives could thus idealize their marriage as he idealized his own. The Iveses must also have enjoyed sharing with the Bellamanns an atmosphere of genteel culture—an atmosphere in which the interest in the arts and humanities was too earnest to be effeminately dilettantish and too well-bred to be exuberantly strident. Ives found such an atmosphere satisfying, for it gave him a sense of participating in high culture while avoiding extremes that would have been threatening and distasteful to him. And Bellamann, after all, was an eminently respectable writer and lecturer on music who became chairman of the examining board of the Juilliard Musical Foundation and dean of the Curtis Institute of Music; he was quite at home in the conventional world of the arts.

But there was another side to Bellamann, a side reflected in the poems that he published in avant-garde magazines and in his interest in the new psychology. It must have been very difficult for him to avoid condescension toward Ives when their cultural dialogue entered nonmusical realms in which his knowledge was considerably greater than Ives's and his tastes correspondingly more advanced. Ives's songs *Yellow Leaves* and *Peaks* are settings of two of Bellamann's more "proper" poems; but Ives must have had reservations about the style, the sensual images, and the general aestheticism of some of Bellamann's more "modern" verse.[25] Ives apparently complained about this aspect of Bellamann's work to his friend Furness, for Furness wrote back: "If Bellamann was able to sense this [the essential drive back of all of Ives's work] and, what is infinitely more difficult, to a certain extent define it, I am sure he gives evidence of a very penetrating and aggressive, masculine perception, *even tho he may run, as you suggest, toward the effeminate in his own work.*" [26] Here, as elsewhere, Ives had pinned the label of effeminacy upon what was really a threat to the genteel tradition in the arts.[27]

Bellamann, however, was not really close to the principal figures in the new musical avant-garde, such as Edgard Varèse and Aaron Copland, and thus he was not in a position to introduce Ives's music to those who could secure a hearing for it. Bellamann did write further about Ives in the 1920s and early 1930s; [28] and in 1933, after Ives had secured a following among the avant-garde, Bellamann contributed an article about him to the highly respected *Musical Quarterly*.[29] This article had the important effect of enlarging Ives's reputation by placing his name before a wide audience of professional and amateur musicians with generally conservative tastes. On the other hand, Bellamann probably did not see Ives as "the great American composer," as he revealed in an article on American music that he published in 1934: "How good is American music? . . . Have we produced a composer who is as good in his field as Poe or Whitman or Emerson or Hawthorne in the literary field? Apparently not. We have no composer who is as good a composer as Albert Ryder was a painter." [30]

The Iveses and the Bellamanns seem to have drifted apart after 1933. Bellamann gave up the profession of music in order to devote his time wholly to writing. Ives had once chosen to believe that Bellamann was a high-minded artist who found the business side of his art distasteful.[31] In fact, however, Bellamann gradually gave up writing poetry and turned to the more commercially viable novel form; and with his novel *Kings Row* (1940), he finally achieved fame and success. *Kings Row* frankly revealed the darker side of small-town life. With its large cast of characters driven by such motives as incest, homosexuality, and sadism, the novel became a best seller and was later made into a movie. It is doubtful that the Iveses read it.

There were several significant similarities between Bellamann and Clifton Joseph Furness, whose friendship Ives also acquired in the early 1920s. Both men were academics. Both divided their professional lives (and their personal interests) between literature and music. Both stood midway between the avant-garde and the genteel world of the arts. They were close enough to the avant-garde to be able to appreciate it, and thus to appreciate Ives's music, but they were too far away from it to pose a threat to Ives's values—or to be able to do much for his music. Both gave Ives a comfortable sense of being able to share with others the appreciation of high culture, while they only occasionally alarmed him with a too exuberant enthusiasm for the modern. These similarities between the two men are indicative of what Ives was looking for in a musical friend in the early 1920s.

When Clifton Furness received his copy of the *Concord* Sonata in the spring of 1921, he was twenty-three years old and about to receive his A.B. degree from Northwestern University. Immediately impressed by the sonata, Furness introduced it into music courses that he was teaching at Northwestern; and on August 3, 1921, he played *The Alcotts* at a lecture-recital.[32] He wrote to Ives about these activities, and a correspondence ensued between the two men.

Furness's letters suggest that he was a very repressed young man who sought to sublimate his impulses through the pursuit of art on a high spiritual plane and through intellectual and spiritual relationships with others. He was bursting with ideas, opinions, and feelings that he wanted to share with a kindred spirit. In Ives's music and in the *Essays before a Sonata,* Furness thought he detected a soul mate. Without knowing anything about Ives—even how old he was—Furness signed his first letter to him, "Your sincere fellow-seeker in the Quest."[33] In his second letter, he gushed that the *Essays* "aroused so many thrills of intellectual comradeship that I am still vibrating" with them. "You don't mind," he asked, "my rambling attempts to get across to you something of my reaching toward you?" And he sent along to Ives a fragment of autobiography.[34] Ives was pleased by the younger man's interest, but he found his self-revelation a bit embarrassing. Commending the autobiography for "a strong kind of frankness," he added: "Perhaps, if it were more suffused with 'A Reticence Which Kindleth Imagination,' as some Victorian has said (I forget who), it might gain in some ways."[35]

In 1922 Furness secured, with Ives's help, a position as teacher of English and music at the Horace Mann School for Boys in New York

City. Once settled in the East, he became a frequent visitor at the Iveses' home during the 1920s. The close "intellectual comradeship" of the two men was based on far more than Furness's interest in Ives's music. Ives probably had deeper and lengthier discussions of philosophy and aesthetics with Furness than with anyone else whom he encountered during his adult life. Furness later recalled with pleasure "our high bold talk and music-making" [36] and "those hours . . . when we snatched thoughts in-the-making out of clear brains over the breakfast coffee." [37]

There were two great sources of inspiration for Ives's music: transcendentalist philosophy and the religiodemocratic life of a New England town. Furness, like Bellamann, was relatively indifferent to the latter,[38] but keenly appreciative of the former. He fully agreed with Ives's Platonic notion that the underlying "substance" of music (what Furness called the "Archetype idea" [39]) was the important part of it, and that the formal or technical working out of this idea was relatively unimportant. Thus Furness justified program music only when (as in Ives's works) the "subject portrayed in the music" served as a "mystic symbol" of higher spiritual values; but he felt that an extramusical program was unjustified if the composition was merely a realistic picture of something "sensuous." [40] It was the "Big Things" [41]—innate ideas, the role of the spiritual in music—that the two men talked about and agreed upon when they were together.[42]

But Furness—again, like Bellamann—was willing to pursue the arts far beyond the limits of Ives's comprehension or tolerance. In New York City the young man attached himself to the fringes of several avant-garde groups, such as the Provincetown Players and the Russian artistic figures in exile.[43] In particular, Furness was interested in primitivism in the contemporary arts, for in the primitive he found the ecstasy of direct contact with the mysterious and the elemental.[44] But the unrestrained passion and sensuousness of primitivism were naturally threatening to Ives. When a critic suggested in the 1940s that his orchestral piece *Thanksgiving* was "dithyrambic," Ives was distressed and wrote that the music was "hardly 'Dithyrambic' nor anything of a reflection of the wild sallies of a band of revellers for Bacchus." [45]

Closely related to Furness's interest in primitivism was his unbounded admiration for Walt Whitman. Furness's transcendentalism, unlike Ives's, did not prevent him from reveling in Whitman's sensuous and lusty verse; in fact, Furness became the leading scholarly authority on Whitman. In his second letter to Ives, who was then still a stranger to him, he wrote: "At random—where do you line up with Walt Whitman? I can pretty well judge from certain implications in your writing, but nothing for or against him would vitally affect our relation." [46] Ives replied cautiously that he thought Whitman's work might be too wrapped up in his own personality; and he passed along Mrs. Ives's judgment on Whitman: "She doesn't like the over-human leer in his face." [47] Furness remarked to Ives that "to me he [Whitman] seems more god, to you more man." [48] And years later Furness recalled that "one of our few differences of opinion" had been "about Whitman and my thesis on him at Harvard." [49]

In spite of occasional differences on emotional and aesthetic grounds, however, the two friends always held a philosophical and moral idealism in common—though Ives, who was a bit suspicious of the occult, could not follow Furness in his pursuit of the mystical cult of anthroposophy. Furness knew how to overcome their differences in age and temperament. Although he sometimes introduced Ives to recent developments in the arts,[50] he generally centered their relationship around the art that they loved in common. It is unlikely that Furness consciously condescended to Ives in their conversations. On the contrary, he seems to have derived genuine inspiration from the friendship; and his own thinking about art undoubtedly reflected Ives's aesthetic philosophy.

Furness admired Ives's music (though he offered frank criticisms of it), and he continued to talk about it and play it informally for others. (He even played part of the *Concord* Sonata for the inmates of a girls' reformatory! [51]) He undoubtedly regarded Ives as a great creative figure in American music.[52] But Furness had many enthusiasms, of which Ives's music was only one. In his letters to Ives, he preferred to share these enthusiasms with Ives as an equal, rather than to treat him as a great composer whose compositions were worthy of special attention. Furthermore, like many American figures in the arts during the 1920s, Furness had little interest in a specifically *American* culture. Thus he devoted relatively little energy to promoting the cause of Ives's music.

Furness, a lifelong bachelor, had no wife to bring into his relationship with the Iveses; but he did introduce them to his quite genteel parents, who visited frequently at West Redding during the 1920s and 1930s. Furness's father was a bumbling but well-meaning idealist whose great ambition was to teach the "correlation between growing things and spiritual truth." [53] Ives took to him immediately. Later, when Ives's music had been "discovered," it was suggestive of his whole relationship to American culture that he gave his friendship to Furness's father while keeping at a distance some of America's leading creative artists; the latter threatened his values and style of life, while the former did not. Furness and his father were also not above borrowing money from Ives. Over a period of years, he loaned them several hundred dollars.[54] He was to show a similar generosity toward many of his new musical friends.

It was through Clifton Furness that Ives met two other musicians who were interested in contemporary music. One was Elliott Carter, who was then a mere student of Furness's at the Horace Mann School for Boys, but who later became one of America's most distinguished composers. During the middle twenties, Ives befriended the musically precocious boy and took him to some of the New York concerts given by the Boston Symphony Orchestra, to which the Iveses were subscribers. Carter has recalled that after the concerts, he and Ives would discuss the contemporary works that they had heard; Ives would persistently condemn the composer in question, such as Ravel, for taking refuge in only one chord or one musical device.[55] (Although Ives apparently did attend some symphony concerts in the middle 1920s, he claimed in the early 1930s that he had heard nothing by Schoenberg or Hindemith and only two works by Stravinsky: the *Firebird* Suite and *Le Chant du rossignol.*[56]) The last time Carter had any real personal relationship with Ives was when he was an undergraduate at Harvard in the late 1920s; [57] but later, after he had made his own mark as a musician, he played an important role in the career of Ives's music, both as critic and as champion.

It was apparently also through Furness that Ives was introduced to Katherine Heyman, a pianist whose career was dedicated to performing the music of the mystical Russian composer Alexander Scriabin. She held a sort of salon at her New York apartment, and Ives was occasionally a guest there during the 1920s. Miss Heyman mastered parts of the *Concord* Sonata and sometimes played them on these afternoons.[58] Since she and the members of her circle (such as Furness) were deeply involved in theosophy and the mystical element in music, they naturally admired Ives's transcendental compositions.[59] Whether he felt comfortable with their theosophical mystifications is more doubtful, although Ives did become a patron of Miss Heyman's Scriabin activities.[60] But in any case, the Heyman group was pursuing its own special concerns and was far from being in the front ranks of the musical avant-garde.

In 1927 Furness left New York City to do graduate work in English at Harvard. From 1930 on, he was supervisor of academic studies at the staid New England Conservatory of Music in Boston. Year after year he told Ives that his biography of Whitman was nearing completion and that he was looking for a publisher; but when he died, the huge manuscript was still chaotic and unfinished.[61]

Furness always stood too much on the fringes of the musical world to be able to do much for the cause of Ives's music. His greatest help to Ives was the encouragement that he gave him when others were rejecting his compositions. Furness remained on close terms with the Iveses until his death in 1946. That his relation to Ives was principally a personal one is suggested in something that he wrote to the Iveses in 1938: "If there is anything I can do, ever, for either of you, that a son could do, I would like to do it."[62]

There were a few other musical figures who took some interest in Ives's work during the early and middle 1920s, chiefly through seeing or receiving copies of his books of music. The violinist Jerome Goldstein, for example, played the Second Violin Sonata at a modernist recital (given at eleven o'clock on a Tuesday morning!) in New York City in 1924.[63] One critic, Winthrop P. Tryon, of the *Christian Science Monitor,* discussed this violin sonata with amazing understanding in his review, concentrating on Ives's background and the cultural influences that had acted upon him; and Tryon was to continue to write sympathetically about Ives's compositions.[64] Such scattered efforts, however, failed to generate any permanent interest in Ives's music. It was only when Ives met E. Robert Schmitz that he encountered a man who had both a persistent admiration for his works and the means of securing an audience for them.

Schmitz was a renowned French pianist, a noted interpreter of Debussy's compositions, who had been living and concertizing in America since the end of World War I. In 1920, drawing on the American friendship for France that had arisen during the war, Schmitz founded the Franco-American Musical Society, a federated group of music clubs located in several large American cities. Its purpose was to introduce to American audiences music that was little known to them, particularly contemporary European music, which was preferably to be presented through the medium of the composers themselves. The society was remarkable for its concentration on the Midwest and West, rather than merely on New York City. While recent French music was always emphasized, the purposes of the society broadened with time, and its name was changed to Pro Musica in 1925. Regarding music as a means of overcoming national and cultural barriers and of promoting international understanding, Schmitz set up chapters in Paris (where American music was presented) and Tokyo. Perhaps Pro Musica's greatest service during the 1920s was to present in America a number of important European modernists—Ravel, Prokofiev, Bartók, Milhaud, Respighi, and others—in performances of their own works.

For support of its socially proper concerts, Pro Musica was heavily dependent upon wealthy subscribers who were amateur lovers of music. But Schmitz, as president of the national organization and director of its activities in New York City, saw to it that the music performed in New York was chosen by composers and professional musicians whose taste was not conventional; and he tried to ensure that the same policy would be followed in the other chapters around the country. In these respects, Pro Musica stood somewhere between the frankly avant-garde and composer-controlled International Composers' Guild, on the one hand, and the frankly conservative and patron-controlled Philharmonic Society of New York, on the other.[65]

It is not certain how Ives first came into contact with Schmitz.

Perhaps it was through Bellamann, or perhaps through Ives's sending a copy of the *Concord* Sonata to Schmitz.[66] One story has it that
the meeting occurred by accident when Schmitz came to the offices
of Ives & Myrick to take out an insurance policy.[67] In any case, when
the two men met in the autumn of 1923, Schmitz showed an immediate interest in Ives's compositions, while Ives expressed a desire to
take part in Schmitz's organization.[68] Ives's pleasure at meeting
Schmitz—and his intense sense of musical isolation—are revealed in
his sketch for a letter to Schmitz after their first meeting: "It was a
great pleasure and a help to me to meet you—and interesting to find
a man and a professional musician so interested in such a comprehensive scale and not only in his career. This is not a criticism of the
professional artist, for I've known almost none—that is, personally."
Ives concluded: "You will let me know when I may see you again." [69]

Ives was naturally impressed by Schmitz's enthusiasm for experimental music and by the internationalism of his cultural ideals. He
was elected a director of Schmitz's society in 1925 and also served on
the smaller Executive Committee.[70] He gave vital financial aid to Pro
Musica.[71] At the same time, a personal friendship grew up between
the two men. Schmitz's daughter has recalled that when she and her
parents would visit the Ives family at their home, her father and Ives
would hover over the piano together, playing and discussing Ives's
compositions.[72] Schmitz's letters to Ives, however, suggest that the
two men did not talk about great thoughts and great art, as Ives did
with Furness.

In 1925 Schmitz presented Ives to his society in the role of composer. At that time it was believed by some musical experimenters
that composed music would develop in the direction of quarter
tones. (The interval, or difference in pitch, between any two adjacent keys on a normally tuned piano is called a half tone; a quarter
tone, which is not obtainable on such a piano, is simply one-half of a
half tone.) Ives, whose interest in quarter tones dated back to his
father's influence, had composed a quarter-tone piece about
1913–1914; now, his interest rekindled by his association with
Schmitz's group, he composed two more. Of these three pieces, the
Chorale was given at a lecture by Schmitz in New York City in February, 1925; [73] and a few days later, the Chorale and the Allegro

were played at a New York concert of the Franco-American Musical Society.[74] These performances were given on two specially tuned pianos. Ives even contributed a theoretical article on quarter tones to the *Franco-American Musical Society Quarterly Bulletin.*[75]

Quarter-tone experiments would inevitably seem mere novelties to the audiences and critics at Schmitz's concerts. But Schmitz also made possible one of the great milestones in the career of Ives's music—the first really public performance of one of his works for full orchestra. Pro Musica had larger financial resources than the avant-garde organization with which Ives was later to be associated; as a result, it could hire a moderately large orchestra in New York City. At a Pro Musica concert held in Town Hall on January 29, 1927, Schmitz presented the first two movements of Ives's Fourth Symphony, his most mature and advanced orchestral work and the one of which he was proudest. The conductor Eugene Goossens led fifty players from the New York Philharmonic through the two movements, Schmitz himself playing one of the piano parts.[76] It was Ives's fantastic and devilishly difficult second movement—with its clashing harmonies, intricate cross rhythms, and quarter-tone chords—that was bound to challenge the attention of the listeners; moreover, the reputation of Pro Musica, the scale of the concert, and the nature of the audience ensured that the program would be reviewed by the leading New York critics.

For some of them the cacophony was too much to be borne. "Pro-Musica or Anti?" asked Pitts Sanborn, critic for the *New York Telegram;* he referred to Schmitz and his colleagues as "the pianists implicated" in the Ives performance.[77] In a similar vein, Ives's old bête noire the *Musical Courier* once again attacked him in an editorial. The anonymous writer called "Mr. Ives' dreadful symphony" a "desperate effort . . . to be American." The composer "lacked both talent and technic to accomplish his aims." A truly American music, the editorial concluded, must use the national idiom; but it must certainly *not* do so by quoting hymns and folk tunes.[78]

On the other hand, Robert A. Simon, of the *New Yorker,* while finding the music "rather too peculiar" and fearing that "so much eccentricity is likely to degenerate into mannerism," nevertheless expressed a desire to hear more Ives: "He seems to be thumbing his nose most of the time, but, after all, it is his own nose." [79] Even the venerable W. J. Henderson, of the *Sun,* wrote that "at first hearing it [the symphony] seems to possess strong individuality." [80] And Olga Samaroff, writing in the *New York Evening Post,* found these merits in the work: "sincerity—freshness of musical utterance (it was written before many of its devices became modern conventions); no significance likely to be lasting but decided interest as a milestone in national development." [81]

The two most positive reviews, however, came from the two men who were soon to become (if they were not already) the most influential of the New York music critics: Olin Downes, of the *New York Times,* and Lawrence Gilman, of the *New York Herald Tribune.* [82] In spite of its "ineptitudes" and "incongruities," Downes preferred the Ives symphony to an opera by Milhaud that was heard on the same program: "It rings truer, it seems to have something more genuine behind it." He felt that "there is something in this music; real vitality, real naivete and a superb self-respect." Ives "looses his rhythms," wrote Downes, with "a 'gumption,' as the New Englander would say, not derived from some 'Sacre du printemps,' or from anything but the conviction of a composer who has not the slightest idea of self-ridicule and who dares to jump with feet and hands and a reckless somersault or two on his way to his destination." [83]

Equally full of insight and even more favorable was Lawrence Gilman's review. Gilman was not surprised that Ives had used " 'modernistic' devices a good many years ago," for "his writing in this symphony has a sureness of touch which is not that of a neophyte learning an unfamiliar technique." "This music," Gilman felt, "is as indubitably American in impulse and spiritual texture as the prose of Jonathan Edwards; and, like the writing of that true artist and true mystic, it has at times an irresistible veracity and strength, an uncorrupted sincerity." The symphony, he noted, was "evidently built upon a far-reaching spiritual plan. It has, as Emerson said of Whitman, a long foreground. We repeat that we should like to hear the entire score." [84]

Here, then, was the first opportunity for a serious audience to hear one of Ives's major orchestral works—and the best of the critics liked it! But hardly anything came of these favorable reviews. Gilman and Downes were busy men who generally attended only the musical performances of leading artists and prominently sponsored organizations; and Ives lacked both the institutional resources and the personal temperament to bring more of his music to their attention. A decade later, the composer Wallingford Riegger wrote to Ives about a talk that Olin Downes had recently given before the Professional Musicians' Club: "When it was over, we brought up your name. He [Downes] has not heard or seen a single work of yours! He all but beat his breast and is very anxious to make amends." [85] Gilman, too, took no further notice of Ives's compositions until 1939. Perhaps, after all, Ives was not yet ready to make contact with the musical public and with the critics who served it. Perhaps it was first necessary for him to find champions among the avant-garde.

After the Town Hall concert, the *Pro-Musica Quarterly* carried an article by Henry Bellamann on Ives's music.[86] Pro Musica also presented one more work by Ives in New York City. It was played by the pianist Anton Rovinsky, an avid performer of experimental music, who had discovered Ives when a friend had given him a copy of the *Concord* Sonata.[87] Rovinsky had made contact with Ives, and at a Pro Musica concert at Town Hall on November 14, 1928, he played *The Celestial Railroad*, Ives's piano fantasy that bore the name of Hawthorne's famous story.[88] The piece occupied only a small place on the program, and it attracted little attention. It was actually a piano arrangement from portions of the second movement of the Fourth Symphony, the very movement that had been performed at the previous Town Hall concert. (Both works were ultimately derived from the *Hawthorne* movement of the *Concord* Sonata.) This time, however, W. J. Henderson was unfavorable: "What it had to do with Hawthorne could only be conjectured. It certainly had more than seven gables anyhow." [89] Pitts Sanborn called it "an interminable noise." [90]

It was remarkable that E. Robert Schmitz, a Frenchman, should have been among the first to recognize the importance of Ives's music, which is so American in character. Yet a question naturally suggests itself. Why did Schmitz not do more for Ives's music from 1923 to 1929? One reason was that Schmitz, both as a well-known concert pianist and as president of Pro Musica, could not afford to become too closely identified with outlandish music; the nature of his audiences set limits on how far he could go.[91] It is also true that Pro Musica was mainly concerned with presenting unfamiliar *European* music—not *American* music—to American audiences; nor was it exclusively concerned with *contemporary* music. But there may have been yet another reason. Years later, one of Ives's younger champions wrote to Mrs. Ives: "Somehow one gets in the habit of expecting givers to be otherwise useless people and when such a one as your husband with his great talent and achievements and his great warm nature, comes along it is hard to reconcile the generosity with the man." [92] Perhaps this was just the trouble: that in Schmitz's mind (as perhaps also in Katherine Heyman's), Ives's role as wealthy patron tended to overshadow his role as great composer.

Schmitz himself lent some support to this hypothesis. In 1926, when he and Ives were interested in having a special quarter-tone piano constructed for Pro Musica's use, Schmitz wrote to Henry Mason, president of the Mason & Hamlin Company, suggesting that this piano firm undertake the job. He noted that "one of our directors and a personal friend, Mr. Charles Ives of Ives and Merrick [*sic*], 46 Cedar Street, New York, is disposed to give a certain sum of money representing a part of the expenses for construction." He then continued significantly: "Mr. Ives is a business man but has been a steady friend of our Society." [93] He did not mention that Ives was a musician. Additional evidence of Schmitz's viewpoint lies in the fact that while he had Ives elected to the Board of Directors of Pro Musica, where Ives sat with other wealthy society people, Schmitz never placed him on the International Advisory Board or the Central Technical Board, both of which contained only composers and other musicians.[94] Again, the Paris chapter of Pro Musica presented a number of works by American composers, but Ives was apparently not among them.[95]

Although Ives was a director of Pro Musica, he was remarkably isolated from the musical life of that organization; he seems to have dealt with it almost entirely through his personal friendship with Schmitz. Of the many renowned European composers whom Pro Musica brought to New York City, Ives apparently met only Darius

Danbury: Chapel Place viewed from Main Street, 1892. On the left, the house in which Charles Ives was born. Behind it, the house in which he and his family lived from 1889. On the right, the First Congregational Church. *Photograph from the John Herrick Jackson Music*

George E. Ives in his bandmaster's uniform, about 1890.
Photograph from the John Herrick Jackson Music Library, Yale University

Charles E. Ives at about the age of fourteen. *Photograph from the John Herrick Jackson Music Library, Yale University*

Charles and Harmony Ives on their wedding day, June, 1908 (an enlargement of a portion of a group wedding picture). *Photograph from the John Herrick Jackson Music Library, Yale University*

Charles and Harmony Ives at their West Redding home,
probably in the late 1920s. *Photograph from the John Herrick*
Jackson Music Library, Yale University

A page from Ives's own ink copy of the last movement of
his First Piano Sonata. *Copyright 1954 by Peer International
Corporation. Used by permission*

The Iveses' home in West Redding. *Photograph by Lee Friedlander, courtesy of Columbia Records*

Ives's bulletin board on the door of his music room at West Redding. *Photograph by Lee Friedlander, courtesy of Columbia Records*

Henry Cowell at about the time he first met Ives. *Photograph courtesy of Broadcast Music, Inc.*

Charles Ives in 1947. *Photograph by Frank Gerratana, courtesy of Broadcast Music, Inc.*

Milhaud.[96] Furthermore, some of the leading figures in American contemporary music were closely associated with Pro Musica: Edgard Varèse and Carlos Salzedo (the leaders of the International Composers' Guild), the music critic Paul Rosenfeld, the composer Wallingford Riegger. Salzedo and Rosenfeld actually sat with Ives on the Board of Directors.[97] Yet Ives did not establish musical contact with any of them through Pro Musica; it was only later, when Henry Cowell presented Ives to them as first and foremost a great composer, that all these men participated in the "discovery" of Ives's music. Taken as a whole, then, the evidence suggests that during the years when Schmitz was the principal mediator between Ives and the world of music, other musicians retained the impression that Ives was merely a wealthy businessman who wrote amateurish and highly eccentric compositions.

With the onset of the Great Depression in 1929, Pro Musica's organization in New York City lost many of its wealthy subscribers and soon collapsed. Shifting his base of operations to Hollywood, California, Schmitz kept some of the western chapters going, and these chapters occasionally presented works by Ives in the 1930s. During the course of that decade and the next, however, Schmitz and Ives gradually lost contact with each other. But even before 1929, Ives had found in Henry Cowell a more dedicated and persistent champion of his music.

By late 1927, Ives must have concluded that his seven years of efforts to find an audience for his music had largely failed. Although he did not realize it, the trouble was that he had not found a base of support among the avant-garde—the composers and other musicians who could secure frequent performances of his works and also disseminate information about him throughout the larger musical world. He needed, above all, a mediator with the avant-garde, someone more effective than Bellamann, Furness, or even Schmitz. Without the accident of such a man's happening along, Ives might have continued indefinitely as an obscure amateur composer. But in 1927 he found his mediator in Henry Cowell. Next to Ives's decision to send out his compositions in the early 1920s, his meeting Cowell was the most important event in the history of his musical recognition.

Born in California in 1897, Henry Cowell lacked all but the bare rudiments of formal education in his childhood and early youth. The resultant freedom and sense of self-direction help to explain why, at the age of fifteen, he was already shocking audiences with his piano compositions that contained the device known as the tone cluster—a group of adjacent notes that are played simultaneously (as a single chord) with the fist, the flat of the hand, or the whole forearm. By the middle 1920s, his piano recitals of his own works— which, in addition to employing tone clusters, called for stroking or plucking the piano strings—had earned him an international reputation as the "bad boy" of music. When he made his European debut in 1923, the Leipzig audience rioted.

Like Stravinsky, Cowell obviously possessed a large capacity for self-advertisement; but he also had a scholarly bent and a very large measure of altruism. His remarkable mind, inventive yet also analytical, carried him far beyond the confines of traditional Western music; he was fascinated by both new mechanical instruments and non-Western music systems. Cowell searched constantly for what he called "new musical resources." These resources were new approaches to harmony and rhythm, new instruments—in short, any means for producing new sounds and combinations of sounds and thus for expanding the expressive capacities of music.

Early in his career Cowell began to devote much of his enormous energy to promoting the compositions of other innovative composers. In 1925 he founded the New Music Society of California for the purpose of giving concerts of experimental works. Two years later, with his society firmly based in San Francisco, Cowell began publishing the quarterly *New Music*. This unique periodical was devoted entirely to the printing of the actual scores of contemporary compositions, particularly those by Americans, beginning with Carl Ruggles's *Men and Mountains* in October, 1927. Commercial publishing houses usually would not touch such scores. For nine years Cowell edited *New Music* without including in it a single composition of his own.

By the winter of 1926–1927, Cowell had heard enough about Ives to want to meet him; [98] but when he attempted, through a mutual friend, to contact him in New York City that winter, Ives was ill and could not see him.[99] Back in California the following summer and trying to launch *New Music,* Cowell wrote to Ives asking him to subscribe. He also asked permission to place Ives's name on his society's advisory board, and he suggested that Ives submit some of his compositions for possible publication.[100] Ives, who must have been very much flattered, took two subscriptions, praised the purposes of the quarterly, and offered his cooperation.[101] This correspondence prepared the way for the first meeting between Ives and Cowell, which took place toward the end of 1927 when Cowell was again in New York City.[102] It was the beginning of a momentous musical collaboration.

When he saw Ives's scores, Cowell immediately recognized them as works of remarkable originality and great creative significance, and he determined to gain for them the public recognition and acceptance that they deserved.[103] Such a purpose could never have been accomplished, however, if Ives had been unwilling to entrust to Cowell his compositions and his reputation. But Ives liked and trusted Henry Cowell from the very beginning. Not only was Cowell altruistic, fearless, and broad-minded in his approach to music, but he was also a person who could be—and was, often—welcomed into the Iveses' home. On the one hand, Cowell was not an obvious "artist"; that is, he was not cursed with the "Byronic fallacy," the tendency to be utterly wrapped up in one's own personality.[104] He was just the opposite: utterly businesslike, efficient, and impersonal in his approach to his own and others' music. On the other hand, Cowell was not so cold-bloodedly "modern" (or, at least, not so impolitic) as to reject those gentler aspects of life that meant so much to Ives. Cowell also had little use for theosophy or transcendentalism, but he was quite capable of getting along with composers who were deeply involved in these philosophies.

Of course, Ives and Cowell were of two entirely different generations and styles of life. In their letters to each other, they rarely discussed philosophy, aesthetics, and the other "Big Things." In a sense, though, they had much in common, musically speaking. Both men believed that American composers must stop being mere imitators of European styles, whether traditional or modern, and must develop their own independent modes of musical expression, built up out of the distinct American experience. Both had worked out their own innovations independently, apart from the influence of European modernists; and both had separately hit upon the tone cluster as a musical device. Both found inspiration in folk or vernacular musical sources, although down to the 1930s Cowell's sources were more Irish than American. Unlike Ives, Cowell did not have an essentially philosophical or religious attitude toward music; but he shared with Ives an eclectic experimentalism that caused him to reject the more formalistic musical styles that occupied Europe in the 1920s. Like Ives, he had a large tolerance for many different kinds of approaches (except the merely conventional) to expressiveness in music. Both men believed that if only it could be heard and known, the good music would ultimately drive out the bad.

Cowell, then, at once took up the role of mediator between Ives and the American musical world. He was able to overcome Ives's suspicions about avant-garde organizations and his scruples about using his personal fortune to promote his own music. Ives soon entrusted to Cowell not only his musical reputation, but also his money. Though always remaining anonymous, he became in effect one of the leading patrons of experimental music in the country. In 1928 he promised to guarantee *New Music* financially,[105] thus making it possible for Cowell to publish scores by leading American modernists right through the Depression. This backing, which increased in amount as the Depression deepened, even allowed *New Music* to branch out into other ventures: a separate series of orchestral works and a series of phonograph records. By the end of 1932, when the Depression was at its worst, Ives was committed to supplying Cowell with $1,500 a year for *New Music* and other purposes; he was also counting on contributing an additional $900 that year to the "surplus account" that he entrusted to Cowell.[106] In 1938, even after Cowell had disappeared from the musical scene and his personal activities had ceased, Ives was still giving *New Music* $1,500 a year, which was the great bulk of its annual income.[107] Finally, Ives was continually providing Cowell with money—often separate from the funds just mentioned—for projects not directly connected with *New Music:* the giving of concerts, scholarships to Cowell's lectures at the New School for Social Research, the purchase of copies of Cowell's book *New Musical Resources* in large quantities.[108] In 1929 Ives gave Cowell a concise summary of the nature of their collaboration: "You give time, physical and mental energy, and I wampum." [109]

The first result of this collaboration was the decision to publish in *New Music* the second movement of Ives's Fourth Symphony, which had been played at the Pro Musica concert in 1927. Ives himself oversaw the engraving of the score in New York and bore the cost of publication.[110] The work occupied the whole issue of January, 1929.[111] It was the first publication of one of Ives's compositions (aside from his private editions) since 1903. The appearance of the score in *New Music* was of some significance, for Cowell's quarterly was distributed in important musical circles; in Europe and other parts of the world, it often came to be relied on as representative of contemporary American composition. On the other hand, very few people are able to read an orchestral score, particularly one as complex as Ives's. The actual *performance* of his works was still a pressing necessity.

Paul Rosenfeld once compared Henry Cowell's disinterested zeal for the promotion of modern music to the devotion of a saint.[112] Brushing aside Ives's nonprofessional status, his personal eccentricities, his financial success in business, and his patronage of others' music, Cowell went directly to the heart of the matter: the intrinsic value of Ives's compositions. It was Ives the serious composer, Ives the great but neglected American pioneer of experimental music, whom Cowell presented to his fellow musicians; naturally, he also helped Ives to think of himself in the same way.

In 1928 Cowell began to write about Ives in journals that were devoted to music, intellectual matters, or the avant-garde, as well as in the articles on music that he contributed to the *Americana Annual*.[113] He emphasized Ives's essential Americanness, pointing out that he had found his inspiration in the "unnotatable differences that create an American idiom in folk-music," the "mistakes" in rhythm and intonation of country fiddlers and hymn-singing congregations. According to Cowell, Ives had developed his remarkable technical innovations out of this idiom of the American "folk." He had been the real pioneer in the use of many ultramodern devices; and yet his music was different from that of the European modernists, for it was distinctively American in both technique and feeling. Cowell called him "the father of originality in American music." [114]

Meanwhile, Cowell continued to concertize extensively at home and abroad. Through his many lectures and recitals (as well as through his articles) he carried Ives's name to cities and towns around the United States, to Latin America, to Europe, and even (in 1929) into the Soviet Union. [115] He also placed Ives's compositions in the hands of performers (such as the violinist Dorothy Minty and the pianists Arthur Hardcastle and Keith Corelli) who actually played them, particularly at concerts of the New Music Society of California. [116] Cowell knew everyone in the musical avant-garde; and within four or five years, largely through his efforts, nearly everyone in the avant-garde knew about Ives. It was Henry Cowell who laid the basis for Ives's present-day musical reputation.

Cowell had an active organization on the West Coast; but in order to lay siege to the musical capital of the country, New York City, he needed a means by which he might give New York performances of the music of Ives and other experimenters. In 1928, with the help of Edgard Varèse, an organization for just that purpose fell into Cowell's lap.

Varèse, a Frenchman who composed ultramodern music full of the sounds of the machine age (including sirens), had come to the United States in 1915 at the age of thirty-two. In 1921, along with his close friend the harpist Carlos Salzedo, Varèse founded the International Composers' Guild; and between 1922 and 1927, this group introduced a large amount of contemporary (chiefly European) music at concerts in New York City. Varèse, however, was tremendously egotistical and tended to dominate any group with which he was associated. In 1923, therefore, the members of the Guild who objected to his way of doing things (and especially to his preference for the most radically experimental of contemporary compositions) broke off and formed the League of Composers, which had much the same goals as the Guild and which also published the important journal *Modern Music*. [117] This split into two avant-garde musical groups in New York City became basic and had lasting repercussions. Aaron Copland later pointed out that all organizations which subsequently promoted new music in the United States down through the early 1930s tended to be allied with either the Guild group or the League group.[118] Pro Musica, for example, had close connections with Varèse and Salzedo.

In November, 1927, Varèse suddenly announced that the active life of the Guild was at an end. Its original purpose, he declared rather optimistically, had been attained: through its concerts, contemporary composers had secured an audience for their works, and the large orchestras were now ready to perform them. Only a few months later, however, Varèse founded the Pan American Association of Composers; it was a similar group, but one whose purpose was limited to securing performances for composers of the Western Hemisphere. In forming it, Varèse was closely associated with Carl Ruggles, the Mexican composer Carlos Chávez, and Henry Cowell.[119] Ives, who had just met Cowell, accepted his invitation to become a composer member.

Hardly had Varèse founded the Pan American Association than he returned to France, remaining there for five years. Cowell soon assumed command of the group, with the titles of Acting President and Director of the North American Section. During the years that he directed its activities, from 1929 to 1933, the Pan American Association became the most important of the organizations performing experimental American compositions, although it suffered an odd neglect. Wallingford Riegger, who served as its treasurer, described the association:

> We had rejected the neo-classicism of a war-weary Paris, and had struck out for ourselves, each in his own way. We formed, of the remains of the International Composers Guild and the Pro-Musica Society, a new organization, the Pan-American Association of Composers (which included Latin-Americans) and gave numerous concerts here and abroad.
>
> It was undoubtedly the most anomalous chapter in American music, or in music anywhere. Here was a group of serious composers, literally making music history and yet without the slightest show of interest on the part of those newspaper pundits who are supposed to keep their readers informed. We gave, at no end of effort and sacrifice, concerts of our own and of Latin-American

works, with a generous sprinkling of works by younger American composers. In justice I must say that once we did obtain a review. It was of a program given at the New School for Social Research, and appeared in the New York *Post,* but unfortunately the day before the concert, which had been postponed at the last minute! [120]

The Pan American Association, obscure though it was, would have expired without financial backing; but the patronage of the wealthy, so abundant in the twenties, dried up when the Depression struck. It was Charles Ives's large but anonymous contributions that allowed Cowell to carry on the extensive activities of the association.[121]

With typical altruism, Henry Cowell energetically took up the cause of four older composers—Ives, Riegger, Carl Ruggles, and John Becker—who lacked the temperament to promote their own compositions. All four composers had rejected the traditional approaches to music that they had been taught and had worked out their own modernism in America independently (for the most part) of the new European trends. Unlike Ives, the other three of these older men had embraced a frankly experimental approach to composition only after World War I; but all four were being neglected in the 1920s, when the musical styles of Paris were in vogue among the younger avant-garde. Cowell brought the four together in the Pan American Association, which performed their works in New York City. At a concert in April, 1930, for example, Cowell programmed three of Ives's short songs in their trumpet-and-piano arrangements.[122] It was a small beginning, but a portent of greater things to come.

While Cowell championed these older friends and encouraged some younger ones, he felt a distinct antipathy for certain of the American composers of his own generation, the generation that came to maturity in the 1920s. A number of these men, such as Aaron Copland, had received their formative musical training in Paris or at the American Conservatory at Fontainebleau; and Cowell was suspicious of the musical trends that came out of France after World War I. It is important to understand Cowell's attitude toward much of the European and American music composed during the 1920s and early 1930s, because his views tended to influence Ives in a vague way, even though Ives knew little of the music in question.

By smashing the old rules of music, the European musical revolution of the 1910s had opened up to the composer a vast range of new technical possibilities. Henry Cowell reveled in these "new musical resources," believing that they expanded the expressive capacity of music, and he approached them in a spirit of free eclectic experimentalism. Edgard Varèse, with whom Cowell was musically allied, also welcomed the new atmosphere of musical freedom and took advantage of it by developing his own remarkable innovations. But certain important European composers were disturbed by the technical chaos that seemed to have been loosed—a technical chaos that was only added to the already existing emotional and aesthetic chaos of nineteenth-century romanticism. After World War I, therefore, these European composers (and their American followers) began to advance various musical styles that emphasized such virtues as order, control, form, and simplicity.

The breakdown of the older harmonic system had resulted in the chaos of atonality, the absence of a central key or tonal center to which the tones of a piece of music are related. Arnold Schoenberg's twelve-tone system, which he developed during the 1920s, imposed upon the freedom of atonality a new principle of harmonic order and control, based upon the composer's own arrangement of the twelve notes of the chromatic scale into a particular tone row. Largely confined to Germany and Austria in the 1920s, the twelve-tone system achieved its full influence in Europe and America only after World War II.

A second tendency of the 1920s was neoclassicism, a movement particularly associated with Igor Stravinsky and centered in Paris. Less specifically concerned with harmony than was Schoenberg's system, neoclassicism put forth a new approach to aesthetic ideals, form, and expressiveness in music. It was clear (as one can see in many of Ives's works) that the adoption of the new technical means in music had not necessarily put an end to some of the more unfortunate expressive features of nineteenth-century romanticism: bombastic self-assertion, sentimentality, intense emotional subjectivity and self-revelation, reliance on literary programs, and general looseness of form. The neoclassicists proposed a return to the artistic ideals (and often to the specific musical forms) of the preromantic era. Music was to be more objective and less personal, more concerned with form and less with content, more abstract and less programmatic, more craftsmanlike and less Byronic. While not rejecting the recent technical innovations, neoclassic composers usually approached them in a manner that was too conservative for Henry Cowell. Neoclassicism was the most influential tendency in Western serious music between the wars. It shaped the work of composers as different as the Spaniard Manuel de Falla and the German Paul Hindemith. In America its influence was felt by many of the younger men, especially by Roger Sessions and Walter Piston.

A third tendency of the post–World War I period, also centering in Paris, aimed at writing works that were designedly unpretentious and that often poked fun at more self-important music. In its reaction against bombastic romanticism, this trend toward simplicity and satire was not unrelated to neoclassicism; it also reflected the widespread disillusionment in Europe after World War I and the influence of the Dada movement. Erik Satie, the French composer of *Three Pieces in the Shape of a Pear,* was the father of this musical tradition, which was carried on by his disciples known as *Les Six.* Satie's principal American follower was Virgil Thomson; among Thomson's often amusing compositions were several with texts by his friend Gertrude Stein.

Of these three tendencies, Henry Cowell simply rejected the first, was irked by the second, and found the third especially offensive. Among a number of the younger American composers of the late 1920s and early 1930s—including those, like Copland, who had achieved a certain success—Cowell found too much of a tendency to be corrupted by neoclassicism and French training, or to treat music as a mere superficial amusement, or to use the jazz devices that were then so much in vogue among the European and American avant-garde. He felt that Americans (like Copland) who were influenced by European modernists were scarcely more original—that is, more indigenously American—than Americans (like Deems Taylor) who were influenced by traditional European composers. Cowell inevitably contrasted many of the American modernists unfavorably with Charles Ives, who had remained in America and developed a distinctive style based on music from his own racial and cultural background—or with Carl Ruggles, who did not use hymn-tune and folk-tune material, but who had also built up his own style in America without dependence on European influences. Cowell stated the contrast bluntly:

> The real division among the modern American composers now, a sharp one, is between those who regard music as something for the purpose of amusement, and those who regard it as a medium for expressing greater depths of feeling. The former group, that work together closely, is composed of men who have studied for the most part in Paris, and have become distinctly influenced by certain modern French philosophical trends. The latter group are for the most part made up of men who have studied in America, and who, although often cruder in technique than the others, are building up a style distinctly rooted in the feelings and traditions of this country.[123]

The charge of clever superficiality that Cowell made against this American music of French derivation was very similar to the charge of "softness" that Ives leveled at Gertrude Stein's modern poetry a few years later.[124] The two men agreed that art could and should express "greater depths of feeling."

The League of Composers proved considerably more hospitable than Cowell's group to American compositions of French or neoclassic tendency. Aaron Copland, in fact, was the most important composer in the League, which inevitably became the rival of the Pan American Association of Composers in the period from 1929 to 1934. While publicly serving on the League's advisory board, Cowell privately expressed a petty hostility toward Copland and other composers in the League [125]—a hostility that sometimes led Ives to regard musicians who were active in the League as just so many "ladies." [126]

There were, nevertheless, certain real distinctions between the two groups. First, the League was bigger and more highly organized, and it had many wealthy patrons; its concerts tended to take on the character of social events. The Pan American Association, on the other hand, was smaller and more austere, and its concerts remained obscure. Second, the League did not restrict itself to American works. In time, its relative success caused it increasingly to perform the music of European modernists who had already achieved recognition; thus Varèse saw the League as the embodiment of "the smart, the fashionable, the Vanity Fair of music." [127] The Pan Americans, concentrating on music of the Western Hemisphere, tended to present compositions that were more vital and audacious. Third, the Pan American Association would seem, in retrospect, to have had the more important composers; certainly it had those who were more experimental and less influenced by neoclassicism. The League had Copland, but the Pan Americans could boast a whole group of first-rate (although largely unrecognized) men: Ives, Varèse, Ruggles, Riegger, and Cowell.[128] Fourth, the League had, since its founding, contained many composers, active members, and patrons who were Jews; it was sometimes privately called the "League of Jewish Composers." [129] On the other hand, several of the leading Pan Americans—Cowell, Ruggles, Adolph Weiss, but *not* Ives—had tendencies toward anti-Semitism.[130]

If the Pan Americans hoped to have their orchestral works performed, they would require a conductor. He would need to have not only considerable talent, but also a willingness to devote himself to unpopular modern music. In his travels Henry Cowell had already met such a man: the young Boston conductor Nicolas Slonimsky, founder of the Chamber Orchestra of Boston. When Cowell told Ives that Slonimsky would like to conduct one of his works, Ives was so flattered that he rescored his First Orchestral Set, *Three Places in New England,* for chamber orchestra and sent it off to the conductor.[131] Remarking later to Slonimsky that "you aren't afraid to ferret out a non-entity and do the unpopular thing," Ives added: "You're the only conductor that ever asked me to do anything. This score would never have gotten off the shelf, if it hadn't been for you." [132]

Meanwhile, Cowell and Ives had decided to submit their music to the United States Section of the International Society for Contemporary Music. The American activists in this European-based society tended to be close to the League of Composers; nevertheless, Cowell and Ives hoped that their works would be selected for performance at the society's annual festival in Europe. Ives submitted *Three Places in New England;* and Slonimsky, who was by now familiar with the score, came down to New York, was introduced to Ives by Cowell, and conducted the work in a rehearsal arranged by the United States Section on February 16, 1930.[133] Shortly after, Ives revealed to Slonimsky that he cared very much whether or not his music was performed: "I think Henry C. told you that both his and my things were accepted by the committee—*you did it,* as far as my music was concerned." [134] The international jury in Europe, however, subsequently turned down the two works; and Ives, in writing to Cowell, phrased his bitter disappointment in the classic, Europe-defying American vernacular:

> The action of the "Non-Contemporary Society of Music and Commercial Travelers" is a good one—for our vanity. It will be well, I suppose, not to throw anything wet at them. We can be good sports, as the man said when the undertaker came in—and when they ask for more "American beauties," we can say "Nix on that Stuff—You know me Al!"—and Johnny Spiel auf will put it to American music. In a new country like ours, children should be obscene and not heard. But the real cause of the situation is the Republican Party—they kept us out in the L. of N. [League of Nations] chorus, and we are still out.[135]

But with Henry Cowell's encouragement, Ives did not retreat after this unsuccessful attempt to find an audience for his compositions. Besides, he had discovered a conductor who liked his music; and he himself liked and admired Slonimsky very much, regarding him as a man of great courage. Born in Russia in 1894, the brilliant but erratic conductor had been in America since 1923. He had an infectious sense of humor, and Ives loved to joke with him. He was immediately admitted into the Ives family circle. Later, when Slonimsky married, Ives took a doting interest in his wife and especially in his little daughter, Electra.

Ives now offered to finance a concert in New York's Town Hall for Slonimsky and his Chamber Orchestra of Boston (whose members were players in the Boston Symphony Orchestra). It cost Ives more than $1,500, an enormous sum during the Depression. During 1930 the two men carefully laid their plans for the concert, finally sending out huge quantities of the program book to colleges and music institutions as propaganda.[136]

The concert, which included the first public performance of *Three*

Places in New England as well as pieces by Ruggles and Cowell, took place on January 10, 1931.[137] Ives attended, and he later described his reaction to it in the third person:

> At this concert he [Ives] sat quietly through the "boos" and jeers at his own music—but when that wonderful orchestral work "Men and Mountains" of Carl R[uggles] was played, a sound of [a] disapproving hiss was heard near him. Ives jumped up and shouted: "You g-ddarn, sissy-eared mollycoddle—when you hear strong masculine music like this, stand up and use your ears like a man— and don't 'flibby' faint over backwards." [138]

Pleased by a performance that, although not formally polished, had been full of spontaneous dedication, Ives told Slonimsky afterward: "This was just like a town meeting—everyone for himself. Wonderful how it came out!" [139]

The Town Hall concert attracted little attention from the New York critics. Slonimsky, however, repeated the work two weeks later at a concert given by his orchestra in Boston.[140] Here, where he had musical connections, the works that he played were reviewed more extensively. The critic of the *Boston Post,* noting that Slonimsky had included "the lunatic fringe of modern music" in his program, was not very favorable to *Three Places in New England.* The first movement (*The "St. Gaudens" in Boston Common*) was "thickly and monotonously dissonant" and "bore no observable relation to its subject matter," while the conclusion of the third (*The Housatonic at Stockbridge*) "might have provoked the thought that the Housatonic was in the throes of an ice-jam." Yet at the end of this same third movement "came measures genuinely beautiful, measures of a nostalgic melancholy"; and the second movement (*Putnam's Camp*) was "an ingenious and sometimes humorous parody of the efforts of a country band." [141] This was the review of a literal-minded critic who was looking for the most easily assimilable parts of the work. More sympathetic was the critic of the *Boston Herald,* for whom the whole set (but particularly *Putnam's Camp*) was "modern in the exact manner of those painters whose canvases—so redolent of this chaotic age— are a patchwork of jagged fragments overlapping, dovetailing, with an added complexity which painting cannot rival, namely that of a bewilderingly crowded simultaneity, an extraordinary contrapuntal freedom." [142] Here was an irony that Ives would have to face repeatedly. His music was actually inspired by the old-fashioned America of the nineteenth century; but he *expressed* that inspiration in such a way that critics often took his work to be representative of the modernity of the twentieth century. The critic of the *Boston Evening Transcript* took an opposite view, however, when he remarked that "in all three pieces more or less romantic brush was tangled about the modernistic saplings." He found the first movement "lugubrious" and "semi-articulate," and the second "clumsy"; of the third, he remarked that "as long as Mr. Ives is as respectful as he was of bar-lines and symmetrical phrases, he is far from being a practising modernist." [143]

Slonimsky conducted the work again in New York in February and then in Havana in March.[144] In the meantime Cowell, Ives, and Slonimsky were conceiving a plan to lay musical siege to Europe itself. Since the International Society for Contemporary Music was unwilling to introduce their compositions into Europe, the Pan Americans would themselves present their orchestral works in the capital cities of the Continent. Cowell would arrange the concerts through his European contacts, Slonimsky would conduct them, and Ives would pay for them. Cowell knew that the well-known conductors of American orchestras, who had almost all been born in Europe, would not perform the work of American modernists until it had been first approved by the powerful European censor-critics. He believed that the comparatively few works of American classical music which Europe had so far heard had been imitative of European styles, especially older and more conservative styles; naturally, then, Europeans tended to think that the only really indigenous and original American music was jazz. Cowell wanted them to hear the works of Pan Americans likes Ives and Ruggles, who had been writing a "distinctively American" serious music for some time. Besides, hiring players and putting on a concert would be much less expensive in Europe than in the United States. Since France rather than Germany had come to dominate European and American music after World War I, it was decided to storm Paris first.[145] Accordingly, in May, 1931, Slonimsky was dispatched to Paris to make final arrangements and rehearse the musicians.

The Paris concerts of the Pan American Association of Composers were given on June 6 and 11, 1931. Slonimsky conducted *Three Places in New England* and other works by the inner circle of Pan Americans, along with some Latin American pieces.[146] It was the musical fulfillment of a promise that had been made by Emerson nearly a hundred years before: "We will walk on our own feet; we will work with our own hands; we will speak our own minds." Ives and his fellow American composers were at last confronting the European musical Establishment on its home ground.

These concerts attracted a good deal of attention among musicians in Paris.[147] But if the Pan Americans hoped to convince Paris that they were writing a truly indigenous music, independent of European influences, then they certainly failed. After hearing the music, a number of the critics clearly felt that the Americans, for all their revolutionary fervor, had rejected traditional European models only to replace them with modernist European models.[148] They excepted Varèse's highly original music from this judgment; in fact, of the works presented by Slonimsky, it was Varèse's which received the greatest critical acclaim. Varèse, of course, was a Frenchman who had returned to live in Paris and whose works had already been performed there. But after Varèse it was Charles Ives, a composer previously unknown in Europe, whose work proved most interesting to the critics. The antecedence in time of his modernism was generally acknowledged. Several of the critics were fascinated by the similarity between the technical devices used in *Three Places in New England*— especially the complex rhythms and polytonality of *Putnam's Camp*— and those used by Stravinsky in *Le Sacre du printemps*. The American primitivism of Ives inevitably reminded them of the primitivism in Stravinsky's great pioneering work, which had provoked a scandal in Paris eighteen years before. What was amazing was that Ives had anticipated Stravinsky by nearly a decade, since the materials for *Putnam's Camp* dated from about 1903–1904.

Three important critics bestowed noteworthy praise upon Ives's composition. Boris de Schloezer, while admitting that Ives was deficient in "technical knowledge and skillfulness," nevertheless saw in him "a real forerunner, a bold talent." Schloezer felt that the other native North Americans whose works had been heard were mere imitators of the European modernists, while Ives had discovered modern techniques on his own by courageously following his lonely musical path. But mere antecedence in the use of these techniques was not the only thing that distinguished Ives from the others, for in his case, "despite his awkwardness, or rather just because of his awkwardness, this modernism acquires a flavor all its own." [149] Paul Le Flem, the critic for *Comoedia,* also singled out Ives for both his pioneering of the modern idiom and his greater natural talent. Comparing Ives's work with the "scientific" approach taken by Cowell, Ruggles, and Adolph Weiss in their music, Le Flem wrote that Ives seemed to be "the most spontaneously gifted musician, whose truculent boldness, although occasionally awkward, is not inconsistent with the feelings that he is trying to express." But Le Flem did not take Ives to be merely a primitive or folk artist: "He is as scholarly as his companions and handles polytonality without its exploding in his hands. But he knows how to temper his science with something sensitive, fresh, and lively, something which is not a mere laboratory leftover." [150] Émile Vuillermoz, the critic of *Excelsior,* was less willing to set Ives above the other composers. He called the whole first concert, at which Ives's work was played, an "astonishing revelation." [151] But he also bestowed particular praise upon *The Housatonic at Stockbridge* (the third movement of Ives's set) for its "wonderful color"; the careful use of each instrument for its special tonal quality was "the orchestration of a painter." [152]

The real hero of these concerts was Slonimsky. He had admitted to Ives that he was using his genius for promotion and advertisement in order to stir up curiosity in Paris about the concerts; [153] but Ives was too loyal and grateful to him to be disturbed. Slonimsky's efforts were rewarded by the practically universal critical acclaim that he received for conducting these difficult works. At one point in *Putnam's Camp,* for example, he had to conduct two march meters simultaneously, the one going at a rate one and a third times as fast as the rate of the other. He gratefully admitted that he owed his overnight success to Ives's generosity.[154] His patron, of course, rewarded him with the personal gift of a check.[155]

Ives was quite pleased with the results of the Paris concerts. There were, however, two American articles about them that aroused his wrath. Henry Prunières, the Paris musical correspondent of the *New*

York Times, wrote of Ives: "There is no doubt that he knows his Schönberg, yet gives the impression that he has not always assimilated the lessons of the Viennese master as well as he might have." [156] Similarly, the charge of being mere imitators of the European modernists was leveled at the Pan Americans as a group by the septuagenarian critic Philip Hale in an editorial in the *Boston Herald.* Hale had not attended the Paris concerts, but his conservative taste was offended by Slonimsky's choice of American works, for "the composers represented were not those who are regarded by their fellow-countrymen as leaders in the art, nor have they all been so considered by the conductors of our great orchestras." [157]

Incensed by these criticisms, Ives unburdened himself in a letter to E. Robert Schmitz in which he castigated Prunières.[158] This letter was then expanded into the first draft of a letter addressed to "Dear Sirs and Nice Ladies," which was in turn developed into an extensive musical autobiography to which he was still adding material in 1934. Ives's original purpose in writing this manuscript was to make it clear that only a handful of American conductors had ever even *seen* any of his compositions and that he had developed his musical style independently of such Europeans as Stravinsky and Schoenberg.[159] The document inevitably ramified, however, into a rambling discussion of Ives's whole musical life and work, including sections on each of his major compositions, on his father, on Horatio Parker, on his musical recognition (or lack of it), and on many other matters. The *Memos* (to use Ives's title) are curious because of their inconsistency of tone, which ranges from the rhetorical and didactic to the intimate and allusive. As with so many of Ives's writings on political and musical subjects (and as with so much of his music), it is hard to tell whether these memoirs were intended for the public or were merely written to give Ives a private opportunity for "getting something off the chest." [160] At any rate, the *Memos* (which were finally published in 1972) are the most valuable source for Ives's life as a musician, particularly because of the light they shed on his musical isolation during the first two decades of the century.

Encouraged by the relative success that they had had in stirring up Parisian interest in the Pan Americans' music, Ives, Cowell, and Slonimsky continued their efforts on the Continent. While he was in

Europe toward the end of 1931, Cowell set up several more Pan American concerts.[161] One concrete result of Slonimsky's "triumph" in Paris, moreover, was that he was actually invited to conduct two regular concerts of the Orchestre Symphonique de Paris, one of the great orchestras of Europe. The "catch" was that the orchestra would not provide for the many rehearsals that were necessary to master the difficult works on Slonimsky's programs. Ives had to put up the money for the extra rehearsals.[162]

These two Paris concerts were given on February 21 and 25, 1932. Acting with foolhardy disregard of his future career as a conductor, Slonimsky chose to load his programs (especially the first one) with avant-garde compositions, and he thus alienated his audience.[163] Perhaps, too, Slonimsky and his Pan American music were considerably less attractive as a novelty than they had been the preceding June. For the first concert, Ives and Slonimsky put together a "suite" of somewhat disparate works by Ives. The short first and third sections from the Set for Theatre Orchestra (*In the Cage* and *In the Night*) were chosen, and sandwiched between them was the world premiere of *The Fourth of July*, a very complex work that was certain to challenge both players and audience.[164] Critical attention at this first concert naturally centered on Béla Bartók's First Piano Concerto, in which the composer himself was soloist. *The Fourth of July*, nevertheless, attracted the admiring notice of several critics with its brilliant massing of orchestral forces at the end, climaxing in the representation of a skyrocket going up over the church steeple and then the sudden quiet of the fall of the exploded fireworks through the night sky. Once again Boris de Schloezer (a personal friend of Slonimsky's) offered a thoughtful and long-range critique:

> Ives, who is familiar to us through Slonimsky's concerts of last year, stands totally apart: [like the other Americans played at these concerts,] he too is inclined to abuse material means, but he is not an imitator; he has something to say. Ives is a musical painter, if one may use such an expression, an impressionist; he is, however, not without moments of naive realism. His art is at times coarse and clumsy, but in him there is genuine strength and inventiveness, thematically as well as rhythmically, in no way taking fashion or authority into consideration. Ives's suite *The Fourth of July* (the Ameri-

can national holiday) is based on national motifs; in this regard Ives
is, perhaps, the only one among the composers of North America
whose work is profoundly national, and in him there is something
reminiscent of Walt Whitman.[165]

Meanwhile, Cowell (with Ives's financial help) had arranged two
concerts for Slonimsky in Berlin and one in Budapest; they were
devoted entirely to the work of the Pan Americans. Slonimsky repeated the Ives "suite," which he had just given in Paris, at a concert
on March 5, 1932, for which Berlin's renowned Philharmonic Orchestra was hired; [166] and he conducted the suite again, with the
Hungarian Symphony Orchestra, on April 2.[167]

Among both its audiences and its critics Paris had not been lacking
in outright opponents of the American modernists; but Berlin,
which had once been a principal center of influence upon European
music, proved considerably more conservative and less enthusiastic
than Paris. In fact, at the concert of March 5, the audience responded to the last work, Varèse's *Arcana,* with whistling and other
oral expressions of distaste.[168] The critics, too, tended rather uncritically to accept the works played as typical of American modernity—
and to condemn them accordingly (including Varèse's work). After
hearing at a single concert not only Ives's suite, but also such striking
and difficult works as Ruggles's *Sun-treader,* Cowell's *Synchrony,* and
Varèse's *Arcana,* the Berlin critics generally ignored Ives or passed
rather quickly over his compositions, although there were a few favorable nods in his direction. It is likely that *The Fourth of July,* with
its program based upon the details of an American national holiday
and its aggressive quotation of tunes familiar only to Americans, did
not find in Europeans the immediate response that it might have
aroused in an American audience.

One of the more thoughtful and sympathetic reviews of the Berlin
concerts was by the critic Jerzy Fitelberg. He was doubtful about the
obvious desire of the Pan Americans to experiment, but he selected
Henry Cowell's *Synchrony* and Ives's suite as having "made the greatest impression" among the works by twelve different composers that
had been heard. He found Ives's suite "striking." *The Fourth of July*
"is unquestionably noisy but the real spirit of a musician comes
through." *In the Night* "is built entirely on tonality; a breath of ro-

manticism pervades this last movement of the suite." Fitelberg felt that "these three movements are as inconsistent in style as if they had been written by different composers; perhaps this is why the work fails to express its musical idea precisely." He did not realize, of course, that *The Fourth of July* had been written later than the other movements and had not originally been intended to be played with them. Fitelberg concluded of Ives that "a will to experiment is present, although restrained by the musical element." [169]

The Berlin concerts can hardly be said to have marked a success for Ives and the other Pan Americans. Looking back at the concerts after the space of a year, during which time Berlin had heard a number of more conservative and European-sounding works by Americans, the great German musicologist and critic Alfred Einstein concluded that Slonimsky had been "an extraordinarily fine conductor," but that "the dose of revolutionary music was just too big" for Berliners. Einstein paid Ives a compliment (in Ives's terms, at least) when he wrote that "the radical group of [American] composers is, in its lack of traditional values, very international [that is, apparently, non-German] and very American—Mr. Charles Ives being, in my estimation, the most original and national." Einstein felt that "the distressing part lies in the fact that Germany now means very little to modern musical America." [170]

In spite of Einstein's observation, Cowell wanted to present more music by the Pan Americans in Germany. [171] By early 1933, Cowell felt he had the powerful Berlin critic H. H. Stuckenschmidt convinced that the nonexperimental American compositions which were being heard in Germany were not America's most original musical product, so that Stuckenschmidt was calling for more works by the Pan Americans. [172] But even as Alfred Einstein was lamenting the lack of German influence upon American music, a political regime was closing down upon Germany that would soon drive Einstein himself from the homeland of his beloved culture and would make it impossible for experimental music to be played there any more.

Taken as a whole, the European concerts given by the Pan American Association of Composers in 1931 and 1932 were a bold venture—a venture which, in spite of Ives's heavy expenditures of money, ultimately failed. In a very limited sense, of course, Cowell and his associates could take comfort in the reception that their works received on the Continent. The European critics, at least, did not ignore the Pan Americans, as American critics had done. In Ives's case this result of the European venture was an especially fortunate one. Before the first Paris concerts, Ives had still been widely regarded in America, even among the avant-garde, as an amateur and a crank who did not know what he was doing; [173] the major European critics, however, knowing nothing about him, did not take him for a mere primitive or an eccentric when they heard his compositions, but assumed instead that he was a serious professional musician. This critical reaction to his work in Europe undoubtedly contributed to his being taken more seriously in the United States. More important, it must have given a large boost to his own respect for himself as a composer. Since apparently the *Memos* were written and dictated mainly in March, April, and May of 1932, it was probably the results of the European concerts that made Ives realize that his compositions were destined to find a significant audience and that it was important to set down data about his life and works.

Cowell and Slonimsky, however, could hardly have been satisfied with their minimal success in Europe, for they had been playing for much larger stakes. They had hoped, in the first place, to conquer Europe—that is, to create a demand in Europe for the orchestral works of the Pan Americans. In the second place, they had intended to use their conquest of Europe as a means of conquering America; they had counted on securing major orchestral performances in the United States for the Pan Americans, on the strength of their newly won European reputations.[174]

They failed, however, to achieve either of these goals. Europeans could not help admiring Slonimsky's brilliance as a conductor, but they had definite reservations about the music that he insisted on performing; moreover, the economic depression and the growing nationalism of the European states during the 1930s created an increasingly unfavorable climate for the performance of American orchestral works after the Pan American Association retired from the field. For example, European recognition of Ives's music during the rest of the decade was restricted to a few performances of his songs in Paris and Vienna, performances made possible largely through Cowell's publication of the songs in *New Music*.

In America the Great Depression had a similar effect on the Pan Americans' hopes, for it dried up the patronage of the wealthy which had formerly supported avant-garde activities. Slonimsky was engaged for a few concerts with the Los Angeles Philharmonic and at the Hollywood Bowl, but otherwise the straitened financial circumstances of the major American orchestras caused them to avoid experimental music that might alienate their audiences. Even the growing American nationalism of the thirties, which should have been an ally of Cowell and his group, proved to be just the opposite, for it encouraged the composing of a simpler music that could be understood by a broader segment of the American people.

8

THE AVANT-GARDE
AND THE MUSICAL PUBLIC
1932–1939

❦

THE EUROPEAN CONCERTS given by the Pan American Association of Composers in 1931 and 1932 failed to achieve their intended results. Less than a month after the last of Slonimsky's European concerts, nevertheless, Ives achieved a triumph in America which compelled the avant-garde to take him seriously and to accept his works as the product of first-rate talent, if not of genius. But this event—the performance of his songs at the Yaddo festival—occurred independently of the European concerts. In fact, it was arranged not by the Pan American Association, but by Henry Cowell's principal rival, Aaron Copland.

While the European concerts were going on, Henry Cowell was continuing his efforts to promote Ives's music in America. During 1932 *New Music* published three of Ives's compositions: the Set for Theatre Orchestra; *Lincoln, the Great Commoner,* for chorus and orchestra; and *The Fourth of July.* Ives's songs reached a wider audience when *New Music* issued *Thirty-four Songs* (1933) and *Eighteen Songs*

(1935),[1] both of which were taken largely from the plates of Ives's earlier *114 Songs. Washington's Birthday* was published in 1937. Cowell also edited the symposium *American Composers on American Music* (1933), a book which contained both his own essay on Ives and an essay by Ives on "Music and Its Future." [2]

Cowell pressed Ives to issue his scores in *New Music;* but Ives hesitated, obviously feeling that it was improper for a supposedly independent publication which he was subsidizing to contain too much of his own music.[3] It is unfortunate that Ives did not decide to publish more of his compositions during the early and middle 1930s; if he had, he would have been spurred on to get more of his manuscripts into a final form and have fair copies of them made while his eyesight was still good enough to correct them. Back in the twenties, he had begun to have photostats made from his manuscripts, so that he could give photographic reproductions to musicians who were interested in his music. But the manuscript copies (made by himself or his copyists) from which these photostats were reproduced were often in a condition that was not satisfactory to Ives: they were inaccurate, incomplete, confused, partly illegible, or not copied in the most playable form. Most musicians found Ives's scores perplexing enough in their finished form, without the additional problems of these disordered manuscripts. It is true that during the 1930s, he had good copies made of a number of his shorter works written for chamber orchestra or a few players; but he neglected important compositions in the larger forms, such as the Second and Third Symphonies and the First Piano Sonata. Many of his most important works were still in disorder in the 1940s, when performers were more apt to request them; Ives had nothing to give them but his infamous photostats, whose very appearance was often enough to frighten away all but the dedicated.[4] And for both published and unpublished orchestral works, the only instrumental parts available were too often poorly made and unwieldy to play from.

Cowell was also busy promoting Ives performances in the Western Hemisphere during the early 1930s, although a full orchestra was not available to him in the United States. Slonimsky conducted the first real public performance of *Washington's Birthday* at a concert given by Cowell's New Music Society of California in September,

1931.[5] In December of that year, *Decoration Day* was premiered by the Havana Philharmonic Orchestra under the baton of Amadeo Roldán, Cowell's colleague in the Pan American Association of Composers.[6] The following February, at a concert of the Pan American Association in New York City, the Set for Theatre Orchestra was given its first complete public performance; and Slonimsky conducted *Washington's Birthday* at a similar concert in New York in November, 1932.[7] Cowell also put the contralto Radiana Pazmor in touch with Ives; and as a result, she gave the premiere of *General William Booth Enters into Heaven,* usually regarded as Ives's best song, at a concert of the New Music Society of California in September, 1933.[8] And these were only the most important of the Ives performances engineered by Cowell in the early 1930s. Furthermore, when Cowell launched New Music Quarterly Recordings in 1934, he saw to it that among the early releases were Slonimsky's performances of *In the Night* and the "Barn Dance" section from *Washington's Birthday,* as well as Pazmor's performance of *General Booth.*[9]

As a result of his brief moment of fame in Europe, Nicolas Slonimsky was invited to conduct the regular concerts of the Philharmonic Orchestra of Los Angeles on December 29 and 30, 1932.[10] Heedless of his own career, Slonimsky refused to stick to standard orchestral fare and recklessly programmed the second and third movements of *Three Places in New England* as well as a work by the modernist Roy Harris. These were the first public performances of an Ives work by one of the major American orchestras—and the last until 1948. Naturally, hisses and boos mingled with the applause from the audience, but on the whole the occasion was a success for Slonimsky.[11] One critic, José Rodriguez, was so struck by Slonimsky's courage that he took the occasion to denounce the conservative, European-born conductors who controlled the great American orchestras for their refusal to perform pioneering American music.[12] Ives's heart was warmed when he read Rodriguez's review.[13] The musical life of Los Angeles was, however, little influenced by Slonimsky's efforts. It is true that Rodriguez helped to get him some conducting engagements at the Hollywood Bowl during the following summer; [14] but again Slonimsky truculently programmed modern music that was beyond the understanding of either orchestra or audience,[15] after which he returned to musical obscurity and Los Angeles to more traditional symphonic fare.

In spite of all the energies expended by Cowell and Slonimsky, the attention of those who were interested in modern music still centered on Aaron Copland and the League of Composers. They were much better known than the Pan Americans and were regarded as the mainstream, so to speak, of the musical avant-garde. It is not surprising, then, that Ives's first great success among the American avant-garde—the event which clinched all of Cowell's previous efforts—should have come through the sponsorship of Aaron Copland.

Copland had been relatively indifferent to Ives's music during the first four years of Cowell's attempts to interest other musicians in that music. By 1932, however, through the growing curiosity about Ives and the efforts of his own younger colleagues to direct his attention to Ives's work, Copland had discovered that *114 Songs* contained some remarkable compositions.[16] Copland was then serving as principal organizer of the First Festival of Contemporary American Music, which was to be held on the estate called Yaddo at Saratoga Springs, New York, in the spring of 1932. Having decided to present some of Ives's songs at Yaddo, he carefully chose seven of them in such a way as to represent a wide variety of styles, moods, and subjects. All seven were among Ives's very best songs, and they ranged from the delicate art song *Evening* to the rollicking cowboy ballad *Charlie Rutlage*.[17] Naturally, they lacked the forbidding complexity of his most advanced orchestral works, and they impressed the listener less as forerunners of subsequent modernist developments than as finished compositions of intrinsic beauty. At the afternoon concert on May 1, the baritone Hubert Linscott sang the seven songs, accompanied at the piano by Copland himself.[18]

The invited audience and the critics present were highly impressed, and *Charlie Rutlage* had to be repeated. The songs received several admiring reviews, including a discerning criticism by Alfred H. Meyer in the *Boston Evening Transcript:* "Nothing heard at the festival showed higher imaginative powers than the songs of Ives. The variety of expression to be found in the seven is little short of amazing. In all one discovers equal mastery, equal accomplishment. . . .

These songs, one feels, are first-rank work." [19] "The melody is strikingly unconventional and economical," wrote Meyer in another review, "with marvelously apt certainty of expressive touch. The accompaniments often contain shrewdly chosen bits of realistic suggestion." [20] Clearly, Meyer saw in Ives not a primitive, but an artist of great subtlety. On the other hand, Arthur Mendel, of the *Nation,* chose to emphasize the "recognizably American twang" of *Charlie Rutlage;* but he found in the whole group of songs "startling imagination, vitality, and humor." [21] Robert Pitney, of *Hound & Horn,* also thought that "one of the unforgettable things taken away from Yaddo was Charlie Rutlage with its distillation of the true flavor of the West; the false fronts of clapboards, the smell of dusty saddles and the clank of harness against a horizon of immense blue." In these seven songs Pitney "heard the great work of a curious genius" and realized that Ives had "established twenty years ago many of the conventions that others firmly impressed and fixed in our minds." [22]

The festival certainly awakened greater interest, even in the popular press, than the Pan Americans were ever able to arouse. It was not principally the established professional critics, however, who carried the gospel of Ives away from Yaddo. In fact, only a handful of representatives of the newspapers even bothered to attend, and during the festival Copland charged newspaper critics in general with being prejudiced against American music because (in their ignorance of it) they still thought of it in terms of the weak compositions of twenty years before.[23] But at that time Aaron Copland probably had a greater influence than did anyone else upon the American musical avant-garde. By performing Ives's music, he brought it to the respectful attention of a wide range of musicians and others who were interested in contemporary music.[24] Wallingford Riegger, a Pan American who served as an advisory member of the festival, wrote to Ives (whom he had never met) afterward:

> Your beautiful songs that were given at Yaddo aroused not only enthusiasm and wide-spread interest on the part of the audience (of about 200 discriminating music-lovers) but keen appreciation in the numerous composers present. About 16 of these remained a few days after the festival and your songs were a constantly recur-

ring subject. I had some of your scores, but I found that they were pretty well known already.

There was much curiosity about the facts of your life—musical and otherwise—concerning which my information is extremely meagre. In the New Republic I see an article about you by Paul Rosenfeld is soon to appear. I am sure this will swell the ranks of those who are eager to know about one who I think will be increasingly regarded as *the* outstanding figure in the musical history of this country.[25]

Widespread interest in Ives's works among the American musical avant-garde began with the Yaddo festival. The festival was the decisive event that brought to fruition the efforts which Cowell and others had been previously making on behalf of Ives. A good deal was to be written and published about Charles Ives during the next year or so.

About the time of Yaddo, a small group of avant-garde critics— men who lay outside Cowell's circle—began to take up the cause of Ives's music. The most influential of them, and possibly the most incisive, was Paul Rosenfeld, music critic for the *New Republic*, who wrote about Ives and other modernist composers in that journal.[26] Rosenfeld had been contemptuous of the first two movements from Ives's Fourth Symphony when he had heard them at the Pro Musica concert in 1927, noting that "besides being literary [they] are badly orchestrated as though Schumann had done the instrumentation, doubling all the parts."[27] But by 1932, having heard *Three Places in New England* and the Set for Theatre Orchestra and having examined the second movement of the Fourth Symphony more closely in *New Music*, Rosenfeld had changed his mind. He had probably encountered *Three Places in New England* at one of Slonimsky's New York concerts in early 1931, and this composition had been the "actual cause of the present writer's conversion to the Ivesian faith and his happy conviction of the composer's possession of creative forces." He called *The Housatonic at Stockbridge* "the hero of the suite and easily one of the freshest, most eloquent and solid orchestral pieces composed in America."[28]

The "great place" that Ives occupied as a composer, according to Rosenfeld, was due not only to his being "the pioneer in atonality," but also to his filling "the even more enviable position of one of the few originally gifted composers of impressionistic or descriptive or imitative music borne [*sic*] in America." It had been in listening to "the sounds of life" around him, thought Rosenfeld, that Ives's "imagination was actually touched by dissonant idiom." Thus the critic shrewdly speculated that Ives had produced his pioneering atonal and polytonal compositions by pursuing "the strongly imitative inclination of his eminent talent," rather than (as in Schoenberg's case) through experiment based upon theory.[29]

Rosenfeld also understood very well the awful isolation in which Ives had composed and something of its effect upon him. Yet he felt that for Ives there had been no alternative: "In the nineteen-tens, there was no preparation for him in Europe," not to speak of America. "But Ives had to give an integration of many hitherto disparate layers of American experience, through the medium of tone. And Wagner and Strauss and Debussy had shut behind them the doors through which they had passed, once and for all time." [30]

Thus Rosenfeld believed that Ives had been *compelled* to work in isolation, that he had accepted the burden of that isolation, and that he had triumphed over it. The record of that triumph lay in *114 Songs,* which Rosenfeld called "a sort of notebook exposing the whole of a creative mind." He grasped one of the most fundamentally animating ideas of Ives's life when he noted that in its very heterogeneity, *114 Songs* was "another worthy confession and consequence of the old national belief that all things possessing breath of their own, no matter how dissimilar, are ultimately compatible." To Rosenfeld, then, Ives was "the 'old master' of modern American music." [31] "It is precisely for his utter faithfulness to spirit," he wrote, "that we rejoice in and honor him today." [32]

These important articles by Paul Rosenfeld, which appeared in the *New Republic* in 1932 and 1933, revealed the beginnings of an "Ives Legend." Rosenfeld did, however, make a mistake when he found subtlety, rather than relative naiveté, in the extramusical programs and connotations of Ives's works. The song *In Flanders Fields,* for example, uses portions of several patriotic tunes—particularly *The Red, White, and Blue,* oddly harmonized and with its melody at one point put into the minor key. Rosenfeld, noting that the song bore the date "1919" in *114 Songs,* assumed that Ives's use of patriotic tunes in this way expressed his disillusionment with the results of World War I; and he described the song as "savagely sardonic." [33] In fact, it had been composed at the moment of America's entrance into the war in 1917, and 1919 was only the date of its revision. It was really a heartfelt expression of Ives's sincere grief for the fallen soldiers and of his identification of himself with their noble purpose. The music reflected exactly the sentimental attitude of the popular poem of which it was a setting, an attitude which younger intellectuals like Rosenfeld generally scorned after the war.

Paul Rosenfeld was less than sixteen years younger than Ives, but he was at least a generation removed from him in his values and world view. He did not understand that Ives was temperamentally incapable of writing "savagely sardonic" music or of sharing in the fashionable postwar disillusionment of young intellectuals. There is, of course, humor in much of Ives's music; but many of his works are confusing because they combine a highly sophisticated musical talent with a straightforward and simple approach toward matters which he considered serious. When he wished to express a serious idea or attitude which lay close to his heart, Ives often turned to the traditional music (especially the vernacular-tradition music) with which that idea or attitude was identified in his mind. But his musical understanding was so superior to the music which he was quoting that he could hardly avoid writing a "takeoff" of that music. People who heard his compositions sometimes assumed that he also intended a takeoff of the idea or attitude with which the music was connected. For Ives, however, the term *takeoff* could mean not only a caricature, but also a reflection (or even an idealization) of something. His takeoff of the music with which a serious idea or attitude was associated was usually not intended to satirize that idea or attitude, but was rather the most effective way he knew of showing how much that idea or attitude really meant to him.

A good example is the song *General William Booth Enters into Heaven,* where Ives's dissonant takeoff of the evangelical hymn tune *Cleansing Fountain* ("There is a fountain filled with blood . . .") was actually a means of profoundly identifying himself with the spirit of General Booth and the Salvation Army. He made the identification by calling up a tune which had meant a great deal to him at the camp meetings in his boyhood. The listener, however, might easily conclude that Ives's intention in the song was to scoff at enthusiastic religion. Similarly, the critic Alfred H. Meyer, reviewing the Yaddo festival, incorrectly assumed that there was an "almost Rabelaisian" musical burlesque of religious sentiment toward the end of the song *Charlie Rutlage*.[34] In fact, the final lines of the song, which imagine Charlie in heaven, were intended by Ives to be sung in all seriousness. Critics like Meyer sometimes saw humor or sarcasm in Ives's music when it was not there, because they lacked his old-fashioned reverence for the events and ideas that he treated. One critic showed admirable prudence when he wrote of *Washington's Birthday*, "One can only hope that Ives' intentions were as humorous as they seemed to be." [35]

During 1932 Ives also found champions in the music critics of the magazine *Trend*. Published irregularly in New York City from 1932 to 1935, this journal was devoted almost exclusively to the avant-garde in the arts and drew into its pages such younger talents as Paul and Percival Goodman and Buckminster Fuller. The music critics for *Trend*, Harrison Kerr and Arthur V. Berger, reported faithfully on the concerts of the Pan American Association of Composers, which the New York newspapers generally neglected. Kerr pointed out that the League of Composers was presenting mainly European music that was fashionably or acceptably modern and that its leaders were not drawing into their organization the more able of the younger American composers. Kerr and Berger both felt that the League was performing only mediocre American works, while the Pan Americans were presenting the most vital and important contemporary American music, a category in which these critics included the music of Ives.[36] "If the Pan American Association did nothing more than present the music of Charles Ives," wrote Kerr, "its existence would be justified. The perverse fate which brings recognition to this man, so slowly and so grudgingly, should be sufficient evidence against those smug individuals who assure us that true merit never goes unrecognized in these enlightened day[s]." [37]

As for Berger, he had written about Ives even before Yaddo, when he had been a mere nineteen-year-old critic for the New York

Daily Mirror. Hearing the Set for Theatre Orchestra at a Pan American Association concert in February, 1932, Berger immediately recognized its merit and referred to Ives as "this cyclopean figure . . . in our midst." [38] Reviewing the Yaddo festival, he described Ives as "the great American tone painter." [39] Arthur Berger was perhaps the first American music critic to write of Ives with a full appreciation of his genius. [40]

Berger's youth is a reminder that a new generation of young composers, born about 1910 and therefore a decade younger than Copland and Cowell, had begun to appear in America by 1932. Reaching maturity during the Great Depression, they had little connection with the artistic climate of the Roaring Twenties. In 1932, eight of these young people—Bernard Herrmann, Jerome Moross, Lehman Engel, Irwin Heilner, Henry Brant, Elie Siegmeister, Vivian Fine, and Israel Citkowitz—came together to form the Young Composers' Group, with which Arthur Berger was also closely associated. To a large extent, the Young Composers' Group transcended the rivalry between the League of Composers and the Pan American Association. Aaron Copland was these young composers' mentor and originally brought them together. But it was Henry Cowell who set up their first group concert at the New School for Social Research; [41] and several of them had musical ideals which drew them toward Cowell and his circle rather than toward the League. The eight were linked together by their youth, their Jewish background, and a common participation in music education and musical life in New York City. They disagreed among themselves on many musical matters; but it is significant that several of them chose Charles Ives, a man nearly forty years older than they, as the symbol of their musical ideals and struggles. [42]

To understand their turning to Ives, it is necessary to realize the social and cultural situation that faced young Americans in the arts who were coming of age in 1932 and early 1933. The business-dominated order of the 1920s had collapsed both functionally and morally, but the Hoover administration was still in power and the New Deal had not yet made its appearance. Young American creative artists and intellectuals were searching for something new to believe in, but nothing concrete had yet appeared. They certainly rejected the example of their predecessors of the 1920s, who had removed themselves artistically (and often physically) from American vernacular life while at the same time accepting the patronage of the wealthy as a means of supporting their hedonistic and superficially disillusioned existence. These young people of 1932–1933 wanted to express their hostility to the business order not by fleeing it, but by creating a new native art of social consciousness, an art inspired by the life of the common people of America. They rejected Europe and European influences, which had meant so much to the cosmopolitan artists of the 1920s. They intended to live and study in America, and they were searching idealistically for a way to make their country a better place.[43]

It is understandable, then, that the young composers adopted Ives as their symbol of artistic integrity. Not to speak of his isolation even earlier, he had been rejected throughout the 1920s by both the entrenched musical conservatives and the newer exponents of the fashionably modern, because both of these groups had taken their cues from Europe. Ives had courageously kept his ideals pure and clean, even at the cost of isolation, during that hedonistic decade. Of course, Ives was also a member of the business community, which was the very embodiment of the order that had dominated the 1920s. The young composers, however, saw him not as a businessman, but as an independent American artist who had suffered neglect because he had remained true to himself.

Some of these young composers saw symbolic significance not only in Ives the creative artist, but also in Ives's music, which they found interesting for both its early experimentation and its aesthetic point of view. Here their attitude was a reversal of that of the young composers of the 1920s. Although Copland later regretted that the composers of his generation had not known Ives's music in the 1920s, the fact is that even after Schmitz brought that music forward, only the American-trained Henry Cowell took up its cause in the latter years of that decade. The other advanced composers (with their European training) who came of musical age in the twenties paid little attention until Aaron Copland performed the songs at Yaddo in 1932, while the more conservative composers were obviously not sympathetic to Ives's modernism. In order to understand how the shift from the artistic climate of the 1920s to that of the 1930s brought with it a shift in attitude toward Ives's compositions, it is helpful to remember the two quite different characteristics of his music that immediately strike even the casual listener: innovation and aesthetic naiveté. The apparent conflict between these two characteristics has again and again aroused misunderstanding and hostility among those who attempt to evaluate his compositions.

Ives's pursuit of experiment and technical innovation certainly did not run counter to the avant-garde movement of the 1920s, although even musicians who were sympathetic to modernism found his compositions that were then available terribly unclear and confused in texture.[44] Nor was it Ives's Americanness per se that separated him from the advanced tendencies of the time, for there was much concern in the twenties about the native composer's finding an American "voice." Virgil Thomson even used hymn tunes in a somewhat Ivesian way at that time, while a rural American background was clearly recognizable in the compositions of Roy Harris. Both these composers, however, studied in France with Nadia Boulanger, and apparently neither saw in Ives a kindred spirit during the latter 1920s or the early 1930s. In general, moreover, the native land which was expected to inspire an advanced American composer in the twenties was modern urban America, with its clattering machinery, its skyscrapers, and its jazz.[45] Ives's Americanness was more naively old-fashioned, and it was just this aesthetic naiveté that cut him off from the advanced trends of the period. One of his most obviously naive qualities was his eclecticism. The young composers of the twenties were searching above all for a consistent style; but in Ives's music one found Lisztian romanticism, popular hymn tunes and marches, and extraordinary innovations in harmony and rhythm, all jumbled together in apparent stylistic confusion. The twenties saw an increasing interest in musical form and in absolute (rather than programmatic) music; but Ives had clearly relied less on a formal design than on an extramusical program to hold many of his compositions together. These programmatic elements, moreover, embodied points of view that were out of favor among sophisticated young intellectuals and creative artists in the twenties: a sentimental attachment to America, an idealization of the life of the small town

246

and of the American common people, a call for political reform, a deep religious feeling, and an admiration for genteel nineteenth-century literary figures like Emerson.

The Great Depression brought a startling reversal of the attitudes of the twenties among a yet newer generation of young artists and intellectuals. America, the common people, and political change now came to be looked upon with great favor. Ives's extramusical programs and his naive Americanness, which had rendered him *persona non grata* among the avant-garde of the 1920s, had by 1932–1933 helped to make his music the object of a minor cult among a new generation of composers (without, however, having yet had much effect on their own compositions). Calling Ives "the Walt Whitman of American music," Bernard Herrmann acted as their spokesman in a newspaper interview in 1932:

> "By golly," said Herrmann, "Mr. Ives puts cowboy themes and hillbilly songs and camp-meeting hymns into his symphonies. Those are the tones of our country and we love them. Mr. Ives writes about everything from Nelly, the Poor Working Girl, to the How and Why of Life. . . .
>
> ". . . We know that Mr. Ives belongs among the immortals and some day all the rest of America will know it. America will know it when it can appreciate the meaning of a new American tone, of a new dissonance. His music is our music. It is not European." [46]

Not only did the programmatic and naively American aspects of Ives's music arouse the enthusiasm of several of these young composers, but (as Herrmann implied) its experimental aspect also found favor with them at this time. Moross and Heilner even claimed to be using Ives's compositions as models in the construction of their own works.[47] It is true that within a year or two, as the Americanist trend continued, there would appear a distinct tendency for American composers to retreat from the extremes of complexity and dissonance—a tendency to write a simpler and more functional music which might find an audience among "the people." But in 1932 and early 1933, in spite of their newly discovered sympathy for the common people of America, the members of the Young Composers' Group were still thinking in terms of a difficult, sophisticated, or self-consciously artistic music that would be presented to an exclusive audience through such avant-garde institutions as the League of Composers, the Pan American Association of Composers, and the New School. Their situation at this transitional point in time closely reflected that of their mentor, Aaron Copland.[48] Since new institutional channels to the masses had not yet been opened up to them, they had not yet thought seriously about the changes that their music would have to undergo if they wanted it to be understood by the people.

Of the eight members of the Young Composers' Group, only Bernard Herrmann and Jerome Moross actually knew Ives personally in 1932–1933. The two young men had accidentally discovered Ives's privately printed music in the latter 1920s, and Herrmann had made contact with Ives on his own at that time; several years later, Moross met Ives through Henry Cowell. Perhaps the fact that both were mere boys made it easier for Ives to accept their first advances without feeling threatened. It was these two young composers who helped to direct Copland's attention to *114 Songs* in the early 1930s.[49]

Ives liked Herrmann and Moross, and both of them admired and performed his music. Herrmann, in particular, was strongly influenced by the aesthetic judgments of the *Essays before a Sonata;* [50] and he devoted a good deal of effort to the promulgation of Ives's work. Having assembled a chamber orchestra, he conducted in 1933 the first public performance of the third movement from Ives's Fourth Symphony, an early and relatively simple fugue based on hymn tunes.[51] He continued to perform this fugue, later adding the Prelude (first movement).[52] Herrmann worked for the Columbia Broadcasting System for many years, and during the 1930s and 1940s he was responsible for the broadcast of a number of Ives's compositions.[53] A third member of the Young Composers' Group, Lehman Engel, met Ives and performed his music later in the 1930s.

The tributes that were paid to Ives and his music by these young composers were an important part of the Ives Legend. That legend grew mightily among the avant-garde in 1932 and 1933, and it has since reached gigantic proportions. It received its classic statement as early as the beginning of 1934 in an article by R. D. Darrell that appeared in a review of recorded music:

IVES, Charles: To my mind (and in the opinion of many others) the most original and most characteristically "American" composer the United States has yet produced. Largely self-taught, a business man rather than a professional musician, tied to no schools and refusing to propagandize his own music, he has been an almost unknown name until the last few years when the younger school of radical composers has suddenly awakened to the fact that Ives is its spiritual father. He was—and still is—years ahead of his time, anticipating many of the "discoveries" of Schönberg, Strawinski, and their followers. And yet his music is steeped in purely American feeling. We are just beginning to catch up with Ives, but his will be a powerful voice in the future. It is to professional musicians' lasting disgrace that they have consistently ignored his work. Few of his major works have even been performed; none of course has been recorded, but the N.M.Q.R. [New Music Quarterly Recordings] promises to make a beginning. One of his songs, probably *General Booth,* will be included in the first batch of N.M.Q.R. releases (1934), and it is devoutly to be hoped that this society will get the backing it needs to record some of his works in the larger forms. The future generation is going to have sardonic contempt of us for ignoring Ives and his music so long.[54]

Darrell's statement contained the major elements of the Ives Legend. First, there was Ives's precedence as a musical pioneer and "father of the moderns." Second, there was his pre-eminence as a fundamentally *American* composer. Third, there was his self-chosen isolation from the professional world of music, implying a touch of healthy primitivism, but viewed most of all as a choice of great integrity on Ives's part. Fourth, there was the disgraceful neglect of his music, a neglect for which professional musicians were to blame. Fifth, there was his discovery by the younger composers of the early 1930s, who felt a deep kinship with him. Sixth, there was the slow recognition of his music, resulting from others' appreciation of his genius rather than from his efforts in his own behalf. (Darrell would have been surprised to learn that New Music Quarterly Recordings was being backed by Ives himself.) Seventh, there was the certainty that music lovers of the future would finally understand and vindicate him. Eighth, there was the flagellation of American culture (past and present) for neglecting him.

This appearance in 1934 of the full-blown Ives Legend in a magazine aimed at the record-buying public is a significant indication of how far Ives's reputation had come since 1931.[55] But the Ives cult, although it permanently lifted him from obscurity so far as the avant-garde was concerned, actually proved to be short-lived. As a movement of widespread interest in Ives among the musical avant-garde, the Ives cult appeared suddenly about the time of the Yaddo festival in 1932, flourished mightily during the season 1932–1933, and then began to die down. By the middle of 1934, it had become largely quiescent.

The young composers and others who took up Ives's cause in 1932 and early 1933 were living through a period of transition between two distinct cultural climates. Having broken free of the cynicism of the 1920s, they were looking for something genuine in which they could believe; yet all they could see around them was a failed civilization. Under these circumstances, they turned to Ives as a symbol of integrity. But beginning in 1933, the New Deal and other developments provided many young people with the sense of purpose that they needed, thus completing the transition from the individualistic cultural climate of the 1920s to the more collectivist one of the 1930s. The avant-garde soon found other concerns than the reclusive Ives, and interest in him waned.

The members of the Young Composers' Group, for instance, turned to their careers and went their separate ways. Like other composers of their own generation (and like some of the older composers, such as Copland), they found their art strongly influenced by the political, social, and cultural milieu of the middle and latter 1930s. Some composers of the period found inspiration in Communist or other collectivist ideology, in left-wing political activity, in the ideal of a music written for the working class, and in a revival of interest in American folk music. Some, both as composers and as performers, threw themselves into institutional channels which might reach a wider audience for serious music: the WPA's Federal Music Project and its other artistic activities, the theater and dance, the radio, the phonograph recording, and the movies. Of the three members of the Young Composers' Group who knew Ives personally, Herrmann composed for the radio and later for the movies

(*Citizen Kane*); Moross for the theater, the dance, and the radio; and Engel for the theater (including the Federal Theatre Project) and later, during World War II, for United States Navy films.[56]

This new cultural milieu, with its emphasis on organization and collective action, was obviously alien to Charles Ives, who was now sixty years old and as individualistic as ever. There was, furthermore, little place for Ives's complex and difficult scores in the new scheme of things, for the new idea was to leave behind the avant-garde societies with their special audience and to compose a simpler music that would appeal to the largest possible number of people. Even Herrmann and Engel, in the Ives performances for which they were responsible during the 1930s, gave their preference to a few of his simpler works.

In the end, it is doubtful that Ives's compositions had very much influence on the style of the younger composers who discovered him in the early 1930s. Part of the reason was that so much of his work remained unplayed and unpublished, then and for many years thereafter.[57] As for the influence of Ives's Americanness upon them, it must be remembered that his America lay in the rural past, theirs in the urban present. There was of course no lack of interest among American composers of the 1930s and 1940s in capturing the spirit of an older rural or small-town America in their works; Copland's music of the period is only the best-known example of that interest. But whether younger composers approached the older and simpler America critically or merely nostalgically, they generally approached it as outsiders; Ives, on the other hand, approached it as an insider— not as an unreflective insider, to be sure, but certainly as one who had grown up in the way of life that he was portraying. Interestingly enough, the comparison between the two approaches is all in Ives's favor. Not only in their challenging and experimental qualities, but also in their sheer effectiveness as musical expressions of the older America, works such as the First Piano Sonata and *The Fourth of July* were not equaled or surpassed by any of the new music of simplicity that was composed three decades later.

While Ives was enjoying the experience of being discovered by the American avant-garde, the active life of the Pan American Association of Composers—and with it the conducting career of Nicolas Slonimsky—were drawing to a close. The years of Cowell's leadership of the association (1929–1933) constituted an exciting and vital period in the development of American music, with the members involved in presenting some of the most significant works of the twentieth century—music by Ives, Varèse, Cowell, Riegger, Ruggles, and Carlos Chávez, in many cases played for the first time anywhere. In March, 1933, when Slonimsky gave the world premiere of Varèse's *Ionisation* (a work for forty-one percussion instruments alone, which is regarded as one of the most revolutionary and seminal compositions of the twentieth century), the regular Pan American players in New York could not handle the score; so Slonimsky enlisted the services of the composers Paul Creston, William Schuman, Carlos Salzedo, and Henry Cowell as percussionists! [58]

Since 1930 Cowell had also been director of music at the New School for Social Research. Founded in 1919 by a group of liberal intellectuals, this institution for higher adult education had become extremely important in the cultural life of New York City by concentrating its attention on contemporary developments in the social sciences, the humanities, and the arts. Cowell proceeded to make it the country's principal center for experimental American music, since the music conservatories were too timid to assume this role. He secured performances for new American works through a wide range of concerts at the New School, such as those of the Pan American Association and the Young Composers' Group. He also attempted to create an audience for these works through an extensive series of courses aimed at inculcating an understanding and appreciation of contemporary music.[59] Endowed with immense energy, he was simultaneously directing the various projects of *New Music* and running the New Music Society of California.

The event which brought a number of Cowell's efforts to a halt was the return of Edgard Varèse from France to the United States in September, 1933. Although he had resided abroad for five years, Varèse had retained the title of International President of the Pan American Association; and now, with the aid of the faithful Salzedo, he resumed control of the organization. In April, 1934, he put on two New York concerts that were heavily weighted with his own works, Ives contributing a substantial sum to help make up the deficit in the association's budget that was incurred as a result of these concerts.[60]

At the first of these concerts, Slonimsky conducted Ives's *In the Night* and two of his short pieces for chorus and instrumental ensemble.[61] The concert did not go well, and the fault seemed to be Slonimsky's. Ives discovered afterward, for example, that the performance of *In the Night* had been all wrong. In publishing this piece in *New Music,* Ives had disregarded the convention by which, in writing the part for the horns pitched in F, the composer writes the note C if he wishes the horn to play F. Ives had written the *actual notes* that the horn was to play, and Slonimsky had not bothered to read the note explaining the fact. The result was that the entire horn part, which is the basic melody of the piece, had been played in the wrong key.[62] Carl Ruggles was particularly incensed at the way Slonimsky had mishandled his *Portals* at the same concert. A month after the concert, when Wallingford Riegger was arranging for a recording of works by Ives and Ruggles to be made for New Music Quarterly Recordings, he decided to exclude Slonimsky from the project altogether and replace him with someone else.[63] Ives, who was paying the fees of the performers for the recording, successfully interceded for Slonimsky so far as his own works were concerned; he was much too loyal to the conductor to hold the April concert against him. But Carl Ruggles held out adamantly and successfully against Slonimsky's conducting *his* piece on the same recording.[64]

It was, however, Varèse's temperament, not Slonimsky's "slump," that brought about the collapse of the Pan American Association. Edgard Varèse was a man of incredible self-esteem and gigantic will. He had to dominate any group or activity in which he took part, imposing his own opinions and standards upon his associates. Ives, disturbed by Varèse's method of re-establishing his authority over the Pan American Association,[65] even submitted himself to the embarrassing ordeal of confronting Varèse directly concerning his dictatorial practices: "I tried to tell him that 'an Association' to us in this country means a comprehensive group in which all members have a say." [66]

Then in that same spring of 1934, *Trend* magazine carried an article on Varèse in which the author's statements about the Pan American Association were obviously Varèse's own opinions. Varèse implied that Cowell's leadership of the group had been weak and ineffective, but that he himself was already restoring it to the vigor that it had shown when he had first founded it.[67] This gratuitous insult to Cowell, which was just the reverse of the truth, revealed the arrogance of which Varèse was capable. Ives was naturally angered when his friend was treated by Varèse in such a "stupid and unfair way." [68] More significant than the alienation of Ives and Cowell, however, was Varèse's entering a period of profound depression and musical unproductiveness at about this time.[69] As a result of his personal problems and the lack of financial support for concerts during the Depression, the Pan American Association of Composers, which had done so much to secure performances of contemporary American music, became inactive after 1934.

With the demise of the organization, Nicolas Slonimsky no longer had regular opportunities for conducting. In spite of his ability, he had alienated himself from the musical Establishment by consistently identifying himself with avant-garde music. At about this time Ives decided to publish *Three Places in New England,* at his own expense, through the music publishing house of C. C. Birchard & Company in Boston; and he gave Slonimsky the job of helping him prepare the score for publication.[70] Slonimsky soon gave up his conducting career and turned to the editing and compiling of musical reference works, in which he was to distinguish himself for many years. After 1935 his relationship with Ives became much less close than it had been, but the two men remained friends until Ives's death.

Even as Ives's music was being drawn into the current of his country's cultural life, his personal existence was becoming calmer and more withdrawn from the rapidly changing society around him. The gradual decline of his health during the 1920s compelled him to remain away from Ives & Myrick much of the time, and he finally retired from business at the beginning of 1930. From then on, he lived a quiet and secluded domestic life with his wife and daughter. Each spring they moved to West Redding; each autumn they returned to their Manhattan house, where they spent the winter months.

During the 1930s Ives suffered from a number of physical ailments. It is surprising that he lived so long after his retirement; his wife's care was probably the principal reason for this longevity. He had a continuing heart condition, the result of his heart attack in 1918. He had diabetes, for which Mrs. Ives had to give him shots of insulin. As a result of the diabetes, cataracts were forming on both his eyes. His hands shook, so that he found it difficult to write; it was because of difficulties in shaving that he grew his famous beard. Finally, he developed a sort of blurred hearing, so that some musical sounds seemed distorted when he heard them.[71]

In 1932, less than two weeks after the Yaddo festival, the Iveses sailed for Europe, where they remained for more than a year while Ives tried to recover his health. They spent the winter of 1932–1933 at Taormina, Sicily. Thus Ives was out of the country during the very year when the Ives cult in America got started and reached its peak among the avant-garde. Indeed, his absence may actually have appeared to offer proof of his isolation and lack of any desire for public praise, qualities that were becoming an integral part of the Ives Legend. Charles Ives was already a figure of some mystery. Of course, the year during which Ives, his wife, and his daughter traveled in Europe was also one of intense political and economic crisis for that continent. The Iveses even stayed in Germany for several weeks during the summer of 1932. But Ives gave no indication that he grasped what was going on around him.

The debilitating effect of Ives's physical illness should not be over-emphasized. He traveled extensively throughout Europe with his family in 1932 and 1933. He made two subsequent trips to Great Britain, the second as late as 1938. Even in the early 1940s, he was still capable of going to a recording studio and making private recordings, in which he played his own works on the piano.[72] He also took walks near his home in New York. His growing social isolation, then, had emotional as well as physical causes.

From the time of his marriage, Ives generally avoided participation in society, and after 1931 he hardly ever went out for musical or social purposes.[73] If one wanted to meet him, therefore, it would have to be in his home. As interest in Ives's music increased during the early 1930s, there were naturally a number of composers and other musicians who did wish to meet him. Aside from the inner circle of Pan Americans, however, Ives preferred not to meet new people if they were musicians. It is true that he admitted Bernard Herrmann and Jerome Moross into his home, and even after 1936 he agreed to meet a few of the younger men who were propagating his music: John Kirkpatrick, Lehman Engel, Goddard Lieberson, and Lou Harrison. But among musicians the opportunity of meeting Charles Ives came to be considered a rare privilege indeed.[74]

Ives and his wife had to keep visitors away in part because of their fear for his health. When he had the opportunity to discuss issues with people, he was apt to grow so excited that he would become short of breath and have to lie down.[75] Yet there was also another motive for Ives's unwillingness to meet new people. It lay in his old tendency to judge musicians by his personal standards rather than by purely professional ones. In spite of his long neglect at the hands of other musicians, he was not now anxious to have direct dealings with people who were far removed from him in age, background, and outlook, although he was certainly flattered by their praise. This personal standard of judgment was applied even when Aaron Copland himself sought to meet Ives. When Slonimsky tried to arrange such a meeting, Ives asked him one question about Copland, in all seriousness: "Is he a good man?" Slonimsky, of course, replied that he was; but somehow the meeting never took place.[76]

Ives also began to receive a good deal of musical correspondence in the 1930s, and he got into the habit of having his wife or daughter answer his letters for him. Again there was a physical reason: Ives did not type, and his palsy allowed him to make only shaky "snake tracks" when he tried to write with a pen on smooth paper. But the method that he worked out for dealing with the situation only emphasized his desire for isolation from his correspondents. Ives would laboriously write out a reply in pencil on rough, lined paper, often preparing one or more revisions of this "sketch." His wife would then transcribe it onto writing paper. Ives would begin his sketch somewhat as follows: "I am writing for Mr. Ives as he is not at all well . . ."; and he would continue, entirely in the third person, with such remarks as "Mr. Ives deeply appreciates your interest in his music." [77] What he had devised, perhaps unconsciously, was a means of maintaining personal control over what happened to his music while at the same time keeping correspondents at one remove from himself by forcing them to deal with his wife. The persons who received these replies from Mrs. Ives generally had no idea what an important part Ives had played in writing them. Their natural reaction was to send subsequent communications directly to Mrs. Ives.

These correspondents and would-be visitors were younger composers and others interested in contemporary music.[78] Ives's attitude toward them raises the question of what he thought about the great movement of modern music that had swept over Europe and America since the 1910s. Of course, by his own testimony, he had heard very little of this music. He went to scarcely any concerts during the 1930s. The last public performances of his own work that he is known to have attended were Slonimsky's concerts in New York and Boston of January, 1931. Probably the last public musical event of any kind at which he was present was a Sibelius program in London in 1934; it was typical of Ives that he first chose an obviously conservative concert like this one and then, having found an easy target, relieved his pent-up feelings with a fierce diatribe against the triteness of the music played.[79]

Ives took an almost perverse pleasure in having seen or heard nothing by Schoenberg or Hindemith and scarcely anything by Stravinsky. It certainly required an effort for him to be so ignorant of the work of these Europeans, for he subscribed to the *Musical Quarterly;* furthermore, his close friends Furness and Cowell knew all about the latest developments in European music.[80] Ives, however, was willing to make the effort. The truth is that he had little or no interest in modern music as a whole. When he thought of "modern music," he meant *his* music. When he participated in the struggle for modern music, he was actually reliving his own earlier struggle, the struggle of his music against the "lily pads," which he had carried on without allies. Nor did he make any attempt to see or hear or learn about the advanced music that was being written in the United

States.[81] It is safe to say that with the exception of Carl Ruggles, Ives gave financial support to certain American composers because he liked them as persons or because he was told that they were rebels against musical conservatism, not because he knew and admired their compositions.

In spite of his lack of knowledge, however, Ives did make a few judgments about modern music. In his *Essays before a Sonata* (printed in 1920), he wrote of Hawthorne: "His intellectual muscles are too strong to let him become over-influenced, as Ravel and Stravinsky seem to be by the morbidly fascinating—a kind of false beauty obtained by artistic monotony." [82] Then in his *Memos* (written principally in 1932), he leveled the charge of "soft ears" against the same two composers. He recalled that when he had first heard something by Stravinsky ("a part of *Firebird*") around 1919 or 1920, it had seemed "morbid and monotonous" to him. "The idea of a phrase, usually a small one, was good enough and interesting in itself, but he kept it going over and over, and [it] got tiresome." It had reminded him of "something I'd heard of Ravel, most of whose music, that I've heard, is a kind I can't stand, weak, morbid, and monotonous—pleasing enough if you want to be pleased." [83]

Adding a section to the *Memos* in August, 1934, however, Ives saw things somewhat differently: "The trouble with modern music is that [it's] somewhat too intellectual—the brain has [been] working a little more than that bigger muscle underneath (what you may call it, spirit, inner blast, soul?)." He went on to point out that this fault in modern music was just the opposite of the fault in much nineteenth-century music, which had been "soft, easy entertainment—no brain or any other muscle of man required." [84] Apparently the old charge of "soft ears" had suddenly become inappropriate to a whole new body of music, but it is doubtful that Ives felt as much at home with the new music as he had with the old "easy-on-the-ears" works that he loved to denounce.

What did Ives mean by saying that modern music was "too intellectual"? Perhaps he had in mind the neoclassicism of Stravinsky's second major period, or Schoenberg's twelve-tone system; he had probably read about these movements or heard about them from Furness and Cowell. On the other hand, he would almost certainly have regarded neoclassicism as merely "soft"; and when he himself had once used a procedure that foreshadowed the twelve-tone row, he had warned that to rely on such a scheme was "too easy." [85]

Perhaps Ives was thinking of Henry Cowell's compositions when he accused modern music of being "too intellectual." In a continuation of the same passage, he referred to Cowell as "one of the best" of the modernists.[86] It is unlikely that Ives would have implied a criticism of his friend Cowell, but probably he was not entirely satisfied with Cowell's compositions (some of which he did get to hear). Henry Cowell was very Ivesian in his technical experimentation, and his works are full of programmatic elements and nonformal free expressiveness; but they lack that fundamentally spiritual or moral or philosophical approach—that "substance"—which Ives thought so important in music.[87] Probably Ives was making this very point in general, without specific reference to Cowell, when he criticized the overly intellectual nature of modern music: he was lamenting that modern works were not inspired by profound spirituality or noble philosophies. If he was indeed asserting that these elements were absent from modern music, then he was largely correct.

It is quite possible, on the other hand, that Ives's judgments about modern music were based less on his opinions of the music itself than on his opinions of the men who wrote it. While Ives heard very little contemporary music in the late 1920s and early 1930s, he did meet during that period several of the most important experimental composers in America. Among them was one of the great creative giants of twentieth-century music: Edgard Varèse. An examination of the gulf that lay between Ives and Varèse will yield several important conclusions about Ives's anomalous place in modern American culture.

On the surface Varèse and Ives would seem to have had a great deal in common. Varèse was only nine years younger than Ives and was a thoroughly masculine and virile person. No man was ever less of a "lily pad," in personality or in music, than he. His artistic ideals, moreover, resembled Ives's in a number of respects. He too shunned the effete and decadent in music and strove for what was vital and "strong." Varèse despised the neoclassicism and "clever Parisian tricks" [88] that were highly admired in the 1920s and 1930s—

despised, indeed, all academic systems, believing (with Ives) that they hampered the freedom of the composer. He agreed with Ives that there was a large audience for their sort of music, but that conductors and virtuoso performers, intent upon increasing their own prestige, prevented that music from ever reaching its audience. Like Ives he used a sexual simile for the performer, likening him to "a eunuch who can very well theorize about love, but who can't make a life." [89] Ives would have agreed perfectly with three of his aphorisms:

> Sometimes one sees so far that expression refuses to follow as though it were afraid.
>
> I have known fierce and uncompromising traditionalists who proclaimed the unchanging dogmas of schools that were. Each trafficked in a corpse. Yet when business began appreciably to fall off, they would quaintly admit that the time had come for the dead to die.
>
> No matter how consummate a work of art may seem, it is only an approximation of the original conception. It is the artist's consciousness of this discrepancy between his conception and the realization that assures his progress. [90]

There was even a similarity between the two composers in their tendency to embody their philosophical visions in their compositions. Thus a work like Varèse's unfinished *Espace* has its counterpart in Ives's unfinished *Universe* Symphony.

In spite of these similarities, however, Charles Ives detested Edgard Varèse. He seems to have had only two meetings with Varèse, both of them in 1934.[91] Yet nearly ten years later, in 1943, he began a sketch for a letter to Varèse with the words "Varase—Go to Hell!!" (It was not, of course, actually sent in that form.) Varèse had written asking to make a personal visit to Ives, but Ives did not mention the request in the reply that he wrote out for his wife to send, for he obviously had no intention of granting it.[92] It is true that Ives had resented Varèse's egotism and his cavalier treatment of Henry Cowell in 1934, but that resentment was hardly sufficient to explain his holding a grudge against the man a decade later. After all, Cowell's and Ives's friend Carl Ruggles experienced Varèse's domineering leadership in both the International Composers' Guild and the Pan American Association of Composers; yet years later, Ruggles still expressed admiration for Varèse.[93] Varèse, moreover, was always friendly to Ives and made a number of attempts to interest others in Ives's music and to have it performed.[94] In fact, the letter to which Ives sketched such an insulting reply contained a request for information about Ives and his works, to be used in some lectures that Varèse was to give on American music.[95] Ives's continued hostility toward Varèse can only be satisfactorily explained by postulating some deeper antipathy in him.

Again and again Ives insisted that what he found objectionable in many musicians was the effeminacy, conventionality, and commercialism of the compositions that they wrote and performed; and he traced those elements back to the musicians' personal conduct of life. Varèse's qualities, both musical and personal, were just the opposite of those that Ives found objectionable, and thus there was every reason why Ives should have admired Varèse. Yet he did not, for he found Varèse's qualities—Bohemianism, unconventional morality, and lack of gentility—equally objectionable; they formed a style of life which was just as threatening to him as was that of the "lily pad." If one wished to get close to Ives, one dared not be either too refined or too unrefined.

Naturally, Ives did not apply these standards to farmers, servants, employees, and others who had never had the opportunity to become genteel; with them he could carry on an apparently easy banter on their own level. He was careful, however, to protect himself from those (especially artists and intellectuals) who had been raised to gentility but had become alienated from it. Similarly, Ives was happy to patronize ragtime music so long as he could think of it as the "shuffling lilt of a happy soul just let out of a Baptist Church in old Alabama." But when intellectuals began to express an unpatronizing admiration for ragtime and it threatened to engulf the higher reaches of American culture, then Ives found himself retreating into gentility and quoting with approval the "soft-eared" Daniel Gregory Mason in depreciation of this urban music.[96]

Varèse's style of life was that of the Bohemian and the rebel.[97] He hated his father. He received his musical education in Paris just after the turn of the century and participated fully in that city's cultural ferment. His first wife was an actress; they separated and were divorced because of a desire to pursue their individual careers. His second wife, Louise Norton, was part of the literary and artistic "rebellion" in New York before World War I and later became known for her translations of modern French literature; she and Varèse lived together before they were married. Varèse loved the modern city and disliked the countryside. Shunning nostalgia or an easy optimism, he fully accepted the inevitability of the machine age even as his music spoke of the agony of men in that age. His friends were Debussy, Picasso, Cocteau, Malraux, Joseph Stella, Henry Miller. He moved easily among intellectuals and artists in both Europe and America, exchanging ideas with them; and these associations kept him within the vanguard in all the arts. He was, in short, the self-conscious artist, striking the pose of the artist, living fully the life of the artist, and issuing manifestoes to the world in the name of his art. The contrast of this mode of life with that of Ives is extraordinary. Carl Ruggles, who was friendly with both men, must have had to reorient himself completely when he went from the presence of one into the presence of the other.

The essential difference between Ives and Varèse lay in Varèse's conscious artistic alienation from the bourgeoisie, his parents' social class. This alienation was made much easier and more palatable for him because the arts had traditionally held a more central place in the European countries than in the United States. Although he did plenty of starving in garrets in his younger days, Varèse was in fact assured at an early point in his life that his society recognized and respected him as an artist. Partly through choosing out and educating an artistic elite based on merit, the European system actually encouraged the formation of a separate and special social group of self-conscious artists and intellectuals who felt free to thumb their noses at the bourgeoisie. The associations that he had with other "free" creative artists also gave Varèse the courage to move beyond all his contemporaries in his musical ideas. And yet the whole system did not have for Europeans the popular connotations of uselessness and aristocracy which a similar system would have had in the United States. In the absence of such a system, the American creative figure of Ives's generation too often lacked even the assurance that his society accepted him as an artist or the support and encouragement of other free artists; thus he often lacked the confidence to make a break with the respectable middle class.

Having taken up the Bohemian way of life and found refuge among other artists and intellectuals, Varèse could afford to espouse left-wing political causes and vaguely to identify himself with the masses, since he was well protected from having to deal with them as equals. It is the pattern of many modern radical intellectuals and artists. Theoretically identified in spirit with the masses and alienated from the bourgeoisie, he was in fact alienated aesthetically and intellectually from both, having found the separate existence of the artist.

Ives was theoretically alienated from no class, for he made no distinction between the middle class and the masses; they all made up "the majority," with which he identified himself. Indeed, he was so busy worrying about sexual categories in art and politics that he was conveniently freed from considering categories of social class. He never allowed himself to feel conscious alienation, with all its disturbing implications. In fact, however, he too was separated from the masses—separated from them by his genteel and dignified style of life, which was that of the conventional American bourgeois of the early twentieth century. Of course, he would certainly never have *thought* of himself as a bourgeois.

In this position Ives was threatened from two sides at once. On one side there was the role of Establishment artist, the role of Horatio Parker or David Stanley Smith. This role, with its suggestions of effeminacy and aristocracy, threatened Ives because it implied that the creative artist was necessarily undemocratic and separated from the majority. But it was easy for Ives to counter this threat simply by attacking these men as *artists* ("lily pads") and asserting that he himself was a different kind of artist, an artist of the people. Thus he obscured what really separated him from the majority: the *personal* and *social* middle-class gentility that he shared with Parker and Smith.

On the other side there was the role of Bohemian artist, the role of Edgard Varèse. This role, with its subtle combination of primitivism and unsentimental modernity, was equally threatening to Ives, because it implied that gentility was not a style of life suited to a creative artist like himself. Here, however, Ives had no weapons with which to counter the threat; he could hardly attack Varèse as an *artist*. He had no choice but to abandon his own position as creative artist and retreat into Philistinism; from that position he could attack Varèse as a *person*. Ives was so anxious to hold on to his identity as a common man and his identity as a refined gentleman, both at the same time, that his identity as a creative artist was often lost in the process.

These needs explain why Ives found it difficult to meet and feel easy with other musicians. He was really comfortable only with a man who was both conventional in his personal life and radical in his musical outlook, and there were few such men. Even a Frenchman could gain his confidence if he conformed, as E. Robert Schmitz did, to the genteel pattern of life; and Cowell and Slonimsky, although their styles of life were much more unconventional than Ives's, made special efforts to bridge the gap between themselves and the older man. Varèse, however, although friendly, was incapable of such an approach; and so Ives kept him at a distance.[98] Ives expressed his feeling that modern music was "too intellectual" only a few months after his encounters with Varèse; when he wrote these words, perhaps he had in mind Varèse's approach to the life of a creative artist.

Of course, it is still possible that Ives objected more strongly to Varèse's personal idiosyncrasies of temperament than to his broader definition of the role of the artist in society. But the exact nature of Ives's feeling of dislike for Varèse is less important than Varèse's being representative of a number of avant-garde composers whose lives were touched in various ways by Bohemianism. Ives had as little as possible to do with most of them. Perhaps the most interesting case is that of Wallingford Riegger. Riegger's personal life was entirely acceptable to Ives, but the two men never succeeded in establishing a friendship.[99]

From one point of view, Wallingford Riegger and Charles Ives were strikingly alike. Not only were they both composers of highly experimental and innovative music, but they also shared such personal qualities as middle-class family background, shyness, integrity, independence, gentility and respectability, devotion to wife and chil-

dren, generosity, humor, optimism, scorn of glamour and easy popularity, devotion to the highest artistic ideals.[100] Even their political
convictions carried them in the same direction. Riegger, moreover,
recognized this similarity between them. After the Yaddo festival in
1932, he wrote to Ives: "I know we are total strangers to each other,
but I feel, through your music and what I have heard about you,
that we have much in common." [101] Riegger also had a high regard
for Ives's music, for which he tried to secure a wider hearing. Although normally reticent, he reacted ecstatically in 1949 to a performance of the First Piano Sonata. "It was one of the few high spots in
my whole musical career to have heard it," he wrote to Ives. "I suppose I'm gushing like a school girl, but I still can't get over the indescribable grandeur of your work." [102] Ives likewise thought highly of
Riegger. In a sketch for a letter to Riegger in 1948, he wrote: "Mr.
Ives greatly admires your music and your personality." [103] He had
probably never heard the music, but the remark about personality
was an extraordinary one for Charles Ives to make. Ives would also
have been proud of Riegger's conduct before a subcommittee of the
House Un-American Activities Committee; summoned for questioning in 1957 about former Communist party membership and activities, the old man refused to answer the subcommittee's questions,
risking punishment by basing his refusal solely on the First Amendment and on his respect for his own integrity.[104]

There was every reason, then, why Riegger and Ives should have
become friends. Yet they were never close. Although drawn together
by their common involvement in Cowell's activities, they saw each
other a few times at most.[105] Both were reticient men, to be sure; but
it is likely that they kept their distance from each other because one
or both of them sensed a fundamental difference between them—a
difference having to do with their attitudes toward their era and
toward themselves as artists.

Although he was only ten and a half years younger than Ives,
Riegger was in spirit of a different generation. He had made his
philosophical peace with the modern age and all its terrors, and he
seems not to have indulged himself in a nostalgia for the past out of
which he had come. While his personal style of life remained close to
that of his nineteenth-century Protestant background, he apparently

grew away from the religious and philosophical underpinnings of that older mode of life in a way in which Ives did not. His music, also, is essentially different from Ives's in the sense that it is animated by a more modern spirit.

Even more important, Riegger accepted himself as an artist. As a young man he faced much the same set of choices about his career that Ives did, but his decisions were very different. Lacking Ives's facility and early maturation as a composer, Riegger knew that he would have to devote his full time to music if he hoped to produce anything of value. He chose to become a musician—an artist—with the full knowledge that it was to be a lonely and materially unrewarding vocation. He suffered the indignities of a life of public neglect with humor and humility. Avoiding Ives's simplistic notions about democracy and art, Riegger also accepted that conscious alienation from the general culture of his time which is necessary to the truly creative artist if he is to be integrated with himself. And he did all this without the paranoia that attacked Ives whenever he was confronted with the fact that he was an artist.

As a professional musician Riegger took a vigorous part in the artistic and intellectual life of New York City from the 1920s on. Having achieved personal acceptance of himself as an artist—having achieved a physical and spiritual separation of himself from nonartists and nonintellectuals—Riegger was prepared to reintegrate himself into his democratic heritage by joining other artists and intellectuals in leftist movements during the 1930s. His political activities were certainly more effective than Ives's, which were largely exercises in talking to himself. Riegger identified himself with the aspirations of the masses, but only *as an artist*. Ives, on the other hand, refused to accept himself as an artist (and therefore as an alienated man), but instead tried confusedly to see himself as just one more element in the "majority mind."

In contrast with Ives, then, Riegger can be said to have achieved meaningful success, both as a man and as an artist, in spite of adversity. Riegger achieved actual separation from the people; but at the same time, he identified himself with them and with positive goals that he imputed to them. This combination seems to be self-contradictory, but it is probably the only possible solution for the radical intellectual or artist in America if he is to achieve integration with his democratic tradition without destroying his freedom as a creative person and wounding his aesthetic sensibility. It is, in fact, the solution that most radical intellectuals and artists have arrived at in the twentieth century.

Since the cultural distance that separated Ives from both Varèse and Riegger has been examined, it should also be pointed out that Ives did form close friendships with two other composers in Henry Cowell's circle: John J. Becker and Carl Ruggles.

Becker was the midwestern pillar of Cowell's musical organizations. When Cowell first put him in touch with Ives, Becker was living in St. Paul, Minnesota, where he served as chairman of the Fine Arts Division at the College of St. Thomas. Unfortunately, there was scarcely anyone in the Midwest who could understand the experimental music that he was writing. Becker was no Bohemian, but rather an academic with a doctorate in music and a strong interest in all the arts. There were certain similarities between him and Henry Bellamann, though Becker lacked the talent and inclination to write a best-selling novel.

Before actually meeting Ives, Becker gratified him by conducting (in St. Paul in 1931) what was probably the first public performance of *In the Night;* [106] and he continued to foster an interest in Ives's works in the Midwest. The two men only saw each other on rare occasions, when Becker made trips to the East; but they carried on a large correspondence during the 1930s.[107] Ives seems to have paid relatively little attention to Becker's compositions, but he was strongly impressed by the man's ideals and his philosophy of the arts. Becker was a devout Roman Catholic. In fact, the contrapuntal style that he liked to employ was modeled upon the music of the great Catholic polyphonists of the sixteenth and seventeenth centuries; yet although he was attracted by these older forms, his harmonies followed the advanced trends of the twentieth century. Like Ives he believed that the arts were essentially spiritual in nature and closely akin to religion, and he had a missionary's conviction of the importance of education in the fine arts for young people.[108]

Even more significant, from Ives's point of view, was Becker's devotion to his wife and four children.[109] He was utterly melted by the picture of Becker's struggling to support his family while remaining true to his austere artistic ideals and refusing to truckle to the conservative musical Establishment. When Becker lost his teaching position during the Depression, Ives gave him financial help, partly for working on some of Ives's scores in order to get them into playable shape.[110] Eventually Becker became state director for Minnesota of the WPA's Federal Music Project.

Henry Cowell worked hard to secure an audience for Becker's music, and Becker was so grateful that he named one of his sons for Cowell.[111] But most modernists seemed to feel that Becker lacked the talent for composition that the others in Cowell's circle had.[112] His compositions, therefore, were seldom performed. Even the Pan Americans left his music out of their European programs, although he was a member of their association. Becker came to feel that, isolated as he was from the centers of musical activity, he was being deliberately slighted by an inner group that controlled the field of contemporary music.[113] Ives did not like to become too closely involved in other people's problems, and after a while he probably got tired of hearing about Becker's many troubles.[114] At any rate, the frequency of their correspondence declined markedly in the 1940s, although the two families continued to write to each other and Becker saw Ives a few more times before the latter's death.

Of all Ives's composer friends, it was Carl Ruggles with whom he had the warmest relationship.[115] When he met Ruggles through Henry Cowell's musical activities, about 1930 or 1931, Ives discovered in him many qualities that he greatly admired. They were, in fact, qualities that Ives also saw in himself. It is true that Ruggles was self-consciously a professional composer (and an amateur painter as well); he was, moreover, friendly with many figures in the vanguard of the arts.[116] But Ruggles was first and foremost a New Englander, with all the individualism, straightforwardness, and crusty humor that his place of origin connotes.

Ives and Ruggles could be bad boys together, "cussing" at the "lily pads" and playing pranks on the proper people in the musical Establishment. Once when Ruggles and his wife were visiting Charles and Harmony Ives during Ives's last years, the two aged composers began marching around the luncheon table and singing Reeves's *Sec-*

ond Connecticut March (the piece that Ives had quoted in *Decoration Day*). Their wives, doing just what they were expected to do, played Aunt Polly to the men's Tom Sawyer. Mrs. Ruggles's reaction was: "Those two *boys!*" Mrs. Ives remained calm and paid no attention.[117] It is interesting that Ruggles even had a pronounced inclination toward the risqué, being renowned for his dirty stories; it was a part of himself that he must have kept carefully hidden from Charles Ives.

Besides the safe rebelliousness that Ives and Ruggles were able to enjoy together, they also shared another and entirely different quality: each man was something of a transcendentalist visionary in search of the sublime. Like the innovations which Ives had worked out earlier, Ruggles's experiments were largely independent of outside influences. His compositions conjure up New England in all its cragginess; yet they do not quote from other music. And in contrast to Ives's comparatively offhand approach to composition, Ruggles's method was to choose every note of his small body of works with extreme care, working very slowly and constantly revising. Ives praised this music highly, though it is uncertain how much he knew of it. Yet Ruggles's titles alone, with their connotations of spiritual striving, would have been enough to win Ives's enthusiasm: *Angels, Vox Clamans in Deserto, Portals, Evocations*—but above all, *Sun-treader* and *Men and Mountains. Sun-treader* was named from a line of poetry by Ives's hero Robert Browning: "Sun-treader, life and light be thine for ever!" *Men and Mountains,* a work which Ives heard performed and which he admired very much, took its title from William Blake: "Great things are done when Men & Mountains meet." Ives himself had long used the symbol of the mountain to suggest spiritual transcendence and the hard and lonely way of truth.[118]

Ruggles, in turn, came to admire at least some of Ives's music.[119] But he tended to be a perfectionist in his attitude toward others' music as well as toward his own. Thus he lacked the practical ability to organize and carry on musical activities, and he depended on people like Varèse and Cowell to disseminate his works. Ives helped in every way he could, particularly in the matter of *Sun-treader,* which was Ruggles's masterpiece. His money made it possible for Slonimsky to give (in Paris) the first performance of this work and for Cowell subsequently to publish it in *New Music*.[120] He also took advantage of opportunities to recommend Ruggles for the recognition that he thought he deserved.[121] Carl Ruggles's friendship meant a great deal to Ives, and the two composers remained close until Ives's death.

In the summer of 1936, the Iveses were appalled to learn that Henry Cowell had been arrested in California for a homosexual offense involving a minor. He was tried and sentenced to serve up to fifteen years in San Quentin Prison.[122] It is difficult to think of anything Cowell could have done that would have been more threatening to both of Ives's great commitments—his commitment to gentility and his commitment to masculinity. John Becker first informed Mrs. Ives, the more "practical" member of the family, of what had happened; and for a while she protected her innocent husband from the shocking knowledge. When she finally told him, Ives felt that he had been personally betrayed by a man to whom he had entrusted his friendship and his music. Cowell's other musical friends were sympathetic to his situation and regarded his imprisonment as a temporary absence, at the end of which they expected him to resume his musical offices and activities. The Iveses, however, were so repelled by his unspeakable practices that they decided to have no communication with him while he was in prison; they would not even talk about Cowell's offense. Charles Ives determined that he would never see Henry Cowell again.[123]

Cowell chose Gerald Strang, a young Los Angeles composer, to run *New Music* for him while he was in San Quentin. But Strang lacked Cowell's energy and organizing ability, and *New Music* declined in both the efficiency of its operation and the number of its subscribers.[124]

Meanwhile, Lehman Engel, who had been a member of the Young Composers' Group, had secured from Ives the score of *Psalm 67*, the bitonal work for unaccompanied chorus that had been composed in the 1890s. Engel was the conductor of the Madrigal Singers, who gave New York concerts under the auspices of the WPA's Federal Music Project. This group performed *Psalm 67* several times during 1937,[125] and through these performances Engel earned Ives's friendship and the privilege of a visit with him.[126] The next year Engel headed a group of composers (including Aaron Copland) who set up the Arrow Music Press in New York for the publication of contemporary music. Ives decided not only to publish *Psalm 67* and some of his other compositions (at his own expense) through this nonprofit firm, but also to subsidize its publication of works by other composers.[127]

Ives did not abandon *New Music* in California. But faced with the fact of the quarterly's obvious decline, he for once imposed his will upon it by cutting its subsidy sharply. Then with the aid of Becker and Riegger, of the editorial board of *New Music,* he took several more steps in 1939 that he considered necessary: he gently compelled Gerald Strang to discontinue the separate and expensive series of orchestral scores that *New Music* had been issuing; he tried to bring about a more efficient operation of *New Music* on Strang's part; and he helped to initiate the process by which the distribution of *New Music* would eventually be taken over by a music distribution center in New York City. Such a center for the distribution of American music (the American Music Center) was being set up in close cooperation with the Arrow Music Press.[128]

With Cowell in prison and Varèse in eclipse, the former hostility between the League of Composers and the composers connected with the Pan American Association died down in the latter 1930s. It was a time when the avant-garde rivalries of the earlier part of the decade gave way to a more hardheaded uniting of American composers for their own economic protection and benefit.[129] New organizations like the American Composers Alliance, the Arrow Music Press, and the American Music Center brought together composers from both Cowell's group and the League group. Ives cannot have been entirely sympathetic to the realistic and self-interested character of these new musical organizations; but he was enough of a businessman to realize that *New Music* could not remain a viable enterprise if it did not take advantage of the wider and more efficient distribution of which the American Music Center would be capable.

Lehman Engel was one of the few bright spots in Ives's musical life during the years immediately following Cowell's arrest.[130] In fact, the period from 1933 through the end of 1938 witnessed a pronounced decline in interest in Ives's music. In contrast to the vigorous activity of 1931–1932, when a number of Ives's most important orchestral works were performed for the first time before a serious public audience, the period from the spring of 1934 until well into the 1940s saw no such first performances (and very few performances at all) of his compositions for full or chamber orchestra. Nor did more than three or four of his other instrumental works receive a first hearing in public during this same period until John Kirkpatrick played the complete *Concord* Sonata in 1938. With only a handful of performances of his compositions taking place each year and with the bulk of his music still not having been publicly heard, Ives was already acquiring the reputation of being a composer who was more talked and written about than played.[131] For example, when the WPA's Federal Music Project gave a week-long festival of American music in New York in 1936, performing compositions which represented the historical development of American music as well as contemporary compositions, Ives's work was completely left out.[132] His songs, which were now in print in three published collections, were given a number of times during these years. For a time during the 1930s, indeed, it seemed that Ives would become known mainly as a composer of art songs. He was still remembered best for the songs that had been sung at Yaddo.

The avant-garde's loss of interest in Ives during the middle 1930s can be traced, as has already been suggested, to the new social and cultural currents that were affecting composers and other creative artists.[133] These currents encouraged a new simplicity in American music at the expense of the complexity and difficulty that had previously characterized avant-garde compositions. The basic shift in America's cultural and intellectual life during the 1930s was a response to the human misery at home during the Great Depression and to the determined effort of the New Deal to overcome that misery. The shift involved a turning away from the sophisticated cosmopolitanism of the 1920s and a search for inspiration in the past and present life of America itself. Henry Cowell had believed that the growth of such a national consciousness among American composers would produce an advanced music based on indigenous American materials, much as the experimenters Ives and Bartók had earlier worked from indigenous music in the United States and Hungary.[134] But Cowell's expectations of a new experimentalism were not fulfilled. The reason was that the new cultural nationalism coincided with a greatly increased interest in political radicalism and collectivism. The new love and hope for America inevitably became allied with a new feeling of ideological attraction to the common people of America; and it was only a short step from exalting the common people to writing a simpler and less dissonant music that they could understand.

There were also more practical reasons for the trend toward musical simplicity. The financial crisis greatly reduced the patronage of the wealthy, which had been crucial during the 1920s in supporting experimental composers and avant-garde societies (like Pro Musica) that had very limited audiences. This decline of private patronage prompted Aaron Copland, among other composers, to begin composing for a new and larger audience, an audience which lay entirely outside the avant-garde:

> During these years I began to feel an increasing dissatisfaction with the relations of the music-loving public and the living composer. The old "special" public of the modern music concerts had fallen away, while the conventional concert public continued apathetic or indifferent to anything but the established classics. It seemed to me that we composers were in danger of working in a vacuum. Moreover, an entirely new public for music had grown up around the radio and phonograph. It made no sense to ignore them and to continue writing as if they did not exist. I felt that it was worth the effort to see if I couldn't say what I had to say in the simplest possible terms.[135]

Following the decline of the exclusive avant-garde societies and organs,[136] the extensive activities of the WPA in the arts began in 1935. There was also a new interest in music making by amateur and school groups. At about the same time, opportunities for composers were opening up through phonograph recordings and in the expanding industries of radio broadcasting and sound films. The mass audience, if it could be reached, offered the composer a whole new field for useful work. The change in Copland's own style of composition was especially notable. The harsh and forbidding works that he had been composing around 1930, such as his Piano Variations, gave way about 1935 to more ingenuous and easily understood compositions like the music for the film *Our Town* and the scores for the ballets *Billy the Kid, Rodeo,* and *Appalachian Spring.* These compositions dealt with American subject matter and incorporated American tunes, they focused on the life of common people, and their relatively simple style was aimed at a mass audience.

Like so much else in American culture, even the new trend toward musical simplicity and functionalism can in part be traced to a European source. That source was not so much neoclassicism per se as it was the German movement of the 1920s that centered around *Gebrauchsmusik. Gebrauchsmusik* (literally, "music for use") was essentially a functional, unpretentious, and uncomplex music that could be easily played (often by amateurs) and easily understood. The *Gebrauchsmusik* movement involved German composers as different from one other as Paul Hindemith and Kurt Weill; the latter's *Die Dreigroschenoper (The Threepenny Opera)* is a good example of the genre. *Gebrauchsmusik* clearly had an effect on Copland and other Americans of the 1930s, finding perhaps its principal American exponent in the young composer Marc Blitzstein. Obviously influenced by Weill's example, Blitzstein wrote semipopular operas that forsook "art for art's sake" in order to preach a leftist morality. Weill himself, driven out of Germany by the Nazis, came to the United States, where he achieved considerable success in composing Broadway musicals and an American folk opera.

It is certainly true that listeners heard a new and distinctively American sound in the music of Copland, Harris, and other native-born composers of the 1930s. But it is equally true that these composers turned away from many of the revolutionary musical procedures that had been introduced during the preceding twenty or twenty-five years. They made a partial retreat back toward the harmonic and melodic style of the nineteenth century, which was, after all, the style that common people enjoyed most. It seems ironic that the 1920s, a period of political and social conservatism, should have produced a great outpouring of radical and innovative music in America, while the New Deal era, a period of political and social radicalism, should have fostered a music that was stylistically conservative. Yet this apparent contradiction between the ideological tone of each era and the style of music which it produced actually made a good deal of sense, given the cultural implications of leftist and collectivist ideology. It was no accident that the Soviet Union, in working to build a revolutionary socialist society, found it necessary to curb the avant-garde tendencies of its composers and to force them to write a music that the Soviet people could understand.

In the light of this trend toward simplicity in American music, it is not difficult to understand why so little was done to advance the cause of Ives's music from 1934 through 1938, following the decline of the earlier Ives cult. In the early 1930s, Cowell and others had presented Ives's music as essentially an experimental body of work that made use of new musical resources. Ives had thus acquired a reputation as a composer of complex and difficult works. It is true that Ives's compositions were based upon extramusical American programs, which were much in vogue during the 1930s. But the difficulty that Ives's American programs presented to many people was noted by Aaron Copland in a shrewd comment that he made in 1937 about *Washington's Birthday:* "What is most striking . . . is the contrast between the 'homely' program attached to the piece and the incredibly complex means for achieving it." [137] The American composers of serious music whose works attracted the most attention during the middle and latter 1930s—men like Copland, Harris, Thomson, and Blitzstein—tended to embody their relatively simple American "messages" in relatively simple music. Ives's music was anything but simple; and to the arbiters of musical fashion at the time, the combination of simple programs and very complex music seemed inappropriate. In particular, the concerts of the Federal Music Project, which put a certain emphasis on American works, shamefully neglected Ives's orchestral music. Of course, Ives was not the only composer whose work went against the new cultural grain of the middle 1930s. Ruggles and Varèse were other experimenters who also suffered neglect at the hands of the avant-garde during this period. Indeed, it was a time when the avant-garde tried to forget that it *was* the avant-garde.

Another reason for the neglect of Ives's music in this period—a reason more peculiar to Ives's own special situation—was that the very physical condition of his scores violated the *Gebrauchsmusik* ideal. Not only were they too difficult to be played by amateurs, but only a few of them had even been published, and many of the rest were available only in photostats of disordered, incomplete, and confusing manuscripts; instrumental parts were also poorly made or difficult to obtain. In 1938 the music director of the Columbia Broadcasting System suggested that someone "spend his time making Charles Ives' later scores more practical for performance." [138] He was perhaps expressing a desire not only that the scores be simplified, but also that clear and complete copies of them be made in a form that was as easy as possible for the players to read. Ives's eyesight, however, no longer allowed him to undertake the task of getting his more confused manuscripts "in shape"; he needed the help of someone who really understood his music. Cowell had made a beginning of the job, completing an arrangement of *Calcium Light Night* (an evocation of the ceremonies accompanying the announcement of elections to Yale's junior fraternities) and sending the orchestral score to Ives just before his arrest in 1936.[139] But now Cowell was gone, and Ives believed that he and Cowell would never collaborate again.

And here, certainly, was another important reason why Ives's musical reputation languished from 1936 to 1939: the absence of Henry Cowell. A few days after he learned of Cowell's arrest, Ives received a letter from the United States Section of the International Society for Contemporary Music inviting him to submit compositions for possible performance at the society's 1937 festival in Paris. Ives's music might well have been played—as Ruggles's *Sun-treader* had been at the 1936 festival—if he had submitted something. But he refused to answer the letter, undoubtedly recalling his unhappy previous experience with this organization; and he damned its officers and directors as a bunch of "ladies." [140] There was now no Henry Cowell to advise him against such precipitate action.

Cowell had been the great sponsor and promoter of Ives's music. He had drawn Ives into the modern music movement, giving him for the first time a sense of participating in a definite "cause" and belonging to a special "crowd" of modern composers.[141] It was only because Cowell had brought Ives's personal wealth to the aid of *New*

Music and the Pan American Association that Ives's orchestral scores had ever been published and played in the late 1920s and early 1930s. There was no one else who could assume Cowell's role in Ives's musical life. Slonimsky had given up his career as a conductor and rarely saw Ives any more. Ruggles and Becker had enough to do just furthering their own careers as composers. Bernard Herrmann and Lehman Engel did what they could for Ives's music, but Henry Cowell was really irreplaceable.[142]

Feeling that he had been made the victim of Cowell's "treachery," Ives may even have decided that now he must stay away from *all* musicians, including modernists. Once his working relationship with Cowell had ended, he rarely took the initiative in promulgating his own music, apparently retreating again to the position that those who were interested would have to approach *him* if they wanted his scores. At the same time, he made it harder and harder for people to make contact with him, either personally or by correspondence. His increasing isolation was self-chosen; yet Ives must have been a lonely man in the years that followed Cowell's arrest and imprisonment.

Then in early 1939, just when it seemed that the musical avant-garde had become lukewarm about Ives, his work made a sudden and decisive breakthrough to the musical public.

The vehicle of the sudden fame that came to Ives in 1939 was his *Concord* Sonata. The instrument of that fame was the young American pianist John Kirkpatrick.

It was in Paris, in 1927, that Kirkpatrick had first become interested in a copy of the *Concord* Sonata that belonged to his friend Katherine Heyman. At her suggestion he wrote to Ives about the work, and Ives sent him a copy of the sonata and the book of essays; but for Kirkpatrick the music's "penetration was gradual." [143]

During the 1930s Kirkpatrick, although not a pianist known to the average concertgoer, became closely identified with the performance of American music, particularly works by the contemporary composers Aaron Copland and Roy Harris. But as a close friend of Copland's and a product of the American Conservatory at Fontainebleau, Kirkpatrick was not drawn into Henry Cowell's circle and did not become personally acquainted with Ives in the early thirties.

His admiration for *Concord*, nevertheless, continued to grow. By 1933 he was playing *The Alcotts*, the shortest and easiest movement of the sonata, in recital. By the beginning of 1934, he had decided to learn the entire sonata.[144] By 1935 he had mastered the much more formidable *Emerson* movement and was giving it before audiences; he included it in his New York recital at Town Hall on January 28, 1936, which Mrs. Ives and her daughter, Edith, attended.[145] Kirkpatrick had, in the meantime, begun a correspondence with Ives (through Mrs. Ives and Edith) and was deluging him with questions about his music. In May, 1937, he was rewarded for his efforts in behalf of Ives's music—and for his importunities—by a personal visit to Ives at his house in New York City.[146]

By June, 1938, Kirkpatrick had mastered the difficulties of *Hawthorne* and *Thoreau* and was able to play the complete sonata (not yet from memory) at a private lecture-recital in Stamford, Connecticut.[147] At another private recital, held in Cos Cob, Connecticut, on the following twenty-eighth of November, he performed the whole sonata from memory—an extraordinary feat of interpretative powers, technical skill, and memorization, which no one (except possibly Ives himself) had ever before successfully attempted.[148] Paul Rosenfeld attended this Cos Cob recital and reported in *Modern Music* that the sonata contained "possibly the most intense and sensitive musical experience achieved by an American." *Thoreau* "seemed music as beautiful at the very least as any composed by an American." Rosenfeld felt that Ives had undergone a genuinely nationalistic experience, that of the individual who "imaginatively . . . grasps the forces and the values of the individuals who existed on his soil before him, the forces and values of the group, race or nation incarnate in them; recognizing their survival in the best of himself and comprehending them with love." Ives had thus imaginatively grasped the Concord transcendentalists' mystical sympathy with Nature; and having comprehended it, he had successfully communicated the experience in his sonata, particularly in *Thoreau*.[149]

By this time Kirkpatrick's wealthy patroness had promised him another Town Hall recital, and he had decided to devote the whole program to only two works: a Beethoven sonata and *Concord*.[150] Neither the *New York Times* nor the *Musical Courier* even bothered to send a reviewer to this recital of January 20, 1939, and there is no reason to think that this first complete New York performance of *Concord* would have caused any stir had it not been for the interest of one man. But that man was Lawrence Gilman, of the *New York Herald Tribune*, at that time probably the most influential music critic in America.

Gilman had earned his great reputation largely for his graceful prose style and for his authoritative knowledge of Wagner's operas. He had always been friendly to new music; but for years he had devoted his critical attention to the great orchestral and operatic performances in New York, to the neglect of less prominent performances by avant-garde groups like the Pan American Association. When Gilman saw the advance announcement of the program for Kirkpatrick's New York recital, he evidently remembered his favorable impression of two movements from an Ives symphony that he had heard at a Pro Musica concert twelve years before, and he decided that he wanted to hear *Concord*. Not wishing to confront the sonata unprepared, he secured a copy of it from the Iveses so that he might study it before the recital. In his correspondence with Mrs. Ives, he recalled having known her in his student days in Hartford, more than forty years before.[151]

Gilman was deeply moved by Kirkpatrick's performance of *Concord*.[152] The morning after the recital, in a long two-column review in the *Herald Tribune*, he ecstatically lauded this "music by an unexampled creative artist of our day, probably the most original and extraordinary of American composers":

> This sonata is exceptionally great music—it is, indeed, the greatest music composed by an American, and the most deeply and essentially American in impulse and implication. It is wide-ranging and capacious. It has passion, tenderness, humor, simplicity, homeliness. It has imaginative and spiritual vastness. It has wisdom and beauty and profundity, and a sense of the encompassing terror and splendor of human life and human destiny—a sense of those mysteries that are both human and divine.

Most impressed by the movement inspired by Emerson's thought, Gilman found in it "a quality of musical utterance which is altogether extraordinary and unique" and "pages in which the expressional power of musical speech is mysteriously extended and released." Genuinely indifferent to acclaim, Ives was "one of the pioneers of modern music, a great adventurer in the spiritual world, a poet, a visionary, a sage, and a seer"—yet "as unchallengeably American as the Yale Fence." As for Kirkpatrick, who had overcome the "appalling" obstacles of this "almost unplayable" sonata: "His performance was that of a poet and a master, an unobtrusive minister of genius." [153]

These remarkable words of praise, backed up as they were by Gilman's powerful reputation as a critic, naturally created a sensation. "Enthusiastic messages coming in all day," Ives telegraphed to Kirkpatrick on the day that the review appeared; he was, of course, deeply grateful to both Kirkpatrick and Gilman.[154] Gilman's review sent Olin Downes, the critic of the *New York Times,* to the back issues of his newspaper, and he proudly produced the favorable review that he had written about Ives's Fourth Symphony in 1927. Having publicly ignored Ives during the intervening twelve years, Downes now devoted his entire Sunday column to what he was able to learn about the life and work of "the mysterious Mr. Ives." He pictured for his readers an "obstinate, fanatical, visionary and crotchety" man who had sacrificed much in order to compose his remarkable music—a nonconformist who was "as American as Samuel Clemens." But Downes could not say much about the *Concord* Sonata, for he had neglected to go and hear Kirkpatrick play it.[155] *Time* magazine also climbed on the bandwagon, in its issue of January 30, 1939, with an article on "one of the most individual and authentically American of all U.S. composers," accompanied by a rare photograph of Ives. Quoting Gilman's laudatory opinion, *Time* contributed enormously to the spread of the Ives Legend with its sketch of the paradoxical pioneer modernist who was both a successful insurance man and a philosopher-recluse.[156] As for the Communist *New Masses,* its critic declared: "If American music has a Tom Mooney, it is Charles Ives." [157]

After Kirkpatrick's recital Gilman urged him to give a repeat performance of *Concord,* and an all-Ives program was arranged for

Town Hall in February; according to the program announcement, this second recital by Kirkpatrick was given "by general request," but the "request" was actually Gilman's.[158] Ironically, Gilman suffered a heart attack before it took place, and he died the following September. He had lived just long enough to proclaim Ives's greatness.

At the all-Ives concert of February 24, 1939, Kirkpatrick accompanied the mezzo-soprano Mina Hager in two groups of Ives's songs. But it was his repetition of *Concord* that drew not only New York's leading critics but also large numbers of the curious, eager to be associated with Ives's sudden recognition. "The hall was packed," reported Olin Downes. "Literati and cognoscenti were present in larger numbers than had been witnessed since the last Town Hall concert of the League of Composers." The enthusiasm of the audience caused several of the songs to be repeated. Downes himself, while he felt that Ives was not altogether uninfluenced by other composers or able completely to express his ideas in music, nevertheless concluded that the sonata was "a creation spun out of a man's home memories and consciousness—not a fabric of tone to fit a model outside of himself. An American composer thus dares be himself." [159] Downes was particularly appreciative of Ives because he himself had long been looking for a vital and distinctively American art music, one that had developed out of the music of America's people and was infused with the spirit of their national life.[160]

Interest in Ives and his works remained strong for some time after the two Town Hall recitals. Kirkpatrick was invited to give the *Concord* Sonata on a number of occasions in 1939, including a performance (sponsored by Emerson's grandson) at the First Parish Church of Concord, Massachusetts.[161] The Yale Class of 1898 gave a dinner in Ives's honor (which Ives did not attend), at which a number of its members sat dutifully through Kirkpatrick's performance of the whole sonata.[162] There was now some demand for copies of *Concord*, which still existed only in Ives's private edition, and it was decided that Lehman Engel's Arrow Press would publish a new edition of the work.[163] A concert artist as popular and well known as the baritone John Charles Thomas found it advantageous to include some Ives songs in a New York recital, while Jascha Heifetz showed a sudden interest in looking at his works for violin.[164] The poet Muriel Rukeyser even published a five-page poem called "Ives." [165]

It is obvious that the widespread recognition of Ives in 1939 was almost entirely the result of the interest of one man, Lawrence Gilman. It is important, nevertheless, to note the influence of a cultural trend of the 1930s which has already been alluded to and which undoubtedly influenced both Gilman and those who listened to what he had to say. In 1939 the name of Ives spread beyond the confines of the purely musical avant-garde to a portion of the more general musical public. A crucial part of his new audience consisted of intellectuals, writers, and other creative artists who would ordinarily not have followed the development of the modern music movement; and it was just these groups who, during the course of the thirties, had been rediscovering American values, American traditions, and particularly pre-twentieth-century American literature.

Back in the 1920s, younger American intellectuals and creative artists had experienced a revulsion against their country's supposedly repressive traditions of Puritanism and Victorianism. As an essential part of this revulsion, the writers of antebellum New England, such as Emerson and Longfellow, had often been disparaged in the twenties for their gentility and their uncritically optimistic view of life. When, for example, Jerome Goldstein had given a performance of Ives's Second Violin Sonata in 1924, it had drawn this cynical review:

> Charles Ives is an American, and a 100 percenter, according to his sonata. In it New England stands forth in all its glory and bigotry (Thy Will Be Done). Instead of mounting a pulpit to harangue hepatically, Mr. Ives chose to gun his shoulder and forth with the pilgriming ones. From the services he has brought back a musical "History of New England." In it are pages of revival meetings, Boston Tea Parties, boiled dinners, and those innumerable inrushes of the soul which Emerson received—or said he did.[166]

The coming of the Depression, however, soon dispelled this cynical sophistication by refocusing the attention of intellectuals and creative artists upon America and the problems of its common people.

By the latter thirties, with Europe being drawn into the vortex of war, Americans on several different intellectual levels were celebrating the special unifying virtues of American democracy and nostalgically seeking its origins in American history, traditions, and culture.[167] No event marked the intellectuals' rediscovery of America more clearly than the publication in 1936 of *The Flowering of New England,* by Van Wyck Brooks. Having for years castigated his country for its lack of a viable literary tradition, this critic now reversed himself in the thirties and concluded that the American writer did have a "usable past" after all, and a very remarkable one at that. In *The Flowering of New England,* which became a best seller and won a Pulitzer prize, Brooks located that usable past among the very writers of New England whom Ives had celebrated in his *Concord* Sonata.

Many who heard the sonata in 1939 undoubtedly found its terrible complexities incoherent and incomprehensible; and yet the Americanness of Ives's music, its evocation of the American past, outweighed these disadvantages and ensured a certain receptiveness to it once Gilman had spoken. Ives's musical innovations were duly applauded, but it was the fundamental Americanness of his music (which was itself, of course, an aspect of its originality) that now proved most attractive to a larger audience, much as it had earlier fascinated several members of the Young Composers' Group. What Bernard Herrmann had said of Ives in 1932 now took on new significance: "One of his sonatas is called 'Concord, Mass.'—now if that isn't American, what is?" [168]

Gilman himself, in his *Herald Tribune* review, noted that the sonata had been a forerunner of Brooks's "celebrated masterpiece." [169] Nor did Gilman make more than passing reference to the actual musical materials of the work in his review, choosing instead to devote most of his discussion of the composition to quotations from *Essays before a Sonata* that set forth its literary program. It was the sonata's compellingly successful evocation of extramusical ideas and images (particularly the mysticism of the transcendentalists) that captivated Gilman. Similarly, Muriel Rukeyser filled her poem about Ives with the loving images of rural New England that his music evoked for her.

Not all critics, however, could agree with Gilman's aesthetic principles or with his assessment of the *Concord* Sonata. Ives's innovations per se were no longer the central issue, for by now the more astute critics accepted "modern music." The question that now arose was the old one of substance versus manner, but with a new twist. In his *Essays before a Sonata,* written just after World War I, Ives had thought of "manner" largely in terms of musical mannerism. He had deplored such excesses of nineteenth-century romanticism as the use of brilliant orchestral effects and superimposed local color that would easily please an audience, the display of technical proficiency for its own sake, and the blatant intrusion into music of the personality of the performer or composer. Against such "manner" Ives had upheld the importance of the spiritual and moral basis ("substance") of musical composition. But with the more general twentieth-century revulsion against romanticism—and particularly with the rise of neo-classicism in the 1920s—many younger composers had come to reject not only old-fashioned mannerism, but also the emphasis on what Ives called "substance." Their point of view (which Ives would probably have dismissed as simply another kind of overinsistence on manner) discounted extramusical connotations, no matter how spiritual and exalted they were, and regarded music (in the words of Roger Sessions) "as something other than a means of evocation, [as] an art completely self-sufficient as a mode of expression." [170]

In spite of trends toward program music and Americanism in the latter 1930s, a number of composers and critics continued thus to uphold coherence, form, and the realization of a purely *musical* purpose as the supreme values in composition. They would have found incomprehensible Ives's comment in 1935 that he preferred the printed version of *Emerson* to certain variants that existed in manuscript because the latter, although they "may be better or worse music as such than the printed movement," contained "some things that seem to have more to do with music, as such, than with Emerson." [171] For some who had doubts about his music, therefore, the question was not whether Ives quoted hymn tunes, band marches, and the opening notes of Beethoven's Fifth Symphony (to suggest Emerson's "spiritual message" of "the Soul of humanity knocking at the door of the Divine mysteries" [172]). The question was whether these quotations had been made an integral part of a musical fabric that was satisfying and beautiful in itself—satisfying and beautiful without any need to refer to the extramusical associations evoked by the quoted material.

Among older critics it was Oscar Thompson, the distinguished reviewer for the New York *Sun*, who applied this standard most succinctly to the *Concord* Sonata:

> The sonata . . . is essentially a work of associations, and there may be a need to guard against a tendency to evaluate it on a literary or fanciful basis rather than a musical one. What, one wonders, would be the purely musical reaction of a trained and responsive listener from abroad who had never so much as heard of Concord, Emerson, Hawthorne, the Alcotts or Thoreau? This question of association, which may be largely extra-musical in its promptings, remains one of the perplexities of music criticism. An earnest effort last night to hear this sonata purely as music left with this reviewer substantial doubts as to whether the work possesses the basic stuff to make a strong and intelligible appeal direct to the ear, without which the most ingenious of program music is unable to maintain itself.

The songs given at Kirkpatrick's second New York recital also raised for Thompson the problem of extramusical association, particularly in their use of musical quotations. Referring to the song *Down East* (which quotes the tune of Lowell Mason's hymn *Bethany*), he questioned "whether the appeal of this song is not primarily sentimental rather than musical." The songs as a group he found notable for their "melody—now distinctive, now close to the banal. . . . But they are not profound songs. They lack the emotional and musical substance of the songs of the masters. With their quips, verbal or musical, some of them smack more of the drawing room than of the concert hall." [173]

A younger critic who found fault with *Concord* was Elliott Carter, writing in *Modern Music,* the organ of the League of Composers. His critique takes on greater significance in the light of his later emergence, in the 1950s, as perhaps the most important American composer of his generation. Carter suggested an alternative to Ives's aesthetic principles: "While the Concord school was at its height, Poe was inaugurating the idea: 'take care of the manner and the matter will take care of itself.' " Carter felt a similar opposition between manner and matter when he contrasted Nadia Boulanger, his former teacher, with Charles Ives.[174]

Carter had come a long way since the days of his adolescent friendship with (and enthusiasm for) Ives, whom he had not seen for years. After he had entered Harvard in 1926 and begun the serious study of music, he had come to feel the need for a more methodical and precise approach to composition than he found in Ives. He had become, in fact, temperamentally incapable of appreciating what he regarded as the disorganization and methodless confusion of Ives's music.[175]

Now, upon hearing Kirkpatrick perform *Concord* in its entirety, Carter confessed that he was "sadly disappointed" in the work. Because it lacked a coherent and appropriate form, it was unable "to fill out the broad, elevated design forecast in the composer's prefaces." While Ives's "music is more often original than good," Carter admitted that "the good is really very personal and beautiful" and that "there is . . . much good in the sonata." But its "impressionistic content" was hindered by the fact that "in form and esthetic it is basically conventional, not unlike the Liszt sonata, full of the paraphernalia of the overdressy sonata school." "Behind all this confused texture there is a lack of logic which repeated hearings can never clarify." Nor did Carter like the musical quotations: "The esthetic is naive, often too naive to express serious thoughts, frequently depending on quotation of well-known American tunes with little comment, possibly charming but certainly trivial." Thus Carter felt that "it is not possible on the basis of the music we know to rank him among the great originals of American art, with, for instance, Ryder and Whitman. Unlike theirs his work, though original, falls short of his intentions." Carter concluded that "the present canonization is a little premature." [176]

But Carter would not stop with a criticism of the music itself. Not really in sympathy with the musical trends of the late thirties in America, he was obviously disturbed by the sudden and unexpected appearance of what he saw as uncritical praise of Ives's work. Apparently, too, he still felt the need to purge himself of his youthful enthusiasm for Ives. Drawing somewhat unfairly upon his earlier friendship with the older composer, therefore, he sketched a picture of Ives at home in the middle 1920s, excitedly playing portions of his works (including *Concord*) on the piano for young Carter. He suggested that since Ives had constantly revised his compositions, "adding dissonances, harmonies and complicated rhythms to a fundamentally simple work," the dates attributed to his innovations were perhaps too early. And he pictured himself, even at that tender age, questioning Ives about the impracticability of his scores for performance, the "complicated textures" that "would never sound," and his generally vague and improvisatory approach to the notation of his works.[177]

The questions about Ives's music that were raised in 1939 have been debated ever since. Certain critics would continue to find his music ill organized, undisciplined, bloated with everything that it had occurred to him to throw into it. But it is not likely that Ives was disturbed by the debate. His music had won the respect of two powerful newspaper critics, Gilman and Downes, and it had been belatedly accorded the public recognition that was its due. The composer who had very likely feared in 1919 that his music would die with him was now, in 1939, assured of a permanent place in the history of American music.

9

RECOGNITION

SINCE 1939

❦

NEARLY THREE YEARS WENT BY between John Kirkpatrick's New York performances of the *Concord* Sonata in early 1939 and America's entry into World War II in late 1941, an event which naturally brought a pronounced decline in activities on behalf of contemporary music. But while interest in Ives's music was much greater during these three years than it had been before, the actual dissemination and performance of his compositions failed to keep pace with the new interest. The description of Ives as a composer more talked and written about than played became even more appropriate after the Kirkpatrick concerts than it had been previously. Kirkpatrick himself played *Concord* (or individual movements of it) in various parts of the country, but few other musicians showed an inclination to tackle his major works that were already available for performance. And of his numerous important compositions that were still in manuscript and unknown, only the Third and Fourth Violin Sonatas were uncovered and played publicly in these years.[1]

It is especially surprising that the conductors of America's larger orchestras did not seize upon Ives's orchestral works during the prewar and war years. As the United States faced an increasingly Nazified Europe, Americans became intensely concerned with an appreciation of their own country and its uniquely democratic heritage. As one aspect of this nationalism, the enthusiasm for American music, particularly for its "folk" and popular sources, reached a climax in the early 1940s, and Ives's compositions for orchestra would surely have spoken very directly to this enthusiasm. But the orchestral works which Ives had published during the 1920s and 1930s had generally been his more difficult works, such as the second movement of the Fourth Symphony, *Three Places in New England,* and *The Fourth of July;* even in the early forties, the conductors of major orchestras still found them too formidable and confused to be played successfully. On the other hand, his early and more conservative Second and Third Symphonies, with their many quotations from well-known American tunes and their general aural accessibility to both performers and audience, would have fitted perfectly into the Americanist cultural atmosphere; had these symphonies been readily available for performance in the early forties, they would almost certainly have been given by one of the larger orchestras. But Ives had lost the professionally copied scores of both these works some thirty years before, and he had nothing left but his own rougher pencil copies, so that a good deal of work on the scores (not to speak of the preparation of instrumental parts) would have been required prior to any performance. His adolescent Variations on *America* could also have been a popular success during these patriotic years; in the 1960s it was to become, in an orchestral version by William Schuman, one of Ives's most frequently performed compositions. But in the early 1940s, the Variations on *America* was only an unknown organ work, neglected among Ives's manuscripts.

The failure to take advantage of the widespread curiosity about Ives that appeared in 1939 was due in large part to the composer's own extreme isolation from other musicians. Another heart attack in the fall of 1938 was followed by further such attacks,[2] marking the beginning of an even greater retreat into privacy and quiet. There was no more traveling abroad; and after his daughter's marriage in

1939, Ives apparently found the daily company of his wife alone sufficient for his declining years, although Mrs. Ives herself continued to attend church and to see people outside their home. Hostile to the radio, unwilling to meet new people, rarely seeing his old friends, carefully protected by his wife from any disturbing outside influence, Charles Ives lived in extraordinary isolation from the world during the 1940s. He was certainly not indifferent to his growing fame, and he spent a fair amount of time writing out his wife's replies to his correspondence and making sure that published and private comment on his works (especially favorable comment) was gathered together and copied. But while isolation enhanced the aura of legend that surrounded his name, it also hindered the progress of his musical recognition.

It was widely known that Ives was old and sick and ought not to be disturbed, and those who did decide to bother him sometimes found it difficult to get their messages through to the old man. Correspondence from prospective performers of his compositions would be sent to West Redding when the Iveses were in New York or to New York when the Iveses were in West Redding. When it was finally received, an answer would often be delayed for some time, or the correspondence might even be left behind in the next move from one house to the other. Ives could easily become confused about the location of scores and instrumental parts for his works—or even about the location of his original manuscripts, the pages of many of which had been lost over the years. He was constantly explaining in the sketches that he wrote for his wife's letters that his health no longer allowed him to attend to things as he would have wished to. A case in point is the new edition of the *Concord* Sonata, which was planned for 1939 to meet the demand for the work created by John Kirkpatrick's performances in January of that year. It was first arranged that Kirkpatrick would help prepare the new edition, which was to incorporate revisions that Ives insisted upon to bring the printed version closer to his original conception of the work.[3] When Kirkpatrick procrastinated, Ives decided to do it himself with the help of his copyist, George F. Roberts.[4] But he kept making changes in the score,[5] the war intervened, and the new edition was not finally published by the Arrow Music Press until 1947, more than eight years after the Kirkpatrick performances which it had been intended to follow up!

The new interest that many musicians showed in Ives's music in 1939 came at a time when Ives had been deprived of the services of Henry Cowell, who had formerly played so energetically and well the role of mediator between such musicians and the reclusive composer. If the recognition of his music was to go forward, Ives would obviously need someone to take up this role that Cowell had been forced to relinquish. But no such person had appeared by May, 1940, when Cowell was granted a parole from prison.[6] Cowell's recovery of his position in the musical world was extraordinary for a man who had spent nearly four years in San Quentin. In October, 1941, he was piano soloist at the opening concert of the New York Philharmonic's centennial season. In 1943 he joined the government as a music consultant in the Office of War Information. In 1951 he was inducted into the National Institute of Arts and Letters.

This remarkable pattern of musical rehabilitation was a tribute to Cowell's indomitable courage and energy, but it would not have been possible without the help of a number of musicians—such as Leopold Stokowski, Percy Grainger, and Gerald Strang—who took a "modern" view of his original offense and who felt that his possible "moral turpitude" should be forgotten in view of his altruism and his genuine contributions to music. The Iveses, however, took a very different view of the matter. It was a view which Cowell could not ignore, not only because of Ives's financial backing of *New Music,* but also because of Cowell's very sincere desire to re-establish his friendship with Ives.

Since California required that Cowell have a job waiting for him in order to be paroled, the Australian-American pianist and composer Percy Grainger made Cowell his secretary and assistant.[7] Grainger and his wife lived in White Plains, New York, and soon after moving east to live with them, Cowell resumed the direction of *New Music* and moved it east with him, locating the quarterly's main offices in the American Music Center in New York City. Gerald Strang was all too happy to relinquish his authority to Cowell, but Ives expressed his preference for a board of editors with no editor in chief or chairman.[8] Cowell did not openly flout this wish, although he had *New*

Music stationery printed showing himself as editor and the others as associate editors.[9] But it soon became clear that Cowell was once again running *New Music* just as he wished it to be run. Ives recognized this *fait accompli* in October, 1941, when he sent the year's checks for *New Music* to Cowell in New York rather than to Strang in California.[10]

The problem of Cowell's personal relationship to Ives was not so easily solved. Even while Cowell had still been in prison, Ives had retreated somewhat from his original position by sending him a Christmas gift and writing a letter to recommend his parole.[11] But in her correspondence with Cowell after his parole, Mrs. Ives (pleading her husband's ill health) made it clear that Ives did not wish to see Cowell.[12] Then in September, 1941, Cowell wrote to Mrs. Ives to announce his impending marriage to Sidney Robertson.[13] In reply he received a letter of congratulations signed by Charles Ives himself, expressing the hope that the Iveses would see Cowell and his new wife in New York the following winter.[14] In this incident Ives and his wife revealed the narrow conventionality of their moral and social views. It was not enough for them that Cowell had paid his debt to society; they demanded something more. They could not, of course, be certain of his inner moral rehabilitation; but what they wanted was assurance of his outward conformity to the genteel social and moral conventions that they prized, and this assurance they received with his marriage.

The two old friends saw each other for the first time in six years on April 14, 1942,[15] and their musical collaboration was resumed for the rest of Ives's life. Each needed the other in a rather different way. Ives required Cowell's help in the promulgation of his music, and he felt gratitude and even affection toward the younger man, though it is doubtful that their relationship was ever again what it had been before Cowell's imprisonment. Cowell, for his part, had enormous admiration for both Ives's musical genius and his character as a man. It is likely that the resumption of their friendship had become a point of personal honor with Cowell, a means of assuring himself that he had finally passed successfully through his terrible ordeal. That his wife, an ethnomusicologist, got along well with Mrs. Ives certainly increased Cowell's closeness to the Iveses.

Reflecting the temper of the times, Cowell's own music had become somewhat less experimental and had taken on a definite Americanist note during his imprisonment and after his parole. In the 1940s he composed a number of pieces with the title Hymn and Fuguing Tune, using as a sort of model the fuguing tunes composed by New Englanders of the late eighteenth and early nineteenth centuries, particularly those of William Billings. It is interesting that this earlier New England music to which Cowell reverted had never had much influence on Ives, since it had largely disappeared from the New England churches before he had been born.[16]

Even before their reunion, Cowell had again taken up the cause of Ives's music. For example, he showed the Fourth Violin Sonata to the violinist Joseph Szigeti, who played it in a recital at Carnegie Hall in 1942 and recorded it for a joint venture of New Music Recordings and the League of Composers.[17] Szigeti thus became the first leading concert artist (aside from E. Robert Schmitz) to identify himself publicly with a major Ives composition. During the war, Cowell also worked on getting the score of Ives's *Robert Browning* Overture into shape.

As World War II drew to a close, a number of developments pointed to the likelihood that with the resumption of musical activities after the war, Ives would finally receive the recognition and important performances that had so long been denied him. There was actually a fairly widespread feeling in the modern music movement that he had been unduly neglected. In early 1946, for example, *Modern Music* published the replies of ten composers and critics to a request that they name the ten most neglected pieces of contemporary music. Seven of them (including Aaron Copland, Paul Rosenfeld, and Leonard Bernstein) named works by Ives.[18] For another thing, Bernard Herrmann, ever an Ives enthusiast, had become influential both as a composer and as a symphonic conductor for the Columbia Broadcasting System. At the same time, Henry Cowell was turning over the direction of *New Music* to a group of younger composers—especially Elliott Carter and Lou Harrison—who were determined to "do something" for Ives's music. Carter had once again shifted his opinion about that music.[19] Never really reconciled to Ives's aesthetic position, he nevertheless came to believe that Ives was an important figure in American musical culture and that he deserved more of a hearing than he had yet received; on the other hand, Carter felt that after his 1939 review of *Concord* he could never see Ives again.[20] In 1944, on the occasion of Ives's seventieth birthday, Cowell and Carter wrote to him to suggest than an organization of his musician friends be formed for the purpose of securing more performances of his works.[21] Ives reluctantly agreed that something of the sort was indeed desirable.[22] Both he and Mrs. Ives also seemed to realize that if they did not now make a determined effort to get the more important of his neglected manuscripts into finished shape, it would probably never be done.[23] Thus Ives's election to the National Institute of Arts and Letters in December, 1945,[24] ushered in the most active period of the recognition and performance of his music.

Elliott Carter was particularly appalled at the confused state of some of Ives's manuscripts that had been deposited (in photostatic copies) at the American Music Center in New York. At first Carter thought that he could be the one to get them into better shape while Ives was still alive to approve what was being done; but he proved temperamentally unfit to make the many editorial decisions that were involved, and the task fell instead largely to Lou Harrison.[25]

Harrison and his friend John Cage were a sort of second generation of West Coast experimental composers, pursuing lines of development that had earlier been laid down by Henry Cowell. At Cowell's suggestion, Harrison had written to Ives in the 1930s, when he had still been in his teens, and had begun receiving photostats of Ives's compositions, which had had a deep influence upon him. Later, during the war, he had moved to New York, where Cowell had given him the job of orchestrating Ives's War Song March (*They Are There!*) and preparing it for performance. (This work for chorus and orchestra was commissioned by the League of Composers and was to be given by the New York Philharmonic, but it was never played.) Although he met Ives only once, Harrison was very closely associated with his music during the 1940s.[26]

Harrison was also responsible for the first important performance after the war of a previously unknown Ives work. Asked to be guest conductor with the New York Little Symphony in 1946, Harrison decided to give the first public performance of the Third Symphony, a work for chamber orchestra that had been completed some thirty-five years before. He was willing to do work on the manuscript that no conductor of a major orchestra could be bothered with. Harrison deciphered Ives's old pencil score of the symphony, did some editing of it,[27] copied out the parts, and conducted the work in Carnegie Chamber Music Hall on April 5, 1946.[28] With its simple camp-meeting tunes quoted in an appropriately naive context, the work created a minor sensation and was favorably reviewed by the critics. The reviewer for the *Times,* noting that "it possessed a freshness of inspiration, a genuineness of feeling and an intense sincerity that lent it immediate appeal and manifested inborn talents of a high order," found it "music close to the soil and deeply felt." [29]

A month later the symphony was repeated on an all-Ives program (with which Elliott Carter was closely connected) in Columbia University's Second Annual Festival of Contemporary American Music.[30] Critics were now calling for further performances of Ives, and the symphony received a special citation from the Music Critics Circle of New York.[31] But most important of all, a Pulitzer prize was awarded to the Third Symphony in May, 1947. This award marked another major milestone in the process of Ives's recognition, for it carried his name into daily newspapers all over the country.

Realizing that another chapter in the Ives Legend was being written, Ives played his part to the hilt in an interview that he granted to a reporter from the Bridgeport *Sunday Herald.* Probably he did not intend that the interview be reported so literally, but the paper quoted him as scoffing at the Pulitzer prize as "a badge of mediocrity" and pictured him lambasting the National Institute of Arts and Letters, of which he was a member.[32] Again in 1949, when he was interviewed by Howard Taubman, of the *New York Times,* Ives put on much the same act that his other occasional visitors of the period testify to: he wore old clothes, cracked jokes, made up and sang songs in disparagement of the "old ladies," brought forth his political views, waved his cane in excitement, and from time to time became so violently enthusiastic or indignant that he lost his breath and frightened his guest into thinking that the old man was having a physical attack.[33] In acting this way, not only was he living up to the myths that had been spread about him, but he was also repeating, out of habit, the pattern of defenses that he had adopted forty years before against forces and people that had threatened to wound him deeply. The defenses were now so ingrained that no one could any longer get through them to the sensitive inner man. Did that inner man, indeed, any longer exist?

The great increase of public interest in Ives after he received the Pulitzer prize necessitated a new method for making his music available for performance. Inherently hostile to the commercialization of serious music and to such notions as copyright, royalties, and performance fees, Ives had up until this time subsidized the publication of his own works by *New Music* and the Arrow Press, noncommercial and avant-garde enterprises. As for the distribution of his compositions, he had handled it largely himself. To those who had written him inquiring about his music, he had sent free of charge the appropriate published works or photostats of manuscripts, relying for this purpose on the assistance of the *New Music* office, the American Music Center, and the Quality Photoprint Studio. But the Iveses were becoming too old and slow to continue this procedure, while on the other hand the commercial publishing houses, which had facilities for a more widespread distribution through ordinary sales, were now willing to handle his works on the usual business basis. Relying heavily on Cowell's assistance and advice, Ives began in the late forties to sign contracts with a number of commercial publishing firms, and his scores were thenceforth published with greater frequency than they had been before. Ives soothed his own conscience by assigning his royalties to Cowell, Harrison, and other musicians who had performed particular works or assisted in their publication.[34]

Lou Harrison continued to do his "excavations" of Ives's works from the manuscripts, a task for which he had a distinct talent. Of all Ives's major compositions that were still in manuscript, the one that was probably in worst shape was the First Piano Sonata. Harrison patiently deciphered it,[35] and his friend William Masselos gave the first complete performance in Febuary, 1949, in New York.[36]

As for Henry Cowell, the Iveses relied ever more heavily upon him in the late forties and early fifties. He relieved them, for example, of the burden of some of Ives's musical correspondence;[37]

and he sorted through the negative photostats of Ives's manuscripts at the Quality Photoprint Studio in New York, trying to bring some order into the mass of material that had been accumulating there for more than twenty years.[38] But not even Cowell was allowed to go through the disordered piles of Ives's original music manuscripts, which the aged composer jealousy guarded in his barn at West Redding as a sort of private preserve.[39]

Ives was also jealous of his public reputation. He wanted publicity about him to be accurate and high-minded, and he attempted to keep some control over the performance and publication of his compositions. But his desires in these matters were often not fulfilled because of his inaccessibility and the need to rely on protracted and confusing correspondence in order to check things with him. Unfortunately, since he was no longer physically able to go over carefully the work that was being done on his scores, a number of his compositions were published in his last years or after his death in versions which were not entirely in accord with his manuscripts or with his own conception of how they should be played.

Beginning with the Pulitzer award, the last seven years of Ives's life finally brought him some of the honors and recognition that he had been entitled to decades before. His enthusiasts were no longer limited to younger composers and avant-garde critics. In fact, during the latter forties and much of the fifties, the trend among younger composers and the avant-garde was definitely away from the Americanist and programmatic tendencies of the thirties and the war years—away, that is, from one important aspect of Ives's music—and toward more systematic and absolute approaches to composition, particularly toward development of the twelve-tone (or serial) approach. Leading exponents of serialism in the period, such as the composer Milton Babbitt, clearly did not regard the long-neglected and eccentric Ives as having laid down the lines that later American composers were likely to follow.[40] The composer-critic Arthur Berger, like Elliott Carter before him, even reversed his judgment about the composer whom he had helped to discover in 1932. In Ives's music Berger now found crudeness in the use of modernistic devices, lack of coherent form, awkwardness, and excessive indulgence in self-expression for its own sake; he blamed these faults on Ives's nonprofessional approach to music, which had denied him the critical reaction of an audience.[41] He even suggested that Ives had been more conservative and less innovative than was generally supposed.[42] (Later, again like Carter, Berger was to change his opinion about Ives once more.[43])

But outside the avant-garde, among a larger audience composed of many conductors, performers, critics, and lay listeners, Ives came into his own in these postwar years. This was the period of the cold war, when a feeling of insecurity in the present promoted nostalgia for a past that had been secure. The historian Richard Hofstadter observed in 1948 that "this quest for the American past is carried on in a spirit of sentimental appreciation rather than of critical analysis. . . . The two world wars, unstable booms, and the abysmal depression of our time have profoundly shaken national confidence in the future. . . . If the future seems dark, the past by contrast looks rosier than ever; but it is used far less to locate and guide the present than to give reassurance."[44] For many in the concert audience and the growing audience for recordings, Ives's compositions helped to fulfill a longing for a nearly forgotten American past— helped to fulfill it most of all through their quotation of American tunes that were no longer so familiar as they had been in Ives's youth, but which for that very reason were more pregnant with nostalgia and a sense of "rootedness." Thus Olin Downes remarked of *The Alcotts,* which struck him as something like an improvisation on tunes recalled from childhood, that "one is none too sure of the utmost logic or sequence and development in the . . . movement," but "the music moves one, perhaps past entirely objective analysis."[45] These postwar audiences were also more sophisticated than ever before about "modern" music, although they still preferred Ives's more easily understood works, like the Third Symphony.

Except for the performance of two movements from *Three Places in New England* when Nicolas Slonimsky had guest-conducted the Los Angeles Philharmonic in 1932, no Ives composition had been performed by a major American symphony orchestra down to 1948. This neglect had not been entirely Ives's fault. He had never quite gotten over the feeling, ingrained in his youth, that the great metropolitan orchestras were the proper vehicles for the performance of classical music in America; and he had thus abased himself repeatedly, over a period of more than thirty years, by offering or sending his compositions unsolicited to the conductors of major orchestras, only to have them rejected or ignored.[46] It is particularly interesting that both Leopold Stokowski and Serge Koussevitzky, the two conductors of great orchestras who were most closely identified with contemporary music, had shown no public interest in his compositions during the 1930s and 1940s; their neglect had probably resulted largely from their not being close to Henry Cowell and his circle. When the Boston Symphony did finally play an Ives work in 1948, it was programmed not by the regular conductor, Koussevitzky, but by the associate conductor, Richard Burgin. Burgin chose *Three Places in New England* and conducted it in February, 1948, with the Boston Symphony in both Boston and New York.[47] Once again the critics were favorable; indeed, the critic of the *Christian Science Monitor* publicly retracted a disparaging comment that he had made about the first and third movements when Slonimsky had conducted the set in Boston seventeen years before.[48] Apparently the ears of even conservative critics had undergone some stretching during the interim. These Boston Symphony concerts were also the occasion for another article in *Time* about Ives.[49] The next year, on the occasion of his seventy-fifth birthday, he was the subject of a feature article in the *New York Times Magazine*,[50] and a photograph of him was published in *Life*.[51]

The New York Philharmonic had played an awe-inspiring role in the musical life of Ives's younger days, and so it must have been particularly gratifying to him when *the* orchestra finally performed one of his compositions. But when, following the preparation of the score by Cowell and Harrison,[52] Leonard Bernstein premiered the Second Symphony as guest conductor with the Philharmonic on Washington's Birthday in 1951,[53] Ives could not bring himself to attend, although his wife was there. Still, he did for once overcome his aversion to the radio sufficiently to listen later to a broadcast of Bernstein's performance of the work. Obviously pleased by the performance, he was yet not too overawed to inform Bernstein (through his wife's letter of appreciation) that the allegro movements had been "too slow." [54]

Much of the public and even critical reaction to Bernstein's performances of the Second Symphony was out of all proportion to the merit of a work that was not only obviously dated and derivative in its nineteenth-century European romanticism, but also far less interesting than many of Ives's later orchestral compositions. It was as if Ives were being deliberately compensated for the long neglect of his more daring works. For Olin Downes, of the *New York Times,* the symphony was "an immense structure" whose "tonal speech" was "by turns, rudely, tenderly, fantastically and cantankerously Yankee"; the third movement he found "of unique inspiration and a noble elevation of thought." Ives had done far more than merely quote old American tunes in the manner of a folklorist, for "these tunes, with their profound meanings to a creative artist, are matters of reference." Overemphasizing somewhat the audaciousness of the work, Downes suggested that it had been far in advance of American musical knowledge and practice at its time of composition (the turn of the century) and was still "an astonishing work today." [55] Even the very sophisticated composer Virgil Thomson, Gilman's successor as principal critic for the *New York Herald Tribune,* was captivated by the symphony: "Orchestrally, harmonically and melodically the symphony is both noble and plain. It speaks of American life with love and humor and a deep faith. It is unquestionably an authentic work of art, both as structure and as communication." Thomson noted with approval that the work was "in a tradition of American music that is not afraid to speak from the heart." [56]

It is obvious that the Second Symphony, which nearly anyone could enjoy without much effort, was being praised more for its broader cultural values than for its musical values per se. Fondly recalling his father's musical life in Danbury, Ives in this symphony had glorified the life of the Connecticut country people of his childhood. With its naive American awkwardness and its quotation of the old religious and secular tunes, the symphony seemed in 1951 a thin, threadlike connection between the present and a beloved but now forever vanished past. And how democratic to incorporate popular American tunes into the context of a nineteenth-century European symphony! It was now pointed out that Ives alone had spoken in the true accents of America even back at the turn of the century, but that he had never been able to find an audience among other Americans because the musical institutions of the country had been monopolized by conservative and Europe-worshiping pedants. That the Second Symphony had lain neglected for fifty years while its composer had remained indifferent to self-promotion and had apparently even treated his music nonchalantly, but that this same composer was still alive and that after long years of neglect his countrymen were finally discovering that he had all along embodied the American spirit magnificently in his music—these circumstances gave the Ives Legend a compelling power over the imagination.[57] Ives could now truly be hailed as the father of American music.[58] As for the American national culture, it could be flayed for having so long neglected its most original composer, but also congratulated for having produced him in the first place.

After the Boston Symphony and the New York Philharmonic had played Ives's orchestral works, other symphony orchestras around the United States and even in Europe slowly began to program them also, particularly (at first) the Second Symphony. But there was one more honor that would probably have meant more to Ives than any other: an honorary doctorate from his alma mater. By the early 1950s, the conservative regimes of Horatio Parker and David Stanley Smith were things of the past at Yale. Important people on the music faculty—especially Richard Donovan, a composer who had long been associated with Cowell and *New Music*—were interested in securing for Ives an honorary degree. But when members of the music faculty proposed Ives's name for the 1953 commencement, their nomination ran afoul of Yale's rule that no alumnus might receive an honorary degree in a year in which his class was holding a reunion.[59] (Ives's class was holding its fifty-fifth reunion in 1953.) The honorary Doctor of Music degree was offered him the next year, in 1954; [60] but as Mrs. Ives ruefully noted, it was "too late." [61] Yale required that all honorary degrees be received in person, and Ives was by now too ill to go through with the ceremony.[62] In fact, he did not even live until commencement day. Operated on for a double hernia in May, he was not strong enough to survive the shock of the operation. Charles Ives died at Roosevelt Hospital in New York City on May 19, 1954, in his eightieth year.

Two events that followed closely upon Ives's death laid the basis for a yet more widespread knowledge of the man and his works. One was the publication in 1955 of the book *Charles Ives and His Music,* by Henry and Sidney Cowell, which included a biographical section written largely by Mrs. Cowell (and based upon part of Ives's autobiographical *Memos*) as well as an extensive analysis of the music by her husband. Although it gave a somewhat idealistic and sentimentally popular view of Ives's life and contained numerous mistakes of fact, the book did serve to crystallize the Ives Legend into a coherent form and to spread knowledge about the composer and his compositions to many who had previously had only a vague idea about him. The Cowells presented Ives as "one of the four great creative figures in music of the first half of the twentieth century," along with Schoenberg, Stravinsky, and Bartók.[63]

The second event that paved the way for a broader recognition of Ives was his wife's gift of his music manuscripts in 1955 to Yale University, where this Ives Collection was housed in a special room in the music library. The manuscripts, however, were old and in great disorder, and they had not been cared for properly; their usefulness would be very limited unless they could be put in some sort of order. Henry Cowell was Ives's musical executor, but the Cowells' busy lives precluded their doing the necessary work on the collection. That task fell instead to John Kirkpatrick, who (although he had not been trained as a musicologist) was the only one willing to devote the necessary time, effort, patience, and persistence to the job.

During the 1940s, Kirkpatrick had shifted his major attention from giving piano recitals to teaching at Cornell University. Although he had certainly been less close to Ives than Cowell had been, he was in fact the only musician friend who attended Ives's funeral.[64] Shortly after, with Mrs. Ives's permission, he began sorting the manuscripts in the barn at West Redding. After devoting enormous amounts of time to the project over the next several years, Kirkpatrick produced in 1960 his "Temporary Mimeographed Catalogue" of the Ives music manuscripts and related materials at Yale, a work of monumental scholarship in which each page—indeed, each fragment—of music paper was minutely described and related to the corpus of Ives's compositions. Distributed to universities, music schools, and music libraries around the country, the catalogue not only enabled scholars who came to Yale to work more effectively with the manuscripts, but also allowed those in other places who had never seen the manuscripts to order photostats of them from Yale with a good deal of foreknowledge of what they were getting; incidentally, it brought to public notice a number of previously unknown (but mainly minor) Ives compositions. Both Ives scholarship and Ives performances, therefore, were enormously advanced by the appearance of this extraordinary catalogue.

Pursuing unstintingly his study of many aspects of Ives's life and work, John Kirkpatrick became recognized in the 1960s as the leading authority on Charles Ives and his music. Deeply sympathetic to the religious and philosophical bases of Ives's compositions, Kirkpatrick made it his main work in life to guard the Ives legacy and to extend the knowledge of it. In 1968 he finally came to Yale as curator of the Ives Collection. Besides his critical editing of a number of Ives's compositions, based on a careful comparison of all known sources, Kirkpatrick edited the complete text of Ives's *Memos*, which (annotated and amplified with many footnotes and appendices) was published in 1972. Howard Boatwright, an Ives enthusiast on the Yale music faculty, had already brought out a new edition of the *Essays before a Sonata*, along with a number of Ives's shorter writings, in 1962.

During the 1950s and 1960s, Ives's compositions appeared with increasing frequency in America on the programs of symphony orchestra concerts and solo recitals, although the leading virtuoso instrumentalists were still reluctant to attempt music that was more difficult and less gratifying to audiences than the standard repertoire. Among the major symphony orchestras, Leonard Bernstein and the New York Philharmonic became particularly closely identified with Ives's compositions. Somewhat symbolically, especially because he himself had been born in America, Bernstein conducted the Second Symphony in 1958 at the opening concerts of his first season as music director of the Philharmonic.[65] In succeeding years, under his regime, several other works by Ives were given by the orchestra, including *The Unanswered Question,* which Bernstein conducted on the orchestra's tour of Europe, the Middle East, and the

Soviet Union in 1959.[66] "More and more," wrote Herbert Kupferberg, of the *New York Herald Tribune,* in 1962, "Charles Ives is emerging as *the* American composer." [67]

The high point of this recognition of Ives by the symphony orchestras of America came in 1965 with the premiere of his Fourth Symphony, which had been completed in 1916. Of his larger finished works, this was his most advanced and probably the one of which he had been proudest. The first three movements had previously been played separately, but the fourth movement had never been publicly performed until Leopold Stokowski conducted the whole symphony with his American Symphony Orchestra in Carnegie Hall on April 26, 1965. Stokowski had shown little interest in Ives until just before the composer's death, but he was always ready to give a first performance that could be accompanied by a great deal of publicity, for which he had a definite genius. The advance publicity for this premiere played up the forty-nine-year delay in performance, the terrible difficulty of the symphony, and the great effort needed to get the score into playable shape; it even included a false press report that part of the manuscript had been lost.[68] The performance itself, employing as it did a chorus and large orchestra (with pianos and extra percussion) and two assistant conductors to handle the many conflicting rhythms, created a sensation. "The work is a masterpiece," wrote Harold C. Schonberg, principal critic of the *Times.* "It has tremendous personality and authentic stature." [69] William Bender, who reviewed the concert for the *Herald Tribune,* agreed that the symphony "is by all odds a masterpiece." [70] The work was recorded; and a one-hour television program about Ives, centering around Stokowski's performance of the symphony, was subsequently shown throughout the country on National Educational Television. The splash made by this premiere brought another major widening of the circle of Ives's admirers. *Newsweek* noted afterward that "Ives' pre-eminence among American composers is now beyond question." [71]

By the latter 1960s there was so much action on the Ives front that it could be said that the actual availability of the composer's music to audiences had finally begun to catch up with his reputation. On February 23, 1967, for example, the Columbia Broadcasting System televised an hour-long program called "Charles Ives, American Pioneer," a New York Philharmonic young people's concert in which Bernstein brought his eminent talents to the task of explaining and popularizing Ives's life and work.[72] According to the survey of American symphony orchestra programs made by Broadcast Music, Inc., for the 1969–1970 season, Ives stood fortieth on the list of all composers and fourteenth on the list of twentieth-century composers in the frequency of performance of his works.[73] But by this time the principal audience for Ives performances was no longer to be found in the concert hall, but rather among the owners and borrowers of phonograph records.

Because Ives's compositions were for so long a time too difficult for most performers, phonograph records proved to be of particular importance in the dissemination of his music. They also made it possible for this music to be heard in places besides New York City and the other centers for the performance of contemporary works. And yet, beginning with the first New Music Quarterly Recordings in the 1930s and continuing throughout the 1940s and well into the 1950s, Ives's recorded music was mainly issued on esoteric labels of limited distribution. The exception among the large commercial companies was Columbia Records, where the Ives enthusiast Goddard Lieberson held an influential position, eventually becoming president; over the years Columbia issued several recordings of major Ives works, including Kirkpatrick's performance of *Concord* (1948) and Bernstein's of the Second Symphony (1960). In spite of the long-playing revolution, however, relatively few recordings of Ives were commercially available at any one time until the 1960s. Then, beginning about the time of Stokowski's premiere of the Fourth Symphony in 1965, Columbia produced a spate of Ives recordings: orchestral works conducted by Stokowski, Eugene Ormandy, and especially by Bernstein; a new version of *Concord* by Kirkpatrick; and a number of other works. Other major companies rushed in with their own versions to take advantage of the Ives market. In fact, the production and sale of Ives recordings constituted something of an exception to the general depression in the classical recordings industry that existed around 1970.[74]

An important part of the increasing audience for Ives recordings in these years was made up of young people (both lay listeners and music students) in American colleges and universities. To a generation that regarded classical music as impossibly formal and pompous, Ives's compositions (once they were encountered) seemed a notable exception. Paradoxical as it might seem, there was a certain similarity between his music and the youthful cultural climate that appeared in the sixties. Most obviously there was his quotation of "people's music" as a way of expressing his love of vernacular life. But there was a subtler affinity too. Eclecticism, rhythmic freedom, a general impression of chaos or anarchy, a multidirectional or spatial approach (so well adapted to stereophonic recording in the Fourth Symphony and *The Unanswered Question*), the use of music to communicate ideas and criticize society, the involvement of the performer (and even the listener) in the creative act—these qualities of Ives's music were also important aspects of rock music, which was the crucial unifying element in youth culture and which was approached with great seriousness by many thoughtful young people.[75]

But the cultural climate of the 1960s was not limited in its effects to rebellious youth; it was felt in the very centers of intellectual and creative endeavor. In both Europe and America, the rational (and even total) organization that many composers had sought to achieve in their works after World War II, usually through serialism, had given way by the sixties to a freer, more eclectic, more indeterminate experimentalism. A number of the leading tendencies of advanced composition in the sixties could be found in embryo in works that Ives had composed more than fifty years before: the introduction of aleatory or chance elements into composition (an approach of which John Cage had been the prophet in the fifties), including the practice of the composer's leaving certain choices to the performer; the collagelike combination of formally irreconcilable elements; the production of multidirectional, "layered" music through the spatial separation of sound sources that were not necessarily in strict temporal coordination with one another; the composition of music that quoted from other music; the attempt to bridge the gap between classical and popular music.

Most of these practices were in evidence, for example, in the team-written opera *Reconstruction,* produced in the Netherlands in 1969, which attacked United States imperialism in Latin America and apotheosized the guerrilla leader Che Guevara.[76] What is significant is that two of the composers of the opera, Reinbert de Leeuw and Louis Andriessen, were also the principal organizers of the Charles Ives Society of Amsterdam, founded in 1967.[77] To these musically experimental and politically radical young Dutch composers, Ives seemed a very appropriate culture hero. Indeed, it was in this period of the latter 1960s that Ives came into his own generally in Europe, although his compositions had been performed there earlier.

In America, too, Ives was hailed by many in the musical avant-garde of the 1960s as the prophet of the latest compositional proce-dures. The tendency of his music to imitate the human and natural sounds of his environment—a tendency which Paul Rosenfeld had once seen as impressionism—was now praised by Arthur Berger as an early form of the "action music" of the sixties.[78] John Cage, the more immediate father of that action music, also paid tribute to Ives for his early experimentalism and especially for his "understanding . . . of inactivity and of silence," his realization of the importance of the ability "to listen to the sounds which surround us and hear them as music." [79] Younger composers of the avant-garde, such as Gunther Schuller and James Tenney, took up the cause of Ives's music and got his more experimental works performed. Schuller, who conducted Ives compositions frequently, even tried to show that Ives had written a twelve-tone composition before Schoenberg! [80] The situation was somewhat reminiscent of Ives's brief moment of fame in the early thirties. Now, however, the American avant-garde was more numerous and influential and could make much more of a noise in Ives's behalf; moreover, what advanced people now ad-mired in his music was not so much its Americanness or its "sub-stance" of transcendentalist philosophy as the "manner" in which Ives had handled the musical materials themselves.

Thus, ironically, Ives's music was being taken up again by the avant-garde just when it was also achieving a more popular success with a much broader public. But it was characteristic of the cultural development of the sixties that, at least for a time, the formerly sharp line between avant-garde enthusiasms and the popular fads promoted by the mass media became blurred, much as the older line between cultivated and vernacular had also become blurred several decades before. Aaron Copland thought, however, that youthful musicians in the avant-garde admired Varèse decidedly more than Ives, simply because Ives's music (unlike Varèse's) had been tainted by the acclamation of a larger public.[81] On the other hand, perhaps the more popular interest in Ives's music arose from the same superficial sources as did popular enthusiasm for other serious art forms, especially pop art, that were being exploited commercially—arose, that is, from a discovery of "camp" in Ives's quotations and musical materials.

In a history of twentieth-century music published in 1967, the composer-critic Eric Salzman made a more thoughtful and long-range assessment of Ives's importance. Looking for the antecedents of the experimental music that had proliferated in Western culture since World War II, Salzman found them not only in the Stravinsky-Parisian and Schoenberg-Viennese lines of development, but also in a third group of pioneers who had composed, oddly enough, in the United States. These Americans were particularly notable for having continued to experiment extensively during the period 1920–1945, rather than (as had been generally true of European composers of that time) settling into neoclassicism or the twelve-tone idiom. The principal figures among them in the older generation were Varèse, Cowell, Ruggles, and Riegger; in the younger, John Cage, Lou Harrison, and Henry Brant. But as Salzman implied, the real father of this American experimental tradition had been Charles Ives, "the first composer whose work stands essentially outside the received European tradition." [82] And this relationship held true even though Ives had been so isolated and so long neglected that his actual influence on most of the others had been very limited.

Salzman also felt that Ives's music had influenced his own work and that of other young composers of his generation, the next generation after Cage and Harrison.[83] Yet even after his works had achieved recognition, the intellectual limitations of Ives's musical thought as well as the intuitive and personal nature of his approach to composition seemed destined to deprive him of the direct effect on future generations that composers like Schoenberg and Varèse were likely to have.

From the vantage point of the 1970s, it is possible to look back and note the major milestones in the process of Ives's recognition, a fifty-year process that took him from complete obscurity to a generally acknowledged position as "America's greatest composer." Those major turning points were: his decision to send out *Concord* and *114 Songs* in the early 1920s; the beginning of his collaboration with Henry Cowell in 1927–1928; the performance of his songs at Yaddo in 1932; Kirkpatrick's performances of *Concord* in early 1939; the awarding of the Pulitzer prize for the Third Symphony in 1947; Bernstein's premiere of the Second Symphony with the New York Philharmonic in 1951; and Stokowski's premiere of the Fourth Symphony in 1965.

In the years that followed the last of these events, Ives's fame reached a greater height than it ever had before. People spoke of the "Ives phenomenon." He had become an American cultural property, a part of the national heritage with his appropriate myths and legends—"our Washington, Lincoln and Jefferson of music," as Leonard Bernstein once called him.[84] His name was still not known to the man in the street, and there were even a few dissenting voices which continued to maintain that "Ives is to Mozart what Grandma Moses is to Fragonard." [85] But among musicians and those who knew something about classical music, Ives was very widely admired and even idolized—no longer as simply "America's first great composer," but rather as "America's greatest composer." Many of his admirers, indeed, revealed a sentimental desire to overlook the obvious limitations in his thought and his music and to give him more than his due; it was an unfortunate tendency that could only obscure the truth about his creative life and its terrible contradictions.

Ives would probably have been disturbed by much that had happened to his reputation since his death. He had denounced, in its earlier and less developed forms, the fashionable, publicity-conscious New York world of the arts; he had foreseen, with dread, the growth of the slick, commercially exploitative world of the mass media. Now, inevitably, his name and his music had been drawn into both these worlds, particularly into that increasingly large area in which the two seemed to overlap. And all the while, the religious and philosophical traditions out of which his music had been written seemed to recede further and further into the incomprehensible American past.

As the hundredth anniversary of Ives's birth drew near in 1974, it was clear that the centennial would be marked by appropriate performances and recordings, books and articles, festivals and conferences—all to honor the memory of a great man. A Charles Ives Society was reactivated in the United States, with John Kirkpatrick as chairman of the board of directors and several prominent composers and other musicians among the board members, for the purpose of issuing critical editions of Ives's works.

To attempt to look beyond the centennial and assess the future place of Ives's music in American and Western culture could only result in a guess. Ives's compositions have all along had two very different kinds of appeal: to the lay listener they have conjured up the American past, while to the avant-garde they have been astonishingly daring foreshadowings of later compositional procedures. But the approach to Ives through cultural nostalgia runs the risk that in time, with a sufficient shift in American culture, the quoted tunes will no longer be recognized and Ives's music will seem a mere anachronism; and the approach to Ives through an appreciation of his historical importance in musical development threatens to reduce him to a scholarly footnote in a history of music. Ives's works will only live if performers continue to want to play them and audiences continue to want to hear them. And these conditions will only obtain if the music proves inherently satisfying to the sensitive musical intelligence, apart from all considerations of its extramusical cultural connotations or its significance in music history. Of Ives's works in the larger forms, several seem to meet this criterion: the two piano sonatas, the four violin sonatas, *Three Places in New England*— perhaps also the Second String Quartet, the Fourth Symphony, and some movements of the *Holidays* Symphony. These works are undoubtedly flawed, much as Ives's own creative life was flawed, by the limitations that American culture imposed upon them. But in them Ives came closer than any other American of his time to creating a music comparable to that of the great European composers—a music entirely self-sufficient as pure expression, yet a music arising (naturally and of necessity) out of a long cultural background.

Epilogue

AN INTERPRETATION

❧

In *The Lonely Crowd,* a well-known book on the social psychology of Americans written during the period of increased recognition for Ives's music that followed World War II, David Riesman used Ives as an example of the "autonomous" man—the man who is psychically free to choose whether to conform to the social and cultural norms of his time and place or to transcend them.[1] Ives's autonomy—his independence in working out the problems of the creative artist in America—has been repeatedly emphasized by those who have commented on his remarkable career.

This independence contrasts sharply with the course followed by other American composers early in the twentieth century, who tended to have a good deal of anxiety and uncertainty about their position as creative artists. They looked anxiously to Europe for their artistic standards, even though they feared that they could never equal the finer European artistic accomplishments. In relation to their own country, their position was even more uncertain. They might believe fully in democracy and might desire to find some common ground with their fellow Americans; but they knew there was no real place for them in the culture of their country, and they felt it necessary to keep somewhat aloof from the debasing qualities of American vernacular life.

Charles Ives, however, broke through this whole pattern of anxiety and uncertainty. On the one hand, he declared his independence of European musical standards and procedures. He was not capable of the complete intellectual overhaul of Western music that Schoenberg later effected. But he was freed from that necessity by an American come-outer tradition which held that one might withdraw from existing institutions and systems without feeling obligated to erect new ones in their place; it was enough to follow the promptings of one's own intuition, and this very unsystematic approach enabled Ives to compose music more advanced than anything being done in Europe at the time. On the other hand, Ives proclaimed his solidarity with the American people—not only in the themes and subject matter of his compositions, but also (and more significantly) in his choosing to lead an ordinary life in the workaday business world.

It has been generally assumed that the supreme proof of Ives's independence lay in his ability to weld together into an integral whole these two aspects of his life as an artist—his extreme experimentation in musical techniques and his nonprofessional life as a composer. But a close examination of the texture of his life leads to the conclusion that the two aspects were not really integrated at all; in departing from the usual pattern of life of an American composer of his time, Ives moved simultaneously in two opposite directions. In his experimentalism, he was certainly more independent than his contemporaries among American composers. But in his everyday existence, he was even less autonomous than they, for he succumbed to a series of pressures that his society and culture brought to bear upon him during the course of his life. To see Ives as a middle-class man, a Yale man, a businessman, and a family man is to begin to appreciate how extraordinarily great these pressures were. Their influence upon him was so powerful and baleful as to bear comparison with the more obvious pressures exerted upon a very different sort of composer, the composer of the Soviet Union.

In 1936 the Soviet newspaper *Pravda,* organ of the Communist party, denounced the composer Dmitri Shostakovich for his opera *Lady Macbeth of the District of Mtsensk.* Not only was the opera cacophonous, according to *Pravda,* but it contained "the coarsest kind of naturalism" in both story and music. In place of the socialist realism expected by the Soviet audience, Shostakovich was writing music that "would reach only the effete 'formalists' who had lost their wholesome taste. He ignored the demand of Soviet culture that all coarseness and wildness be abolished from every corner of Soviet life." [2] A week later a ballet by Shostakovich was similarly denounced. In response to these criticisms, the composer withdrew his Fourth Symphony, which was about to be performed, and remained out of public view for nearly two years. At the end of 1937, however, the performance of his Fifth Symphony proved that he was again writing music comprehensible to the Soviet people, and he regained his honored position in the society.

In 1948, the Central Committee of the Communist party of the Soviet Union issued a resolution critical of several Soviet composers. Shostakovich was included in the group, but this time the resolution also denounced Sergei Prokofiev, perhaps the most eminent of the country's composers. Again, cacophonous "formalism" was condemned as "a lowering of the social role of music, . . . limiting that role to the satisfaction of the perverted tastes of individualist 'aesthetes.' " [3] Some of the offenders lost their teaching posts. The composers were quick to confess their mistakes. Prokofiev, in his letter of apology, noted that "the Party resolution has separated the decayed tissue from the healthy"; and he admitted that "elements of formalism" had crept into his music from "contact with certain Western trends." He concluded: "I would like to express my gratitude to our Party for the clear directives set forth in the Resolution, which are helping me in my quest for means of expression that will be comprehensible and close to our people." [4] Prokofiev's Seventh Symphony, written a few years later, proved to be acceptably conservative.

It can be reasonably argued that these experiences undergone by Soviet composers were broadly similar to Charles Ives's experience in the United States. It is not a matter of comparing their music with Ives's music. From the point of view of cultural history, such a comparison would not be relevant, for the music of the Soviet composers played a vital role in Soviet society, while Ives's music had no function in American society during the time when it was written. The real basis of comparison lies in the demands that were made by the two societies upon men of creative musical genius and the actions that such men took in response to those demands. The Soviet Union of the 1930s and 1940s, like the United States of the 1890s, was a society undergoing rapid economic development, a society in which the energies of all citizens had to be directed to the tasks in hand; in particular, each society brought pressure upon its most gifted members to bend their efforts to the common purpose and not to go wandering away in private and irrelevant ventures.

But the means by which these social pressures were applied to the Soviet composers and to Ives were markedly different. In the Soviet Union persons in the arts had a tradition, extending back long before the Bolshevik Revolution, of being a respected group with a special place in the society. The Soviet government was committed to the preservation of that tradition; and it could scarcely have hoped to undermine the composer's confidence in his own role as an artist even if it had wished to. Thus the pressure that it applied to men like Prokofiev was a crude external force, designed to make them follow outwardly the party line of socialist realism. It is very doubtful that the composers believed everything that they said when they were required to denounce their own works.

The pressure brought to bear upon Ives was more insidious and operated more internally, as befitted a society which was decentralized and had more time to accomplish its tasks. In America there was scarcely any tradition of an independent artistic profession with a recognized place in the society; some of the most gifted of American creative artists—men like Hawthorne and Melville—had been wanderers in the wilderness, largely unwanted by their culture. As a self-conscious artist, Ives was truncated not by a government decree, but by the very process of his cultural upbringing in Danbury and later at Yale. The commitments to values and institutions which he imbibed from American culture made it extremely difficult for him even to think of himself as an artist, in spite of his genius; and there was nothing in the American cultural tradition, or in Ives's own personal development, that enabled him to resist those commitments. On the one hand, he learned that he must be masculine; and this commitment caused him to be ashamed of all art music, to regard it as effete, unmanly, and undemocratic. On the other hand, he learned that he should conform to the conventional pattern of middle-class life; and this commitment caused him to live out his life isolated among Philistines, cut off from other avant-garde artists because he regarded them as Bohemians.

The values of masculine self-assertion and of middle-class gentility, seemingly so opposed to each other, were actually both essential to a decentralized capitalist society during its period of most rapid development; such a society was dependent upon individual sources of initiative and entrepreneurship, but it also had to ensure conformity to its social system. Thus nineteenth-century American culture inculcated the two values together. Ives's acceptance of these American values led him into a career in business, and his highly original talents were placed at the service of American capitalism for more than thirty years. Musical composition, for which he had a far greater talent, was carried on in his extra hours and practically in secret, hidden away from the eyes of a society that neither understood nor approved. And in other respects, too, his independent-mindedness took the form of private and "safe" rebellions that offered no practical threat to the dominant values and institutions of his society.

Ives's life was more unstintingly devoted to the purposes of his society than were the lives of the Soviet composers to the essential requirements of theirs, for he never even reached that degree of independence which would have allowed him to define himself primarily as an artist. While Soviet society could only bring external pressure upon its composers—particularly upon those who had grown up before the widespread inculcation of proletarian values—American society made its demands upon Ives internally and from childhood. As an artist, he became literally his own worst enemy. He willingly—even eagerly—subordinated both his art and his life as an artist to a rigid ideology that was based upon nonartistic considerations. And that ideology was remarkably similar to the Soviet musical ideology, as both were similar to Tolstoy's view of art.[5] Ives's distinction between substance and manner had much in common with the Soviet distinction between socialist realism and formalism.

According to his official Soviet biographer, Shostakovich in his early years as a composer made the mistake of writing works which "lack of emotion, and bear the imprint of expressionism or exaggeratedly grotesque eccentricity"; he had an "inability to find positive ideals in life, with the resultant sarcastic denials that at times became an object in themselves." But in maturity, Shostakovich learned to eschew "those elements of purely superficial novelty, the novelty that is mere manner and colour." Becoming "fully appreciative of the ethic purpose of art, of its great role in ideological formation," he would "have nothing to do with the abstract play of sounds" or "art for art's sake." [6] This criticism might well be a passage from *Essays before a Sonata*. When Ives condemned the little of Ravel and Stravinsky that he had heard as "over-influenced . . . by the morbidly fascinating," [7] he was applying much the same standards as were the Soviet officials who condemned the same composers' "formalism." And the double bed in the middle of the stage in Shostakovich's *Lady Macbeth* would have proved as shocking to the prudish Ives as it did to the Soviet arbiters of culture. Shostakovich's New York speech of 1949 (after his "repentance") may or may not have represented his real convictions; [8] but it was very close to what Ives had been saying from the bottom of his heart for more than thirty years. "In modern art, including music," said Shostakovich,

> a fierce, implacable struggle is going on between two philosophies of art. One of them is realistic and is engendered by a harmonic, truthful and optimistic outlook on the world. This is a progressive philosophy that enriches mankind with great spiritual values. The other is formalistic. Formalism we call that art that does not know of love for the people, that is anti-democratic, that takes into account only form and denies content; it is a philosophy that is engendered by a pathologically disturbed, pessimistic concept of reality, by lack of faith in the strength and ideals of man. This is a re-

actionary nihilist philosophy that must lead to the corruption and death of music. The bad features of cosmopolitanism that are profoundly alien to the fate of the nation and of mankind, the decline and emptiness of that pseudoculture that has no roots in the people, in the nation, manifest themselves in the rejection of the broad audience and in the loss of national features.

It may be said with all certainty that even the most talented artist cannot say anything that is really new and really big, cannot find his way to the hearts of the people from the position of formalistic art.

Shostakovich explained realism as "a matter of a lofty and beautiful ability to see the world in all its richness from all angles, an ability to generalize a considerable experience of life and record that which is most important in life. Music must cease to be amusement and a toy in the hands of satiate gourmands and aesthetes, and must again become a great social force that serves man in his struggle for progress, for the triumph of reason." [9]

Of course, Ives's ideology drove his music in a radical direction, while the ideology of the Soviet Union caused its composers to write more conservatively; the Soviet leaders wanted music that the Soviet people could understand, while Ives sought to write music that the American ladies could *not* understand. But it must be remembered that the music of the Soviet composers played an important role in Soviet culture when it was being written, while Ives's music was unknown in American culture at the time of its composition. American society had no use for Ives's radical-sounding music (in spite of its thoroughly American ideology); and so, fittingly, he was recruited to serve his society as a businessman, while his composing was done in private. There was no need for Ives's unconventional music to be disciplined by external forces; since the seeds of doubt about his role as an artist had already been planted within him by his own upbringing, he lacked the will to make his music public or to be publicly identified as an artist. It is in his public role as businessman, not in his private role as composer, that Ives should be compared with the Soviet composers. And in this role of businessman, Ives conformed admirably to the standards of his society.

Ives differed from the official Soviet view in denying that glorification of one's nation could be a worthy purpose for a composer;

nor did he reject individualism per se, but only a kind of morbid subjectivism. And it is clear that if his music had been introduced into the Soviet Union during periods of cultural crackdown, it would have been condemned as formalistic. But these considerations do not obscure the fact that Ives imposed on his music and on his life as an artist an extramusical ideology that reflected the dominant values of American society at the turn of the century. And this ideology was similar in many respects to the official ideology that was imposed later upon Soviet composers; both were products of societies tightly organized to resist decadence. That Ives *voluntarily* imposed such an ideology upon himself is evidence of the greater effectiveness of the American system of "indoctrination."

The great challenge facing Ives as a young composer was the challenge of breaking away from his bourgeois background. In his day it was bad enough for *any* creative artist to be caught in the conventional middle-class mode of life; for an *experimental* artist, it meant almost certain frustration of the artistic impulse—as Ives's years of isolation show. Some American artists who were older than Ives succeeded in breaking away from the limitations of their middle-class backgrounds—the painter John Marin and the photographer Alfred Stieglitz, to name two.[10] But in American music, which was slower than the other arts to reject the conventions of nineteenth-century romanticism and to produce an avant-garde, it is harder to find a precedent that Ives might have followed in breaking with gentility. Among men somewhat younger than Ives, however, both Carl Ruggles (born 1876) and Wallingford Riegger (born 1885) worked out relatively integral lives for themselves as avant-garde artists independent of genteel society.

Yet in fairness to Ives, it should be pointed out that he was ten years older than Riegger; moreover, both Ruggles and Riegger were more patient and meticulous composers than Ives, and neither of them "found" himself—either musically or as an artist in his culture—until after a musical avant-garde had appeared in the 1920s. Ives, who was more musically impatient, had largely burned himself out by 1921. But it was not only the late appearance of a Bohemian avant-garde in American music that was responsible for Ives's remaining trapped among the Philistines. More important was the tight conventionality of his upbringing in Danbury and at Yale; the demands of his environment hardly gave him a breathing space to find out who and what he was.

Ives's four years at Yale were especially crucial in his development. Compared with today's notions of what the college experience should be, his Yale environment was total in its demands upon the student; Ives's susceptibility to those demands determined the pattern of the rest of his life. If his college success had come to him on top of a background of wealth or social position (as was the case with his classmate Gouverneur Morris, who became a professional writer), he might have been able to take his success in stride and rise above it; but Ives lacked the assured background in society that many of the more prominent Yale men possessed, and he undoubtedly entered Yale with uncertainty about his position there. Or if, on the other hand, he had experienced social alienation at college, he might have found it easier to accept that artistic alienation from one's culture which is a natural consequence of composing advanced music; but instead, he attained real social success at Yale. The combination of his limited social background with his success in the Yale system must have made it especially difficult for him to reject the Yale pattern after graduation. His early social success was perhaps his greatest curse.

But Ives should be given credit for not being destroyed artistically by Yale, for preserving his integrity as a creative figure even in the midst of that tight environment. And eventually, in his thirties, he did rebel against the Yale system. The rejection of his music by his peers probably encouraged his sympathy for the underdog, for the led rather than the leaders, although that sort of sympathy was also part of a family tradition. But his rebellion was so long delayed that when it finally came, Ives had already made his commitments to the conventional outward life expected of a Yale graduate and a businessman. His rebellion, therefore, became a kind of one-man guerrilla war against the leaders of the conservative business and professional community, carried on from within that community without outside allies. The inevitable result of such isolated rebelliousness was a certain strident repetitiousness and an inability to make fruitful contact with the leading issues and concerns of his time. Cultural historians obviously find it difficult to relate Ives to the avant-garde movements in the American arts during the early twentieth century. But it is almost equally difficult to fit him into the more general political, social, and cultural concerns of the progressive era, in spite of his reformist enthusiasms. Ives came late to the progressive movement. In his isolation, he concentrated on extreme (and rather abstract) schemes for instituting direct government and limiting personal income and property, schemes that were hardly close to the central concerns of progressivism. And in 1919–1920, while other reformers were losing faith in Woodrow Wilson and in progressivism in general, Ives reached the height of his Wilsonian and reformist idealism, apparently ignorant of the significance of what had happened at Versailles. Music is indeed the most abstract of the arts; it is difficult to believe that work comparable to his in importance could have been done in literature or painting by a man so far removed from the leading artistic and intellectual currents of his time.

Ives never directly approached the problem of the Bohemian versus genteel society, because a red herring was drawn across his path. That red herring was the connotations of effeminacy and aristocracy that Americans attached to classical music. By spending so much of his life wrestling with this false issue, Ives was relieved of having to face the Bohemian alternative to gentility—an alternative that he did not want to face, because of his fundamental commitment to the genteel way of life. It was much easier for him to engage in those ceremonial forms of rebellion—those assertions of his manhood and his democracy—which gave him the satisfaction of feeling ungenteel while offering no real threat to genteel, middle-class society and culture. It is for just these ceremonial gestures—his radical music, his radical rhetoric, his radical political opinions—that he is remembered today, while the conventionality of his everyday life has been forgotten.

Ives's fear of aristocracy and effeminacy in classical music was a false issue because it was peculiar to America. In Europe, artists were not regarded as particularly effeminate or undemocratic. Because of an ancient tradition of aristocratic patronage, artists were a well-established and popularly accepted group there—a self-conscious "class" that took pride in its contributions to the society. This situation made it relatively easy for many nineteenth-century European artists to break with the bourgeoisie and become Bohemians without feeling guilty that they had somehow turned their backs on "the people"; Edgard Varèse's experience in France early in the twentieth century is a case in point. In America, however, the lack of a system of aristocratic patronage meant that artists had had great difficulty in securing an accepted place in the society. In nineteenth-century New England, it is true, a group of esteemed literary men lived in close connection with the leading figures in politics and society. But the situation of literary men was far less favorable in other parts of the country; and even in New England, there was a sharp difference between literature and the other arts. Nineteenth-century composers, in particular, were so unsure of their position that they clung tenaciously to their European connections and their refined mode of life, thus earning the special scorn of men like Ives. American men regarded musicians in general, whether they were Americans or not, as an effete importation from Europe, having little or no relation to democratic life and the tasks confronting a developing society; if they tolerated them, it was only to satisfy the desire of their women for "culture." Thus Walt Whitman, apostle of masculinity and democracy, denounced not only the "syllabub and confectionery of parlor and drawing-room literature for ladies," but also the "male odalisque singing or piano-playing a kind of spiced ideas." [11]

There may indeed be something undemocratic about a separate professional group of artists in a society—a body of people who are governed by their own special standards, who have their own special system of patronage or public support, and who associate mainly with themselves and stay apart from the general life of the society. When Ives reacted with emotional hostility to the typically proud and self-assured European "artist," he was only reflecting a traditional American suspicion of certain kinds of undemocratic and snobbish behavior that do not seem to bother Europeans. But the nineteenth-century American position was not consistent. While Americans thought it unhealthy to have a separate "class" of artists, they did not think it undemocratic to have a separate "class" of

321

wealthy businessmen; yet the latter was surely as inimical to the spirit of democracy as the former. Ives accepted the American viewpoint as his own; in this, as in so much else, he was a good American. The thought of making art his life's work was too much for him, for it seemed to imply that he must cut himself off from the common life of America. But business was not snobbish and aristocratic; one could become a businessman and remain one of the people.

In *The Lonely Crowd*, David Riesman expressed admiration for Ives's "autonomy" in refusing "to take the cultural definitions of what constitutes 'work' for granted." In transcending "the requirement that all recruitable emotional energies be harnessed by endless reciprocal chain in work," Ives " 'worked' by heading an agency that sold half a billion dollars' worth of insurance, and he 'played' by composing some of the more significant, though least recognized, music that has been produced." The mistake in this view lies in Riesman's thinking that Ives viewed himself mainly as a composer, that he was willing "to justify [his] work primarily by its pay check." In fact, Ives felt compelled to be a businessman; business was not a sideline that supported his music. "Ives felt, and feels, not in the least guilty," wrote Riesman, "about the money he made or about the fact that he lived a 'normal' American life, rather than a Bohemian one." [12] This is hardly the point. What Riesman did not realize is that Ives *would* have felt guilty had he been a professional musician or a Bohemian. His being in business and living "a 'normal' American life" were not concessions that he made to American society in order that he might be free to compose. They were a means of affirming to himself and others that he was an American, an affirmation that he would have found it nearly impossible to make if he had been a professional musician. In this respect, Ives's business career is not really comparable to Thoreau's work as a surveyor or to Hawthorne's as a customhouse official.

After Ives began to be discovered as a composer, he presented his life as having been a unified and happy one. According to him, he had indeed been the autonomous man, satisfying the demands of American society and at the same time writing his pioneering compositions. Today it is widely believed, especially by those who admire his music, that Ives had the best of both worlds—the normal American world and the world of the avant-garde. But this is a sentimental view. It ignores the hard choice with which Ives's society confronted him at the turn of the century—a choice between being an artist and being a good American. Ives chose to be a good American.

Because he could not accept himself as an artist—because he could not place his art first in his life—Ives brought tragedy upon himself. It is not possible to determine what effect his choice had on his music. But on his life as an artist and as a man the effect is clear. Seeking a unified life, he lived instead a fundamentally divided one, in which his daily work and his art were separate from each other. Fearing to associate with artists and intellectuals who were removed from the people, he became himself utterly isolated, lacking any contact with those who might have encouraged his thinking about art and society or even his musical innovations. Rejecting the inevitable alienation of the artist from his society, Ives asserted his oneness with the majority even as he became increasingly trapped in middle-class gentility. This gentility, in turn, made it impossible for him to follow the shift in American popular culture in the 1920s; cut off from vernacular life, he became more and more a recluse.

After World War I, American society and culture became less dominated by the work ethic and more concerned with consumption, leisure, and "finding oneself." More breathing spaces were offered to the young person of creative talent as he was growing up; there was a wider range of possibilities for personal fulfillment. When a new generation of American composers (born during the period 1893–1900) came to the fore in the 1920s, its members were not confronted by the same heavy demands for both masculinity and gentility that had confronted Ives; perhaps this is why a number of the composers in this and succeeding generations felt freer to pursue homosexuality, or Bohemianism, or both.

The rebellion that began in the American arts during the 1910s came to fruition in the 1920s, producing (even in music) an avant-garde art that was worlds apart from the art of the genteel tradition. It was as if a line had been drawn across American culture separating past from present. On one side of that line stood Charles Ives. On the other side stood the younger composers and other musicians who reveled in the new music. Yet it was from the ranks of these younger men that Ives's discoverers had to come during the 1920s and 1930s. Some of them paid little attention to him. Others admired him from a distance, held back by his obvious hesitation about having personal contact with them. A few actually came to know him, but even they could not deal with him so frankly (in the manner of one artist speaking to another) as they could with their fellow members of the avant-garde. Ives enjoyed the recognition that he received through the efforts of these younger people; but he did not really understand the avant-garde musical world in which that recognition was first achieved. With most of the modernists he was perhaps even less comfortable than he had been with the traditionalists of his own generation and before.

The cultural barrier between Ives and these younger musicians was partially overcome because of the extraordinary character of his music. Some of them hailed him as a sort of father of American music, as the only American who had composed truly original music before 1920. Some thought they had found a kindred spirit from the older generation, assuming that such modern music must have been produced by a very modern mind. The exceptional autonomy or artistic independence of his creative years was generally emphasized. As the Ives Legend was elaborated by younger musicians during the 1930s and later, Ives's earlier life was interpreted so that it accorded with his radical music and his radical rhetoric. The tremendous pressures that had narrowed his creativity, stifled his autonomy, and driven him into artistic isolation were overlooked.

In his later years, then, the relationship between Charles Ives and American culture was just the opposite of what it had been in the earlier part of his life. In his earlier years, both his music and his thought reflected the dominant (and traditional) values and way of life of his time and place; particularly in his thinking about the artist and society, he accepted the prevailing American attitudes so completely and literally as to become a virtual prisoner of his culture. But his compositions had no reciprocal influence upon his culture at that time; only in the insurance business was his influence felt. In the last two or three decades of his life, on the other hand, Ives's compositions were drawn increasingly into the mainstream of his country's concert life and musical heritage. But the composer himself, unable to understand the new America, was at the same time withdrawing ever further from interaction with the rapidly changing society around him.

NOTES

🌿

Notes to Chapter 1: Danbury

1. The standard history of Danbury, from which most of the present account of the town is drawn, is James Montgomery Bailey, *History of Danbury, Conn., 1684–1896*, from notes and manuscript left by him, compiled with additions by Susan Benedict Hill (New York: Burr Printing House, 1896).

2. *Ibid.*, p. 559.

3. *Ibid.*, pp. 560, 561, 562; the population figure for 1890 given in Bailey is corrected in U.S., Census Office, *Report on Population of the United States at the Eleventh Census: 1890*, pt. 1, p. 80. The corrected figure is used here.

4. The generalizations in this paragraph are based upon data and examples given in Bailey, *History of Danbury*, esp. chaps. 25, 26, 28, 30–37, 40–43, 48, 53.

5. *Ibid.*, chap. 31.

6. Quoted *ibid.*, p. 244.

7. *Ibid.*, p. 496.

8. *Ibid.*, p. 212.

9. *Ibid.*, p. 327.

10. This percentage is computed from: U.S., Census Office, *Report on Population of the United States at the Eleventh Census: 1890*, pt. 1, p. 525. The figures used are not for

the *town* (that is, the whole township) of Danbury, but rather for the incorporated *city* of Danbury, which excluded the more rural regions of the town. In 1890 the city of Danbury contained 16,552 of the town's 19,473 people: *ibid.,* p. 80.

11. Ives wrote these words on the back of the last page of the earlier manuscript version of the "Thoreau" section of his *Essays before a Sonata;* this manuscript is in the "Concord Essays" file, Ives Collection, John Herrick Jackson Music Library, Yale University, New Haven, Conn. (hereafter cited as Ives Collection).

12. *Danbury News,* July 16, 1890, p. 4.

13. Interview with Amelia Ives Van Wyck by Vivian Perlis, November 7, 1968, Tape #2A, Ives Oral History Project (hereafter cited as Van Wyck interview). The originals of this taped interview and others cited hereafter are in the Ives Collection.

14. Information about members of the Ives family is taken, where not otherwise indicated, from Bailey, *History of Danbury,* and from the Van Wyck interview, November 7 and 21, 1968, Tapes #2A, #2B, and #2C.

15. Bailey, *History of Danbury,* p. 551.

16. Quoted *ibid.,* p. 432.

17. Van Wyck interview, November 21, 1968, Tape #2B.

18. *Danbury Times,* April 12, 1860, p. [2]; *Jeffersonian* (Danbury), May 21, 1862, p. [2].

19. For the traditional story about this incident, see "Col. Wildman Reminisces," *Danbury Evening Times,* August 2, 1932; a copy of this article is in Scrapbook No. 3, p. 145, Ives Collection.

20. George E. Ives, Notebook 5 (7A1v), p. 34, Ives Collection.

21. See "Danbury's Delight Is All for Music," *New York Herald,* January 5, 1890, Connecticut Edition section, p. [2].

22. Charles E. Ives, *Memos,* ed. John Kirkpatrick (New York: W. W. Norton & Company, Inc., 1972), p. 45.

23. Charles E. Ives, "Some 'Quarter-Tone' Impressions," *Franco-American Musical Society Quarterly Bulletin,* March, 1925, p. 27.

24. Ives, *Memos,* p. 115.

25. Henry Cowell and Sidney Cowell, *Charles Ives and His Music,* paperback ed. with additional material (New York: Oxford University Press, 1969), p. 20.

26. Charles E. Ives, "Conductor's Note" (1929) to 2d movement of Fourth Symphony, reprinted in Charles Ives, *Symphony No. 4* (New York: Associated Music Publishers, Inc., c1965), p. 13.

27. On a page of corrections to a biographical article about himself, in the "Autobiographical" file, Ives Collection, Charles Ives recalled that he had been playing in one of the two bands during an incident of this sort and that it had been musically suggestive for his own composition, particularly with respect to the approach and then the dying away of the other band.

28. Interview with Philip Sunderland by Vivian Perlis, November 29, 1968, Tape #3, Ives Oral History Project (hereafter cited as Sunderland interview).

29. *Ibid.*

30. *Danbury Evening News,* December 7, 1891, p. 1.

31. Ives, *Memos,* p. 45.

32. Clipping of obituary in Scrapbook No. 5, p. 19, Ives Collection.

33. Sunderland interview, November 29, 1968, Tape #3.

34. Van Wyck interview, November 7 and 21, 1968, Tapes #2A, #2B, and #2C.

35. Bailey, *History of Danbury,* pp. 497, 522.

36. *Ibid.,* pp. 422–23.

37. *Danbury Evening News,* November 5, 1894, p. 1.

38. Van Wyck interview, November 21, 1968, Tape #2B; Sunderland interview, November 29, 1968, Tape #3.

39. Sunderland interview, November 29, 1968, Tape #3.

40. Van Wyck interview, November 21, 1968, Tape #2B.

41. Sunderland interview, November 29, 1968, Tape #3.

42. Personal information from Amelia Ives Van Wyck, via John Kirkpatrick.

43. *Danbury Evening News,* August 12, 1890, p. 4; *Evening News* (Danbury), March 16, 1888, p. 3; *Danbury Evening News,* August 30, 1890, p. 4.

44. Van Wyck interview, November 21, 1968, Tapes #2B and #2C.

45. Letter of Amelia Ives Brewster to Charles E. Ives, April 8, 1908, in custody of John Kirkpatrick.

46. Van Wyck interview, November 21, 1968, Tape #2C.

47. *Ibid.,* Tape #2B.

48. Ives, *Memos,* p. 114.

49. Cowell and Cowell, *Charles Ives and His Music,* p. 11.

50. E.g., Ives, *Memos,* pp. 45, 114–15; enclosure in letter of Charles E. Ives to John Tasker Howard, June 30, 1930, published *ibid.,* app. 11, pp. 236–37.

51. The following discussion is based upon H. Wiley Hitchcock, *Music in the United States: A Historical Introduction,* 2d ed., Prentice-Hall History of Music Series (Englewood Cliffs, N.J., 1974), esp. chap. 3.

52. John Philip Sousa, *Marching Along* (Boston: Hale, Cushman and Flint, 1928), p. 132, quoted *ibid.,* p. 120.

53. Gilbert Chase, *America's Music, from the Pilgrims to the Present,* rev. 2d ed. (New York: McGraw-Hill Book Company, 1966), p. 131.

54. Harold Schonberg, "Gustav Mahler as Conductor," *HiFi/Stereo Review,* August, 1967, p. 48.

55. Walter Damrosch, *My Musical Life* (New York: Charles Scribner's Sons, 1923), p. 323.

56. Hitchcock, *Music in the United States,* p. 53.

57. The program for this concert of March 7, 1888, is in Scrapbook No. 6, p. 29, Ives Collection; the Toy Symphony was probably composed by Leopold Mozart.

58. *Ibid.*

59. The program for this recital of May 11, 1887, is in Scrapbook No. 6, p. 35, Ives Collection.

60. *Evening News* (Danbury), October 21, 1889, p. 3.

61. Personal information from Harmony T. Ives, via John Kirkpatrick.

62. *Danbury Evening News,* June 12, 1890, p. 4.

63. Ives, *Memos*, pp. 130–31; the words in brackets have been added by the editor of the *Memos*, John Kirkpatrick.

64. *Danbury Evening News*, June 28, 1890, p. 4; June 30, 1890, p. 4.

65. The photograph, taken on November 26, 1892, is in the Ives Collection.

66. Cowell and Cowell, *Charles Ives and His Music*, p. 27.

67. Charles E. Ives, undated sketch for letter of Harmony T. Ives to E. Power Biggs in answer to Biggs's letter of April 15, 1948, Ives Collection.

68. Quoted in Patricia Ashley, "Roy Harris," *Stereo Review*, December, 1968, p. 66.

69. Ives, *Memos*, p. 30.

70. Charles E. Ives, *Essays before a Sonata* (New York: Knickerbocker Press, 1920), pp. 91–92.

71. Ives, *Memos*, p. 29.

72. Charles E. Ives, memo on p. 7 of sketch of 2d movement of Second String Quartet (2A3ii), Ives Collection.

73. Charles E. Ives, memo on p. "4" of sketch of *Varied Air & Variations* (3B20), Ives Collection; Ives, *Memos*, p. 43; Charles E. Ives, memo on p. [3] of sketch of Study #20 (3B17), Ives Collection.

74. Personal information from John Kirkpatrick.

75. Ives, *Memos*, pp. 45–46.

76. Bailey, *History of Danbury*, p. 328.

77. *Evening News* (Danbury), January 17, 1888, p. 3.

78. Personal information from John Kirkpatrick.

79. *Danbury Evening News*, September 23, 1890, p. 4.

80. Charles E. Ives, undated 1st sketch for letter of Harmony T. Ives to Claire R. Reis in answer (2d answer) to Mrs. Reis's letter of October 22, 1945, in "League of Composers" file, Ives Collection.

81. Ives, *Memos*, pp. 132–33.

82. Charles E. Ives, "Diary of a Commuter" (D9), memo of June 5, 1914, Ives Collection.

83. Lou Harrison, jacket notes for *Sonatas for Violin and Piano*, by Charles Ives (Philips World Series Stereo/PHC 2-002).

84. Cowell and Cowell, *Charles Ives and His Music*, p. 27.

85. Charles E. Ives, sketch of *Slow March* (6B10), Ives Collection.

86. Charles E. Ives, *Schoolboy March* (1D1), Ives Collection. This composition may have been nothing more than a title page.

87. *Evening News* (Danbury), January 17, 1888, p. 3; *Danbury News*, December 26, 1888, p. 1; *Evening News* (Danbury), October 10, 1889, p. 3; Charles E. Ives, entries for May 25, [1890], and June 15, 1890, in account book containing Baptist church services, etc. (D4), Ives Collection.

88. Charles E. Ives, memo on p. [2] of ink copy in E♭ by Price of *At Parting* (6B10c), Ives Collection.

89. The photograph is in the Ives Collection.

90. Sunderland interview, November 29, 1968, Tape #3.

91. The program for this concert is in the file of programs and reviews, Ives Collection.

92. Charles E. Ives, entry for July 5, [1891], in account book containing Baptist church services, etc. (D4), Ives Collection.

93. Unsigned jacket notes for *Variations on "America,"* by Charles Ives–William Schuman (Louisville Orchestra First Edition Records Lou-651).

94. Ives, *Memos,* p. 38.

95. Unsigned "Note" in *Variations on "America" (1891) for organ/"Adeste Fidelis" in an Organ Prelude (1897),* by Charles Ives (New York: Music Press, Inc., c1949), p. [ii].

96. Charles E. Ives, undated [May or June, 1948] sketch for letter of Harmony T. Ives to E. Power Biggs, Ives Collection.

97. Quoted in unsigned "Note" in *Variations on "America" (1891) for organ/"Adeste Fidelis" in an Organ Prelude (1897),* by Charles Ives (New York: Music Press, Inc., c1949), p. [ii].

98. E.g., letters of Charles E. Ives to George E. Ives, May 9, 1893, and February 24, 1894, Ives Collection.

99. Personal information from Harmony T. Ives, via John Kirkpatrick; cf. letter of Charles Bonney to Charles E. Ives, March 6, 1893, in custody of John Kirkpatrick.

100. E.g., letter of Charles E. Ives to George E. Ives, November 19, 1893, Ives Collection.

101. Letters of Charles E. Ives to Mary P. Ives, undated [March 22, 1894], and to George E. Ives, October 30, [1893], Ives Collection.

102. Letter of Charles E. Ives to George E. Ives, March 29, [1894], Ives Collection.

103. *Ibid.*

104. Letter of Charles E. Ives to George E. Ives, April 12, 1894, Ives Collection.

105. Letter of Charles E. Ives to George E. Ives, May 8, [1894], Ives Collection.

106. Letter of Charles E. Ives to George E. Ives, May 2, 1894, Ives Collection; letter of Charles W. Whittlesey to Charles E. Ives, March 4, 1895, in custody of John Kirkpatrick.

107. Letter of J. B. Ryder to Charles E. Ives, July 12, 1894, in custody of John Kirkpatrick; letter (with enclosed bills and receipt) of Edward H. Hume to George E. Ives, July 16, 1894, in custody of John Kirkpatrick; letter (with enclosed bill) of Edward H. Hume to George E. Ives, October 5, 1894, in custody of John Kirkpatrick.

108. Letter of Charles E. Ives to George E. Ives, undated [August 3, 1894], Ives Collection.

109. Letter of Edward H. Hume to George E. Ives, October 5, 1894, in custody of John Kirkpatrick.

110. *Ibid.*

111. Charles E. Ives, undated [January, 1930] sketch for letter to John C. Griggs, Ives Collection.

112. Letter of Charles E. Ives to Joseph Hopkins Twichell, dated "Saturday afternoon" [November 23, 1907], published in Ives, *Memos,* app. 16, p. 261.

113. Interview with Chester Ives by Vivian Perlis, May 7, 1969, Tape #10B, Ives Oral History Project (hereafter cited as Chester Ives interview).

114. Ives, *Memos,* app. 13, p. 249.

115. Cowell and Cowell, *Charles Ives and His Music,* p. 27.

116. Ives, *Memos,* p. 46.

117. *Ibid.,* pp. 42–43.

118. *Ibid.,* p. 44 and n. 5.

119. *Ibid.,* p. 47.

120. Charles E. Ives, explanatory memo for *Psalm 67* (5C24), Ives Collection.

121. Ives, *Memos,* p. 48, n. 2.

122. Charles E. Ives, explanatory memo for *Psalm 67* (5C24), Ives Collection.

Notes to Chapter 2: Yale

1. Ives, *Memos,* p. 48.

2. Ives's courses and grades are given in the " '98" section of the ledger entitled "Record of Scholarship. Yale College. 1896–1900," in the Yale University Archives, Yale University Library, New Haven, Conn. The required and elective courses are described in the appropriate issues of the annual *Catalogue of Yale University.*

3. Ives, *Memos,* p. 116.

4. Bruce Simonds, quoted in Isabel Parker Semler, in collaboration with Pierson Underwood, *Horatio Parker: A Memoir for His Grandchildren Compiled from Letters and Papers* (New York: G. P. Putnam's Sons, 1942), p. 271.

5. Ives, *Memos,* pp. 116, 48–49.

6. Charles E. Ives, memo on p. 1 of pencil sketch of Fugue in E♭ (3D15), Ives Collection.

7. Ives, *Memos,* p. 49 and n. 3.

8. *Ibid.,* pp. 49, 115.

9. *Ibid.,* pp. 51, 87.

10. Quoted *ibid.,* p. 132, n. 1.

11. Charles E. Ives, memos on p. 1 of score-sketch, and title page of full score, of 3d movement of Second Symphony (1A2iii), Ives Collection.

12. Ives, *Memos,* p. 52.

13. Charles E. Ives, memo on sketch of first state with original opening (27 measures headed: "II") of 3d movement of Second Symphony (1A2iii), Ives Collection.

14. John Tasker Howard, *Our American Music: Three Hundred Years of It* (New York: Thomas Y. Crowell Company, 1931), p. 337.

15. Charles E. Ives, memo on title page of full score of Postlude in F (1B1), Ives Collection.

16. "Record of Scholarship. Yale College. 1896–1900," Yale University Archives, Yale University Library; *Catalogue of Yale University, 1898–99,* pp. 444–47; *Catalogue of Yale University, 1900–1901,* pp. 439, 442. Grades between 350 and 400 were the equivalent of an A; between 300 and 350, a B; between 250 and 300, a C; and between 200 and 250, a D. The lowest passing grade was 200.

17. Charles E. Ives, memo on p. [1] of ink copy in A♭ by Price of *Ich grolle nicht* (6B27a), Ives Collection.

18. Ives, *Memos,* p. 49.

19. Howard, *Our American Music,* p. 338.

20. Ives, *Memos,* pp. 47–48.

21. William Lyon Phelps, quoted in Semler, *Horatio Parker,* p. 94.

22. David Stanley Smith, "A Study of Horatio Parker," *Musical Quarterly* 16 (April, 1930): 157.

23. Howard, *Our American Music,* p. 337.

24. Semler, *Horatio Parker,* pp. 94, 279.

25. Horatio Parker, "Our Taste in Music," *Yale Review* 7 (July, 1918): 782.

26. The dissertation is quoted and discussed in Ives, *Memos,* app. 15, pp. 253–54.

27. See the entries throughout his memorandum book of "Programs of Music at Center Church, New Haven Ct, 1896–97," Ives Collection.

28. Ives, *Memos,* p. 116.

29. Letter of John C. Griggs to Charles E. Ives, August 27–28, 1921, Ives Collection.

30. Charles E. Ives, undated [January, 1930] sketch for letter to John C. Griggs, Ives Collection.

31. Ives, *Memos,* pp. 57, 120; cf. Charles E. Ives, memo on 2d sketch of Interlude for hymn *Bethany* (3D6ii), Ives Collection.

32. Charles E. Ives, memos on title page of First String Quartet (2A1) and on p. 1 of score by Copyist 9 of original 3d movement (2A1iii), and title page of score of original 4th movement (2A1iv), of First String Quartet, Ives Collection. The title page of the whole quartet and the score by Copyist 9 of the original third movement exist only in negative photostats.

33. Charles E. Ives, memos on p. 1 of copy by Copyist 9 of keyboard arrangement of original 2d movement (2A1ii) of First String Quartet and on title page of First String Quartet (2A1), Ives Collection.

34. The first movement, which may have been written later than 1896, was subsequently detached from this work and became the third movement of the Fourth Symphony; it was from a "Fugue for Parker," who probably did not appreciate its hymn-tune subjects: Charles E. Ives, memo on title page of First String Quartet (2A1), Ives Collection.

35. These two organ pieces were later (1904) worked together into the orchestral composition *Thanksgiving,* the fourth of the *New England Holidays.*

36. Ives, *Memos,* pp. 38–39, 130. On p. [1] of the sketch of the Postlude (3D18) in the Ives Collection, the work begins with a C *major* (not a C *minor*) chord with a D minor chord over it. Cf. Ives, *Memos,* p. 130.

37. Ives, *Memos,* p. 39.

38. Charles E. Ives, memo on p. 1 of ink copy of movement #6 (Aria for Tenor) of *The Celestial Country* (5A1), Ives Collection.

39. Charles E. Ives, memo on p. [1] of sketch of *Harvest Home* (5B2i), the first of Three *Harvest Home* Chorales, Ives Collection. Since part of the manuscript of these three works was later lost, however, Ives may have changed them in the direction of greater musical radicalism when he reconstructed them later; cf. John Kirkpatrick, jacket notes for *Charles Ives: Music for Chorus* (Columbia MS 6921).

40. Charles Edmund Merrill, Jr., and Charles E. Ives, "A Scotch Lullaby," *Yale Courant* 33 (December Third Week, 1896): 125–27.

41. C. E. Merrill, Jr., and C. E. Ives, "A Song of Mory's," *Yale Courant* 33 (February Fourth Week, 1897): 280–81.

42. Even genteel household music took on a vernacular quality in the undergraduate setting. The large quantity of vocal music—particularly vocal music of a romantic, sentimental character—that Ives produced at Yale was in part undoubtedly a response to the musical taste of his peers.

43. George Wilson Pierson, *Yale: College and University, 1871–1937*, vol. 1: *Yale College: An Educational History, 1871–1921* (New Haven: Yale University Press, 1952), p. 17; *Yale Banner* 56 [1897–98]: 257.

44. *The Yale Class Book: '98*, p. 143.

45. Surviving music and programs can be found in Music for Fraternity Shows (4A), Ives Collection.

46. *Yale Daily News,* November 29, 1897, p. [1]; January 24, 1898, p. [1].

47. Ralph Joseph Moore, Jr., "The Background and the Symbol: Charles E. Ives: A Case Study in the History of American Cultural Expression" (Senior essay, American Studies Department, Yale College, 1954), p. 27. Moore's thoughtful essay has proved extremely helpful in bringing to light a variety of sources for Ives's years at Yale.

48. S. B. Hill (words) and C. E. Ives (music), *William Will: A Republican Campaign Song* (New York: Willis Woodward & Co., c1896); C. E. Ives, *For You and Me!* (New York: Geo. Molineux, c1896). Among the materials for the March *Intercollegiate* (1D5) in the Ives Collection are negative photostats of a set of published parts that are in the library of the Columbia Broadcasting System, New York City. These parts are headed "March (Two-Step)—'Inter-Collegiate,' " with Ives's name, and one of them bears a copyright date of 1896. It was Ives's recollection that this march had been published by Pepper & Co. of Philadelphia; cf. Cowell and Cowell, *Charles Ives and His Music,* p. 105, note.

49. Thomas G. Shepard, composer, compiler, and ed., assisted by James W. Reynolds, *Yale Melodies: A Collection of the Latest Songs Used by the Yale University Glee Club* (New Haven: Thomas G. Shepard, 1903), pp. 88–92.

50. Ives, *Memos,* pp. 56–57.

51. Charles E. Ives, "In the Alley," *114 Songs* (Redding, Conn.: C. E. Ives, 1922), pp. 119–21.

52. Ives, *Memos,* pp. 39–40.

53. *Ibid.,* pp. 40–41.

54. Charles E. Ives, memos on p. 1 of full score of 1st movement (1A2i), p. 1 of full score of 3d movement (1A2iii), title page of 2d [?] sketch of 1st movement (1A2i), title page of score-sketch of 2d movement (1A2ii), page [1] of score-sketch of 4th movement (1A2iv), and p. 6 of full score of 5th movement (1A2v), of Second Symphony, Ives Collection.

55. Henry Seidel Canby, *Alma Mater: The Gothic Age of the American College* (New York: Farrar & Rinehart, Inc., 1936), pp. 87–88, 92, 89, 90.

56. Charles E. Ives, memos on pp. [4] and [5] of complete [?] sketch, and separate memo entitled "Songs & cheers . . . ," for *Yale-Princeton Football Game* (1B3), Ives Collection; Ives, *Memos,* p. 40. Cf. *ibid.,* p. 61.

57. Quoted in Charles E. Ives, memo on p. 3 of complete [?] sketch of *Yale-Princeton Football Game* (1B3), Ives Collection.

58. Ives, *Memos*, p. 61.

59. The following discussion of Yale draws upon Pierson, *Yale College*, pp. 3–106.

60. During Ives's years at Yale, each sophomore was to omit one subject (of his choice) from the six basic studies: Greek, Latin, English, French or German, mathematics, and physics.

61. Canby, *Alma Mater*, chap. 3.

62. *Ibid.*, p. 58.

63. *Ibid.*, pp. 82, 72–73.

64. Quoted in Edwin E. Slosson, *Great American Universities* (New York: Macmillan Company, 1910), p. 66.

65. Canby, *Alma Mater*, chap. 2.

66. *Ibid.*, p. 38.

67. Cf. Pierson, *Yale College*, p. 33.

68. *Yale Banner* 54 [1895–96]: 231.

69. Canby, *Alma Mater*, p. 26.

70. Maurice F. Parmelee, "Yale and the Academic Ideal," *Yale Courant* 43 (December, 1906): 129; cf. Pierson, *Yale College*, pp. 240–41.

71. Lewis Sheldon Welch and Walter Camp, *Yale: Her Campus, Class-rooms, and Athletics* (Boston: L. C. Page and Company, 1899), pp. 101–2.

72. Cf. Canby, *Alma Mater*, pp. 81–82.

73. G[eorge] Santayana, "A Glimpse of Yale," *Harvard Monthly* 15 (December, 1892): 94.

74. *Ibid.*, pp. 92, 95.

75. Pierson, *Yale College*, p. 19.

76. Cf. Slosson, *Great American Universities*, p. 67.

77. Edwin S. Oviatt, "On Shams," *Yale Literary Magazine* 61 (January, 1896): 132.

78. Owen Johnson, *Stover at Yale*, with an Introduction by Kingman Brewster, Jr., paperback ed. (New York: Collier Books, 1968).

79. There were only two until 1895.

80. On the sophomore societies, see (in addition to *Stover at Yale*) Nathan Ayer Smyth, "The Democratic Idea in College Life," *Yale Literary Magazine* 61 (April, 1896): 274–76. Although Ives's class was little touched by it, discontent with the sophomore societies later became so strong among the undergraduates that the faculty abolished the societies in 1900. The junior fraternities, on the other hand, were much less exclusive organizations that took in more than a third of the class.

81. Johnson, *Stover at Yale*, pp. 19–21.

82. *Ibid.*, pp. 41, 153–54, 281.

83. *Yale Banner* 54 [1895–96]: 265.

84. He also went out for pitcher on the Freshman Baseball Nine, but was unsuccessful: *Yale Daily News*, February 16, 1895, p. [1]; February 28, 1895, p. [1]; March 15, 1895, p. [1]. In his senior year, after the members of the senior societies from his class had been chosen, Ives rowed with his class's crew in the Fall Regatta and was a substitute on the class's football team: *Yale Daily News*, October 16, 1897, p. [1]; *Yale*

Banner 56 [1897–98]: 226. Part of the essay on Emerson in his later *Essays before a Sonata* "was from an article handed in to the Yale Literary Magazine when I was a Senior, and promptly handed back": Ives, *Memos*, p. 83.

85. *Yale Daily News*, May 28, 1897, p. [1]. This was the Tap Day of Owen Johnson's freshman year, and his reactions to it may have been the basis for the description in chap. 14 of *Stover at Yale*.

86. Ives was also an abysmal student at college. Out of 292 men who graduated from Yale College in 1898, 230 got some form of honors in their studies; Ives was one of the 62 who received no honors: *Yale Banner* 57 [1898–99]: 151, 159–61.

87. *The Yale Class Book: '98*, p. 159; *Yale Banner* 56 [1897–98]: 147, 149, 151.

88. Thomas B. Davis, Jr., *Chronicles of Hopkins Grammar School, 1660–1935, Containing a Life of the Founder Together with School Records and Reminiscences Covering 275 Years* (New Haven: [Hopkins Grammar School], 1938), pp. 457–58, 564–66.

89. *Catalogue of* Π. Σ. T. (New Haven: Hopkins Grammar School, 1896), pp. 14, 10.

90. *Yale Banner* 55 [1896–97]: 251.

91. Letter of Charles E. Ives to George E. Ives, October 24, 1894, Ives Collection.

92. *A Catalogue of the Members of* H BOYΛH *of Yale, 1900*, pp. 161–62, 166.

93. *Ibid.*, p. 164; *The Yale Class Book: '98*, p. 109; *Yale Banner* 56 [1897–98]: 222. Twichell's father was a member of the Yale Corporation; and he himself, as a class deacon, an activist in the YMCA, and the son of a clergyman, probably qualified for membership in the politically powerful "Dwight Hall ring": *Yale Banner* 56 [1897–98]: 200; Pierson, *Yale College*, p. 13.

94. *Yale Banner* 55 [1896–97]: 175; *ibid.* 56 [1897–98]: 149.

95. *Ibid.* 55 [1896–97]: 179; *Danbury Evening News*, October 15, 1892, p. 4; letter of Charles E. Ives to George E. Ives, October 24, 1894, Ives Collection; *Catalogue of* Π. Σ. T. (1896), p. 16.

96. *Yale Daily News*, October 21, 1897, p. [1].

97. Interview with Louise Garbarino Berneri by Vivian Perlis, March 23, 1972, Tape #56, Ives Oral History Project.

98. *Horoscope*, May, 1897, p. 8; a copy of this booklet is in the Yale University Archives, Yale University Library.

99. Quoted in Ives, *Memos*, app. 17, p. 267. John Kirkpatrick has generously shared his letters from Dr. Park and his notes on conversations with him.

100. Ives put these words into the mouth of "George" on pp. 39–40 of an early dialogue version (c. 1919) of his essay "The Majority"; the surviving portion of the manuscript is in the folder marked "Majority—early dialogue version," in the Ives Collection. "George" is obviously Ives himself.

101. *Yale Daily News*, February 4, 1895, p. [2]; June 4, 1895, p. [2].

102. Ives, *Memos*, p. 41.

103. *The Yale Class Book: '98*, pp. 157–60.

104. Canby, *Alma Mater*, pp. 75–76.

105. Letter of Sidney R. Kennedy to Charles E. Ives, April 21, 1950, in "Yale 1898" file, Ives Collection.

106. Charles E. Ives, memo on p. 11 of ink copy of *The All-enduring* (6B23), Ives Collection.

107. *Ibid.*

108. Ives, *Memos,* p. 61.

109. Johnson, *Stover at Yale,* pp. 262–63. Moore, "Background and the Symbol," chap. 6, shows undergraduate aversion to serious music by quoting the unsuccessful attempts of the *Yale Daily News* to induce students to attend concerts at the university.

110. Charles E. Ives, memo on p. 4 of score-sketch of *Country Band March* (1C14), Ives Collection.

111. Charles E. Ives, memo on sketch of measures 10–13 and 20–21 of *On the Antipodes* (6B71), Ives Collection.

112. Ives, *Memos,* pp. 130–31.

113. An early example was his so-called Postface in *114 Songs,* pp. 261–62. Cf. Charles E. Ives, undated [November, 1940?] sketches for letter of Harmony T. Ives to Peter Yates, Ives Collection.

114. E.g., Mrs. Ives stated in 1963 that Ives's "father had wanted him to be a concert pianist"; she is quoted in Ives, *Memos,* p. 103, n. 7.

115. *Ibid.,* p. 130.

116. William Kay Kearns, "Horatio Parker 1863–1919: A Study of His Life and Music" (Ph.D. diss., University of Illinois, 1965), pp. 120, 129–31.

117. E.g., Cowell and Cowell, *Charles Ives and His Music,* pp. 36–37.

118. Burnet C. Tuthill, "David Stanley Smith," *Musical Quarterly* 28 (January, 1942): 64.

119. E.g., letter of J. Moss Ives to Charles E. Ives, August 18, 1919, in Scrapbook No. 5, p. 64, Ives Collection.

120. U.S., Census Office, *Report on Population of the United States at the Eleventh Census: 1890,* pt. 1, pp. 80, 525; U.S., Census Office, *Census Reports: Twelfth Census of the United States, Taken in the Year 1900,* vol. 1: *Population,* pt. 1, pp. 89, 649.

121. Pierson, *Yale College,* p. 25.

122. Canby, *Alma Mater,* pp. 71–72.

123. Santayana, "Glimpse of Yale," p. 95.

124. Quoted in Henry Bellamann, "Charles Ives: The Man and His Music," *Musical Quarterly* 19 (January, 1933): 48.

Notes to Chapter 3: The Composer

1. Ralph Waldo Emerson, "The American Scholar," in *The Prose Works of Ralph Waldo Emerson,* new and rev. ed., 2 vols. (Boston: James R. Osgood and Company, 1875), 1:45, 61–62.

2. Aaron Copland, *The New Music, 1900–1960,* rev. and enl. ed. (New York: W. W. Norton & Company, Inc., 1968), pp. 17, 24.

3. *The Journal of Henry D. Thoreau,* ed. Bradford Torrey and Francis H. Allen, 14 vols. (Boston: Houghton Mifflin Company, 1949), 12:389–90.

4. Edward N. Waters, "The Wa-Wan Press: An Adventure in Musical Idealism,"

in *A Birthday Offering to [Carl Engel]*, ed. Gustave Reese (New York: G. Schirmer, Inc., 1943), pp. 214–33.

5. Aaron Copland, *Music and Imagination* (Cambridge, Mass.: Harvard University Press, 1952), pp. 103–4.

6. Ives, *Essays before a Sonata,* pp. 92–96; letter of Charles E. Ives to John Tasker Howard, June 30, 1930, published in Ives, *Memos,* app. 11, p. 240.

7. Emerson, "American Scholar," p. 60.

8. *Journal of Thoreau,* 4:471–72.

9. Ives, *Memos,* p. 87.

10. Lou Harrison, "On Quotation," *Modern Music* 23 (Summer, 1946): 167–68.

11. Ives's aesthetic views are discussed below, chap. 6.

12. Ives, *Memos,* p. 52.

13. "Notes on Fourth Violin Sonata," in *Sonata No. 4 for Violin and Piano: "Children's Day at the Camp Meeting,"* by Charles Ives (New York: Associated Music Publishers, Inc., c1942), p. 21. Ives incorrectly identified the quoted hymn tune as Lowell Mason's *Work Song.*

14. *Ibid.*

15. Lou Harrison's comments on Ives's technique of "recomposition" are in his jacket notes for Ives's *Sonatas for Violin and Piano* (Philips World Series Stereo/PHC 2-002).

16. Ives, *Memos,* pp. 128–30. On the other hand, his settings of the Psalms and his *Harvest Home* Chorales had been among his most experimental works during his years as a church organist; but some of these works had probably never been performed.

17. Charles E. Ives, memo on p. 7 of 2d ink copy of 1st movement of First Piano Sonata (3A1i), Ives Collection.

18. Ives, *Memos,* p. 75.

19. Quoted in Van Wyck Brooks, *The Ordeal of Mark Twain* (New York: E. P. Dutton & Company, 1920), p. 177.

20. Thornton Wilder, *Three Plays: Our Town, The Skin of Our Teeth, The Matchmaker* (New York: Harper & Row, Publishers, 1957), pp. 81–82, 45, xii.

21. In a memo in Mrs. Ives's hand in the "Memos about Music" file, Ives Collection, Ives explained that the sonata contrasted the exuberant life of the young people with the deep religious life of their elders; the older people would indicate to the boys that it was time to end their barn dance by humming the chorus of a hymn.

22. Charles E. Ives, *"Three Places in New England": An Orchestral Set* (Boston: C. C. Birchard & Company, c1935), p. 20.

23. Ives, *Memos,* pp. 96, 97.

24. Charles E. Ives, "Diary of a Commuter" (D9), memo of June 5, 1914, Ives Collection.

25. Ives, *Essays before a Sonata,* p. 50.

26. Ives, *Memos,* p. 104.

27. Charles E. Ives, typed postface (longer version) added as p. 35 to bound photostats of full score by Hanke of *The Fourth of July* (1A4iii), Ives Collection. Ives went on to say that not all these things and events were in the music.

28. *The Writings of Mark Twain,* Stormfield Edition, 37 vols. (New York: Harper & Brothers, 1929), vol. 16: *Pudd'nhead Wilson and Those Extraordinary Twins,* pp. 223–25.

29. Cf. Ives, *Memos,* p. 71.

30. Ives, *Essays before a Sonata,* p. 1.

31. *Ibid.,* pp. 48–49.

32. E.g., *ibid.,* p. 77.

33. Cf. *ibid.,* pp. 20–23, 66–67.

34. Ives, *Memos,* pp. 129–30.

35. Ives, *Essays before a Sonata,* pp. 36–37.

36. Ives, *Memos,* p. 97.

37. Ives, *Essays before a Sonata,* p. 36.

38. These program notes, originally written by Henry Bellamann in consultation with Ives, were revised by Ives and printed as "Notes on Fourth Symphony" in *New Music* 2 (January, 1929): [ii]. This issue of *New Music* contains the second movement of the symphony.

39. *Ibid.*

40. *Ibid.*

41. *Ibid.*

42. Ives, *Memos,* p. 66.

43. *Ibid.,* pp. 106–7.

44. Cowell and Cowell, *Charles Ives and His Music,* p. 201.

45. Quoted in Ives, *Memos,* app. 19, p. 279.

Notes to Chapter 4: The Businessman

1. Van Wyck interview, November 21, 1968, Tape #2C.

2. Interview with Julian S. Myrick by Vivian Perlis, November 4, 1968, Tape #1B, Ives Oral History Project (hereafter cited as Myrick interview).

3. Morton Keller, *The Life Insurance Enterprise, 1885–1910: A Study in the Limits of Corporate Power* (Cambridge, Mass.: Harvard University Press, Belknap Press, 1963), chap. 15.

4. *Ibid.,* pp. 265–68, 275; Shepard B. Clough, *A Century of American Life Insurance: A History of the Mutual Life Insurance Company of New York, 1843–1943* (New York: Columbia University Press, 1946), pp. 228–32, 276–77.

5. Myrick interview, December 11, 1968, Tape #1C.

6. Letter of T. T. Johnson to Charles E. Ives, January 6, 1907 [rightly 1908], copy in Scrapbook No. 8, p. 1, Ives Collection; Ives, *Memos,* app. 18, p. 270.

7. Letter of George T. Dexter to Charles E. Ives and Julian S. Myrick, December 21, 1908, in "Ives & Myrick" file, Ives Collection; Keller, *Life Insurance Enterprise,* pp. 67–69; Clough, *Century of American Life Insurance,* pp. 163–65, 277–78.

8. Keller, *Life Insurance Enterprise,* pp. 275, 285–86; Clough, *Century of American Life Insurance,* chap. 13.

9. Sales figures for 1909 through 1928 are given in an Ives & Myrick circular

headed "In the Past, Present, and Future Tense," in the "Ives & Myrick" file, Ives Collection.

10. "Ives & Myrick and J. I. D. Bristol Lead," *Eastern Underwriter,* January 2, 1920, p. 1.

11. "To Continue Ives & Myrick Name," *Eastern Underwriter,* January 23, 1942, p. 3; "Ives & Myrick Gain," *New York Herald Tribune,* January 22, 1929, p. 38.

12. Myrick interview, November 4, 1968, Tape #1B; interview with Peter M. Fraser by Vivian Perlis, November 21, 1969, Tape #30A, Ives Oral History Project (hereafter cited as Fraser interview); "In the Past, Present, and Future Tense," in "Ives & Myrick" file, Ives Collection.

13. Quoted in "To Continue Ives & Myrick Name," p. 3.

14. Ives, *Memos,* p. 103, n. 7.

15. Fraser interview, November 21, 1969, Tape #30A; interview with George A. Hofmann by Martha Maas, September 13, 1969, Tape #23B, Ives Oral History Project (hereafter cited as Hofmann interview); interview with Charles J. Buesing by Martha Maas, September, 1969, Tape #21, Ives Oral History Project (hereafter cited as Buesing interview).

16. From the back of p. 35 of the early dialogue version of "The Majority," in "Majority—early dialogue version" file, Ives Collection.

17. These quotations and ideas are from pp. 2–4 of Ives's pamphlet *The Amount to Carry—Measuring the Prospect,* copies of which are in the Ives Collection.

18. *Ibid.,* pp. 4–9, 12–17.

19. *Ibid.,* p. 4.

20. A copy is in Scrapbook No. 8, p. 67, Ives Collection.

21. These letters are in one of the folders labeled "Biography—Ives, C. E.," in the Historical Collection of the Research Library of the Mutual Life Insurance Company of New York, in New York City (hereafter cited as Mutual Library).

22. Hofmann interview, September 13, 1969, Tapes #23A, #23B, and #23C; Fraser interview, November 21, 1969, Tape #30A; Myrick interview, November 4, 1968, Tape #1B.

23. Clough, *Century of American Life Insurance,* p. 282.

24. Keller, *Life Insurance Enterprise,* pp. 72–74, 289; Clough, *Century of American Life Insurance,* pp. 168, 276, 279–84.

25. Hofmann interview, September 13, 1969, Tapes #23A, #23B, and #23C; Buesing interview, September, 1969, Tape #21.

26. Hofmann interview, September 13, 1969, Tapes #23B and #23C; Buesing interview, September, 1969, Tape #21.

27. Myrick interview, November 4, 1968, Tape #1B.

28. Myrick interview, December 11, 1968, Tape #1C.

29. Copies of this memorandum (c. 1920) are in a folder marked "Organization," in the Historical Collection of the Mutual Library.

30. Biographical information on Myrick is taken from John P. Brion, *Mr. Life Insurance: Julian S. Myrick, Mutual of New York,* an undated pamphlet issued by the Mutual Life Insurance Company of New York.

31. Quoted in Bellamann, "Charles Ives: The Man and His Music," pp. 47–48.

32. Ives, *The Amount to Carry—Measuring the Prospect,* pp. 13, 15, 16, 17.

33. See Ives's letter to agents of July, 1916, on p. 43 of Julian Myrick's scrapbook labeled "Ives-Myrick Scrapbook No. 1, 1918–1948," in the Mutual Library.

34. From p. 38 of the early dialogue version of "The Majority," in "Majority—early dialogue version" file, Ives Collection.

35. See Ives's memoranda on the recruiting of agents, on p. 13 of his "Business Scrap Book," in the Mutual Library.

36. See pp. 7–8 of his speech (written for Myrick to deliver) on "Life Insurance in Relation to Inheritance Taxation," in Scrapbook No. 8, p. 54, Ives Collection.

37. Charles E. Ives, marginal memo on sketch dated August 14, 1919, for letter to Julian S. Myrick, Ives Collection.

38. Charles E. Ives, "Diary of a Commuter" (D9), memo of February 25, [1914], Ives Collection.

39. Charles E. Ives, memo on patch toward bells (measures 244–47) of *Thanksgiving* (1A4iv), Ives Collection.

40. Robert H. Wiebe, *The Search for Order, 1877–1920* (New York: Hill and Wang, 1967), pp. xiii–xiv.

41. Richard Hofstadter, *The Age of Reform: From Bryan to F. D. R.* (New York: Alfred A. Knopf, 1955), pp. 213, 221.

42. See George E. Mowry, *The Urban Nation, 1920–1960* (New York: Hill and Wang, 1965), pp. 2–3, 34, 35, 40, 44, 73.

43. Charles E. Ives, undated [fall, 1949?] sketch (beginning "Deer, Hen, Cow-Eel!") for letter to Henry Cowell, Ives Collection.

44. Wiebe, *Search for Order,* p. 145.

45. Letter of Charles E. Ives to John J. Becker, undated [March, 1934], in answer to Becker's undated letter of [March 9, 1934], copy by John Kirkpatrick in his custody.

46. Wiebe, *Search for Order,* p. 123.

47. Chester Ives interview, May 7, 1969, Tape #10B.

48. Charles Ives, "The Majority," in his *Essays before a Sonata, The Majority, and Other Writings,* ed. Howard Boatwright (New York: W. W. Norton & Company, Inc., Norton Library, 1970), p. 189.

49. Ives, *Memos,* app. 19, pp. 274–77.

50. The poem was written during the summer of 1907 on stationery of the Henry Street Settlement; a copy by John Kirkpatrick is in his possession.

51. Her essay "The Nurse's Gain," written in 1900 upon her graduation from nursing school, is given in Ives, *Memos,* app. 19, pp. 275–76.

52. Charles E. Ives, entry for New Year's, 1918, in "Our Book" (D7), p. [41], Ives Collection.

53. Clough, *Century of American Life Insurance,* p. 244; Ives's memorandum on the Mutual Life Insurance Company of New York (c. 1920), in a folder marked "Organization," in the Historical Collection of the Mutual Library.

54. Ives's political views are discussed below, chap. 5.

Notes to Chapter 5: The Political and Social Thinker

1. With the manuscripts of Ives's Studies for piano (3B17), in the Ives Collection, is a copy of the published edition of his piece *The Anti-abolitionist Riots,* on which he noted in pencil, on p. [ii], this description of his grandfather. The incident referred to was probably the mobbing of an abolitionist speaker in Danbury in 1838; see Bailey, *History of Danbury,* pp. 166–67.

2. Letter of Harmony T. Ives to John Kirkpatrick, October 11, 1935, published in Ives, *Memos,* app. 8, p. 201.

3. Ives, *Memos,* p. 53 and app. 14.

4. S. B. Hill (words) and C. E. Ives (music), *William Will: A Republican Campaign Song* (New York: Willis Woodward & Co., c1896), pp. 2–3. There is a copy of this published song in the Ives Collection (6B24).

5. Letter of Harmony Twichell to Charles E. Ives, dated "Wed. evening" [January 15, 1908], part of which Mrs. Ives allowed John Kirkpatrick to copy.

6. See his marginal comments about Roosevelt on p. 2 of the typescript of "Stand by the President and the People," Ives Collection.

7. Charles E. Ives, memos on sketch of [*Vote for Names*] (6B48a), Ives Collection. This song has been published by Peer International Corporation (New York, c1968).

8. Charles E. Ives, [*Election Memo*] (7C23), Ives Collection.

9. Charles E. Ives, *"Three Places in New England": An Orchestral Set* (Boston: C. C. Birchard & Company, c1935), p. 1. The second line of this excerpt appears to have been added later.

10. Verses 1–4 and 7–8 are taken from the published version of the song for voice and piano: Ives, *114 Songs,* pp. 1–5; verses 5 and 6 are taken from Charles E. Ives, sketch of verses 5 and 6 of the poem, and pp. 9–11 of full score in pencil, of *Majority* (5B10), Ives Collection.

11. Charles E. Ives, "Diary of a Commuter" (D9), memo on Wilson and Mexico of [July, 1914], Ives Collection.

12. Charles E. Ives, pp. [1]–[2] of pencil sketch (and memos thereon) of *Sneak Thief* (5B9a), Ives Collection.

13. Ives, *Memos,* pp. 92–93.

14. Charles E. Ives, "Diary of a Commuter" (D9), memo on Mexico of April 15, [1914], and undated memo on politicians and war in continuation thereof, Ives Collection.

15. Charles E. Ives, "Diary of a Commuter" (D9), memo of June 11, 1915, Ives Collection.

16. Charles E. Ives, memo written on back of envelope postmarked February 26, 1917, in "Diary of a Commuter" papers (D9), Ives Collection.

17. *Evening Post* (New York), December 4, 1916, p. 8; a clipping of this letter in Scrapbook No. 1, p. 7, Ives Collection, has "C. E. I." written under "Fundamental."

18. Charles E. Ives, memo on p. [2] of ink copy of *Tom Sails Away* (6B59), Ives Collection.

19. Robert Endicott Osgood, *Ideals and Self-interest in America's Foreign Relations: The Great Transformation of the Twentieth Century* (Chicago: University of Chicago Press, 1953), pp. 241–42, 257, 261–62.

20. Ives, *114 Songs,* pp. 107–11. *He Is There!* was related in both music and ideas to *Sneak Thief.*

21. Charles Ives, "Stand by the President and the People," in his *Essays before a Sonata, The Majority, and Other Writings,* ed. Boatwright, pp. 136–38.

22. A typescript of the document, with Ives's memos and corrections thereon, is in the "People's World Union" file, Ives Collection.

23. Ives, *Memos,* p. 112.

24. Interview with Richard Ives by Vivian Perlis, June 2, 1969, Tape #11, Ives Oral History Project. One of these circulars is in Scrapbook No. 8, p. 72, Ives Collection.

25. Letter of Charles E. Ives to C. C. Whittelsey, September 4, 1918, copy by John Kirkpatrick in his possession.

26. Charles E. Ives, entry for February 18, 1919, in the Iveses' diary of vacation at Asheville in 1919, etc. (D10), p. [25], Ives Collection.

27. Ives, "The Majority," in his *Essays before a Sonata, The Majority, and Other Writings,* ed. Boatwright, pp. 161, 154.

28. *Ibid.,* pp. 162–63, 182–86, 165–74.

29. But in the "Political Misc." file, Ives Collection, is a political sketch of 1938 (on paper of the Hotel Moorlands, Surrey, England) in which Ives discussed a minimum property right for the poor, except those who shirked work, as a means of giving everyone a stake in society and dispersing the decision-making power.

30. Ives, "The Majority," pp. 142, 196, 189–90.

31. Bellamann, "Charles Ives: The Man and His Music," p. 46.

32. Charles E. Ives, undated sketch for letter to Clifton Joseph Furness in answer to Furness's letter of August 11, 1922, Ives Collection.

33. Van Wyck interview, November 21, 1968, Tape #2C.

34. Charles E. Ives, memo on p. 1 of sketch of 1st movement of Second String Quartet (2A3i), Ives Collection.

35. E.g., Ives, *Essays before a Sonata,* p. 64.

36. Gilbert Highet, *Talents and Geniuses: The Pleasures of Appreciation* (New York: Oxford University Press, 1957), pp. 54–55.

37. Cf. Copland, *The New Music,* pp. 45, 85–92, 171–76.

38. Ives, *Memos,* app. 3, p. 164.

39. Charles E. Ives, memo on pp. 10–11 of full score in pencil of *Majority* (5B10), Ives Collection.

40. The "Twentieth Amendment" file, Ives Collection, contains the circular and Ives's correspondence and other papers relating to his proposed amendment, including the letter of William Howard Taft to Charles E. Ives, June 19, 1920, and several drafts for Ives's reply thereto.

41. *Globe and Commercial Advertiser* (New York), October 28, 1920, p. 16.

42. See the "Harding Election" file, Ives Collection, for this letter of October 19, 1920, to the newspapers.

43. Ives, *114 Songs,* pp. 50–55. This work was first composed for chorus and orchestra.

44. *Ibid.,* p. 55.

45. E.g., Charles E. Ives, memo beginning "Politics is a magnate [*sic*] for small minds . . . ," in "Emasculating America" file, Ives Collection.

46. E.g., letter of Charles E. Ives to Nicolas Slonimsky, undated [May 27, 1930], copy by John Kirkpatrick, Ives Collection; Ives, *Memos,* p. 90.

47. Interview with Brewster Ives by Vivian Perlis, January 24, 1969, Tape #4A, Ives Oral History Project.

48. J. Moss Ives, *The "Ark" and the "Dove": The Beginning of Civil and Religious Liberties in America* (London, New York, and Toronto: Longmans, Green and Co., 1936).

49. Chester Ives interview, May 7, 1969, Tape #10B.

50. Charles E. Ives, memo beginning "This reminds me of an Englishman . . . ," in "Emasculating America" file, Ives Collection.

51. His membership certificate is in Scrapbook No. 5, p. 30, Ives Collection.

52. *New York Times,* May 14, 1922, sec. 8, p. 8. The letter is signed "Another Yale Graduate," but is identified as Ives's in Scrapbook No. 1, p. 105, Ives Collection.

53. His comments are on a letter that he received from Twyeffort, Inc., August 5, 1935, in the "Emasculating America" file, Ives Collection; see also his marginal comments on an advertisement for the Yale Club in New York, in Scrapbook No. 1, p. 92, Ives Collection.

54. E.g., letter of Charles E. Ives to John J. Becker, May 23, 1931, copy by John Kirkpatrick in his custody.

55. E.g., Ives, *Memos,* pp. 133–34.

56. There are several of Ives's memos against the airplane in the "Emasculating America" file, Ives Collection.

57. Interview with George Grayson Tyler by Vivian Perlis, March 18, 1969, Tape #8, Ives Oral History Project (hereafter cited as Tyler interview).

58. Charles E. Ives, memo beginning "Freds and Fellow Citeesons!" in "Emasculating America" file, Ives Collection.

59. Interview with Nicolas Slonimsky by Vivian Perlis, January 29, 1969, Tape #5A, Ives Oral History Project (hereafter cited as Slonimsky interview).

60. See his comments on a 1936 newspaper photograph of marching German soldiers, in Scrapbook No. 1, p. 33, Ives Collection.

61. This new line of thinking is described in Osgood, *Ideals and Self-interest,* pp. 381–402; cf. *ibid.,* pp. 10–17.

62. See the "Letter to Roosevelt, etc." file, Ives Collection, which contains a copy of Ives's letter to Franklin D. Roosevelt of January 6, 1938, and its accompanying document.

63. See the Iveses' correspondence with Charles Edmund Merrill, Jr., June–August, 1940, in the "Yale 1898" file, Ives Collection.

64. The leaflet, issued by the Keep America Out of War Congress and the Youth Committee Against War, is in the large brown envelope labeled "Newspapers: Politics, War, etc.," Ives Collection.

65. Various versions of the new proposal are in the "People's World Union" file, Ives Collection.

66. Letter of Claire R. Reis to Charles E. Ives, July 13, 1943, in "League of Composers" file, Ives Collection; letter of Alice M. Kyne to Charles E. Ives, June 15, 1944, in "N" file, Ives Collection.

67. Charles E. Ives, *"They Are There!" A War Song March* (New York: Peer International Corporation, c1961), pp. 5–6, 17–18.

Notes to Chapter 6: The Self-conscious Artist in Isolation

1. Ives, *Memos*, pp. 128–30.

2. Charles E. Ives, memo on pencil copy of *Adeste Fidelis* in an Organ Prelude (3D19), Ives Collection.

3. Ives, *Memos*, p. 58.

4. The program is in the file of programs and reviews, Ives Collection.

5. Ives, *Memos*, pp. 32–34.

6. "A New Cantata," *New York Times*, April 20, 1902, p. 14.

7. "Charles E. Ives' Concert and New Cantata, 'The Celestial Country,' " *Musical Courier*, April 23, 1902, p. 34.

8. This clipping is in the file of programs and reviews, Ives Collection.

9. The program for this concert of May 7, 1902, which was part of an annual festival of the Connecticut Music Teachers' Association, is in the file of programs and reviews, Ives Collection.

10. Ives, *Memos*, p. 68. For some years after 1902, he occasionally supplied at various churches: *ibid.*, p. 128.

11. Aaron Copland, "One Hundred and Fourteen Songs," *Modern Music* 11 (January–February, 1934): 64.

12. Ives, *Memos*, p. 61.

13. *Ibid.*, pp. 118–19, 123, 121, and app. 7, pp. 186–87.

14. *Ibid.*, pp. 99, 87, 123, and app. 7, p. 187.

15. *Ibid.*, p. 34; cf. Charles E. Ives, memo on sketch for measures 22–28 of 2d movement of Set of Three Short Pieces (2B16ii), Ives Collection.

16. Charles E. Ives, memo on p. 1 of full score in ink of 2d movement of Second Orchestral Set (1A6ii), Ives Collection; Ives, *Memos*, p. 59.

17. Ives, *Memos*, pp. 70–71.

18. *Ibid.*, pp. 58, 64, 74, 125.

19. *Ibid.*, pp. 90–91; Charles E. Ives, sketch for postscript to letter of Harmony T. Ives to Elliott Carter, April 9, 1946, Ives Collection; Ives, *Memos*, p. 119.

20. Ives, *Memos*, p. 98; Van Wyck interview, November 21, 1968, Tape #2C; interview with Mrs. Artur Nikoloric by Vivian Perlis, January 29, 1971, Tape #46, Ives Oral History Project; Ives, *Memos*, pp. 121–22; Charles E. Ives, entry for January 26, 1918, in "Our Book" (D7), p. [40], Ives Collection.

21. Harmony T. Ives, entry for March 20, 1910, in "Our Book" (D7), p. [30], Ives

Collection; Ives, *Memos,* pp. 51, 86–87; Charles E. Ives, undated [late 1947 or January, 1948] sketch for letter of Harmony T. Ives to William Malloch, in "Letters about Dissertations" file, Ives Collection. Cf. Cowell and Cowell, *Charles Ives and His Music,* pp. 67–68 and 131, note.

22. Ives, *Memos,* p. 121.

23. Bernard Herrmann, "Four Symphonies by Charles Ives," *Modern Music* 22 (May–June, 1945): 220; Cowell and Cowell, *Charles Ives and His Music,* p. 131, note.

24. Charles E. Ives, undated [c. 1937] sketch for letter of Harmony T. Ives to Walter Damrosch, in "D" file, Ives Collection.

25. Ives, *Memos,* pp. 102–3; letter of Paul Eisler to Charles E. Ives, April 20, 1920, in "N" file, Ives Collection; letter of Charles E. Ives to Paul Eisler, April 22, 1920, carbon copy in "N" file, Ives Collection.

26. E.g., letter of Harmony T. Ives to John Kirkpatrick, October 11, 1935, published in Ives, *Memos,* app. 8, p. 201.

27. Ives, *Memos,* pp. 46, 117, 127, 141–42.

28. Letter of Julian S. Myrick to George A. Knutsen, April 3, 1968, carbon copy in one of the folders labeled "Biography—Ives, C. E.," Historical Collection, Mutual Library; Ives, *Memos,* app. 18, p. 271. Along with the manuscripts of the song *In Flanders Fields* (6B56) in the Ives Collection is a photostat of a statement written out by McCall Lanham on January 1, 1959, concerning his singing of the song on or about April 15, 1917.

29. Charles E. Ives, memo on p. 1 of score-sketch of *The Fourth of July* (1A4iii), Ives Collection. Cf. Ives, *Memos,* p. 65.

30. Ives, *Memos,* pp. 136–38, 27.

31. *Ibid.,* pp. 71, 116–17, 118.

32. *Ibid.,* pp. 126, 70–71.

33. Chester Ives interview, May 7, 1969, Tape #10B; Ives, *Memos,* pp. 118, 114, and app. 19, p. 277.

34. Cowell and Cowell, *Charles Ives and His Music,* p. 74.

35. Enclosure in letter of Gertrud Schoenberg to Charles E. Ives, November 17, 1953, in "S" file, Ives Collection.

36. Letter of Harmony T. Ives to Nicolas Slonimsky, July 6, [1936], copy by John Kirkpatrick, Ives Collection.

37. This discussion of Ives's philosophy of art is based principally upon the Prologue and the Epilogue to *Essays before a Sonata* and the "Postface" to *114 Songs.*

38. Ives, *Essays before a Sonata,* pp. 121, 90.

39. *Ibid.,* pp. 90–91, 3, 99, 4.

40. *Ibid.,* pp. 91, 118–19, 26.

41. Charles E. Ives, sketch (unused) for letter of Harmony T. Ives to Nicolas Slonimsky, July 6, [1936], Ives Collection.

42. Ives, *Essays before a Sonata,* p. 100.

43. Elliott Carter, "Shop Talk by an American Composer," *Musical Quarterly* 46 (April, 1960): 199–200.

44. Ives, *Essays before a Sonata,* pp. 106–10.

45. *Ibid.*, p. 97; Ives, *114 Songs*, p. [261].

46. Quoted in Bellamann, "Charles Ives: The Man and His Music," p. 48.

47. Ives, *114 Songs*, p. [262].

48. Charles E. Ives, "Conductor's Note" (1929) to 2d movement of Fourth Symphony, reprinted in Charles Ives, *Symphony No. 4* (New York: Associated Music Publishers, Inc., c1965), p. 14.

49. Ives, *Essays before a Sonata*, pp. 109–10, 82; Ives, *114 Songs*, p. [262].

50. Van Wyck Brooks, *America's Coming-of-age* (New York: B. W. Huebsch, 1915).

51. Ives, *Memos*, p. 135.

52. Carter, "Shop Talk," p. 199.

53. See Marcus Cunliffe, *The Literature of the United States*, 3d ed. (Baltimore: Penguin Books, 1967), p. 17.

54. Ives, *Essays before a Sonata*, pp. 62, 74.

55. Carter, "Shop Talk," p. 199.

56. Quoted in Bellamann, "Charles Ives: The Man and His Music," p. 47.

57. Ives, *Memos*, p. 126.

58. E.g., H[iram] K. Moderwell, "On Acquiring New Ears," *New Republic* 4 (September 4, 1915): 119–21.

59. Paul L. Rosenfeld, "The American Composer," *Seven Arts* 1 (November, 1916): 89–94; Hiram Kelly Moderwell, "Two Views of Ragtime: I. A Modest Proposal," *Seven Arts* 2 (July, 1917): 368–76.

60. See Henry F. May, *The End of American Innocence: A Study of the First Years of Our Own Time, 1912–1917* (New York: Alfred A. Knopf, 1959).

61. *Ibid.*, pp. 315, 316.

62. Charles E. Ives, "Diary of a Commuter" (D9), memo of June 26, [1914], Ives Collection.

63. Charles E. Ives, "Insert for 2nd Edition of 'Essays before a Sonata' (if there happen to be one)," Ives Collection.

64. Ives, *Memos*, p. 130; Ives, *Essays before a Sonata*, p. 123; letter of Charles E. Ives to Clifton Joseph Furness, October 11, 1921, carbon copy in Ives Collection.

65. Ives, *Memos*, pp. 54, 66, 119; Cowell and Cowell, *Charles Ives and His Music*, pp. 39–40.

66. Letter of Edwards Park to John Kirkpatrick, quoted in Ives, *Memos*, app. 17, p. 263.

67. See the account of a sermon delivered by Mrs. Ives's brother, in the *Danbury Evening Times*, June 30, 1930; a copy of this article is in Scrapbook No. 5, p. 17, Ives Collection.

68. Harmony Twichell, entries for May 23, 1905, and June 22, 1905, in diary for May–June, 1905, and April–October, 1907 (D6), pp. [7] and [46], Ives Collection.

69. Ives wrote this memo on the back of the last page of the earlier manuscript version of the "Thoreau" section of his *Essays before a Sonata*, in the "Concord Essays" file, Ives Collection.

70. Ives, *Essays before a Sonata*, pp. 56–57.

71. See Mrs. Ives's lists of the large amount of serious reading the Iveses did dur-

ing a two-month period in 1919, in Charles E. Ives and Harmony T. Ives, diary of vacation at Asheville in 1919, etc. (D10), pp. [206]–[207], Ives Collection.

72. Letter of Harmony Twichell to Charles E. Ives, dated "Tuesday p.m." [February (18?), 1908], from a transcript by Edith Ives Tyler, part of which Mrs. Ives allowed John Kirkpatrick to copy.

73. Personal information from Harmony T. Ives, via John Kirkpatrick.

74. Interview with Elliott Carter, in Vivian Perlis, *Charles Ives Remembered: An Oral History* (New Haven: Yale University Press, 1974), p. 135.

75. Letter of Harmony T. Ives to Charles E. Ives, dated "Wed. afternoon" [January 24, 1912], part of which Mrs. Ives allowed John Kirkpatrick to copy. Cf. letter of Frederick T. Van Beuren, Jr., to Charles E. Ives, March 3, 1921, in "Yale 1898" file, Ives Collection.

76. Bailey, *History of Danbury,* pp. 280–83.

77. See Charles E. Ives, 3d sketch for letter of Harmony T. Ives to Sol Babitz, September 2, 1941, Ives Collection.

78. J. Moss Ives, "Roger Williams, Apostle of Religious Bigotry," *Thought* 6 (December, 1931): 478–92.

79. Letter of Harmony T. Ives to Charles E. Ives, dated "Wed." [March 4, 1914], part of which Mrs. Ives allowed John Kirkpatrick to copy.

80. The roles that Ives and his wife played in their discussions are undoubtedly reflected in the various dialogue versions of "The Majority," which are published in Ives, *Memos,* app. 9, pp. 205–28.

81. Ives, *Essays before a Sonata,* p. 84.

82. Ives, *Memos,* pp. 82–83.

83. Telegram from Nathan Broder (of G. Schirmer, Inc.) to Charles E. Ives, May 17, 1946, copy in Schirmer file, Ives Collection.

84. Ives, *Essays before a Sonata, The Majority, and Other Writings,* ed. Boatwright, p. 121.

85. Paul Rosenfeld, "Two Native Groups," *New Republic* 75 (July 5, 1933): 209.

86. Ives, *Memos,* pp. 126–27.

87. Ives, *114 Songs,* p. [261].

88. Charles E. Ives, sketch for advance letter (beginning "Dear Sor:") for *114 Songs,* in "Postface to 114 Songs" file, Ives Collection.

89. Ives, *Essays before a Sonata,* p. [iii]; Ives, *114 Songs,* p. [260].

90. Ives, *114 Songs,* pp. [261]–[262].

91. Paul Rosenfeld, "Charles E. Ives," *New Republic* 71 (July 20, 1932): 263–64; Copland, "One Hundred and Fourteen Songs," pp. 64, 61.

92. See the various bills from G. Schirmer, (Inc.), to Charles E. Ives, in the Schirmer file, Ives Collection. The bill of August 31, 1922, indicates that 350 copies of *114 Songs* had already been sent out by that date. A memo by Ives on the back of the first page of his second sketch for the table of contents of *50 Songs,* in the "Postface to 114 Songs" file, Ives Collection, indicates that he intended to send out 1,075 more between December, 1922, and March, 1923.

93. Charles E. Ives, schedule of nine numbered tasks to be undertaken [in 1920], in "Postface to 114 Songs" file, Ives Collection.

94. See Ives's mention of *Who's Who in America* and other sources in memos written on the back of a legal form in the "Postface to 114 Songs" file, Ives Collection; on the obverse side of this form, he gave the number of names of 719 singers that fell under each letter of the alphabet, probably from his *Who's Who* list.

95. See also the small notebook in Ives's desk in his music room at West Redding, in which he wrote down the names and addresses of a number of persons to whom he intended to send the *Essays* or the *Concord* Sonata.

96. Letter of Percy Goetschius to Charles E. Ives, May 20, 1923, and letter of Charles Wakefield Cadman to Charles E. Ives, March 9, [1921], in "Letters acknowledging *Concord* and *Essays*" file, Ives Collection.

97. Wallingford Riegger, "To the New through the Old," *Magazine of Art* 32 (August, 1939): 473.

98. Letter of Thomas S. McLane to Charles E. Ives, March 9, 1921, in "Yale 1898" file, Ives Collection.

99. Letter of Elizabeth Sprague Coolidge to Harmony T. Ives, March 15, 1921, in "C" file, Ives Collection; Charles E. Ives, undated sketch for letter (unsent) to Elizabeth Sprague Coolidge in answer to her letter of March 15, 1921, in "C" file, Ives Collection. John Kirkpatrick has suggested that Mrs. Coolidge's composer friend was Henry Eichheim.

100. William Lyon Phelps, "The Glorious Year A.D. Nineteen-Twenty," *Yale Alumni Weekly* 30 (December 17, 1920): 308.

101. *Sun* (New York), August 29, 1922, p. 19.

102. Charles E. Ives, sketch for letter to the New York *Sun*, September 10, 1922, in "Postface to 114 Songs" file, Ives Collection.

103. See the bill for *50 Songs* from G. Schirmer, (Inc.), to Charles E. Ives, April 16, 1923, in the Schirmer file, Ives Collection. Ives's memo on the back of the first page of his second sketch for the table of contents of *50 Songs*, in the "Postface to 114 Songs" file, Ives Collection, indicates that 500 copies of *50 Songs* were to be sent out by June, 1923. But his memo on the back of the second page of this sketch, in the same file, suggests that only 150 of these copies would go to readers of the *Sun* and that the rest would go to other people. There were actually fifty-two songs in *50 Songs*.

104. "Concord Unconquered," *Musical Courier*, April 28, 1921, p. 22. See also the later criticism of Ives's "insincere experiments" in the *Concord* Sonata as "stupid and worthless": Frank Patterson, "The Perfect Modernist: A Little Primer of Basic Principles (Twelfth Installment)," *Musical Courier*, February 16, 1922, p. 7.

105. "Ives," *Musical Courier*, September 21, 1922, p. 20.

106. A. W. K. [A. Walter Kramer], "A Pseudo-literary Sonata!!!" *Musical America*, April 2, 1921, p. 36. A more straightforward notice of *Concord* was "A Futuristic Sonata," *Musical Advance*, April, 1921, p. [16]. A long but unsympathetic review was Edward [rightly Edwin] J. Stringham, "Ives Puzzles Critics with His Cubistic Sonata and 'Essays,'" *Rocky Mountain News* (Denver), July 31, 1921, sec. 2, pp. 1, 17.

107. Ives's own reactions to criticisms of the *Concord* Sonata have been edited by John Kirkpatrick and published in Ives, *Memos,* app. 7, pp. 185–97.

108. Charles E. Ives, *Second Pianoforte Sonata: "Concord, Mass., 1840–60"* (Redding, Conn.: C. E. Ives, 1920), p. 25, note.

109. Ives, *Memos,* pp. 126–27; cf. *ibid.,* pp. 81–82.

110. Henry Cowell, "Homage to Charles Ives," *Proceedings of the American Academy of Arts and Letters and the National Institute of Arts and Letters,* 2d ser., No. 13 (New York: n.p., 1963), p. 263; Sidney Cowell, "Ivesiana: 'More than Something Just Usual,' " *High Fidelity and Musical America,* October, 1974, p. MA-14.

111. See, e.g., Paul Moor, "On Horseback to Heaven: Charles Ives," *Harper's Magazine,* September, 1948, p. 69.

112. Cowell and Cowell, *Charles Ives and His Music,* pp. 90–91.

Notes to Chapter 7: Openings to the Avant-garde, 1921–1932

1. Copland, *The New Music,* p. 102.

2. Harold Clurman, *The Fervent Years: The Story of the Group Theatre and the Thirties* (New York: Alfred A. Knopf, 1945), chaps. 1 and 2, contains a good picture of the American artistic milieu of the 1920s. Clurman was a close friend of Aaron Copland's.

3. Julia Smith, *Aaron Copland: His Work and Contribution to American Music* (New York: E. P. Dutton & Company, Inc., 1955), pp. 79–80, 97, 100.

4. Copland, *Music and Imagination,* p. 104.

5. This analysis of the American musical scene is based upon Harrison Kerr, "Creative Music and the New School," *Trend* 2 (March–April, 1934): 86–87. In furthering the cause of contemporary music, the avant-garde had the patronage of a number of wealthy people of social prominence.

6. Ives, *Memos,* pp. 133–34.

7. Scrapbook No. 1, p. 43, Ives Collection, contains a printed article directed against "The Wrong Sort of Sex Novel," in the margins of which Ives wrote comments condemning the commercial exploitation of sex. He was apparently denouncing *any* frank treatment of sex in art, commercial or not, for he agreed with the writer of the article that "mere mechanical animalism" was "the least interesting subject in the world."

8. Ives, *Essays before a Sonata,* pp. 113–15.

9. *Ibid.,* p. 115.

10. "Hearing for Unknown Works Offered by Composers Guild," *New York Tribune,* December 3, 1922, sec. 5, p. 6. Ives did, however, take an active part in Pro Musica, another group which presented many contemporary works; see below.

11. Copland, *Music and Imagination,* pp. 100–106.

12. Letter of Henry Bellamann to Charles E. Ives, April 10, 1921, Ives Collection.

13. Letter of Charles E. Ives to Henry Bellamann, undated, in answer to Bellamann's letter of April 10, 1921, carbon copy in Ives Collection.

14. Bellamann's plans to have Miss Purcell play "most of" the sonata "in a lecture we propose to give several times this winter"—but first in Columbia—were mentioned in his letter to Ives of September 19, 1921, Ives Collection. He also cited the Columbia lecture-recital as having been "the first public performance" of the sonata in H. B. [Henry Bellamann], "An American Composer," *State* (Columbia, S.C.), May 22, 1932, p. 23. The Atlanta lecture-recital was reviewed: "Music Club Hears Lecture Recital on Modern Sonata," *Atlanta Constitution,* January 5, 1922, p. 10; and Bellamann discussed it in his letter to Ives of January 6, 1922, Ives Collection. Bellamann may also have included part of the sonata in a lecture-recital on ultramodern music that he gave (again assisted by Miss Purcell) before the Crescendo Club of Charleston on December 17, 1921, although the newspaper account did not mention the work: " 'Ultra Modern Music,' " *Sunday News* (Charleston, S.C.), December 18, 1921, sec. 1, p. 8. Cf. Cowell and Cowell, *Charles Ives and His Music,* pp. 99 and 112, note. In fact, these were not the first public performances of the *Concord* Sonata. Ives recalled that "at an impromptu church concert in New York in the spring of 1914, I played the Emerson and part of the Hawthorne movements"; his recollection was quoted in a letter of Harmony T. Ives to John Kirkpatrick, October 11, 1935, published in Ives, *Memos,* app. 8, p. 201. In 1948 Ives also recalled that he had played *The Alcotts* and *Thoreau* "at an organ recital some thirty years ago": Charles E. Ives, undated sketch for letter of Harmony T. Ives to E. Power Biggs in answer to Biggs's letter of April 15, 1948, Ives Collection. In addition, Clifton Furness played *The Alcotts* at a lecture-recital on August 3, 1921; the program is in Scrapbook No. 6, p. 21, Ives Collection. In a handwritten note at the bottom of his letter to Bellamann of January 9, 1922, a reproduced copy of which is in the Ives Collection, Ives wrote cryptically: "The sonata was played in London recently—by whom, I don't know."

15. Henry Bellamann, " 'Concord, Mass., 1840–1860' (A Piano Sonata by Charles E. Ives.)," review in the *Double Dealer* 2 (October, 1921): 168.

16. *Ibid.,* p. 166; cf. Ives, *Essays before a Sonata,* pp. 92–96.

17. Bellamann, review of *Concord* Sonata, p. 169.

18. Cowell and Cowell, *Charles Ives and His Music,* p. 102, maintains that during the middle 1920s Bellamann attempted to interest his friend Lawrence Gilman, the influential music critic, in Ives's compositions. It is true that Gilman praised the music of Ives that was played at Pro Musica's Town Hall concert of January 29, 1927; but it appears that he took no other notice of Ives's work down through 1938.

19. Letter of William Lyon Phelps to Charles E. Ives, December 7, 1921, Ives Collection.

20. Charles E. Ives, sketch dated August 11, 1922, for letter to Thomas B. Wells, in Bellamann file, Ives Collection.

21. Letter of Katherine Bellamann to Charles E. Ives, October 1, 1923, Ives Collection.

22. Charles E. Ives, sketch dated "Sunday" [October 7, 1923] for letter to Katherine Bellamann in answer to her letter of October 1, 1923, Ives Collection.

23. Letter of Henry Bellamann to Charles E. Ives, June 30, 1932, Ives Collection.

24. Henry Bellamann and Katherine Bellamann, *Parris Mitchell of Kings Row* (New

York: Simon and Schuster, 1948), pp. ix–xi. See also Katherine Bellamann, *A Poet Passed This Way* (Mill Valley, Calif.: Wings Press, 1958), *passim*.

25. E.g., Henry Bellamann, "Decorations for an Imaginary Ballet," *Broom* 1 (December, 1921): 116–18. Ives reported having ordered this issue of *Broom* in his letter to Bellamann of January 9, 1922, reproduced copy in Ives Collection.

26. Letter of Clifton Joseph Furness to Charles E. Ives, May 30, 1923, Ives Collection; italics mine.

27. The assumption is made here that Ives had depreciated Bellamann's poems, not his musical compositions.

28. E.g., Bellamann wrote the program notes for the performance of two movements of Ives's Fourth Symphony which took place at a Pro Musica concert in Town Hall on January 29, 1927. See also Henry Bellamann, "The Music of Charles Ives," *Pro-Musica Quarterly*, March, 1927, pp. 16–22.

29. Bellamann, "Charles Ives: The Man and His Music," pp. 45–58.

30. Henry Bellamann, "How Bad Is American Music?" *Commonweal* 20 (October 26, 1934): 606.

31. Charles E. Ives, sketch dated August 11, 1922, for letter to Thomas B. Wells, in Bellamann file, Ives Collection; Charles E. Ives, undated [autumn, 1922] sketch for letter to Katherine Bellamann, Ives Collection.

32. Letter of Clifton Joseph Furness to Charles E. Ives, August 15, [1921], Ives Collection; the program for the lecture-recital (which does not reveal where it took place) is in Scrapbook No. 6, p. 21, Ives Collection.

33. Letter of Clifton Joseph Furness to Charles E. Ives, August 15, [1921], Ives Collection.

34. Letter of Clifton Joseph Furness to Charles E. Ives, September 10, [1921], Ives Collection.

35. Letter of Charles E. Ives to Clifton Joseph Furness, October 11, 1921, carbon copy in Ives Collection.

36. Letter of Clifton Joseph Furness to Charles E. Ives, December 1, 1930, Ives Collection.

37. Letter of Clifton Joseph Furness to Charles E. Ives and Harmony T. Ives, February 15, 1928, Ives Collection.

38. See Furness's comments on hymn tunes and Ives's Fourth Violin Sonata in his letter to Ives of May 30, 1923, Ives Collection.

39. Letter of Clifton Joseph Furness to Charles E. Ives, November 29, 1927, Ives Collection.

40. Clifton Joseph Furness, "Mysticism and Modern Music: The Future Evolution of Music in the Light of Anthroposophy," *Threefold Commonwealth*, Fifth Year, No. 51 (April, 1926), pp. [2]–[3]; a copy of this article is in the Furness file, Ives Collection. Cf. Ives, *Essays before a Sonata*, pp. 3–10, 98–99.

41. Letter of Clifton Joseph Furness to Charles E. Ives and Harmony T. Ives, May 12, 1937, Ives Collection.

42. Some of Ives's letters to Furness are in the Furnas Memorial Room at the State University of New York at Buffalo.

43. Interview with Elliott Carter by Vivian Perlis, June 20, 1969, Tape #14A, Ives Oral History Project (hereafter cited as Carter interview).

44. See his unpublished manuscript "The Lost Land," in Scrapbook No. 7, p. 13, Ives Collection.

45. Charles E. Ives, 1st sketch for letter of Harmony T. Ives to Elliott Carter, June 12, 1944, Ives Collection.

46. Letter of Clifton Joseph Furness to Charles E. Ives, September 10, [1921], Ives Collection.

47. Letter of Charles E. Ives to Clifton Joseph Furness, October 11, 1921, carbon copy in Ives Collection.

48. Letter of Clifton Joseph Furness to Charles E. Ives, August 11, 1922, Ives Collection.

49. Letter of Clifton Joseph Furness to Charles E. Ives and Harmony T. Ives, January 29, 1939, Ives Collection.

50. Ives later claimed that he had neither heard nor seen any of Schoenberg's music during the 1920s; but Furness was certainly telling him about Schoenberg, and he even invited Ives to attend a performance of *Pierrot lunaire:* letter of Clifton Joseph Furness to Charles E. Ives, January 22, 1923, Ives Collection.

51. Letter of Clifton Joseph Furness to Charles E. Ives, January 21, [1928], Ives Collection; cf. letter of T. Chalmers Furnas to Charles E. Ives, October 24, 1927, in Furness file, Ives Collection.

52. See Clifton Joseph Furness, "Rhythms of Growth: Further Thoughts on Education" (an article from the *Threefold Commonwealth*), a copy of which is in Scrapbook No. 4, p. 48, Ives Collection.

53. Charles E. Ives, letter of recommendation for T. Chalmers Furnas, January 8, 1927, carbon copy in Furness file, Ives Collection.

54. The Furness file, Ives Collection, contains a number of letters that refer to Ives's loans to Clifton Furness and his father, T. Chalmers Furnas.

55. Carter interview, June 20, 1969, Tape #14A. Cf. Elliott Carter, "The Case of Mr. Ives," *Modern Music* 16 (March–April, 1939): 172–75; it is probable that some of Carter's recollections in this article about Ives in the twenties are inaccurate.

56. Ives, *Memos,* pp. 27–29, 138–39.

57. Carter interview, June 20, 1969, Tape #14A.

58. *Ibid.*

59. *Ibid.*

60. Ives jotted down parodies of the mystical outpourings of Dane Rudhyar, an avant-garde composer whom he met during the 1920s; they are written on an envelope and its enclosed prospectus (sent from Rudhyar to Ives in 1929) in Scrapbook No. 1, p. 26, Ives Collection. There is also a parody on mysticism in the section on "labels" in Ives, *Memos,* pp. 78–79. On Ives as Miss Heyman's patron, see, e.g., letters of Katherine Heyman to Charles E. Ives, November 7, [1926], and November 11, 1926, Ives Collection.

61. Gay Wilson Allen, *The Solitary Singer: A Critical Biography of Walt Whitman* (New York: Macmillan Company, 1955), p. x; Malcolm Cowley, "Walt Whitman, Champion

of America," review of *The Solitary Singer: A Critical Biography of Walt Whitman,* by Gay Wilson Allen, in the *New York Times,* February 6, 1955, sec. 7, p. 1.

62. Letter of Clifton Joseph Furness to Charles E. Ives and Harmony T. Ives, December 6, 1938, Ives Collection. Another musical friend that Ives acquired in the twenties, through sending out the *Concord* Sonata, was T. Carl Whitmer, a Pittsburgh organist and composer of Ives's own age. But Whitmer was absorbed in his own career and in Dramamount, an estate near the Hudson River where he hoped to produce his "spiritual music dramas," somewhat as Wagner's operas were produced at Bayreuth; thus he appears to have done little for Ives's music.

63. The relevant portion of the program book for the recital, which took place at Aeolian Hall on March 18, 1924, is in the file of programs and reviews, Ives Collection. Rex Tillson was the pianist.

64. Winthrop P. Tryon, " 'Freischütz' at the Metropolitan—Other Music of a New York Week," *Christian Science Monitor,* March 24, 1924, p. 10. Cf. "Folk Song and Hymn Tunes of America," *Christian Science Monitor,* November 29, 1924, p. 18.

65. Information about Pro Musica has been drawn in part from an unpublished manuscript, "The Story of Pro Musica," lent to Vivian Perlis by Schmitz's daughter, Mrs. Jean Leduc. See also Winthrop P. Tryon, "Pro Musica and Its Plans," *Christian Science Monitor,* June 6, 1925, p. 11.

66. In Ives's desk in his music room at West Redding is a small notebook in which he wrote down (c. 1920) the names and addresses of a number of persons to whom he intended to send the sonata; Schmitz's name is among those listed.

67. Cowell and Cowell, *Charles Ives and His Music,* p. 101.

68. Letter of E. Robert Schmitz to Charles E. Ives, October 4, 1923, Ives Collection.

69. Charles E. Ives, undated sketch for letter to E. Robert Schmitz in answer to Schmitz's letter of October 4, 1923, Ives Collection. In the sketch, Ives crossed out the second of these sentences and changed the first to read: "It was a great pleasure and a help to me to meet you—and interesting to find a man with such a comprehensive range."

70. Letter of Y. Dufour to Charles E. Ives, April 3, 1925, in Scrapbook No. 2, p. 71, Ives Collection; letter of E. Robert Schmitz to Charles E. Ives, March 15, 1926, Ives Collection.

71. E.g., letter of E. Robert Schmitz to Charles E. Ives, December 2, 1926, copy by John Kirkpatrick (made from carbon copy) in Ives Collection. See also interview with Mrs. Jean Leduc (Monique Schmitz Leduc) by Vivian Perlis, May 18, 1971, Tape #55B, Ives Oral History Project (hereafter cited as Leduc interview).

72. Leduc interview, May 18, 1971, Tape #55B.

73. A card announcing this lecture-recital, which took place at Chickering Hall on February 8, 1925, is in Scrapbook No. 6, p. 21, Ives Collection. Ives listed on this card the works played, but he misdated the lecture-recital "1924." The pianists were Hans Barth and Sigmund Klein; it was probably Barth, an associate of Schmitz's, who reawakened Ives's interest in quarter tones.

74. The program for this concert, which took place at Aeolian Hall on February

14, 1925, is in the file of programs and reviews, Ives Collection. Barth and Klein were again the performers.

75. Ives, "Some 'Quarter-Tone' Impressions," pp. 24–33. See also W. P. T. [Winthrop P. Tryon], "New Yorker Writing Music for Quarter-Tone Piano," *Christian Science Monitor,* January 13, 1925, p. 10; Winthrop P. Tryon, "Quarter-Tone Experiments," *Christian Science Monitor,* February 7, 1925, p. 8.

76. The relevant portion of the program book for the concert is in the file of programs and reviews, Ives Collection. Henry Bellamann, a director of Pro Musica, wrote the program notes.

77. Pitts Sanborn, "Pro-Musica or Anti?" *New York Telegram,* January 31, 1927, p. 7. Sanborn arrived late for the concert and heard the Ives movements from outside the auditorium.

78. "The Circus," *Musical Courier,* February 10, 1927, p. 28.

79. R. A. S. [Robert A. Simon], "Musical Events," *New Yorker,* February 12, 1927, pp. 60–61.

80. W. J. Henderson, "Composers Guild Gives Concert," *Sun* (New York), January 31, 1927, p. 25.

81. Olga Samaroff, "Music," *New York Evening Post,* January 31, 1927, p. 7.

82. Two other very favorable and perceptive reviews were Winthrop P. Tryon, "Of Ives and Others," *Christian Science Monitor,* February 3, 1927, p. 6; and Ray C. B. Brown, "Internationalism Is Keynote of Modernist Lists," *Musical America,* February 5, 1927, p. 11.

83. Olin Downes, "Music," *New York Times,* January 30, 1927, sec. 1, p. 28.

84. Lawrence Gilman, "Music," *New York Herald Tribune,* January 31, 1927, p. 11.

85. Letter of Wallingford Riegger to Charles E. Ives, June 12, 1937, Ives Collection. For a somewhat different account of the Downes incident, see letter of Elie Siegmeister to Charles E. Ives, June 15, 1937, Ives Collection.

86. Bellamann, "Music of Charles Ives," pp. 16–22.

87. "Ives Composes Sonata in Modern Style," *Danbury Evening Times,* November 19, 1927. This article (a copy of which is in Scrapbook No. 2, p. 3, Ives Collection) quotes an article in the *Birmingham Age-Herald* concerning Rovinsky's discovery of Ives's music.

88. An announcement of the concert, which incorrectly identifies the piece as the *Hawthorne* movement of the Second Piano Sonata, is in the file of programs and reviews, Ives Collection. This file contains programs for two more occasions when Rovinsky performed the work: his piano recital at the Albany (New York) Institute of History and Art on October 30, 1928, and his piano recital at Town Hall on November 20, 1928.

89. W. J. Henderson, "Pro Musica Opens Its Season," *Sun* (New York), November 15, 1928, p. 25.

90. Pitts Sanborn, "Pro Musica Gives Its First Referendum Program Concert," *New York Telegram,* November 15, 1928, p. 12.

91. Cf. Cowell and Cowell, *Charles Ives and His Music,* pp. 102–3.

92. Letter of Lehman Engel to Harmony T. Ives, June 19, 1940, Ives Collection.

93. Letter of E. Robert Schmitz to Henry Mason, March 19, 1926, carbon copy in Schmitz file, Ives Collection.

94. See the Pro Musica letterheads of letters sent to Ives from 1925 through 1930, in the Schmitz file, Ives Collection. But cf. *Pro-Musica Quarterly,* March–June, 1926, p. 54; here Ives is mentioned under "Activities of Some of the Artist Members."

95. In the unpublished manuscript "The Story of Pro Musica," Ives is not mentioned among the American composers whose works were presented in Paris. The issues of the *Franco-American Musical Society Quarterly Bulletin* (published from 1923 to 1925) and of the *Pro-Musica Quarterly* (published from 1925 to 1929) fail to mention any Ives performances among the activities of the Paris chapter. Cowell and Cowell, *Charles Ives and His Music,* p. 112, note, claims that Schmitz performed part of the *Concord* Sonata "in Paris about 1925."

96. At Pro Musica's Town Hall concert of January 29, 1927, Milhaud conducted one of his own works. It was on this trip to the United States that Milhaud and his wife were brought by Schmitz for lunch at the Iveses' home. See the interview with Darius Milhaud by Vivian Perlis, July 25, 1970, Tape #37A, Ives Oral History Project.

97. See the Pro Musica letterheads of letters sent to Ives from 1925 through 1930, in the Schmitz file, Ives Collection; and the Pro Musica letterhead of the letter of Y. Dufour to Charles E. Ives, April 3, 1925, in Scrapbook No. 2, p. 71, Ives Collection. The issues of the *Franco-American Musical Society Quarterly Bulletin* and the *Pro-Musica Quarterly* also contain lists of the various officials of Pro Musica. Varèse served on the organization's Central Technical Board from before Ives's election to the Board of Directors through 1927. Salzedo served on the Board of Directors and the Central Technical Board from before Ives's election to the Board of Directors until 1930; he was also a vice president of the organization when Ives was first a director. Scrapbook No. 7, p. 56, Ives Collection, contains the minutes of a meeting of the Board of Directors on May 29, 1929; Ives and Salzedo were both present. Scrapbook No. 7, p. 57, Ives Collection, contains the minutes of the annual meeting of the members of Pro Musica, held in New York City on October 23, 1929; Ives, who was still a director, was apparently absent, but the minutes make it clear that Rosenfeld and Riegger were both active in Pro Musica at the time, and Rosenfeld was elected a director at this meeting. Yet Ives seems never in his life to have met Rosenfeld, who did not "discover" him until 1931. And in his letter to Ives of May 4, 1932, in the Ives Collection, Riegger wrote that "I know we are total strangers to each other."

98. For example, Cowell knew something about the two movements of Ives's Fourth Symphony that were performed at the Pro Musica concert in January, 1927: Henry Cowell, "Our Inadequate Notation," *Modern Music* 4 (March–April, 1927): 31. Here he commented on Ives's notation of quarter tones.

99. Letter of Charles E. Ives to Henry Cowell, August 16, 1927, reproduction of typed copy, Ives Collection.

100. Letter of Henry Cowell to Charles E. Ives, July 27, 19[2]7, reproduced copy in Ives Collection.

101. Letter of Henry Cowell to Charles E. Ives, August 20, 1927, reproduced copy in Ives Collection; letter of Charles E. Ives to Henry Cowell, August 16, 1927, reproduction of typed copy, Ives Collection.

102. Cowell and Cowell, *Charles Ives and His Music,* p. 105.

103. Cf. *ibid.,* pp. 104–5.

104. Ives, *Essays before a Sonata,* p. 110.

105. Letter of Charles E. Ives to Henry Cowell, August 12, [1928], reproduced copy in Ives Collection.

106. See Ives's calculations on a piece of note paper containing his undated [mid-December, 1932] sketches for letters of Edith O. Ives to Bernard Herrmann and Jerome Moross, in the Herrmann file, Ives Collection. His $1,500 promised for 1932–1933 included $360 for a concert by the Pan American Association of Composers in November, 1932: letter of Wallingford Riegger to Henry Cowell, October 31, 1932, reproduced copy in Cowell file (as enclosure in letter of Henry Cowell to Charles E. Ives, November 19, 1932), Ives Collection. For Cowell's actually receiving the money promised, see letter of Henry Cowell to Charles E. Ives, April 18, [1933], reproduced copy in Ives Collection; and letter of Henry Cowell to Charles E. Ives, May 16, 1933, reproduced copy in Ives Collection. On the "surplus account," see letter of Charles E. Ives to Henry Cowell, undated [June, 1934], in answer to Cowell's letter of June 6, 1934, reproduced copy in Ives Collection.

107. Enclosure in letter of John J. Becker to Charles E. Ives, Harmony T. Ives, and Edith O. Ives, dated "Thursday" [March 16, 1939], in custody of John Kirkpatrick; letter of Harmony T. Ives to Gerald Strang, December 11, 1938, reproduced copy in "New Music & Strang" file, Ives Collection. The account of Ives's subsidy in Cowell and Cowell, *Charles Ives and His Music,* p. 121, is misleading.

108. E.g., letter of Henry Cowell to Charles E. Ives, November 19, 1932, reproduced copy in Ives Collection; letter of Henry Cowell to Charles E. Ives, January 10, 1931, reproduced copy in Ives Collection; letter of Henry Cowell to Charles E. Ives, April 19, 1930, reproduced copy in Ives Collection.

109. Letter of Charles E. Ives to Henry Cowell, August 29, 1929, reproduced copy in Ives Collection.

110. Letter of Charles E. Ives to Henry Cowell, August 12, [1928], reproduced copy in Ives Collection; letter of Charles E. Ives to Henry Cowell, December 3, 1928, reproduced copy in Ives Collection.

111. Charles E. Ives, "The Fourth Symphony for Large Orchestra," *New Music,* vol. 2, No. 2 (January, 1929).

112. Paul Rosenfeld, *Discoveries of a Music Critic* (New York: Harcourt, Brace and Company, 1936), p. 281.

113. E.g., Henry Cowell, "Four Little Known Modern Composers," *Aesthete Magazine,* August, 1928, pp. 1, 19–20; Henry Cowell, "Music: Three Native Composers," *New Freeman* 1 (May 3, 1930): 184–86; Henry Cowell, "American Composers. IX: Charles Ives," *Modern Music* 10 (November–December, 1932): 24–32; Henry Cowell, "Music," *Americana Annual, 1929,* p. 501; Henry Cowell, "Music," *Americana Annual, 1930,* p. 538.

114. Cowell, "Music: Three Native Composers," p. 185.

115. E.g., letter of Henry Cowell to Charles E. Ives, October 15, [1928], reproduced copy in Ives Collection; Henry Cowell, "Compositores Modernos de los Estados Unidos," *Musicalia* (Havana) 1 (November–December, 1928): 124–27; Henry Cowell,

"Bericht aus Amerika. 2. Die beiden wirklichen Amerikaner: Ives und Ruggles," *Melos* 9 (October, 1930): 417–20; letter of Henry Cowell to Charles E. Ives, March 18, [1930], reproduced copy in Ives Collection. This last letter refers to Cowell's article concerning Ives and other American composers that appeared in *Music and Revolution* (Moscow); a retranslation, "Who Are the Composers in America," is in Scrapbook No. 2, p. 7, Ives Collection. Cowell went to the Soviet Union in 1929.

116. In the file of programs and reviews, in the Ives Collection, there are an announcement for a New Music Society concert in San Francisco on November 27, 1928, at which Dorothy Minty (violin) and Marjorie Gear (piano) performed Ives's First Violin Sonata; and an announcement for a New Music Society concert in San Francisco on September 19, 1928, at which Arthur Hardcastle performed the second of Ives's four transcriptions from *Emerson*. In Scrapbook No. 2, pp. 16–18, Ives Collection, there are a number of newspaper articles concerning Keith Corelli's performances of the *Emerson* movement of the *Concord* Sonata in the South and West during 1928 and 1929; cf. letter of Henry Cowell to Charles E. Ives, July 10, 1928, reproduced copy in Ives Collection. Cowell's letters to Ives during 1928, in the Ives Collection, contain numerous accounts of his attempts to interest his musical acquaintances in Ives's compositions.

117. Fernand Ouellette, *Edgard Varèse*, trans. Derek Coltman (New York: Orion Press, 1968), pp. 44, 65–68.

118. Aaron Copland, "The Composer in America, 1923–1933," *Modern Music* 10 (January–February, 1933): 89.

119. Ouellette, *Edgard Varèse*, pp. 68–69, 97.

120. Riegger, "To the New through the Old," pp. 491–92. The Pan Americans did actually obtain a few genuine New York newspaper reviews, in addition to those in journals devoted to music and the avant-garde.

121. E.g., letter of Wallingford Riegger to Henry Cowell, October 31, 1932, reproduced copy in Cowell file (as enclosure in letter of Henry Cowell to Charles E. Ives, November 19, 1932), Ives Collection; letter of Henry Cowell to Charles E. Ives, November 26, 1932, reproduced copy in Ives Collection. The other principal financial backer of the association was Mrs. E. F. Walton, a wealthy patroness of music.

122. The program for this concert, which took place at Carnegie Chamber Hall on April 21, 1930, is in the file of programs and reviews, Ives Collection. Harry Freistadt (trumpet) and Imre Weisshaus (piano) played a set consisting of *The New River, The Indians,* and *Ann Street*.

123. Henry Cowell, "American Composers," in *Proceedings of the Ohio State Educational Conference, Eleventh Annual Session,* ed. Josephine H. MacLatchy, issued as *Ohio State University Bulletin* 36, No. 3 (September 15, 1931): 379. Cf. Henry Cowell, "Trends in American Music," in *American Composers on American Music: A Symposium,* ed. Henry Cowell ([Stanford University, Calif.]: Stanford University Press, 1933; reprint ed., with a new introduction by the editor, New York: Frederick Ungar Publishing Co., 1962), pp. 3–13. For Cowell's views on neoclassicism, see Henry Cowell, "Music," *Americana Annual, 1932,* pp. 485–86.

124. Ives, *Memos,* pp. 78–79.

125. Letter of Henry Cowell to Charles E. Ives, December 11, 1931, reproduced copy in Ives Collection; letter of Henry Cowell to Charles E. Ives, January 5, 1933, reproduced copy in Ives Collection. The first of these two letters referred pettily to a Berlin concert of 1931 at which works by Aaron Copland, Louis Gruenberg, Roger Sessions, and Carl Ruggles were played; see Julia Smith, *Aaron Copland,* pp. 135–36.

126. See Ives's marginal comments (next to the list of officers and directors of the United States Section of the International Society for Contemporary Music) on a form letter from Dorothy Lawton, July 18, 1936, in Scrapbook No. 3, p. 234, Ives Collection.

127. Quoted in Michael Sperling, "Varese and Contemporary Music," *Trend* 2 (May–June, 1934): 125.

128. Roger Sessions was another important composer who became active in the League. Roy Harris belonged to the Pan American Association, but he was not active in its inner circle.

129. Private information.

130. Letter of Henry Cowell to Charles E. Ives, December 11, 1931, reproduced copy in Ives Collection; letter of Carl Ruggles to Charles E. Ives, August 17, 1933, Ives Collection; letter of Adolph Weiss to Charles E. Ives, March 14, 1943, in "Native American Composers" file, Ives Collection.

131. Letter of Charles E. Ives to Nicolas Slonimsky, July 14, 1929, copy by John Kirkpatrick, Ives Collection; letter of Charles E. Ives to Nicolas Slonimsky, December 29, [1929], copy by John Kirkpatrick, Ives Collection.

132. Letter of Charles E. Ives to Nicolas Slonimsky, December 20, [1930], copy by John Kirkpatrick, Ives Collection.

133. Letter of Charles E. Ives to Nicolas Slonimsky, February 8, [1930], copy by John Kirkpatrick, Ives Collection; letter of Henry Cowell to Charles E. Ives, February 14, 1930, reproduced copy in Ives Collection; enclosure in letter of Charles E. Ives to John Tasker Howard, June 30, 1930, published in Ives, *Memos,* app. 11, p. 238; Henry Cowell, "Music," *Americana Annual, 1931,* p. 513.

134. Letter of Charles E. Ives to Nicolas Slonimsky, February 26, 1930, copy by John Kirkpatrick, Ives Collection.

135. Letter of Charles E. Ives to Henry Cowell, April 17, 1930, reproduced copy in Ives Collection. *You Know Me Al* was a popular book of humor by Ring Lardner. *Jonny spielt auf* was a well-known jazz opera by the Austrian modernist Ernst Křenek.

136. Letter of Nicolas Slonimsky to Charles E. Ives, June 5, 1930, Ives Collection; letter of Nicolas Slonimsky to Charles E. Ives, November 30, 1930, Ives Collection; letter of Nicolas Slonimsky to Charles E. Ives, December 24, 1930, Ives Collection; letter of Charles E. Ives to Nicolas Slonimsky, January 5, [1931], copy by John Kirkpatrick, Ives Collection.

137. The program for the concert is in the file of programs and reviews, Ives Collection.

138. This passage is part of one of several alternative inserts, written out by Ives on yellow legal-sized paper, for p. 3 of Lucille Fletcher's unpublished article "A Connecticut Yankee in Music"; it is in the Fletcher file, Ives Collection.

139. Quoted in Nicolas Slonimsky, "Musical Rebel," *Américas,* September, 1953, p. 41. Cf. Slonimsky interview, January 29, 1969, Tape #5A.

140. The program for this Boston concert, which took place at the Repertory Theatre on January 25, 1931, is in the file of programs and reviews, Ives Collection. Ives also attended this concert: Slonimsky interview, January 29, 1969, Tape #5A.

141. Warren Storey Smith, "Slonimsky Orchestra Makes Bow," *Boston Post,* January 26, 1931, p. 5.

142. S. S. [Stephen Somervel], "Chamber Orchestra of Boston," *Boston Herald,* January 26, 1931, p. 12.

143. H. T. P. [H. T. Parker], "A Mediocre Matinee of Modernists," *Boston Evening Transcript,* January 26, 1931, p. 8.

144. Slonimsky conducted his Chamber Orchestra of Boston in the New York concert, which was held at the New School for Social Research (where Cowell was director of music) on February 7, 1931. The Havana concert, held on March 18, 1931, was one of two chamber-orchestra concerts (using Cuban musicians) that Slonimsky conducted under the auspices of the Cuban Section of the International Society for Contemporary Music. Programs for these New York and Havana concerts are in the file of programs and reviews, Ives Collection. Slonimsky's Havana engagements were probably secured for him by Cowell, who had been in Cuba in December.

145. Cowell and Cowell, *Charles Ives and His Music,* pp. 107–9; Cowell, "American Composers," *Proceedings of the Ohio State Educational Conference,* pp. 377–79; letter of Henry Cowell to Charles E. Ives, February 16, 1931, reproduced copy in Ives Collection. This last letter shows that donations from wealthy patrons were first sought (unsuccessfully) for these concerts, before Ives was called upon to bear their cost; cf. Cowell and Cowell, *Charles Ives and His Music,* p. 107. For Ives's financing of the Paris concerts, see letter of Nicolas Slonimsky to Charles E. Ives, May 19, 1931, Ives Collection; also fragment of letter of Nicolas Slonimsky to Charles E. Ives, undated [perhaps the last page of Slonimsky's original letter of June 21, 1931], Ives Collection; cf. Slonimsky interview, January 29, 1969, Tape #5A.

146. The program for these two concerts, which were given in the salle Gaveau with players from the Straram orchestra, is in the file of programs and reviews, Ives Collection; *Three Places in New England* was played at the concert of June 6.

147. For a general picture of the reaction to the concerts, see letter of Nicolas Slonimsky to Charles E. Ives, June 21, 1931, typed copy in Ives Collection.

148. On this point, Henry Cowell insisted on misrepresenting the reactions of the French critics. See, e.g., Cowell, "Music," *Americana Annual, 1932,* p. 486.

149. Boris de Schloezer, "La Vie musicale à Paris," *Les Beaux-arts* (Brussels), June 26, 1931, p. 1; my translation.

150. Paul Le Flem, "M. Slonimsky a dirigé tout un programme de musique américaine," *Comoedia* (Paris), June 8, 1931, pp. 1–2; my translation.

151. Émile Vuillermoz, "La Musique," *Excelsior* (Paris), June 8, 1931, p. 3; my translation.

152. Émile Vuillermoz, "La Musique," *Excelsior* (Paris), June 15, 1931, p. 3; my translation. Several clippings of other French reviews of the Paris concerts are in the

file of programs and reviews, Ives Collection. See also Carlos Salzedo, "The American Left Wing," *Eolus* 11 (April, 1932): 14–28.

153. Letter of Nicolas Slonimsky to Charles E. Ives, May 19, 1931, Ives Collection.

154. Fragment of letter of Nicolas Slonimsky to Charles E. Ives, undated [perhaps the last page of Slonimsky's original letter of June 21, 1931], Ives Collection.

155. Letter of Charles E. Ives to Nicolas Slonimsky, June 12, [1931], copy by John Kirkpatrick, Ives Collection.

156. Henry Prunières, "American Compositions in Paris," *New York Times,* July 12, 1931, sec. 8, p. 6. Cf. Adolph Weiss, Letter to the Editor, *New York Times,* July 26, 1931, sec. 8, p. 7.

157. Philip Hale, "Mr. Slonimsky in Paris," *Boston Herald,* July 7, 1931, p. 14.

158. Letter of Charles E. Ives to E. Robert Schmitz, August 10, 1931, carbon copy in Ives Collection.

159. Ives, *Memos,* pp. 26–29.

160. *Ibid.,* p. 26. The requests that Ives had begun to receive for information about himself and his music were one reason that he gave for assembling biographical data: *ibid.,* pp. 25–26, 35. But this motive hardly explains many of the digressions in the work.

161. Letter (with enclosure) of Henry Cowell to Charles E. Ives, October 31, 1931, reproduced copy in Ives Collection.

162. Letter of Nicolas Slonimsky to Charles E. Ives, July 14, 1931, Ives Collection; letter of Nicolas Slonimsky to Henry Cowell, January 21, 1932, in Slonimsky file, Ives Collection.

163. Florent Schmitt, "Les Concerts," *Le Temps* (Paris), February 27, 1932, p. 3; Henry Prunières, " 'Elektra' in Paris," *New York Times,* March 20, 1932, sec. 8, pp. 7, 9.

164. The program for the concert of February 21, which took place in the salle Pleyel, is in the file of programs and reviews, Ives Collection. *In the Night* was given the title *Élégie.*

165. B. Shletser", "Muz'ikal'n'iia zametki," *Posledniia novosti* or *Les Dernières Nouvelles* (Paris), March 11, 1932, p. 5; translation by Koit Ojamaa. The Ives Collection contains several clippings of other French reviews of these Paris concerts. See the file of programs and reviews; Scrapbook No. 2, pp. 30 and 32; and Scrapbook No. 3, p. 101.

166. The program for this concert, which was given in the Beethovensaal, is in the file of programs and reviews, Ives Collection. Slonimsky's second concert in Berlin, which was given with a chamber orchestra, took place on March 10.

167. The program for this Budapest concert, which was given by the Pan Americans under the auspices of the Hungarian Section of the International Society for Contemporary Music, is in the file of programs and reviews, Ives Collection. There were two more significant European concerts put on by the Pan Americans in the 1931–1932 season; Slonimsky did not participate in them, but Ives helped to finance them both. The first was a chamber-orchestra concert, at which nothing by Ives was played, conducted by Pedro Sanjuán in Madrid on November 23, 1931: see letter of Henry Cowell to Charles E. Ives, September 1, [1931], reproduced copy in Ives Col-

lection; and letter of Henry Cowell to Charles E. Ives, November 28, 1931, reproduced copy in Ives Collection. The second was a chamber concert held in Vienna on
February 21, 1932, in which Anton Webern participated as conductor; songs by Ives,
Copland, and Alejandro García Caturla were sung by Ruzena Herlinger. The program for this concert, which was given by the Pan American Association under the
auspices of the Austrian Section of the International Society for Contemporary Music,
is in the file of programs and reviews, Ives Collection; see also letter (with enclosure)
of Henry Cowell to Charles E. Ives, October 31, 1931, reproduced copy in Ives
Collection.

168. Herbert F. Peyser, "Music in Berlin," *New York Times,* April 17, 1932, sec. 8,
p. 8.

169. Jerzy Fitelberg, "More Americans and Kurt Weill in Berlin," *Modern Music* 9
(May–June, 1932): 185. The Ives Collection contains a number of clippings of other
German reviews of these Berlin concerts; see the file of programs and reviews and
Scrapbook No. 3, p. 102.

170. Alfred Einstein, "American Music in Berlin," *Christian Science Monitor,* March
6, 1933, p. 4.

171. E.g., Cowell set up a chamber concert, given jointly by the Pan American Association and the Hamburg Chapter of the German Section of the International Society for Contemporary Music, which was held in Hamburg on December 8, 1932.
Cowell played some of his own piano music and accompanied the American soprano
Mary Bell in three songs by Ives; a reproduced page of the program is in the Bell file,
Ives Collection. Again, Ives helped to finance the concert. See letter of Henry Cowell
to Charles E. Ives, November 19, 1932, reproduced copy in Ives Collection; and letter
of Henry Cowell to Charles E. Ives, December 11, 1932, reproduced copy in Ives
Collection.

172. Letter of Henry Cowell to Charles E. Ives, January 26, 1933, reproduced copy
in Ives Collection. Cf. H. H. Stuckenschmidt, "German Season under the Crisis," *Modern Music* 10 (March–April, 1933): 167.

173. Slonimsky interview, January 29, 1969, Tape #5A.

174. E.g., letter of Henry Cowell to Charles E. Ives, August 31, 1931, reproduced
copy in Ives Collection; letter of Nicolas Slonimsky to Charles E. Ives, July 14, 1931,
Ives Collection; letter of Nicolas Slonimsky to Charles E. Ives, January 6, 1933, Ives
Collection.

Notes to Chapter 8: The Avant-garde and the Musical Public, 1932–1939

1. The collection *Eighteen Songs* actually contained nineteen songs.

2. The essay by Ives was a revised version of part of the "Conductor's Note" that
he had written for the *New Music* edition of the second movement of his Fourth
Symphony.

3. Letter of Charles E. Ives to Henry Cowell, July 26, [1935], reproduced copy in
Ives Collection; cf. letter of Henry Cowell to Charles E. Ives, July 31, 1935, repro-

duced copy in Ives Collection. Another reason for Ives's reluctance to publish more of his compositions in *New Music* was that the decline in his eyesight and general health made it difficult for him to attend to such prepublication matters as the correction of proofs.

4. Cf. Carter interview, June 20, 1969, Tapes #14A and #14B.

5. This performance of *Washington's Birthday,* a work scored for chamber orchestra, took place in San Francisco on September 3, 1931; the program for the concert is in the file of programs and reviews, Ives Collection.

6. The program for this concert, which took place in Havana on December 27, 1931, is in the file of programs and reviews, Ives Collection.

7. These two Pan American concerts were held at the New School for Social Research; the Pan American Chamber Orchestra was conducted by Adolph Weiss on February 16, 1932, and by Slonimsky on November 4, 1932. Programs for both concerts are in the file of programs and reviews, Ives Collection.

8. The program for this recital by Pazmor, which took place in San Francisco on September 26, 1933, is in the file of programs and reviews, Ives Collection; Katheryn Foster was the accompanist. Cf. letter of Radiana Pazmor to Charles E. Ives, July 29, 1933, Ives Collection.

9. Cowell also set up a series of radio programs by the Pan American Association on WEVD (New York); songs and pieces by Ives were included. See, e.g., the reproduced copy of the relevant portion of the script for the program of June 4, 1933, in the Bell file, Ives Collection; on this radio program Mary Bell sang five songs by Ives. Members of the Young Composers' Group (see below) participated in these programs.

10. The program for these concerts is in the file of programs and reviews, Ives Collection. Roy Harris, who was then living in the Los Angeles area, helped to secure this invitation for Slonimsky: letter of Nicolas Slonimsky to Harmony T. Ives, November 18, 1932, Ives Collection.

11. Letter of Nicolas Slonimsky to Charles E. Ives, January 2, 1933 [misdated February 2, 1932], Ives Collection.

12. José Rodriguez, "An Old Lady Gets Three Shots in the Arm," *Rob Wagner's Script,* January 7, 1933, pp. 6–7. Rodriguez was probably aiming his remarks at Artur Rodzinski, the regular conductor of the Los Angeles Philharmonic.

13. Letter of Charles E. Ives to Nicolas Slonimsky, February 5, 1933, copy by John Kirkpatrick, Ives Collection.

14. Letter of Nicolas Slonimsky to Charles E. Ives, June 30, 1933, Ives Collection. Rodriguez was a member of the music committee for the Hollywood Bowl concerts.

15. John Weatherwax, "On the Pacific Coast," *Modern Music* 11 (January–February, 1934): 106–7.

16. Bernard Herrmann has recalled that Copland did not at first like Ives's music: interview with Bernard Herrmann by Vivian Perlis, November 12, 1969, Tape #29A, Ives Oral History Project (hereafter cited as Herrmann interview), as revised in Perlis, *Charles Ives Remembered,* p. 156. Jerome Moross has remembered that he and Herrmann (both of whom were members of the Young Composers' Group, which Copland sponsored) attempted to arouse Copland's interest in Ives, encouraged him to have

Ives performed, and lent him a copy of *114 Songs:* interview with Jerome Moross by Vivian Perlis, September 19, 1969, Tape #22, Ives Oral History Project (hereafter cited as Moross interview). Copland himself has simply said that Ives sent him copies of *114 Songs* and *50 Songs:* interview with Aaron Copland by Vivian Perlis, January 30, 1970, Tape #31, Ives Oral History Project (hereafter cited as Copland interview). Cf. Donal Henahan, "He Made Composing Respectable Here," *New York Times,* November 8, 1970, sec. 2, p. 17.

17. The other songs were *The Indians, Walking, Serenity, Maple Leaves,* and *The See'r.*

18. The program for the festival is in the file of programs and reviews, Ives Collection.

19. A. H. M. [Alfred H. Meyer], "Composers Who Spoke Well in Varying Voices," *Boston Evening Transcript,* May 6, 1932, p. 8.

20. Alfred H. Meyer, "Yaddo—a May Festival," *Modern Music* 9 (May–June, 1932): 174.

21. Arthur Mendel, "Music: The American Composer," *Nation* 134 (May 18, 1932): 579.

22. Robert Pitney, "Music Chronicle: Yaddo and Gurre," *Hound & Horn* 5 (July–September, 1932): 666. Another important review was Paul Rosenfeld, "A Musical Tournament," *New Republic* 71 (June 15, 1932): 121.

23. Rosenfeld, "Musical Tournament," p. 119; "Critics of Music Are Denounced by Composers," *New York Herald Tribune,* May 2, 1932, p. 8; Olin Downes, "American Composers and Critics," *New York Times,* May 8, 1932, sec. 8, p. 6; "Critics and American Music; Suggestions from Mr. Copland," *New York Herald Tribune,* May 8, 1932, sec. 7, p. 6; Aaron Copland, "The Composer and His Critic," *Modern Music* 9 (May–June, 1932): 143–47.

24. In the same year the seven songs sung at Yaddo were published by the non-profit Cos Cob Press, with which Copland was closely associated.

25. Letter of Wallingford Riegger to Charles E. Ives, May 4, 1932, Ives Collection. In this letter Riegger asked Ives to set down biographical data about himself, and Ives cited Riegger's request (*Memos,* pp. 25, 26) as the main reason for his decision to write his musical memoirs. In fact, however, he had been writing and dictating the *Memos* for some time before he received Riegger's letter.

26. It should be noted that the *New Republic* announced Rosenfeld's forthcoming article on Ives even before the Yaddo festival took place: *New Republic* 70 (April 20, 1932): iv.

27. Paul Rosenfeld, "Musical Chronicle," *Dial* 82 (April, 1927): 358.

28. Rosenfeld, "Charles E. Ives," p. 263.

29. *Ibid.,* pp. 262–63.

30. *Ibid.,* p. 264.

31. Rosenfeld, "Two Native Groups," pp. 209–10.

32. Rosenfeld, "Charles E. Ives," p. 264.

33. *Ibid.,* p. 263.

34. Meyer, "Yaddo," p. 174.

35. Harrison Kerr, "The League of Composers Presents—Rather Tardily—Mr. Florent Schmitt," *Trend* 1 (January–March, 1933): 142.

36. Kerr, "Creative Music," pp. 87, 89; Arthur V. Berger, "Two Mid-winter Concerts," *Trend* 2 (April–June, 1933): 36–37.

37. Kerr, "League of Composers Presents," p. 142. See also Harrison Kerr, "Die Gurre-lieder and the Festival at Yaddo," *Trend* 1 (June–August, 1932): 57.

38. A. V. B. [Arthur V. Berger], "Pan-American Association," *Daily Mirror* (New York), February 17, 1932 (Extra Edition), p. 18. See also A. V. B. [Arthur V. Berger], "Ruggles Work Performed," *Sunday Mirror* (New York), January 24, 1932 (Extra Edition), p. 28; here Berger referred to "the too infrequently heard [American] composers: Ruggles, Ives, Cowell, Riegger, and others, who are making history in our midst." According to Jerome Moross, it was he and Bernard Herrmann who first interested their friend Berger in Ives's music: Moross interview, September 19, 1969, Tape #22.

39. A. V. B. [Arthur V. Berger], "Yaddo Musical Festival," *Daily Mirror* (New York), May 3, 1932 (Final Edition), p. 18. Cf. A. V. B. [Arthur V. Berger], "The Songs of Charles Ives," *Musical Mercury* 1 (October–November, 1934): 97–98.

40. Irving Kolodin was another perceptive newspaper critic of Ives's music. See his review of *Washington's Birthday:* I. K. [Irving Kolodin], "American Music," *Sun* (New York), November 5, 1932, p. 7.

41. Letter of Henry Cowell to Charles E. Ives, January 5, 1933, reproduced copy in Ives Collection.

42. On the group as a whole, see Rosenfeld, "Two Native Groups," p. 209; Arthur V. Berger, "The Young Composers' Group," *Trend* 2 (April–June, 1933): 26–28; Arthur Berger, *Aaron Copland* (New York: Oxford University Press, 1953), pp. 20–21; and letter of Henry Cowell to Charles E. Ives, January 5, 1933, reproduced copy in Ives Collection. There is also evidence of the attitudes of individual members of the group toward Ives and his music: Bernard Herrmann, "Charles Ives," *Trend* 1 (September–November, 1932): 99–101; letter of Jerome Moross to Charles E. Ives, undated [February 14, 1933?], in "M" file, Ives Collection; letter of Lehman Engel to Charles E. Ives, May 4, 1932, Ives Collection; A. Lehman Engel, "Music Notes," *Symposium* 3 (October, 1932): 495–502; fragment of letter of Irwin Heilner to Henry Cowell, July 14, 1934, in Scrapbook No. 3, p. 161, Ives Collection; letters of Elie Siegmeister to Charles E. Ives, June 15, 1937, and September 21, 1937, Ives Collection; Elie Siegmeister, *Music and Society,* Critics Group Pamphlet No. 10 (New York: Critics Group Press, 1938), p. 56; Elie Siegmeister, "Charles Ives," in *The Music Lover's Handbook,* ed. Elie Siegmeister (New York: William Morrow and Company, 1943), pp. 749–53. For the less friendly attitude of Israel Citkowitz toward Ives's music, see Israel Citkowitz, "Experiment and Necessity—New York, 1932," *Modern Music* 10 (January–February, 1933): 112.

43. For the sharp contrast between the American intellectual and artistic milieu of the 1920s and that of the 1930s, see Clurman, *Fervent Years,* esp. chaps. 1, 2, 23. Cf. Frederick Lewis Allen, *Since Yesterday: The Nineteen-Thirties in America, September 3, 1929–September 3, 1939* (New York: Harper & Brothers Publishers, 1940), chap. 10;

and Robert M. Crunden, *From Self to Society, 1919–1941,* Transitions in American Thought Series (Englewood Cliffs, N.J.: Prentice-Hall, Inc., Spectrum Books, 1972).

44. Copland interview, January 30, 1970, Tape #31.

45. See, e.g., Paul Rosenfeld, *An Hour with American Music,* The One Hour Series (Philadelphia: J. B. Lippincott Company, 1929).

46. "New York Artists Reshape America over the Week End," *New York Herald Tribune,* July 10, 1932, sec. 1, p. 14. Herrmann was joined in his remarks by Moross, Brant, Fine, and Engel. The entire article gives an excellent picture of the ideology of young American creative artists in the summer of 1932.

47. Berger, "Young Composers' Group," pp. 26–27.

48. See Julia Smith, *Aaron Copland,* pp. 119–21.

49. Herrmann interview, November 12, 1969, Tape #29A; Moross interview, September 19, 1969, Tape #22.

50. "New York Artists Reshape America," p. 14.

51. This concert, in which Herrmann conducted his New Chamber Orchestra, took place at the New School, in New York City, on May 17, 1933; the program (dated May 10, although the concert was subsequently postponed one week) is in the file of programs and reviews, Ives Collection.

52. E.g., Herrmann conducted his New Chamber Orchestra in the first and third movements of the Fourth Symphony at a concert in Town Hall, New York City, on February 25, 1934; the program is in the file of programs and reviews, Ives Collection.

53. E.g., a performance of the Fugue from the Fourth Symphony, with Howard Barlow conducting the Columbia Symphony Orchestra, was part of a nation-wide CBS radio broadcast on September 27, 1936; a copy of the relevant portions of the script for this radio program ("Everybody's Music") is in the file of programs and reviews, Ives Collection. Ives's First String Quartet was another work that Herrmann himself conducted (in his own arrangement for string orchestra) over the air.

54. R. D. Darrell, comp., "Living American Composers: A List with Notes on the Recordings or Recording Possibilities," *Music Lovers' Guide* 2 (February, 1934): 173.

55. Henry Bellamann's article on Ives in the *Musical Quarterly* for January, 1933, was another significant extension of Ives's reputation beyond the confines of the avant-garde and its organs.

56. On the developments discussed in this paragraph, particularly as they affected the members of the Young Composers' Group, see Henry Cowell, "Music," *Americana Annual, 1934,* p. 392; Lehman Engel, "New Laboratories and Gebrauchsmusik," *Modern Music* 13 (March–April, 1936): 50–52; Aaron Copland, "Our Younger Generation: Ten Years Later," *Modern Music* 13 (May–June, 1936): 8–9; Siegmeister, *Music and Society,* p. 59 and note; Elie Siegmeister, "Composer in Brooklyn," in *Music Lover's Handbook,* ed. Siegmeister, pp. 771–74; and Hitchcock, *Music in the United States,* pp. 199–201.

57. Cowell and Cowell, *Charles Ives and His Music,* p. 4, note, makes this point, but also detects the influence of Ives's music in certain works written by Herrmann, Moross, and Brant about 1950.

58. Slonimsky interview, January 29, 1969, Tape #5A.

59. Kerr, "Creative Music," pp. 87–90.

60. Letter of Charles E. Ives to Edgard Varèse, undated [April 25 or 26, 1934], reproduced copy in Ives Collection; letter of Edgard Varèse to Charles E. Ives, April 27, 1934, Ives Collection.

61. The two pieces were *The New River* and *December*. This concert conducted by Slonimsky took place in Town Hall on April 15, 1934. The second concert, conducted by Albert Stoessel and featuring the dancing of Martha Graham, took place at the Alvin Theatre on April 22, 1934; as an orchestral interlude, three short works by Ives for instrumental ensemble or chamber orchestra were performed: *Hallowe'en, The Pond,* and *The Gong on the Hook and Ladder.* The programs for both concerts are in the file of programs and reviews, Ives Collection. Ives, who was fiercely loyal to Slonimsky, was offended when Varèse and his associates decided that Fritz Reiner was to conduct the first concert; he may have put pressure on Varèse to have Slonimsky conduct it instead: letter of Charles E. Ives to Nicolas Slonimsky, undated [February 5, 1934?], copy by John Kirkpatrick, Ives Collection.

62. Letter of Charles E. Ives to John J. Becker, August 4–5, 1934, copy by John Kirkpatrick in his custody.

63. Letter of Wallingford Riegger to Charles E. Ives, May 10, 1934, Ives Collection.

64. Charles E. Ives, sketch dated "Sunday" [May 13, 1934] for letter to Wallingford Riegger in answer to Riegger's letter of May 10, 1934, Ives Collection; letter of Wallingford Riegger to Charles E. Ives, May 16, 1934, Ives Collection. From that time on, Ruggles never changed his bad opinion of Slonimsky's abilities as a conductor: interview with Carl Ruggles by Vivian Perlis, February 28, 1969, Tape #6B, Ives Oral History Project (hereafter cited as Ruggles interview).

65. Letter of Charles E. Ives to Henry Cowell, undated [April 27 and 30, 1934], reproduced copy in Ives Collection.

66. Letter of Charles E. Ives to Henry Cowell, undated [end of July or early August, 1934], reproduced copy in Ives Collection.

67. Sperling, "Varese," p. 128.

68. Letter of Charles E. Ives to Henry Cowell, undated [end of July or early August, 1934], reproduced copy in Ives Collection.

69. Ouellette, *Edgard Varèse,* pp. 127–31, 134, 137–40.

70. The Ives Collection contains extensive correspondence between Ives and Slonimsky, from 1933 to 1935, concerning Slonimsky's work on this score.

71. On the state of Ives's health, see Cowell and Cowell, *Charles Ives and His Music,* pp. 123, 127; Tyler interview, March 18, 1969, Tape #8; letter of Harmony T. Ives to Gerald Strang, August 18, 1936, reproduced copy in "New Music & Strang" file, Ives Collection; letter of Edith O. Ives to Lehman Engel, October 16, 1938, reproduced copy in Ives Collection; Charles E. Ives, undated sketch for letter of Harmony T. Ives to Joseph Szigeti in answer to Szigeti's undated letter of [c. March 1, 1942], Ives Collection.

72. Interview with Mary Shipman Howard by Vivian Perlis, September 24, 1969, Tape #24, Ives Oral History Project.

73. On the Iveses' choosing deliberately to lead a life of social isolation, for rea-

sons other than Ives's health, see letter of Edith Ives Tyler to John J. Becker and Evelyn Becker, January 17, 1955, copy by John Kirkpatrick in his custody.

74. See, e.g., letter of Germaine Schmitz to Harmony T. Ives, April 11, 1955, Ives Collection.

75. Cowell and Cowell, *Charles Ives and His Music,* p. 100, note; interview with Lehman Engel by Vivian Perlis, October 12, 1969, Tape #27, Ives Oral History Project (hereafter cited as Engel interview).

76. Slonimsky interview, January 29, 1969, Tape #5A.

77. E.g., Charles E. Ives, undated sketch for letter of Harmony T. Ives to E. Power Biggs in answer to Biggs's letter of April 15, 1948, Ives Collection; cf. letter of E. Power Biggs to Harmony T. Ives, May 7, 1948, Ives Collection.

78. Even George Gershwin made an unsuccessful effort to meet Ives: letter of Charles Martin (of the Florentine Bindery) to Charles E. Ives, May 15, 1934, in Scrapbook No. 3, p. 159, Ives Collection. On a typed extract from this letter, in the "G" file, Ives Collection, Ives noted that he had not acted on Gershwin's suggestion (conveyed through a third party) that he telephone Gershwin.

79. Ives, *Memos,* pp. 135–36.

80. Not long after Ives affirmed that he had "never heard nor seen a note of Schoenberg's music," *New Music* published a piece by Schoenberg: letter of Charles E. Ives to E. Robert Schmitz, August 10, 1931, carbon copy in Ives Collection; Arnold Schoenberg, "Klavierstueck," *New Music,* vol. 5, No. 3 (April, 1932).

81. He did not, for example, acquaint himself with the compositions of his young friends Bernard Herrmann and Jerome Moross. See Herrmann interview, November 12, 1969, Tape #29A; and Moross interview, September 19, 1969, Tape #22.

82. Ives, *Essays before a Sonata,* p. 46.

83. Ives, *Memos,* p. 138. Elliott Carter has recalled that Ives made similar judgments in the middle 1920s about Ravel, Stravinsky, and other contemporary composers: Carter interview, June 20, 1969, Tape #14A.

84. Ives, *Memos,* p. 78.

85. Charles E. Ives, memo on pp. 10–11 of full score in pencil of *Majority* (5B10), Ives Collection.

86. Ives, *Memos,* p. 79.

87. Cf. Charles Seeger, "Henry Cowell," *Magazine of Art* 33 (May, 1940): 288–89, 323–25, 327; and Paul Rosenfeld, "The Winged Mercury," review of *American Composers on American Music: A Symposium,* ed. Henry Cowell, in the *New Republic* 76 (September 6, 1933): 109.

88. Sperling, "Varese," p. 127.

89. Quoted *ibid.,* p. 125.

90. Quoted in Ouellette, *Edgard Varèse,* pp. 141–42.

91. Letter of Charles E. Ives to Henry Cowell, undated [end of July or early August, 1934], reproduced copy in Ives Collection.

92. Charles E. Ives, undated sketch for letter of Harmony T. Ives to Edgard Varèse in answer to Varèse's letter of October 6, 1943, Ives Collection.

93. Ruggles interview, February 28, 1969, Tape #6B. Ruggles was undoubtedly grateful for Varèse's efforts on behalf of his music.

94. See the correspondence in the Varèse file, Ives Collection.

95. Letter of Edgard Varèse to Charles E. Ives, October 6, 1943, Ives Collection.

96. Ives, *Essays before a Sonata,* pp. 113–15. He quoted Mason's *Contemporary Composers* (New York: Macmillan Company, 1918), pp. 248–49. According to Mrs. Ives's list in the Iveses' diary of vacation at Asheville in 1919, etc. (D10), p. [206], Ives Collection, Ives "reread" Mason's book in 1919; its influence appears in several places in *Essays before a Sonata.* Although he was an academic and a musical conservative, Mason had ideals and a cultural background that were similar to Ives's; he was, for example, an admirer of Thoreau and something of an authority on him. It is not surprising that Ives read *Contemporary Composers* with approval, since Mason constantly upheld music of inner spiritual values as opposed to music of external sensuous "effect." Hiram K. Moderwell was the "liberated" intellectual whose admiration for ragtime disturbed Mason and (through reading Mason) Ives: Hiram K. Moderwell, "Ragtime," *New Republic* 4 (October 16, 1915): 284–86; Daniel Gregory Mason, Letter to the Editor, *New Republic* 5 (December 4, 1915): 122.

97. Biographical information about Varèse is drawn from Ouellette, *Edgard Varèse, passim;* and Louise Varèse, *Varèse: A Looking-Glass Diary,* vol. 1: *1883–1928* (New York: W. W. Norton & Company, Inc., 1972), *passim.*

98. See the file of correspondence between the Iveses and Varèse, Ives Collection. Ironically, Varèse had been the founder and first conductor of the New Symphony Orchestra, which gave Ives's *Decoration Day* such a disastrous reading in 1920. But his insistence on performing avant-garde works had forced his resignation soon after the first concerts had been given in 1919; and he had been replaced by a more conservative conductor, Artur Bodanzky, some time before Ives had his brush with the orchestra. See Ouellette, *Edgard Varèse,* pp. 53–54. Thus Ives was not brought into contact with Varèse until after he met Henry Cowell in 1927.

99. The generalizations made here about the relationship between Ives and Riegger are based on the correspondence in the Riegger file, Ives Collection.

100. Biographical information about Riegger is drawn from Riegger, "To the New through the Old," pp. 472–73, 490–92; and Richard Franko Goldman, "Wallingford Riegger," *HiFi/Stereo Review,* April, 1968, pp. 57–67.

101. Letter of Wallingford Riegger to Charles E. Ives, May 4, 1932, Ives Collection.

102. Letter of Wallingford Riegger to Charles E. Ives, February 18, 1949, Ives Collection.

103. Charles E. Ives, undated sketch for letter of Harmony T. Ives to Wallingford Riegger in answer to Riegger's letter of March 7, 1948, Ives Collection.

104. Russell Porter, "Inquiry Charges Red Link in Music," *New York Times,* April 10, 1957, p. 18; Murray Kempton, "A Musical Offering," *New York Post,* April 10, 1957, sec. 2, p. M4.

105. See the correspondence in the Riegger file, Ives Collection.

106. The program for this concert of the St. Paul Chamber Music Society, which took place at the College of St. Thomas on December 7, 1931, is in the file of programs and reviews, Ives Collection.

107. The generalizations made here about the relationship between Ives and Becker are based on the file of their correspondence in the custody of John Kirkpat-

rick. See also interview with Eugene Becker by Vivian Perlis, January 30, 1971, Tapes #47A and #47B, Ives Oral History Project (hereafter cited as Eugene Becker interview); and interview with Evelyn P. Becker by Vivian Perlis, October 15, 1973, Tapes #58A and #58B, Ives Oral History Project.

108. John J. Becker, "Fine Arts and the Soul of America," *Religious Education* 25 (November, 1930): 803–7.

109. E.g., Charles E. Ives, undated [December, 1932?] sketch for letter to Henry Allen Moe in answer to Moe's letter of November 29, 1932, in the file of Ives-Becker correspondence in custody of John Kirkpatrick.

110. Becker also orchestrated Ives's song *General Booth.*

111. Letter of John J. Becker to Charles E. Ives, Harmony T. Ives, and Edith O. Ives, October 31, 1932, in custody of John Kirkpatrick.

112. Even Ives subscribed to this view in private: Engel interview, October 12, 1969, Tape #27.

113. E.g., letter of John J. Becker to Charles E. Ives, December 21, 1936, copy by John Kirkpatrick (made from carbon copy) in his custody.

114. See Charles E. Ives, sketch for letter of Harmony T. Ives to John J. Becker, June 12, 1945, in custody of John Kirkpatrick.

115. The generalizations made here about the relationship between Ives and Ruggles are based on the correspondence in the Ruggles file, Ives Collection, and on personal information from John Kirkpatrick. See also Ruggles interview, February 28, 1969, Tapes #6A and #6B.

116. Biographical information about Ruggles is drawn from Eric Salzman, "Carl Ruggles," *HiFi/Stereo Review,* September, 1966, pp. 53–63; and John Kirkpatrick, "The Evolution of Carl Ruggles: A Chronicle Largely in His Own Words," *Perspectives of New Music,* Spring–Summer, 1968, pp. 146–66.

117. Ives, *Memos,* app. 19, p. 280.

118. E.g., *ibid.,* p. 134.

119. In private, both Ruggles and Becker objected to the practice of quoting hymn and "folk" tunes in serious compositions: interview with Charles Seeger by Vivian Perlis, March 16, 1970, Tape #34C, Ives Oral History Project; Eugene Becker interview, January 30, 1971, Tape #47B. Cowell, with his strong interest in folk music, took the opposite point of view.

120. Letter of Carl Ruggles to Charles E. Ives, March 2, 1932, Ives Collection; letter of Henry Cowell to Charles E. Ives, November 7, 1933, reproduced copy in Ives Collection; letter of Charles E. Ives to Henry Cowell, dated "Sunday" [November 12, 1933], reproduced copy in Ives Collection.

121. The "National Institute of Arts & Letters" file, Ives Collection, contains evidence of Ives's efforts to secure recognition for Ruggles by that body; see also letter of Harmony T. Ives to Carl Ruggles, undated [July, 1954], copy by John Kirkpatrick, Ives Collection.

122. "Teacher Held on Statutory Charge," *San Francisco Chronicle,* May 23, 1936, p. 1; "Cowell Arrested on Coast," *New York Times,* May 23, 1936, p. 5; "Henry Cowell, Composer, Held on Boy's Charge," *New York Herald Tribune,* May 23, 1936, p. 3;

"Cowell, Music Composer, Given Prison Term for Immorality," *San Francisco Chronicle,* July 7, 1936, p. 11.

123. Letter of Harmony T. Ives to Charlotte S. Ruggles, July 3, 1936, copy by John Kirkpatrick, Ives Collection; letter of Harmony T. Ives to Charlotte S. Ruggles, July 12, 1936, copy by John Kirkpatrick, Ives Collection; letter of Harmony T. Ives to Evelyn Becker, August 1, [1936], copy by John Kirkpatrick in his custody.

124. E.g., letter of Gerald Strang to Charles E. Ives, July 23, 1938, reproduction of carbon copy in "New Music & Strang" file, Ives Collection; letter (with enclosure) of John J. Becker to Charles E. Ives, Harmony T. Ives, and Edith O. Ives, dated "Thursday" [March 16, 1939], in custody of John Kirkpatrick.

125. The first performance took place when Engel conducted his Madrigal Singers in an American program at the WPA's Theatre of Music in New York City on May 6, 1937; the program is in the file of programs and reviews, Ives Collection. Engel also conducted *Psalm 67* in a nation-wide radio broadcast over CBS on August 29, 1937: see the announcement (on a post card) in the file of programs and reviews, Ives Collection. A Columbia recording of Engel's performance of *Psalm 67* was later issued; it was the first recording of an Ives composition by one of the large commercial companies.

126. Letter of Harmony T. Ives to Lehman Engel, June 6, 1937, reproduced copy in Ives Collection.

127. E.g., letter of Lehman Engel to Charles E. Ives, March 5, 1939, Ives Collection.

128. Letter of Harmony T. Ives to Gerald Strang, December 11, 1938, reproduced copy in "New Music & Strang" file, Ives Collection; letter of Gerald Strang to Charles E. Ives, December 18, 1938, in "New Music & Strang" file, Ives Collection; letter of Harmony T. Ives to Gerald Strang, March 26, 1939, reproduced copy in "New Music & Strang" file, Ives Collection; letter of Gerald Strang to Charles E. Ives, April 24, 1939, in "New Music & Strang" file, Ives Collection; letter of Gerald Strang to Charles E. Ives, June 12, 1939, in "New Music & Strang" file, Ives Collection; letter of Gerald Strang to the editorial board of *New Music,* July 10, 1939, in "New Music & Strang" file, Ives Collection; Charles E. Ives, 1st sketch for letter of Harmony T. Ives to Gerald Strang, July 20, 1939, in "New Music & Strang" file, Ives Collection; letter of Harmony T. Ives to Gerald Strang, July 20, 1939, reproduced copy in "New Music & Strang" file, Ives Collection; letter of Gerald Strang to Charles E. Ives, September 16, 1939, in "New Music & Strang" file, Ives Collection.

129. Hitchcock, *Music in the United States,* pp. 200–201; William Schuman, "A Brief Study of Music Organizations Founded in the Interest of the Living Composer," *Twice a Year* 5–6 (Fall–Winter, 1940, and Spring–Summer, 1941): 361–67.

130. Another was John Kirkpatrick; see below.

131. E.g., Robert A. Simon, "Musical Events," *New Yorker,* January 28, 1939, p. 44.

132. "American Music Festival Held by Federal Project," *Musical Courier,* May 16, 1936, pp. 5, 29.

133. For the developments in American music during the 1930s that are discussed here, see Roy Harris, "Does Music Have to Be European?" *Scribner's Magazine* 91

(April, 1932): 204–9; Henry Cowell, "Towards Neo-primitivism," *Modern Music* 10 (March–April, 1933): 149–53; Charles Seeger, "On Proletarian Music," *Modern Music* 11 (March–April, 1934): 121–27; Roy Harris, "American Music Enters a New Phase," *Scribner's Magazine* 96 (October, 1934): 218–21; Henry Cowell, "Music," *Americana Annual, 1936,* pp. 472–75; Marc Blitzstein, "Coming—The Mass Audience!" *Modern Music* 13 (May–June, 1936): 23–29; Charles Louis Seeger, "Grass Roots for American Composers," *Modern Music* 16 (March–April, 1939): 143–49; Paul Rosenfeld, "Folksong and Culture-Politics," *Modern Music* 17 (October–November, 1939): 18–24; Aaron Copland, *Our New Music: Leading Composers in Europe and America* (New York: McGraw-Hill Book Company, Inc., 1941), *passim;* Siegmeister, ed., *Music Lover's Handbook, passim;* and Hitchcock, *Music in the United States,* chap. 9.

134. Cowell, "Trends in American Music," in *American Composers on American Music,* ed. Cowell, pp. 3–13, esp. pp. 12–13.

135. Aaron Copland, "Composer from Brooklyn," *Magazine of Art* 32 (September, 1939): 550.

136. E.g., Pro Musica became inactive in New York after 1930; the Pan American Association of Composers became inactive after 1934; *Trend* ceased publication in 1935.

137. Aaron Copland, "Scores and Records," *Modern Music* 14 (May–June, 1937): 232.

138. Davidson Taylor, "Why Not Try the Air?" *Modern Music* 15 (January–February, 1938): 87.

139. Letter of Henry Cowell to Charles E. Ives, April 28, 1936, reproduced copy in Ives Collection.

140. Form letter (and Ives's marginal comments thereon) from Dorothy Lawton, July 18, 1936, in Scrapbook No. 3, p. 234, Ives Collection.

141. E.g., letter of Charles E. Ives to Henry Cowell, April 17, 1930, reproduced copy in Ives Collection; Charles E. Ives, undated [December, 1932?] sketch for letter to Henry Allen Moe in answer to Moe's letter of November 29, 1932, in the file of Ives-Becker correspondence in custody of John Kirkpatrick.

142. While not entirely in sympathy with the new American musical trends of the middle 1930s, Cowell was certainly capable of accommodating himself to them.

143. Ives, *Memos,* app. 8, p. 198.

144. Letter of John Kirkpatrick to Charles E. Ives, January 5, 1934, Ives Collection.

145. Letter of John Kirkpatrick to Harmony T. Ives, dated "Wednesday" [January 29, 1936], Ives Collection. The program for this Town Hall recital is in the file of programs and reviews, Ives Collection.

146. Letter of John Kirkpatrick to Charles E. Ives, July 25, 1937, Ives Collection.

147. Letter of John Kirkpatrick to Charles E. Ives, undated [June 22, 1938], Ives Collection. This lecture-recital took place on June 21, 1938.

148. The program for this recital, which took place at the Old House (a private home in Cos Cob), is in the file of programs and reviews, Ives Collection.

149. Paul Rosenfeld, "Ives' Concord Sonata," *Modern Music* 16 (January–February, 1939): 109–12.

150. Letter of John Kirkpatrick to Charles E. Ives, undated [May 13, 1938], Ives Collection.

151. Letter of Lawrence Gilman to Harmony T. Ives, January 19, 1939, Ives Collection.

152. The program for this Town Hall recital of January 20, 1939, is in the file of programs and reviews, Ives Collection.

153. Lawrence Gilman, "Music," *New York Herald Tribune,* January 21, 1939, p. 9.

154. Telegram from Charles E. Ives to John Kirkpatrick, January 21, 1939, in possession of John Kirkpatrick; letter of Lawrence Gilman to Harmony T. Ives, January 24, 1939, Ives Collection.

155. Olin Downes, "A Lonely American Composer," *New York Times,* January 29, 1939, sec. 9, p. 7. Downes had, however, attempted to meet Ives before 1939: letter of Elie Siegmeister to Charles E. Ives, October 20, 1938, Ives Collection.

156. "Insurance Man," *Time,* January 30, 1939, pp. 44–45.

157. John Sebastian, "Charles Ives at Last," *New Masses,* February 7, 1939, p. 30. "John Sebastian" was actually the composer Goddard Lieberson.

158. Interview with John Kirkpatrick by Vivian Perlis and Leroy Parkins, February 6, 1970, Tape #32C, Ives Oral History Project. The announcement and the program for this Town Hall recital of February 24, 1939, in which Kirkpatrick was assisted by the mezzo-soprano Mina Hager, are in the file of programs and reviews, Ives Collection.

159. Olin Downes, "Concert Devoted to Music by Ives," *New York Times,* February 25, 1939, p. 18.

160. E.g., Olin Downes, "An American Composer," *Musical Quarterly* 4 (January, 1918): 23–36; Olin Downes, "A Nation's Musical Frontiers," *New York Times,* June 3, 1934, sec. 9, p. 5.

161. An invitation to this recital of May 14, 1939, and the program for it are in the file of programs and reviews, Ives Collection.

162. In the "Yale 1898" file, Ives Collection, there is a program (signed by those present) for this dinner, which was held on May 17, 1939, at the University Club, New York City.

163. Letter of Gerald Strang to Charles E. Ives, March 13, 1939, in "New Music & Strang" file, Ives Collection; letter of Harmony T. Ives to John Kirkpatrick, February 2, [1939], in possession of John Kirkpatrick.

164. Thomas sang *The Greatest Man* and *The White Gulls* on a program of American music that he gave at Town Hall on March 24, 1940; the recital is reviewed in Olin Downes, "American Music Sung by Thomas," *New York Times,* March 25, 1940, p. 10. For Heifetz's interest in Ives, see letter of W. R. Magill to Charles E. Ives, February 10, 1939, in "M" file, Ives Collection.

165. Muriel Rukeyser, *A Turning Wind: Poems* (New York: Viking Press, 1939), pp. 115–20.

166. "Concerts for the Month: Jerome Goldstein," *Musical Advance,* April, 1924, pp. [17]–[18].

167. Richard H. Pells, *Radical Visions and American Dreams: Culture and Social*

Thought in the Depression Years (New York: Harper & Row, Publishers, 1973), pp. 310–19.

168. Quoted in "New York Artists Reshape America," p. 14.

169. Gilman, "Music," January 21, 1939, p. 9.

170. Roger Sessions, *Reflections on the Music Life in the United States,* Merlin Music Books, vol. 6 (New York: Merlin Press, [1956?]), p. 132.

171. Charles E. Ives, 1st [?] sketch for letter of Harmony T. Ives to John Kirkpatrick, October 11, 1935, Ives Collection.

172. Ives, *Essays before a Sonata,* p. 45.

173. Oscar Thompson, "Views on an All-Ives Concert," *Sun* (New York), February 25, 1939, p. 28.

174. Elliott Carter, "Further Notes on the Winter Season," *Modern Music* 16 (March–April, 1939): 176.

175. Carter interview, June 20, 1969, Tapes #14A and #14B.

176. Carter, "Case of Mr. Ives," pp. 175–76.

177. *Ibid.,* pp. 172–75.

Notes to Chapter 9: Recognition since 1939

1. The first public performances of both these sonatas were given in Los Angeles in the Fourth Sunday Evenings on the Roof concert series, which was organized by the writer and music critic Peter Yates, an Ives enthusiast. The Fourth Sonata, played by Orline Burrow (violin) and Frances Mullen (piano), was first given on June 25, 1939; an announcement of the concert is in the file of programs and reviews, Ives Collection. The Third Sonata, played by Sol Babitz (violin) and Ingolf Dahl (piano), was apparently first given on August 25, 1940: letter of Gerald Strang to Charles E. Ives, August 29, 1940, in "New Music & Strang" file, Ives Collection; letter of Sol Babitz to Charles E. Ives, November 3, 1940, typed copy in Ives Collection. Frances Mullen (Mrs. Yates) also played the complete *Concord* Sonata in her husband's series in September, 1940: "Sharps and Flats," *Los Angeles Times,* September 22, 1940, sec. 3, p. 5.

2. Letter of Edith O. Ives to Lehman Engel, October 16, 1938, reproduced copy in Ives Collection; letter of Edith Ives Tyler to Radiana Pazmor, March 31, 1940, reproduced copy in Ives Collection; letter of Harmony T. Ives to Henry Cowell, August 14, 1940, reproduced copy in Ives Collection.

3. Letter of Lehman Engel to Harmony T. Ives, March 24, 1939, Ives Collection; letter of Harmony T. Ives to Lehman Engel, July 4, 1939, reproduced copy in Ives Collection.

4. Letter of John Kirkpatrick to Harmony T. Ives, dated "Saturday" [February 17, 1940], Ives Collection.

5. Interview with George F. Roberts by Martha Maas, June 16, 1969, Tapes #12A and #12B, Ives Oral History Project.

6. "Henry Cowell Wins a Parole," *New York Times,* May 9, 1940, p. 12.

7. *Ibid.;* letter of Johanna Magdalena Beyer to Charles E. Ives, May 24, 1940, in "B" file, Ives Collection.

8. Letter of Harmony T. Ives to Henry Cowell, August 14, 1940, reproduced copy in Ives Collection.

9. See the letterhead of the letter of Florence S. Strauss to Henry Cowell, December 2, 1940, in the "New Music & Strang" file, Ives Collection.

10. Letter of Harmony T. Ives to Henry Cowell, September 27, 1941, reproduced copy in Ives Collection; letter of Harmony T. Ives to Henry Cowell, October 30, [1941], reproduced copy in Ives Collection.

11. Letter of Harmony T. Ives to Gerald Strang, December 20, [1939], reproduced copy in "New Music & Strang" file, Ives Collection; letter of Johanna Magdalena Beyer to Charles E. Ives, May 24, 1940, in "B" file, Ives Collection.

12. Letter of Harmony T. Ives to Henry Cowell, August 14, 1940, reproduced copy in Ives Collection; letter of Harmony T. Ives to Henry Cowell, undated [December 20, 1940], reproduced copy in Ives Collection.

13. Letter of Henry Cowell to Harmony T. Ives, September 15, 1941, reproduced copy in Ives Collection.

14. Letter of Charles E. Ives and Harmony T. Ives to Henry Cowell, September 18, 1941, reproduced copy in Ives Collection.

15. Letter of Henry Cowell to Charles E. Ives, April 15, 1942, reproduced copy in Ives Collection.

16. Cf. Charles E. Ives, undated sketches for letter of Harmony T. Ives to "Mr. Belden," in "B" file, Ives Collection.

17. Letter of Henry Cowell to Charles E. Ives, November 26, 1941, reproduced copy in Ives Collection. The program for the Szigeti recital, which took place at Carnegie Hall, New York City, on February 25, 1942, is in the file of programs and reviews, Ives Collection. Andor Foldes was the pianist at the recital and for the recording. The sonata was also published by Arrow Music Press in 1942.

18. "Neglected Works: A Symposium," *Modern Music* 23 (Winter, 1946): 3–12.

19. Elliott Carter, "Ives Today: His Vision and Challenge," *Modern Music* 21 (May–June, 1944): 199–202; Elliott Carter, "An American Destiny," *Listen,* November, 1946, pp. 4–7.

20. Carter interview, June 20, 1969, Tapes #14A, #14B, and #14C.

21. Letter of Henry Cowell to Charles E. Ives, September 21, 1944, reproduced copy in Ives Collection; letter of Elliott Carter to Charles E. Ives, October 20, 1944, in "American Music Center" file, Ives Collection.

22. Letter of Harmony T. Ives to Henry Cowell, September 29, 1944, reproduced copy in Ives Collection.

23. E.g., letter of Harmony T. Ives to Hope Kirkpatrick, February 2, 1946, in possession of John Kirkpatrick.

24. Letter of Henry Seidel Canby to Charles E. Ives, December 20, 1945, in "National Institute of Arts & Letters" file, Ives Collection.

25. Carter interview, June 20, 1969, Tapes #14A and #14B.

26. Interview with Lou Harrison by Vivian Perlis, March 24, 1970, Tapes #36A, #36B, #36C, and #36D, Ives Oral History Project.

27. Letter of Lou Harrison to Harmony T. Ives, undated [February 16 or 17, 1946], Ives Collection.

28. The program for this concert is in the file of programs and reviews, Ives Collection.

29. Noel Straus, "Symphony by Ives in World Premiere," *New York Times,* April 6, 1946, p. 10.

30. The program for this all-Ives concert, which was given at Columbia University's McMillin Academic Theater on May 11, 1946, is in the file of programs and reviews, Ives Collection. Edgar Schenkman conducted a chamber orchestra of students from the Juilliard Graduate School in the symphony. The first public performances of the Second String Quartet and *Central Park in the Dark* were also part of the program. The Third Symphony was published in 1947 by the Arrow Music Press.

31. "Barber Concerto Gets Critics' Prize," *New York Times,* June 28, 1946, p. 16.

32. Ethel Beckwith, "Pulitzer Prize Winner Scoffs at $1,000 Award," *Sunday Herald* (Bridgeport, Conn.), May 11, 1947, pp. 1, 16.

33. Howard Taubman, "Posterity Catches Up with Charles Ives," *New York Times,* October 23, 1949, sec. 6, pp. 15, 34–36.

34. E.g., letter of Wladimir Lakond to Charles E. Ives, May 11, 1951, in "Southern Music Publishing Co." file, Ives Collection.

35. Letter of Lou Harrison to Charles E. Ives, undated [c. February 1, 1949], Ives Collection.

36. The programs for this New York recital by Masselos on February 17, 1949, and for his subsequent Carnegie Hall recital of March 27, 1949 (at which he repeated the sonata) are in the file of programs and reviews, Ives Collection.

37. E.g., letter of Henry Cowell to Charles E. Ives, April 25, 1952, reproduced copy in Ives Collection.

38. Letter of Henry Cowell to Harmony T. Ives, July 16, 1951, reproduced copy in Ives Collection.

39. Cowell and Cowell, *Charles Ives and His Music,* p. 208.

40. On the other hand, and without any sense of incongruity, the choreographer George Balanchine used several Ives compositions for a ballet (*Ivesiana*) whose "modern" subject matter was utterly at variance with the optimistic and homely "substance" of the original music. See Walter Terry, "New York City Ballet," *New York Herald Tribune,* September 15, 1954, p. 26; and Clive Barnes, "Dance: Ives sans Currier," *New York Times,* December 5, 1966, p. 65.

41. E.g., Arthur V. Berger, "Three New Sonatas," *New York Herald Tribune,* November 12, 1946, p. 21; Arthur Berger, "League of Composers," *New York Herald Tribune,* April 7, 1951, p. 7.

42. Arthur Berger, "Ives in Retrospect," *Saturday Review,* July 31, 1954, p. 62.

43. Interview with Arthur Berger by Vivian Perlis, October 19, 1970, Tapes #41A, #41B, and #41C, Ives Oral History Project (hereafter cited as Berger interview).

44. Richard Hofstadter, *The American Political Tradition and the Men Who Made It* (New York: Alfred A. Knopf, 1948), p. v.

45. Olin Downes, "Six Pianists Heard in Special Concert," *New York Times,* December 23, 1948, p. 23.

46. E.g., letter of Charles E. Ives to Walter Damrosch, December 14, 1911, carbon copy in "D" file, Ives Collection; letter of Charles E. Ives to Arthur Judson, March 6, 1923, carbon copy in "N" file, Ives Collection; letter of Leopold Stokowski to Harmony T. Ives, May 12, 1932, in Scrapbook No. 3, p. 191, Ives Collection; Charles E. Ives, undated [c. 1943] sketch for letter of Harmony T. Ives to Serge Koussevitzky, in "K" file, Ives Collection.

47. The program for the Boston concerts, which took place in Symphony Hall on February 13 and 14, 1948, and the program for the New York concert, which took place in Carnegie Hall on February 21, 1948, are in the file of programs and reviews, Ives Collection.

48. L. A. Sloper, "Ives' Orchestral Set Heard at Symphony," *Christian Science Monitor,* February 14, 1948, p. 7.

49. "Double Indemnity," *Time,* February 23, 1948, p. 67.

50. Taubman, "Posterity Catches Up with Ives," pp. 15, 34–36.

51. *"Life* Congratulates . . . . Charles E. Ives," *Life,* October 31, 1949, p. 45.

52. Letter of Wladimir Lakond to Harmony T. Ives, December 13, 1949, in "Southern Music Publishing Co." file, Ives Collection.

53. The symphony was given by Bernstein and the Philharmonic-Symphony Society of New York in Carnegie Hall on February 22, 23, 24, and 25, 1951. An announcement for all four concerts and a program for the first two are in the file of programs and reviews, Ives Collection.

54. Quoted in letter of Harmony T. Ives to Leonard Bernstein, March 11, 1951, reproduction of typed copy in Cowell file, Ives Collection. Cf. Cowell and Cowell, *Charles Ives and His Music,* pp. 135–36. The CBS radio broadcast was heard by Ives on March 4, 1951.

55. Olin Downes, "Symphony by Ives Is Played in Full," *New York Times,* February 23, 1951, p. 33.

56. Virgil Thomson, "Music," *New York Herald Tribune,* February 23, 1951, p. 16.

57. For an example of the appeal that the symphony's Americanism had in the midst of the cold war, see H. E. McMahan, Jr., Letter to the Editor, *New York Times,* March 11, 1951, sec. 2, p. 6.

58. E.g., Cowell and Cowell, *Charles Ives and His Music,* p. 4.

59. Letter of Richard Donovan to Charles E. Ives, March 24, 1953, in "Yale Univ." file, Ives Collection.

60. Letter of Reuben A. Holden to Charles E. Ives, February 15, 1954, in "Yale Univ." file, Ives Collection.

61. See letter of Richard Donovan to Charles E. Ives, March 24, 1953, in "Yale Univ." file, Ives Collection, for Mrs. Ives's comment written at the bottom.

62. Letter of Harmony T. Ives to Reuben A. Holden, March 4, 1954, typed copy in Donovan file, Ives Collection.

63. Cowell and Cowell, *Charles Ives and His Music,* p. 4.

64. Personal information from John Kirkpatrick.

65. Jay S. Harrison, "Philharmonic's Season Begun by Bernstein," *New York Herald Tribune,* October 3, 1958, sec. 1, p. 11. These performances of the Second Symphony at Carnegie Hall were given at a "preview" on October 2 and at regular concerts on October 3, 4, and 5, 1958.

66. "Philharmonic to Play U.S. Work at Each of 50 Concerts Abroad," *New York Times,* June 19, 1959, p. 31; Osgood Caruthers, "Bernstein, on Birthday, Leads Orchestra in 2 Stravinsky Works," *New York Times,* August 26, 1959, p. 25.

67. Herbert Kupferberg, "Ives: Painter in Music," *New York Herald Tribune,* April 1, 1962, sec. 4, p. 6.

68. E.g., Theodore Strongin, "Symphony by Ives to Get Premiere," *New York Times,* April 13, 1965, p. 33. Cf. John Kirkpatrick, Preface to *Symphony No. 4,* by Charles Ives (New York: Associated Music Publishers, Inc., c1965), p. x.

69. Harold C. Schonberg, "Music: Stokowski Conducts Ives's Fourth Symphony in World Premiere after 50 Years," *New York Times,* April 27, 1965, p. 29.

70. William Bender, " 'New' Ives Work: Bravo," *New York Herald Tribune,* April 27, 1965, p. 15.

71. "The Transcendentalist," *Newsweek,* May 10, 1965, p. 101.

72. "Television," *New York Times,* February 23, 1967, p. 71.

73. Broadcast Music, Inc., in cooperation with the American Symphony Orchestra League, *BMI Orchestral Program Survey, 1969–70 Season* (New York: Broadcast Music, Inc., [1970]), pp. 7–8.

74. "Crisis in American Classical Music Recording," *Stereo Review,* February, 1971, pp. 56–84.

75. The connections with Ives mentioned in this paragraph, as well as those discussed in the following paragraphs, were clearly exemplified by the Ives at Minnesota festivals, held at the University of Minnesota in Minneapolis; a schedule of events for the 1971 festival (held in April and May) and reproduced copies of some of the programs are in the file of programs and reviews, Ives Collection.

76. Raymond Ericson, "Horizons Expand in the Mountains," *New York Times,* March 30, 1969, sec. 2, pp. 19, 27; Howard Taubman, "Amsterdam to See an Anti-U.S. Opera," *New York Times,* June 21, 1969, p. 18; Clive Barnes, "Theater: Amsterdam Hit," *New York Times,* July 8, 1969, p. 36; Everett Helm, "Too Many Cooks Make Operatic Hash," *New York Times,* July 13, 1969, sec. 2, p. 17.

77. See the correspondence concerning the society in the "Societies (U.S., Netherlands)" file, Ives Collection; and "Charles Ives Society Founded in Holland," *Sonorum Speculum* (Amsterdam), No. 35 (Summer, 1968), pp. 13–16. De Leeuw also coauthored a book on Ives: J. Bernlef and Reinbert de Leeuw, *Charles Ives,* speciale paperback (Amsterdam: De Bezige Bij, 1969). For another example of enthusiasm for Ives among the European avant-garde of this period, see Hans G. Helms, jacket notes for *"Concord" Sonata: Second Pianoforte Sonata, "Concord, Mass. 1840–1860,"* by Charles Ives (Time Records S/8005).

78. Berger interview, October 19, 1970, Tape #41A.

79. John Cage, *A Year from Monday: New Lectures and Writings* (Middletown, Conn.: Wesleyan University Press, 1967), p. 42.

80. "Evidence Points to Ives as First 12-tone User," *New York Times,* December 1, 1962, p. 17. On Tenney, see Eric Salzman, "Retrospective of Avant-garde Music," *New York Herald Tribune,* December 21, 1963, p. 6; and James Tenney, "Some Notes on the Music of Charles Ives," mimeographed notes to accompany the program of Ives's music given at McMillin Theater, Columbia University, New York City, on May 11, 1963. A copy of Tenney's notes is in the file of programs and reviews, Ives Collection.

81. Ned Rorem, *Music and People* (New York: George Braziller, 1968), pp. 212–13.

82. Eric Salzman, *Twentieth-Century Music: An Introduction,* Prentice-Hall History of Music Series (Englewood Cliffs, N.J., 1967), pp. 142–53.

83. Eric Salzman, "Charles Ives, American," *Commentary,* August, 1968, p. 41.

84. Quoted on the front cover of Charles Ives, *Symphony No. 2,* with jacket notes by David Johnson (Columbia KL 5489).

85. Robert Evett, "Music: Shadow and Substance in Ives," *Atlantic,* May, 1969, p. 110. For another dissenting view, see Virgil Thomson, "The Ives Case," *New York Review of Books,* May 21, 1970, pp. 9–11.

Notes to Epilogue: An Interpretation

1. David Riesman, in collaboration with Reuel Denney and Nathan Glazer, *The Lonely Crowd: A Study of the Changing American Character* (New Haven: Yale University Press, 1950), pp. 287–88, 324–25.

2. Quoted in Victor Ilyich Seroff, in collaboration with Nadejda Galli-Shohat, *Dmitri Shostakovich: The Life and Background of a Soviet Composer* (New York: Alfred A. Knopf, 1943), pp. 204–7.

3. D. Rabinovich, *Dmitry Shostakovich, Composer,* trans. George Hanna (Moscow: Foreign Languages Publishing House, 1959), p. 113.

4. Quoted in Israel V. Nestyev, *Prokofiev,* trans. Florence Jonas, with a Foreword by Nicolas Slonimsky (Stanford, Calif.: Stanford University Press, 1960), pp. 405–6.

5. Cf. Seroff, *Dmitri Shostakovich,* chap. 7. Ives had read Tolstoy's *What Is Art?* But he apparently balked at Tolstoy's extremely narrow definition of good art, which rejected even Beethoven's Ninth Symphony because it was comprehensible to only the few and not the many. See Ives, *Essays before a Sonata,* p. 5.

6. Rabinovich, *Dmitry Shostakovich,* pp. 9, 4.

7. Ives, *Essays before a Sonata,* p. 46.

8. Cf. Boris Schwarz, *Music and Musical Life in Soviet Russia, 1917–1970* (New York: W. W. Norton & Company, Inc., 1972), pp. 246–48.

9. Quoted in Rabinovich, *Dmitry Shostakovich,* pp. 114–15.

10. On the other hand, Ives might be compared with the American painter Louis Eilshemius, who was a decade older than he. Although Eilshemius had been trained in the world of professional artists and was something of a Bohemian, he suffered a long neglect and a belated recognition that were in many ways similar to Ives's. But Eilshemius's creative genius was certainly not on the same high level as Ives's, nor did

his paintings exhibit a pioneering modernism comparable to Ives's. For most of his active career as a painter, Eilshemius's extreme lack of recognition (though difficult to explain) was not basically the result of any experimentalism in his work. See William Schack, *And He Sat among the Ashes* (New York: American Artists Group, 1939).

11. Quoted in Clifton Joseph Furness, ed., *The Genteel Female: An Anthology* (New York: Alfred A. Knopf, 1931), p. xix.

12. Riesman, *Lonely Crowd*, pp. 324–25.

NOTE ON SOURCES

❦

The principal location of primary source materials on Charles Ives, his background, his creative life, and his recognition is the Ives Collection at the John Herrick Jackson Music Library of Yale University, in New Haven, Connecticut. The key to the arrangement of Ives's music manuscripts, which are the heart of the Ives Collection, is to be found in John Kirkpatrick, comp., "A Temporary Mimeographed Catalogue of the Music Manuscripts and Related Materials of Charles Edward Ives . . ." ([New Haven]: Library of the Yale School of Music, 1960); a revision of this catalogue is now in progress. Professor Kirkpatrick, the curator of the Ives Collection, has arranged both the manuscripts themselves and his catalogue according to a coding system, by which each separate composition—that is, all the manuscript pages and fragments connected with that composition—is assigned a separate code number. In citing Ives's music manuscripts in my notes, I have referred to this code number in each case, and I have also followed the description given in the catalogue for each manuscript page. Since one composition is often written on the back of another, however, it is necessary to consult Professor Kirkpatrick's catalogue in order to find the exact location of any given manuscript page. The Ives Collection also contains negative photostats of most of the music manuscripts.

Technically, only Ives's music manuscripts are the property of Yale University. But a large amount of other Ives material is also physically part of the Ives Collection, having been transferred there by Professor Kirkpatrick from the Iveses' home in West Redding (with Mrs. Ives's permission) over a period of years. This material includes correspondence, scrapbooks, diaries, tax records, clippings with marginal comments, manuscripts and typescripts of prose writings, and other jottings on music, politics, and business, as well as a number of photographs of Ives, his family, and his friends. The letters cited in my notes are filed in the collection under the name of Ives's correspondent (or the correspondent's spouse) unless I have specified a different location; my citations of the scrapbooks and diaries use the identifying numbers which Professor Kirkpatrick has assigned to them. The collection also contains an extensive file of programs and reviews of Ives performances and a series of tape-recorded interviews (the Ives Oral History Project) made by Vivian Perlis with about sixty people who had known Ives.

In addition to what is available in the Ives Collection, Professor Kirkpatrick has assembled his own large collection of Ives materials and information; particularly important are his copies of Ives family letters, including a considerable number (which Mrs. Ives allowed him to copy in part) from Harmony T. Ives to her husband both before and after their marriage. Professor Kirkpatrick has shared these materials and his knowledge about Ives with me; he has also made possible several visits to the Iveses' house at West Redding, where I found the books in Charles Ives's library to be of especial interest.

Several other sources of information have proved very valuable: for Ives's Danbury years (particularly for local newspapers), the Danbury Public Library, the Scott-Fanton Museum, and the Ruth A. Haas Library of Western Connecticut State College, all in Danbury, Connecticut; for his Yale years, the Yale University Archives in the Yale University Library; for his career in life insurance, the Research Library of the Mutual Life Insurance Company of New York, in New York City; and for his musical recognition in New York City and elsewhere (particularly for reviews in newspapers and music journals), the New York Public Library.

There are two published collections of Ives's prose writings on music, politics, and business: Charles Ives, *Essays before a Sonata, The Majority, and Other Writings,* ed. Howard Boatwright (New York: W. W. Norton & Company, Inc., Norton Library, 1970); and Charles E. Ives, *Memos,* ed. John Kirkpatrick (New York: W. W. Norton & Company, Inc., 1972), which contains, in addition to the indispensable autobiographical *Memos,* a number of useful appendices prepared by John Kirkpatrick, including several of Ives's shorter writings and notes. Ives's letters to Slonimsky are published in Nicolas Slonimsky, *Music since 1900,* 4th ed. (New York: Charles Scribner's Sons, 1971), pp. 1318–49. Portions of the tape-recorded interviews with those who knew Ives are in Vivian Perlis, *Charles Ives Remembered: An Oral History* (New Haven: Yale University Press, 1974). A list giving the history of Ives's published compositions down to 1960 is in Kirkpatrick's "Catalogue," p. 271. The history of the recording of Ives's works down through 1971 can be followed in Richard Warren, Jr., comp., *Charles E. Ives: Discography,* Historical Sound Recordings Publication Series, No. 1 (New Haven: Historical Sound Recordings, Yale University Library, 1972), which is exhaustive. Frederick Freedman, *Charles E. Ives: A Preliminary Bibliography of the Literature,* Bibliographies in American Music (Detroit: Information Coordinators, Inc., for the College Music Society, forthcoming) should prove very valuable.

SELECTED BIBLIOGRAPHY

Andrews, Kenneth R. *Nook Farm: Mark Twain's Hartford Circle.* Cambridge, Mass.: Harvard University Press, 1950.

Another Yale Graduate [Charles E. Ives]. Letter to the Editor. *New York Times,* May 14, 1922, sec. 8, p. 8.

Bailey, James Montgomery. *History of Danbury, Conn., 1684–1896.* From notes and manuscript left by him, compiled with additions by Susan Benedict Hill. New York: Burr Printing House, 1896.

Bellamann, Henry. "Charles Ives: The Man and His Music." *Musical Quarterly* 19 (January, 1933): 45–58.

———. " 'Concord, Mass., 1840–1860' (A Piano Sonata by Charles E. Ives.)." Review in the *Double Dealer* 2 (October, 1921): 166–69.

———. "The Music of Charles Ives." *Pro-Musica Quarterly,* March, 1927, pp. 16–22.

Berger, Arthur. *Aaron Copland.* New York: Oxford University Press, 1953.

———. "Ives in Retrospect." *Saturday Review,* July 31, 1954, pp. 62–63.

———. "The Songs of Charles Ives." *Musical Mercury* 1 (October–November, 1934): 97–98.

————. "The Young Composers' Group." *Trend* 2 (April–June, 1933): 26–28.

Boatwright, Howard. "Ives' Quarter-Tone Impressions." *Perspectives of New Music,* Spring–Summer, 1965, pp. 22–31.

Booth, Earl Walter. "New England Quartet: E. A. Robinson, Robert Frost, Charles Ives and Carl Ruggles." Ph.D. dissertation, University of Utah, 1974.

Brant, Henry. "Henry Cowell—Musician and Citizen." *Etude,* February, 1957, pp. 15, 47, 58–59; March, 1957, pp. 20, 60–61; April, 1957, pp. 22, 60–61.

Brion, John P. *Mr. Life Insurance: Julian S. Myrick, Mutual of New York.* Pamphlet issued by the Mutual Life Insurance Company of New York, n.d.

Brooks, Van Wyck. *America's Coming-of-age.* New York: B. W. Huebsch, 1915.

————. *The Ordeal of Mark Twain.* New York: E. P. Dutton & Company, 1920.

Call, William Anson. "A Study of the Transcendental Aesthetic Theories of John S. Dwight and Charles E. Ives and the Relationship of These Theories to Their Respective Work as Music Critic and Composer." D.Mus.A. dissertation, University of Illinois at Urbana-Champaign, 1971.

Canby, Henry Seidel. *Alma Mater: The Gothic Age of the American College.* New York: Farrar & Rinehart, Inc., 1936.

Carter, Elliott. "An American Destiny." *Listen,* November, 1946, pp. 4–7.

————. "The Case of Mr. Ives." *Modern Music* 16 (March–April, 1939): 172–76.

————. "Expressionism and American Music." *Perspectives of New Music,* Fall–Winter, 1965, pp. 1–13.

————. "Ives Today: His Vision and Challenge." *Modern Music* 21 (May–June, 1944): 199–202.

————. "Shop Talk by an American Composer." *Musical Quarterly* 46 (April, 1960): 189–201.

Charles, Sydney Robinson. "The Use of Borrowed Material in Ives' Second Symphony." *Music Review* 28 (May, 1967): 102–11.

Chase, Gilbert. *America's Music, from the Pilgrims to the Present.* Rev. 2d ed. New York: McGraw-Hill Book Company, 1966.

Citkowitz, Israel. "Experiment and Necessity—New York, 1932." *Modern Music* 10 (January–February, 1933): 110–14.

Clark, Sondra Rae. "The Element of Choice in Ives's *Concord Sonata.*" *Musical Quarterly* 60 (April, 1974): 167–86.

———. "The Transcendental Philosophy of Charles E. Ives As Expressed in *The Second Sonata for Pianoforte, 'Concord, Mass., 1840–1860.'* " Master's thesis, San Jose State College, 1966.

Clough, Shepard B. *A Century of American Life Insurance: A History of the Mutual Life Insurance Company of New York, 1843–1943.* New York: Columbia University Press, 1946.

Clurman, Harold. *The Fervent Years: The Story of the Group Theatre and the Thirties.* New York: Alfred A. Knopf, 1945.

Copland, Aaron. *Music and Imagination.* Cambridge, Mass.: Harvard University Press, 1952.

———. *The New Music, 1900–1960.* Rev. and enl. ed. New York: W. W. Norton & Company, Inc., 1968.

———. "One Hundred and Fourteen Songs." *Modern Music* 11 (January–February, 1934): 59–64.

Corner, Philip. "Thoreau, Charles Ives, and Contemporary Music." In *Henry David Thoreau: Studies and Commentaries,* edited by Walter Harding, George Brenner, and Paul A. Doyle. Rutherford, Madison, and Teaneck, N.J.: Fairleigh Dickinson University Press, 1972.

Cowell, Henry. "American Composers." In *Proceedings of the Ohio State Educational Conference, Eleventh Annual Session,* edited by Josephine H. MacLatchy. Issued as *Ohio State University Bulletin,* vol. 36, No. 3 (September 15, 1931).

———. "Music: Three Native Composers." *New Freeman* 1 (May 3, 1930): 184–86.

———, ed. *American Composers on American Music: A Symposium.* [Stanford University, Calif.]: Stanford University Press, 1933. Reprint ed., with a new introduction by the editor. New York: Frederick Ungar Publishing Co., 1962.

Cowell, Henry, and Cowell, Sidney. *Charles Ives and His Music.* Paperback ed. with additional material. New York: Oxford University Press, 1969.

Cowell, Sidney. "Ivesiana: 'More than Something Just Usual.' " *High Fidelity and Musical America,* October, 1974, pp. MA-14–MA-16.

Crunden, Robert M. "Charles Ives' Innovative Nostalgia." *Choral Journal,* December, 1974, pp. 5–12.

———. *From Self to Society, 1919–1941.* Transitions in American Thought Series. Englewood Cliffs, N.J.: Prentice-Hall, Inc., Spectrum Books, 1972.

Cyr, Gordon. "Intervallic Structural Elements in Ives's Fourth Symphony." *Perspectives of New Music,* Spring–Summer and Fall–Winter, 1971, pp. 291–303.

"Danbury's Delight Is All for Music." *New York Herald,* January 5, 1890, Connecticut Edition section, p. [2].

Davidson, Audrey. "Transcendental Unity in the Works of Charles Ives." *American Quarterly* 22 (Spring, 1970): 35–44.

Davis, Thomas B., Jr. *Chronicles of Hopkins Grammar School, 1660–1935, Containing a Life of the Founder Together with School Records and Reminiscences Covering 275 Years.* New Haven: [Hopkins Grammar School], 1938.

Downes, Olin. "An American Composer." *Musical Quarterly* 4 (January, 1918): 23–36.

———. "Concert Devoted to Music by Ives." *New York Times,* February 25, 1939, p. 18.

———. "A Lonely American Composer." *New York Times,* January 29, 1939, sec. 9, p. 7.

———. "Music." *New York Times,* January 30, 1927, sec. 1, p. 28.

Edwards, Allen. *Flawed Words and Stubborn Sounds: A Conversation with Elliott Carter.* New York: W. W. Norton & Company, Inc., 1971.

Eiseman, David. "Charles Ives and the European Symphonic Tradition: A Historical Reappraisal." Ph.D. dissertation, University of Illinois at Urbana-Champaign, 1972.

Elkus, Jonathan. *Charles Ives and the American Band Tradition: A Centennial Tribute.* American Arts Pamphlet No. 4. Exeter, England: American Arts Documentation Centre, University of Exeter, 1974.

Evett, Robert. "Music: Shadow and Substance in Ives." *Atlantic,* May, 1969, pp. 110–11.

———. "Music Letter: A Post-mortem for Mr. Ives." *Kenyon Review* 16 (Autumn, 1954): 628–36.

Farwell, Arthur. "Pioneering for American Music." *Modern Music* 12 (March–April, 1935): 116–22.

Fletcher, Lucille. "A Connecticut Yankee in Music." Unpublished article written c. 1939. (Copies in Ives Collection.)

Frankenstein, Alfred. "Taking Cognizance of Tenth Anniversary of New Music Society." *San Francisco Chronicle,* March 31, 1935, p. D3.

Frantz, Donald Howe, Jr. "Search for Significant Form, 1905–1915: An Evaluation of the Symbols of Tradition and Revolt in American Literature, Painting, and Music." Ph.D. dissertation, University of Southern California, 1960.

Freedman, Frederick. *Charles E. Ives: A Preliminary Bibliography of the Literature.* Bibliographies in American Music. Detroit: Information Coordinators, Inc., for the College Music Society, forthcoming.

Furness, Clifton Joseph, ed. *The Genteel Female: An Anthology.* New York: Alfred A. Knopf, 1931.

Gilman, Lawrence. "Music." *New York Herald Tribune,* January 31, 1927, p. 11.

————. "Music." *New York Herald Tribune,* January 21, 1939, p. 9.

Goldman, Richard Franko. "Wallingford Riegger." *HiFi/Stereo Review,* April, 1968, pp. 57–67.

Goss, Madeleine. *Modern Music-Makers: Contemporary American Composers.* New York: E. P. Dutton & Company, Inc., 1952.

Hall, David. "Charles Ives: An American Original." *HiFi/Stereo Review,* September, 1964, pp. 43–58.

————. "Premiere and Cultural Turning Point: Charles Ives' Fourth Symphony: An Account of the History and Preparation of the Score, the Problematic Rehearsals, and the First Performance of an Almost Legendary Work." *HiFi/Stereo Review,* July, 1965, pp. 55–58.

Harris, Neil. *The Artist in American Society: The Formative Years, 1790–1860.* New York: George Braziller, 1966.

Harrison, Lou. Jacket notes for *Sonatas for Violin and Piano,* by Charles Ives. Philips World Series Stereo/PHC 2-002.

————. "On Quotation." *Modern Music* 23 (Summer, 1946): 166–69.

Henderson, Clayton Wilson. "Quotation as a Style Element in the Music of Charles Ives." Ph.D. dissertation, Washington University, 1969.

Herrmann, Bernard. "Charles Ives." *Trend* 1 (September–November, 1932): 99–101.

————. "Four Symphonies by Charles Ives." *Modern Music* 22 (May–June, 1945): 215–22.

Highet, Gilbert. *Talents and Geniuses: The Pleasures of Appreciation.* New York: Oxford University Press, 1957.

Hitchcock, H. Wiley. *Music in the United States: A Historical Introduction.* 2d ed. Prentice-Hall History of Music Series. Englewood Cliffs, N.J.: Prentice-Hall, Inc., 1974.

Hofstadter, Richard. *The Age of Reform: From Bryan to F. D. R.* New York: Alfred A. Knopf, 1955.

Howard, John Tasker. *Our American Music: Three Hundred Years of It.* New York: Thomas Y. Crowell Company, 1931.

————, with the assistance of Arthur Mendel. *Our Contemporary Composers: American Music in the Twentieth Century.* New York: Thomas Y. Crowell Company, 1941.

Ives, Charles E. "The Amount to Carry—Measuring the Prospect." *Eastern*

Underwriter, September 17, 1920, pt. 2 (Life Insurance Salesmanship Edition), pp. 35–38.

———. *The Amount to Carry—Measuring the Prospect.* Pamphlet issued by Ives & Myrick, printed c. 1921–1923.

———. *Essays before a Sonata.* New York: Knickerbocker Press, 1920.

———. *Essays before a Sonata, The Majority, and Other Writings.* Edited by Howard Boatwright. New York: W. W. Norton & Company, Inc., Norton Library, 1970.

———. "The Fourth Symphony for Large Orchestra." *New Music,* vol. 2, No. 2 (January, 1929).

———. *Memos.* Edited by John Kirkpatrick. New York: W. W. Norton & Company, Inc., 1972.

———. *114 Songs.* Redding, Conn.: C. E. Ives, 1922.

———. *Second Pianoforte Sonata: "Concord, Mass., 1840–60."* Redding, Conn.: C. E. Ives, 1920.

———. "Some 'Quarter-Tone' Impressions." *Franco-American Musical Society Quarterly Bulletin,* March, 1925, pp. 24–33.

———. *Sonata No. 4 for Violin and Piano: "Children's Day at the Camp Meeting."* New York: Associated Music Publishers, Inc., c1942.

———. *Symphony No. 4.* Preface by John Kirkpatrick. New York: Associated Music Publishers, Inc., c1965.

———. *"Three Places in New England": An Orchestral Set.* Boston: C. C. Birchard & Company, c1935.

Ives, J. Moss. *The "Ark" and the "Dove": The Beginning of Civil and Religious Liberties in America.* London, New York, and Toronto: Longmans, Green and Co., 1936.

"Ives & Myrick Have Floor in New Building." *Eastern Underwriter,* May 14, 1926, pp. 7, 13.

Johnson, Owen. *Stover at Yale.* Introduction by Kingman Brewster, Jr. Paperback ed. New York: Collier Books, 1968.

Kaplan, Justin. *Mr. Clemens and Mark Twain: A Biography.* New York: Simon and Schuster, 1966.

Kearns, William Kay. "Horatio Parker 1863–1919: A Study of His Life and Music." Ph.D. dissertation, University of Illinois, 1965.

Keller, Morton. *The Life Insurance Enterprise, 1885–1910: A Study in the Limits of Corporate Power.* Cambridge, Mass.: Harvard University Press, Belknap Press, 1963.

Kerr, Harrison. "Creative Music and the New School." *Trend* 2 (March–April, 1934): 86–91.

————. "The League of Composers Presents—Rather Tardily—Mr. Florent Schmitt." *Trend* 1 (January–March, 1933): 140–44.

Kirkpatrick, John. "The Evolution of Carl Ruggles: A Chronicle Largely in His Own Words." *Perspectives of New Music,* Spring–Summer, 1968, pp. 146–66.

————. Jacket notes for *The "Concord" Sonata,* by Charles Ives. Columbia MS 7192.

————, comp. "A Temporary Mimeographed Catalogue of the Music Manuscripts and Related Materials of Charles Edward Ives, 1874–1954, Given by Mrs. Ives to the Library of the Yale School of Music, September 1955." [New Haven]: Library of the Yale School of Music, 1960.

Klein, Howard. "Ives: A White Heat of Conviction." *New York Times,* April 16, 1967, sec. 2, p. 26.

Kumlien, Wendell Clarke. "The Sacred Choral Music of Charles Ives: A Study in Style Development." D.Mus.A. dissertation, University of Illinois, 1969.

Kwiat, Joseph J. "Robert Henri and the Emerson-Whitman Tradition." In *Studies in American Culture: Dominant Ideas and Images,* edited by Joseph J. Kwiat and Mary C. Turpie. Minneapolis: University of Minnesota Press, 1960.

Lang, Paul Henry. "Hidden Wonder in Ives' Scores." *New York Herald Tribune,* October 12, 1958, sec. 4, p. 5.

Layton, Bentley. "An Introduction to the *114 Songs* of Charles Ives." Bachelor's thesis, Harvard University, 1963.

Mannes, David. *Music Is My Faith: An Autobiography.* New York: W. W. Norton & Company, Inc., 1938.

Marshall, Dennis. "Charles Ives's Quotations: Manner or Substance?" *Perspectives of New Music,* Spring–Summer, 1968, pp. 45–56.

Mason, Daniel Gregory. *Contemporary Composers.* New York: Macmillan Company, 1918.

May, Henry F. *The End of American Innocence: A Study of the First Years of Our Own Time, 1912–1917.* New York: Alfred A. Knopf, 1959.

Mellers, Wilfrid. *Music and Society: England and the European Tradition.* 2d ed. London: Dennis Dobson Ltd., 1950.

————. *Music in a New Found Land: Themes and Developments in the History of American Music.* New York: Alfred A. Knopf, 1965.

————. "Music in the Melting Pot: Charles Ives and the Music of the Americas." *Scrutiny* 7 (March, 1939): 390–403.

Mellquist, Jerome, and Wiese, Lucie, eds. *Paul Rosenfeld: Voyager in the Arts.* New York: Creative Age Press, Inc., 1948.

Meyer, Alfred H. "Yaddo—a May Festival." *Modern Music* 9 (May–June, 1932): 172–76.

Moor, Paul. "On Horseback to Heaven: Charles Ives." *Harper's Magazine,* September, 1948, pp. 65–73.

Moore, Ralph Joseph, Jr. "The Background and the Symbol: Charles E. Ives: A Case Study in the History of American Cultural Expression." Senior essay, American Studies Department, Yale College, 1954.

Morgan, Robert P. "Rewriting Music History: Second Thoughts on Ives and Varèse." *Musical Newsletter,* January, 1973, pp. 3–12; April, 1973, pp. 15–23, 28.

Mussulman, Joseph A. *Music in the Cultured Generation: A Social History of Music in America, 1870–1900.* Pi Kappa Lambda Studies in American Music. Evanston, Ill.: Northwestern University Press, 1971.

Myrick, Julian S. "What the Business Owes to Charles E. Ives." *Eastern Underwriter,* September 19, 1930, pt. 2 (Life Insurance Salesmanship Edition), p. 18.

"New York Artists Reshape America over the Week End." *New York Herald Tribune,* July 10, 1932, sec. 1, p. 14.

Newman, Philip Edward. "The Songs of Charles Ives (1874–1954)." 3 vols. Ph.D. dissertation, University of Iowa, 1967.

Osgood, Robert Endicott. *Ideals and Self-interest in America's Foreign Relations: The Great Transformation of the Twentieth Century.* Chicago: University of Chicago Press, 1953.

Ouellette, Fernand. *Edgard Varèse.* Translated by Derek Coltman. New York: Orion Press, 1968.

Parker, Horatio. "Our Taste in Music." *Yale Review* 7 (July, 1918): 777–88.

Parmelee, Maurice F. "Yale and the Academic Ideal." *Yale Courant* 43 (December, 1906): 121–31.

Pells, Richard H. *Radical Visions and American Dreams: Culture and Social Thought in the Depression Years.* New York: Harper & Row, Publishers, 1973.

Perlis, Vivian. *Charles Ives Remembered: An Oral History.* New Haven: Yale University Press, 1974.

———. "Ives and Oral History." *Notes* 28 (June, 1972): 629–42.

Perry, Rosalie Sandra. *Charles Ives and the American Mind.* [Kent, Ohio]: Kent State University Press, 1974.

Pierson, George Wilson. *Yale: College and University, 1871–1937.* Vol. 1: *Yale*

College: An Educational History, 1871–1921. New Haven: Yale University Press, 1952.

Potter, Hugh. "Paul Rosenfeld: Criticism and Prophecy." *American Quarterly* 22 (Spring, 1970): 82–94.

Quandt, Jean B. *From the Small Town to the Great Community: The Social Thought of Progressive Intellectuals.* New Brunswick, N.J.: Rutgers University Press, 1970.

Riegger, Wallingford. "To the New through the Old." *Magazine of Art* 32 (August, 1939): 472–73, 490–92.

Rosenfeld, Paul. "Charles E. Ives." *New Republic* 71 (July 20, 1932): 262–64.

———. *Discoveries of a Music Critic.* New York: Harcourt, Brace and Company, 1936.

———. *An Hour with American Music.* The One Hour Series. Philadelphia: J. B. Lippincott Company, 1929.

———. "Ives' Concord Sonata." *Modern Music* 16 (January–February, 1939): 109–12.

———. "Two Native Groups." *New Republic* 75 (July 5, 1933): 209–10.

———. "When New York Became Central." *Modern Music* 20 (January–February, 1943): 83–89.

Rukeyser, Muriel. *A Turning Wind: Poems.* New York: Viking Press, 1939.

Salzedo, Carlos. "The American Left Wing." *Eolus* 11 (April, 1932): 9–29.

Salzman, Eric. "Carl Ruggles." *HiFi/Stereo Review,* September, 1966, pp. 53–63.

———. "Charles Ives, American." *Commentary,* August, 1968, pp. 37–43.

———. *"Modern Music* in Retrospect." *Perspectives of New Music,* Spring–Summer, 1964, pp. 14–20.

———. *Twentieth-Century Music: An Introduction.* Prentice-Hall History of Music Series. Englewood Cliffs, N.J.: Prentice-Hall, Inc., 1967.

Santayana, G[eorge]. "A Glimpse of Yale." *Harvard Monthly* 15 (December, 1892): 89–97.

Schrade, Leo. "Charles E. Ives: 1874–1954." *Yale Review* 44 (Summer, 1955): 535–45.

Schuman, William. "A Brief Study of Music Organizations Founded in the Interest of the Living Composer." *Twice a Year* 5–6 (Fall–Winter, 1940, and Spring–Summer, 1941): 361–67.

Seeger, Charles. "Charles Ives and Carl Ruggles." *Magazine of Art* 32 (July, 1939): 396–99, 435–37.

———. "Grass Roots for American Composers." *Modern Music* 16 (March–April, 1939): 143–49.

————. "Henry Cowell." *Magazine of Art* 33 (May, 1940): 288–89, 322–25, 327.

Semler, Isabel Parker, in collaboration with Pierson Underwood. *Horatio Parker: A Memoir for His Grandchildren Compiled from Letters and Papers.* New York: G. P. Putnam's Sons, 1942.

Sessions, Roger. *Reflections on the Music Life in the United States.* Merlin Music Books, vol. 6, New York: Merlin Press, [1956?].

Siegmeister, Elie. *Music and Society.* Critics Group Pamphlet No. 10. New York: Critics Group Press, 1938.

————, ed. *The Music Lover's Handbook.* New York: William Morrow and Company, 1943.

Slonimsky, Nicolas. "Composer Who Has Clung to His Own Way." *Boston Evening Transcript,* February 3, 1934, sec. 3, pp. 4–5.

————. *Music since 1900.* 4th ed. New York: Charles Scribner's Sons, 1971.

Slosson, Edwin E. *Great American Universities.* New York: Macmillan Company, 1910.

Smith, David Stanley. "A Study of Horatio Parker." *Musical Quarterly* 16 (April, 1930): 153–63.

Smith, Julia. *Aaron Copland: His Work and Contribution to American Music.* New York: E. P. Dutton & Company, Inc., 1955.

Sperling, Michael. "Varese and Contemporary Music." *Trend* 2 (May–June, 1934): 124–28.

Stambler, Bernard. "Four American Composers." *Juilliard Review,* Winter, 1955, pp. 7–16.

Stone, Kurt. "Ives's Fourth Symphony: A Review." *Musical Quarterly* 52 (January, 1966): 1–16.

Strong, Leah A. *Joseph Hopkins Twichell: Mark Twain's Friend and Pastor.* Athens, Ga.: University of Georgia Press, 1966.

Taubman, Howard. "Forget Posterity." *New York Times,* November 23, 1958, sec. 2, p. 11.

————. "Posterity Catches Up with Charles Ives." *New York Times,* October 23, 1949, sec. 6, pp. 15, 34–36.

Thompson, Oscar. "Views on an All-Ives Concert." *Sun* (New York), February 25, 1939, p. 28.

Thompson, Randall. "The Contemporary Scene in American Music." *Musical Quarterly* 18 (January, 1932): 9–17.

Thomson, Virgil. *American Music since 1910.* Introduction by Nicolas Nabokov. Twentieth-Century Composers, vol. 1. New York: Holt, Rinehart and Winston, 1971.

————. "Cowell's Magazine." *New York Herald Tribune,* November 2, 1947, sec. 5, p. 6.

"To Continue Ives & Myrick Name." *Eastern Underwriter,* January 23, 1942, p. 3.

Trimble, Lester. "Elliott Carter." *Stereo Review,* December, 1972, pp. 64–72.

Tryon, Winthrop P. "Pro Musica and Its Plans." *Christian Science Monitor,* June 6, 1925, p. 11.

Tuthill, Burnet C. "David Stanley Smith." *Musical Quarterly* 28 (January, 1942): 63–77.

Varèse, Louise. *Varèse: A Looking-Glass Diary.* Vol. 1: *1883–1928.* New York: W. W. Norton & Company, Inc., 1972.

Wallach, Laurence David. "The New England Education of Charles Ives." Ph.D. dissertation, Columbia University, 1973.

Ward, Charles Wilson. "Charles Ives: The Relationship between Aesthetic Theories and Compositional Processes." Ph.D. dissertation, University of Texas at Austin, 1974.

————. "The Use of Hymn Tunes as an Expression of 'Substance' and 'Manner' in the Music of Charles E. Ives, 1874–1954." Master's thesis, University of Texas at Austin, 1969.

Warren, Richard, Jr., comp. *Charles E. Ives: Discography.* Historical Sound Recordings Publication Series, No. 1. New Haven: Historical Sound Recordings, Yale University Library, 1972.

Welch, Lewis Sheldon, and Camp, Walter. *Yale: Her Campus, Class-rooms, and Athletics.* Boston: L. C. Page and Company, 1899.

Wiebe, Robert H. *The Search for Order, 1877–1920.* The Making of America. New York: Hill and Wang, 1967.

Yates, Peter. *Twentieth Century Music: Its Evolution from the End of the Harmonic Era into the Present Era of Sound.* New York: Random House, Pantheon Books, 1967.

INDEX

Composers in America (*continued*)
61, 91–92, 93, 193, 198, 221–22, 226–27, 234, 244–45, 246, 247, 250, 251, 272–73, 274, 275; younger men appearing in 1920s, 93, 192–93, 195, 219–22, 244–47, 273, 274, 323 (*see also* Cowell, Henry); Young Composers' Group, 244–48, 250–51, 283; responses to Great Depression and New Deal, 93, 234, 244–48, 250–51, 271, 272–75, 284; resistance to extramusical programs, 284–85, 285–86; avant-garde trends after World War II, 297–98; avant-garde trends of 1960s, 306, 307–8; "Ivesian" experimental tradition, 308. *See also* Cowell, Henry; International Composers' Guild; League of Composers; Modern music movement; Music in America; Pan American Association of Composers

Concord, Massachusetts, 105, 108, 278, 281, 285

Congregational church, 170. *See also* Center Church, New Haven; First Congregational Church, Danbury; West Street Congregational Church, Danbury

Congress. *See* United States Congress

Connecticut Commission for Promotion of Uniformity in Legislation in the United States, 21–22

Constitution. *See* United States Constitution

Coolidge, Calvin, 122, 138

Coolidge, Elizabeth Sprague, 149, 184–85

Copland, Aaron, 91, 92, 191, 192–93, 195, 200, 217–18, 219, 221, 222, 223, 238, 244, 248, 256, 271, 277, 308, 364 n. 24; on Ives, 147, 155, 182–83, 195, 245, 275, 293; and Yaddo festival (1932), 235, 238–39, 245; and simpler music of 1930s, 250, 251, 273–74, 275. Compositions: *Appalachian Spring*, 273–74; *Billy the Kid*, 273–74; music for the film *Our Town*, 273–74; Piano Variations, 273–74; *Rodeo*, 273–74

Corelli, Keith, 217

Cornell University, 302

Coronation (Holden), 62

Cos Cob Press, 364 n. 24

"Cousins' Beach," Westbrook, Connecticut, 21

Cowell, Henry, 156, 213–38 *passim*, 240, 244, 248, 252, 254, 257, 258, 259, 260, 264, 265, 267, 268, 269, 270, 271, 272–73, 276–77, 277–78, 291–93, 294, 299, 301, 302, 308, 370 n. 119, 372 n. 142; hears about Ives in 1920s, 187, 213, 356 n. 98; and Ives's recognition (to 1936), 53, 212, 213–38 *passim*, 240, 245, 252, 275, 276–77, 291, 309, 362 n. 171, 363 n. 9; and Ives's recognition (from 1940), 292, 293, 294, 296–97, 299, 302. Compositions: Hymns and Fuguing Tunes, 293; *Synchrony*, 231. Writings: *American Composers on American Music*, 236; *Charles Ives and His Music*, 302; *New Musical Resources*, 215–16

Cowell, Mrs. Henry (Sidney Robertson), 156, 292, 302; *Charles Ives and His Music*, 302

Creative artists in America: traditional social situation of, compared with Europe, 262–63, 314, 320–22; "highbrow" and "lowbrow," 161; alienation and reintegration of, 263, 266–67, 318; cultural nationalism of, 90, 244–45, 247, 272, 273, 282–83; in 1910s, 166, 171, 172, 318, 323; in 1920s, 194–95, 246–47, 282, 323; response to events of 1930s, 244–45, 247, 250, 272, 273, 282–83; in 1960s, 306, 307–8

Creston, Paul, 252

Cuba, 226, 237

Curtis Institute of Music, 199

Dada, 221

Damrosch, Walter, 27, 152, 153, 192

Danbury, Connecticut, 3–53 *passim*, 77, 88, 95, 96–97, 99, 103–5, 122, 300, 314–15, 319; history, industrial growth, and social structure, 3–9, 96, 100–101, 126, 176–77, 342 n. 1; community improvements in, 9–11, 108, 126; citizens' combined progressiveness and nostalgia, 7–8; non-British immigrants in, 4, 6–7,

tasteful aspects and moral dilemmas of
his work, 85, 114, 119, 163; attitudes
toward fellow businessmen, 119–20,
172–73, 174–76, 319; relations between
business and musical lives, 84–85, 86,
147, 153–54, 159, 162–63, 211–12, 271,
317, 322, 323; semiretirement, 89, 120,
191, 254; retirement, 120, 141, 191, 254
—personal characteristics: early popularity, 76–78, 83, 89; kindness, genuineness, and innocence, 77–78, 114, 117,
178, 179; idealism, 38, 42, 43, 61, 83, 89,
114–15, 129, 132, 134, 139, 140, 142,
143, 144, 203, 245; need to depersonalize activities, 114, 265, 284; ethnic,
religious, and racial tolerance, 7, 78,
127, 128, 140; shyness, 45, 47, 51,
52–53, 57, 62, 77, 82, 114, 125, 150, 174,
179, 181–82, 193; humor, 77, 78, 156,
174, 181–82, 186, 224, 225, 239, 242,
243, 279, 295, 300, 353 n. 60; love of
nicknames and puns, 36, 94, 224; optimism, 105, 125, 135–36, 139, 144, 160,
164; ambition, 84–86, 97; independence and individualism, 78–79, 95, 98,
126–27, 138, 141, 147–48, 156, 165,
175–76, 177, 227–28, 230, 241, 245,
251, 280, 311, 312, 315, 322, 324; un-
conventionality and unpredictability,
78, 169–70, 174; profanity, 165, 178,
268; argumentativeness, cantankerousness, and explosiveness, 78–79, 156,
162, 165, 174, 175, 178, 179, 182, 256,
257, 295; rebelliousness, 36, 45, 47, 62,
147–48, 156, 165, 172–79, 319; "safe"
rebelliousness, 170–71, 172, 178, 195,
257, 258, 268–69, 315, 320; role of
prankish boy, 47, 51–52, 66–67, 78,
81–82, 83, 150, 178, 179, 268–69,
295–96; role of transcendental old man,
178–79, 269, 280, 295–96; escape from
adult male responsibility, 178–79; later
temperament as a pattern of defenses,
179, 295–96; conformity to social and
cultural pressures, 34, 44, 59, 78–79,
81–83, 84–86, 114, 142, 170, 176, 310,
312–13, 314–23, 324; gentility and
middle-class conventionality, 161, 165,

166–69, 170–72, 176, 185, 194–95, 196,
199–200, 201, 261, 263–64, 270, 292,
312, 315, 318–19, 320, 323; fear of
sensuousness, sensuality, and sex, 157,
167–68, 169, 194, 199, 202–3, 269, 270,
316, 350 n. 7; sentimental views of
women and the family, 88, 168–69, 199,
224, 267–68, 312; divided life, 83, 85,
86, 162–63, 312, 323; withdrawal from
world, 88–89, 105, 114, 123–25, 134,
141, 147–48, 164, 173–74, 176, 196,
254, 255–56, 277, 280, 289–90, 297,
323, 325; reading, 88, 172, 174, 269,
369 n. 96; interest in sports, 7, 31–33,
48–49, 67–68, 77, 79, 140, 335 n. 84;
love of countryside and rural life, 88, 96,
99, 101–2, 122, 135–36, 251, 300; as
commuter, 88, 102, 167; nostalgia,
96–97, 101, 107, 108, 122, 156, 300,
310; inaccuracy of memories of past, 16,
46, 96; make-believe railroad, 102; disordered bulletin board, 94; health, 89,
109, 111, 120, 133–34, 141, 156, 174,
179, 180, 191, 236, 254, 255, 256, 276,
289, 290, 295, 297, 301, 362 n. 3;
handling of correspondence, 46,
256–57, 260, 277, 278, 290, 296, 297,
299; charities, 124, 174, 199; gifts and
loans to friends, 204, 228, 268; as patron
of music, 211–12, 215–16, 219, 224,
226, 228, 230, 231, 232–33, 236, 249,
252–53, 258, 269–70, 271, 276–77, 291,
361 n. 167, 362 n. 171
—philosophy and religion: his old-
fashioned mind, 94, 95, 243, 246; separation from current intellectual movements, 94, 143, 171–72, 176, 319–20;
religion, 39–40, 43, 48, 99–100, 105–9,
169, 205, 242–43, 246–47; philosophical
maturation, 106–7; transcendentalism
and mysticism, 38, 41, 61, 93, 99–100,
105, 108, 118–19, 126–27, 136–37, 157,
159, 160, 168, 169, 178, 202, 203, 269,
278, 283, 307, 353 n. 60; belief in men's
innate goodness, 135, 159; belief in
ultimate oneness and natural order of
disparate things, 47, 94, 99–100, 103–4,
136–38, 180–81, 241; symbolism of

139, 161–62, 165, 167, 170, 196, 200, 225, 270, 315, 320; preference for values of popular music, 37, 38, 39–40, 41–44, 46–47, 127, 130, 157, 242–43, 306, 320; resists cultivated-vernacular split, 43, 47, 67–68, 90–91, 130, 161, 306; religious vs. secular compositions, 98–99, 99–100, 104, 106–7, 338 n. 16, 338 n. 21; cultural nationalism, 47, 59, 89–90, 90–91, 92, 93, 160–61, 198, 208, 214–15, 216–17, 221–22, 226–27, 230–31, 232, 239, 241, 246–47, 249, 251, 275, 278, 279, 280, 281, 282, 283, 289, 298, 300–301, 307, 310; on "substance" and "manner" in art, 96, 157–58, 162, 202, 259, 284, 285–86, 315–18, 369 n. 96; his idealization of music and art, 42, 156, 157, 158–59, 160–63, 167–68, 194, 199–200, 201, 202, 222, 259, 269; on program music, 157; on inseparability of art from the common life, 84, 86, 159–64, 182, 193–94, 263, 266, 312, 320, 321, 322, 323; proposes nonprofessional role for creative artist, 83–84, 159–60, 162–63, 182, 312, 321, 322, 323; attitudes toward music profession, 22–23, 43–44, 59–60, 81, 83–85, 162, 164–65, 207, 322; hostility to composers' promoting own music, 35, 153, 180, 181, 187, 193, 196, 215, 236, 249, 271, 277, 294, 301; hostility to commercialism, 35, 42, 83–84, 91, 119, 141, 158, 162, 163, 169, 181, 194, 195, 261, 271, 284, 296, 309, 350 n. 7; refuses to accept alienation from common life, 86, 104–5, 263, 264, 266, 319, 322, 323; refuses to identify himself as artist, 171, 264, 266, 315, 317, 322, 323; fear of Bohemianism, 84, 85, 166–69, 171, 176, 194–95, 199–200, 201, 202–3, 204, 261, 263–64, 315, 320, 322; self-justifications, 164–65, 167, 181, 182, 185; unsystematic and nonintellectual approach to musical innovation, 93, 94–95, 136–38, 241, 258–59, 297, 306, 308, 312; eclecticism, 43, 47, 67–68, 94, 99–100, 103–4, 108, 136–38, 180–81, 215, 246, 287, 306; combines

technical innovation with traditional values, 47, 94, 137, 169, 226, 242, 245–47, 310; separation from current artistic movements, 94, 154, 166–67, 171, 172, 203, 204, 257–58, 319–20, 353 n. 50; artistic naiveté, 94–95, 172, 187, 241–43, 245–47, 286, 300, 308; as artistic "primitive," 94, 228, 249; his position between folk artist and alienated artist, 104–5, 251; and Whitman, 94, 128, 137, 141, 161, 167, 169, 203, 231, 247, 286; judges music and musicians by extramusical standards, 168–69, 196–97, 214, 256, 258, 259, 264, 315–18; and "Ivesian" experimental tradition in American music, 308; opinions about modernist composers, 204, 219, 222, 257–59, 264, 265, 269, 270, 276, 316; compared with Eilshemius, 379 n. 10; compared with Riegger, 264–67, 318; compared with Soviet composers, 312–18; compared with Varèse, 259–64, 308

—as musical performer, 28, 37, 39, 49, 51, 76, 97–98, 145–47, 148, 151, 153, 295, 328 n. 27; church organist, 29–31, 32–33, 44, 45–47, 48–49, 50, 52, 57, 61–64, 67, 78, 97, 98, 145–47, 148, 338 n. 16, 345 n. 10, 351 n. 14; pianist, 29, 45, 51, 65, 66, 68, 148, 149, 151, 152, 153, 155, 207, 255, 278, 286–87, 337 n. 114, 351 n. 14

—as composer: father's influence, 14–16, 23, 36, 42, 45, 51–52, 56, 95, 96–97, 97–98, 101, 207, 229, 300; relation to Yankee composers of fuguing tunes, 293; influence of Danbury's popular music, 37–43, 92, 96–97, 97–98, 99, 100, 103, 105, 107, 108, 141, 215, 216–17, 242–43, 300; influence of "mistakes" in performance of popular music, 41, 43, 92, 97–98, 103–4, 216–17; earliest compositions, 38–39, 44–47, 51–52; music study under Parker, 54–60, 62, 63, 84, 95, 149, 229, 333 n. 34; at Center Church, New Haven, 57, 61–64, 67, 81, 97; and Dr. Griggs, 61–62, 63, 81, 155, 165; and popular music at Yale, 64–68,

292; desire for musical communication and recognition, 148, 149, 150, 152, 153, 155, 163–64, 179–80, 181, 182, 187, 191, 196, 197, 212, 224, 290, 298–99, 324; reluctance to meet musicians and composers, 155, 165–67, 193–96, 204, 211–12, 248, 256, 260, 264, 277, 324, 368 n. 78; reluctance to attend public performances of own works, 153; desire to keep control over his music and reputation, 257, 297; early reviews, 146–47; lack of performances (1902–21), 147, 152, 153; others' rejection of his music, 45, 55–57, 58, 63, 81, 82, 93, 95, 104, 137, 140, 146, 148–56 *passim,* 161, 162, 163–64, 165, 184–85, 186–87, 208, 210, 224, 225, 245, 298–99, 300–301, 319; interest and approval shown by a few, 140, 152, 155, 184; and New York avant-garde of 1910s, 154, 166–67; nadir of reputation, 89; sends out *Essays, Concord,* and *114 Songs,* 134, 179–83, 187–88, 196, 205, 207, 212, 309, 354 n. 62; and others' reactions to *Essays, Concord,* and *114 Songs,* 183–88, 197–98, 201; and avant-garde of 1920s, 183, 187, 191, 193–96, 212, 245–47, 369 n. 98; and younger composers appearing in 1920s, 195, 219, 221–22, 245–47; and Bellamann, 197–201, 210, 351 n. 14, 351 n. 18, 352 n. 28, 366 n. 55; and Furness, 200–205, 351 n. 14, 353 n. 50; and Carter, 204, 285–87, 293–94, 295; and Schmitz and Pro Musica, 206–12 *passim,* 245, 293, 356 n. 95; and Cowell, 212, 213–38 *passim,* 240, 245, 252, 254, 259, 270, 275, 276–77, 291–92, 293, 294, 296–97, 299, 302, 309, 362 n. 171, 363 n. 9, 370 n. 119; and Slonimsky, 223–38 *passim,* 253, 254, 367 n. 61; works performed in Europe (1931–32), 226–33, 361 n. 167, 362 n. 171; writes musical autobiography, 229, 233, 361 n. 160, 364 n. 25; and avant-garde of early 1930s, 217, 233, 235, 238–51 *passim,* 255, 307, 309; and Young Composers' Group, 244–48, 250–51, 283, 363 n. 9; and Varèse's

leadership, 253–54, 260–61, 367 n. 61; friendship with Becker, 267–68, 370 n. 110, 370 n. 112, 370 n. 119; friendship with Ruggles, 268–70, 370 n. 119; and *New Music,* 214, 215, 216, 234, 235–36, 253, 269–70, 271, 291–92, 296, 362 n. 2, 362 n. 3; and Arrow Press, 271, 281, 290–91, 296, 375 n. 17, 376 n. 30; renewed neglect of his music in middle 1930s, 250–51, 271–72, 275–77; recognition in 1939, 277–87, 309; recognition in 1939–45 period, 288–94; recognition since World War II, 294–310; later European recognition, 95, 301, 306–7; shifts to commercial distribution of compositions, 296; music manuscripts given to Yale, 302–3; Ives Legend, 241, 248–50, 255, 280, 290, 295–96, 301, 302, 309, 324

—performances of compositions: in pre-1921 period, 37, 38–39, 44, 45–46, 51, 52, 58, 61, 62, 63, 65, 66–67, 80, 81, 97, 98, 145–46, 147, 148, 149, 150, 151–52, 153–54, 155; in 1921–38 period, 147, 197, 198, 201, 203, 205, 207–8, 210, 212, 217, 219, 223–24, 224–25, 226, 227, 228, 230, 231, 233–34, 236–37, 238, 248, 251, 253, 267, 270, 272, 278, 282, 309, 351 n. 14, 356 n. 95, 361 n. 167, 362 n. 171, 363 n. 9, 366 n. 53, 371 n. 125; in post-1938 period, 143, 248, 278–79, 280–81, 293, 294–95, 296, 299–300, 301, 303–4, 304–5, 307, 309, 351 n. 14, 374 n. 1, 376 n. 30

—publication of compositions, 44, 64, 65–66, 180, 183, 186, 216, 234, 235–36, 254, 271, 281, 289, 290–91, 296, 297, 310, 364 n. 24, 375 n. 17, 376 n. 30

—recording of compositions, 237, 249, 253, 255, 293, 304, 305, 306, 371 n. 125

—compositions: *Adeste Fideles* in an Organ Prelude, 146; *The Alcotts,* 105, 197, 201, 278, 298, 351 n. 14; Allegro (quarter-tone), 207–8; *The All-enduring,* 81; *The Anti-abolitionist Riots,* 128; *At Parting,* 45, 55; "Barn Dance" (from *Washington's Birthday*), 41, 237; *Battell*